DIVIDING THE PUBLIC

A volume in the series
Histories of American Education
Edited by Jonathan Zimmerman and Tracy L. Steffes

A list of titles in this series is available at
cornellpress.cornell.edu.

DIVIDING THE PUBLIC

School Finance and the Creation of Structural Inequity

Matthew Gardner Kelly

CORNELL UNIVERSITY PRESS   ITHACA AND LONDON

Copyright © 2023 by Matthew Gardner Kelly

This book is freely available in an open access edition thanks to TOME (Toward an Open Monograph Ecosystem)—a collaboration of the Association of American Universities, the Association of University Presses, and the Association of Research Libraries—and the generous support of the Pennsylvania State University. Learn more at the TOME website, available at: openmonographs.org.

The text of this book is licensed under a Creative Commons Attribution-NonCommercial 4.0 International (CC BY-NC 4.0) license: https://creativecommons.org/licenses/by-nc/4.0/. To use this book, or parts of this book, in any way not covered by the license, please contact Cornell University Press, Sage House, 512 East State Street, Ithaca, New York 14850. Visit our website at cornellpress.cornell.edu.

First published 2023 by Cornell University Press

Library of Congress Cataloging-in-Publication Data

Names: Kelly, Matthew Gardner, author.
Title: Dividing the public : school finance and the creation of structural inequity / Matthew Gardner Kelly.
Description: Ithaca [New York] : Cornell University Press, 2023. | Series: Histories of American education | Includes bibliographical references and index.
Identifiers: LCCN 2023013369 (print) | LCCN 2023013370 (ebook) | ISBN 9781501773259 (hardcover) | ISBN 9781501773266 (paperback) | ISBN 9781501773280 (epub) | ISBN 9781501773273 (pdf)
Subjects: LCSH: Social justice and education—United States. | Education—United States—Finance. | Education—Economic aspects—United States.
Classification: LCC LC192.2. K45 2023 (print) | LCC LC192.2 (ebook) | DDC 379.1/10973—dc23/eng/20230526
LC record available at https://lccn.loc.gov/2023013369
LC ebook record available at https://lccn.loc.gov/2023013370
DOI: http://doi.org/10.7298/1exm-kp71

To the memory of my mother

Contents

Acknowledgments ix

Introduction: Narratives of State Innocence and the History of School Finance 1

1. Funding for Education, Settler Colonialism, and the "California Experiment" in Common School Centralization, 1848–1865 22

2. Buying and Selling Schools and Racializing Space in a Western State 48

3. Finance Reform and the Contested Meaning of "Public" in the 1870s and 1880s 74

4. State-Sponsored Inequalities, Boosterism, and the Race for Progressive Era School Reform, 1890–1910 106

5. The Rise of the District Property Tax, Educational Expertise, and Rationalized Inequality, 1910–1928 138

6. The Art of Addressing Inequality While Expanding It, 1928–1950 169

Epilogue: Inequity Triumphant 197

Appendix: School Finance Data 203
Notes 209
Index 249

Acknowledgments

While I cannot directly repay the many debts I have accumulated while researching and writing this book, it is a pleasure to express my gratitude here. This book would not exist without the generous support of a long list of people and institutions. If it did, I'm not sure it would be worth reading.

I am grateful to financial support for this book from several sources. The National Academy of Education and Spencer Foundation for a 2021 NAEd / Spencer Postdoctoral Fellowship provided me the time and space I needed to revise this manuscript. The Stanford Interdisciplinary Graduate Fellowship (SIGF) program provided generous support that enabled me to expand the scope of my early research. I'm thankful for the Yu-Ly Interdisciplinary Graduate Fellowship Fund, which supported my years as an SIGF fellow. Grants and support from the Stanford Graduate School of Education, the Technology for Equity in Learning Opportunities at Stanford University (TELOS), and Stanford's Center for Spatial and Textual Analysis (CESTA) provided me with additional resources that helped me complete research and writing for this book. At CESTA, Celena Allen, Amanda Bergado, and Brian Kersey deserve special thanks for their support of this book, and I'm grateful to the four undergraduate research assistants who helped me digitize and map district- and county-level funding data through CESTA: Ngoc Bui, Brandon Leong, Raymond Schneider, and Manami Suenaga. Research assistants at Penn State provided me critical assistance on a series of assorted and often tedious tasks collecting, transcribing, and checking digitized funding data: thank you to Frank Ayata, Elizabeth Cardamone, Zoë Mandel, and Annie Maselli for their help. Thank you to Kim Lawless, dean of Penn State's College of Education, and Gregory Kelly, senior associate dean for research, for supporting my work on a historical monograph and valuing the contributions a historian can offer to educational research. Thank you to Michelle Irwin for helping me process funding to finish revisions. Thank you to Penn State's Office of the Executive Vice President and Provost and Penn State Libraries for making the digital version of this book accessible without charge through the TOME initiative.

This book would not be possible without the work and generosity of librarians and archivists at numerous institutions. The staffs of the California History Room at the San José Public Library, the Santa Clara County Archives, the Santa Clara county clerk and board of supervisors office, the San Mateo County

Historical Society, the Oakland History Room at the Oakland Public Library, the Contra Costa County Historical Society, the UC Berkeley Bancroft Library, the UC Berkeley Earth Sciences and Map Library, the UC Berkeley Microfilm Library, the San Francisco Public Library, the California Historical Society, the California State Library, and the California State Archives all went out of their way to help me complete research for this book. The staffs of the Branner Library, the Green Library, and the Hoover Archives at Stanford provided access to documents, books, and maps. The librarians at Stanford's Cubberley Education Library deserve special thanks. Kelly Roll and Kathy Kerns have enabled my research since my first day of graduate school. I am deeply grateful to them both. Stanford is lucky to have them.

I have benefited greatly from the comments I received on early iterations of each chapter at various conferences over the years. Thank you to Nancy Beadie, Jackie Blount, John Rury, and Christopher Span for providing comments on this work as discussants. Thank you to Esther Cyna, Tina Groeger, and Campbell F. Scribner for organizing and inviting me to join various paper sessions at the annual meetings of the American Educational Research Association, the History of Education Society (HES), and the Organization of American Historians. I was fortunate to receive my historical training from the Stanford University History Department. Thank you to Jennifer Burns, James Campbell, Gordon Chang, Zephyr Frank, Estelle Freedman, Allyson Hobbs, Richard White, and Caroline Winterer for the various courses and conversations that shaped my sense of the historian's craft. I am also grateful for the training I received in history before graduate school. Myra Armstead, Eleanor Aronstein, Mark Lytle, and Robert Culp deserve my thanks for providing that training.

I also benefited from comments on an early version of chapter 2 from Stanford's US History Workshop. Thank you to Alex Stern for organizing the workshop that year. I also received helpful feedback on early versions of chapters 2, 3, and 4 from Fritz Osterwalder, Tom Popkewitz, and Daniel Tröhler at Theory and Data in the History of Education workshops. Thank you to David Labaree for sponsoring my participation in those sessions. I'm grateful for feedback on an early version of the introduction from the History of Education Society West Group. Thank you to Joan Malczewski, Michael Hines, and Linda Perkins for organizing the group and to the many participants who provided helpful feedback. Thank you to Erika Kitzmiller and Matt Lassiter, who provided useful advice and counsel as NAEd/Spencer mentors.

I am grateful to my advisers at Stanford, David Labaree and Leah Gordon. They provided invaluable comments, encouragement, and advice during the messy early years of this book, reading more chapter drafts than they probably care to remember. Thank you to Gordon Chang for his generosity and wise counsel; I'm grateful for helpful feedback he provided on early drafts of the book and the way that feedback pushed my thinking forward. Thank you as well to sean reardon for providing comments.

I owe special thanks to Nancy Beadie, Tracy Steffes, and Jon Zimmerman. Nancy provided helpful comments on multiple early drafts of chapters when they were first presented at HES. In addition, she provided detailed and essential feedback on the full manuscript that helped me substantially improve it. Tracy Steffes provided invaluable feedback on the manuscript as well. She also provided encouragement for the book as a whole that helped me get it out the door. Jon Zimmerman has been a great supporter of this book as well. I'm grateful for his careful reading. Along with comments from anonymous reviewers, comments from Tracy, Nancy, and Jon helped me rewrite, reframe, and improve sections of the manuscript. I am grateful for their sharp reading, constructive comments, and the model for scholarly generosity they provide.

Thank you to Bill Nelson for creating the figures for this manuscript. I am grateful to the comments provided by Eleanor Andrews, an excellent developmental editor who helped me condense and clarify chapters that grew far too long during revision. At Cornell University Press, thank you to Sarah Grossman for speedily processing the manuscript, working with Jon and Tracy to secure exceptionally thoughtful and constructive reader reports, and securing TOME funding for the digital version of the book. I am grateful for her support of the book and patience with my delay revising the manuscript amid Pennsylvania's school funding trial. Also at Cornell University Press, thank you to Jacqulyn Teoh for helping me prepare the book's materials for production, to Karen M. Laun for initiating the production process, and to Mary Kate Murphy for shepherding the manuscript through production. Glenn Novak provided expert copyediting.

I'm grateful to have overlapped with three other doctoral students in the history of education while at Stanford: Ethan Hutt, Ethan Ris, and Laura Marcus. In State College, I've been grateful for mentorship and support for this book from departmental colleagues, especially Gil Conchas, Erica Frankenberg, David Gamson, and Kai Schafft. While finishing this book, I am particularly grateful to have been in community with more colleagues, mentors, neighbors, and friends than I can list here. Gil Conchas, Maria Lewis, Marsha Modeste, and Leticia Oseguera have helped State College feel more like home. Finally, I need to thank Tanner Vea. He is a great partner of eighteen years. I'm glad we have grown up together.

An earlier version of chapter 5 previously appeared in "'Theoretically All Children Are Equal. Practically This Can Never Be So': The History of the District Property Tax in California and the Choice of Inequality," *Teachers College Record* 122 (February 2020): 32 pages. Copyright © by Teachers College, Columbia University (www.TCRecord.org).

Introduction

NARRATIVES OF STATE INNOCENCE AND THE HISTORY OF SCHOOL FINANCE

Located east of Los Angeles, Baldwin Park was a small working-class suburb and home to a large number of Mexican American families by the late 1960s. The infamously elite and almost exclusively white residential community of Beverly Hills was only a few miles away, west of Los Angeles. The stark differences in the wealth and racial composition of Baldwin Park and Beverly Hills reflected the spatial form of racial and economic inequality across California in the second half of the twentieth century. Historians have made the story of that inequality one of the most important stories about the Golden State after World War II, using histories of metropolitan inequality on the Pacific Coast to tell the broader political and economic history of the United States in the postwar era.[1]

This book builds on these well-known accounts of city building and inequality in postwar California by telling a new story about the role that public education played in shaping how the racially segregated, economically divided, and politically fragmented metropolis came to be. It does so in part by upending the conventional story circulating to explain the differences between Baldwin Park and Beverly Hills—a story about California's public school funding system, its legality under the United States Constitution, and its history.

In 1971, California's public school funding system, wherein public schools were primarily funded with local taxes, and its disparate impact on Baldwin Park and Beverly Hills became objects of national discussion because of their role in a state court case on school funding called *Serrano v. Priest*.[2] The Mexican American residents of Baldwin Park paid one of the highest tax rates for public schools in Los Angeles County. But despite that tax rate, the public schools of Baldwin

1

Park had less money to spend than nearly every other public school in the state. The predominately white and affluent Beverly Hills was the real winner. Residents of Beverly Hills paid one of the lowest school tax rates during these years, but the public schools there were spending more than twice as much as those in Baldwin Park.[3]

Most everyone agreed that using local taxes to fund public education created high levels of inequality. They sharply disagreed, however, about whether and to what extent the use of local taxes to finance schools—and the consequent massive inequalities in funding for districts like Beverly Hills and Baldwin Park—violated the United States Constitution. That it did indeed violate the Constitution was the argument that the civil rights attorneys representing twenty-seven Mexican American families from Baldwin Park and other impoverished school districts in Los Angeles County had made when they filed the case in 1968. As California Supreme Court justice Raymond Sullivan later explained in his majority opinion in *Serrano*, the case hinged on "whether the California public school financing system, with its substantial dependence on local property taxes and resultant wide disparities in school revenue, violates the equal protection clause of the Fourteenth Amendment."[4] According to the California Supreme Court, it did.

The decision sent shock waves across the nation. It brought into question the widespread practice of financing education with local taxes and the ways that inequitable funding was both cause and consequence of racial and economic segregation. Following the ruling, one hundred legislative leaders from across the United States gathered in Houston, Texas, for a daylong meeting to discuss "concern over the implications of *Serrano*."[5] Over the next two years, twenty-five similar lawsuits regarding funding were filed in state courts and twenty-seven in federal courts. Eleven state legislatures made modifications to their school funding systems in an effort to avoid litigation by softening the school funding disparities produced by their own reliance on local taxes.[6] Lower courts declared the funding systems of five states unconstitutional—Arizona, New Jersey, Minnesota, Kansas, and, in a ruling that was later overturned by the US Supreme Court, Texas.[7]

Analyses of the history of localized funding for public schools—where the difference between Beverly Hills and Baldwin Park purportedly came from—quickly followed suit, telling a story about how the practice was deeply rooted in the past. At the heart of these analyses was the claim that the historical roots of using local taxes to fund schools absolved the state of responsibility for creating and therefore correcting funding disparities. Columnist Anthony Harrigan declared the ruling "another major blow at local control of schools" and warned that a national ruling paralleling *Serrano* would mean "the end of the last vestige of local control of education—a traditional feature of the American way of life."[8]

In a *Wall Street Journal* article, retired economics professor Harley Lutz ridiculed the idea that "the property tax, work-horse of the tax system, is unconstitutional after so many years of reliable service." According to Lutz, the long history of the local property tax showed there was no viable alternative to it. He also asserted that differences in wealth between communities were "natural and unchangeable," as "Mother Nature is primarily responsible for the differences in real property values," and it "would be as reasonable to hold that the Rocky Mountains are unconstitutional because they are not flat enough to plow as it is to indict the property tax because a given rate of tax will not produce the same revenue."[9] Other editorialists captured the same logic in more compact language, lamenting that *Serrano* and subsequent rulings were helping to "erode" a "tradition of local control over school matters."[10]

This narrative about the deep roots of localized funding had material and constitutional consequences when it was repeated by the United States Supreme Court in 1973, upending the California State Supreme Court's interpretation of the US Constitution in *Serrano*. That case, *San Antonio v. Rodriguez*, came from Texas. It was similar to *Serrano* in many respects. Justice Lewis Powell, who wrote the majority opinion, criticized the lower court in a letter to his clerk, namely how it had relied heavily on *Serrano* in its ruling in *San Antonio v. Rodriguez*.[11] In his opinion, Justice Powell described the purportedly rational basis on which this unequal funding system rested, claiming that Texas—and the entire nation—had always funded their schools with local taxes and that there was no other conceivable way to fund schools. According to Powell, the ensuing inequities were "certainly ... not the product of purposeful discrimination," nor were they produced because of "hurried, ill-conceived legislation." They instead reflected a wise localism in school funding that reflected "what many educators for a half century have thought was an enlightened approach to a problem for which there is no perfect solution."[12] Powell included clear language that the ruling applied beyond Texas.

In declaring local taxation for public schools an esteemed historical tradition, the United States Supreme Court absolved Texas lawmakers of responsibility for the inequalities that their policies produced and what those policies did to children in poor districts—most often children from low-income families and children of color. "The very existence of identifiable local governmental units," Powell claimed, made it "inevitable that some localities are going to be blessed with more taxable assets than others." According to Powell, those differences in wealth had grown, with implications for district resources, as the state had urbanized and become more industrialized. It was these "growing disparities in population and taxable property between districts"—not state policies effectively translating such differences to education funding—that Powell insisted "were responsible in part for increasingly notable differences in levels of local expenditure for education."[13]

The narrative at the heart of *San Antonio v. Rodriguez* claimed that education had started as a local endeavor, and that the massive disparities created by financing schools with local taxes had developed by happenstance, rather than through concerted action. For decades, this narrative has been taken for granted by historians, repeated by education researchers, and used as a rationale for narrowing state responsibility for the rampant inequalities created by funding policies, inequalities felt most often by children from low-income families, and especially children of color from low-income families.[14] State courts in particular have used this narrative to close, at the state level, the same door for mitigating inequality that Justice Powell slammed shut at the federal level in 1973. Indeed, state courts have often insisted that, in deference to tradition, local financing must be maintained, despite the massive inequalities it creates.[15] As legal scholar Richard Briffault has explained, even in cases where state courts are unable to find a textual basis to support local control of financing, they frame it more generally as "a longstanding principle of education finance—in effect, a constitutional norm."[16]

This book shows how this narrative about the supposedly deep roots of localism in school funding is wrong. It demonstrates how the use of local taxes to fund public schools in California—and the massive inequalities it has created and maintains to this day—was not the inadvertent or de facto product of past practices. To the contrary, local financing was adopted in place of well-known alternatives in the 1910s and 1920s, against past precedent and principle at the time. In other words, the notorious inequalities produced by localized funding were not by default but by design. I argue that tracing the contours of that design can show the relationship between public schools and inequality in a new light.

This book also examines the role that the dominant historical narrative has played in maintaining this system of spatial apartheid in education, as the use of history in these high-stakes civil rights cases demonstrates. The same early twentieth-century policy makers who designed the policies described in this book also crafted a misleading historical narrative about localism to help rationalize the new spatialized disparities that those policies were helping to create. This narrative recast those inequalities as inevitable products of changes in property values over time, and it failed to acknowledge how the unequal distribution of wealth between school districts was profoundly shaped by the state. It also naturalized the idea of using local taxes to finance public education, obscuring the fact that this was a policy choice of relatively recent vintage in California.

The historical citations included in Powell's opinion in *San Antonio v. Rodriguez* reflect the power of both this narrative and the influence of one of its popularizers, Ellwood Cubberley. As chapter 5 details, Cubberley was a confidant of state lawmakers, a paid consultant for lobbyists seeking to minimize the tax burdens of public service corporations, and a central figure in the shift toward the use of local taxation to finance public education in California during the early twentieth century. Cubberley was among the first generation of university-based experts in education, founding Stanford University's Education Department and shaping the development of educational administration, school finance, and the history of education as areas of study. Cubberley's writing was an important source for Powell's narrative, as evidenced by Powell's direct citations of Cubberley as well as secondary works that relied solely on Cubberley as their source.[17]

The purported timelessness of localism in most accounts of how public schools were first funded in California—and across the United States—ignores the unambiguous way that nearly every aspect of school funding is structured by state governments. It obscures, from the beginning, how the existence of school districts with divergent levels of taxable wealth stem from state action, and further neglects how state lawmakers can make those differences more or less meaningful for educational provision through polices regulating land use, local governance, and state-level funding. Most importantly, these narratives erase the debate over using local taxes to fund schools in the first place, rendering invisible the deliberate policy-making decisions in the early twentieth century—and their rejected alternatives—that made schools in California increasingly reliant on local taxes.

Consider the state's hand in shaping Baldwin Park School District's poverty and Beverly Hills School District's affluence. First, there were the boundaries of the districts themselves, all structured by the state over time. Here, state involvement was not simply about enabling local activity. School district boundaries were determined by state policy. The residents of what later became the Baldwin Park Unified School District submitted a formal request to the state for a district that was approved in 1888, following a procedure dictated by state law.[18] Government officials invested with powers by the state to consider such requests—the county superintendent of schools and county board of supervisors—decided to approve it, though county officials did not have to approve such requests if they did not deem them appropriate.[19] Similar requests, made on terms dictated by state law, were submitted throughout the next seventy years; only those approved by officials invested with power to approve boundary changes were enacted into law. Even changing the district's name to Baldwin Park—originally Vineland School District—had to be requested and approved. By the late 1950s, the state had modified the boundaries of the school district eleven times. In four cases, it had added territory to Baldwin Park from nearby districts. Seven other changes removed territory from Baldwin Park and placed it inside nearby districts.[20] In

1959, state officials approved a twelfth change to the boundaries of Baldwin Park when it became a unified school district, meaning it would offer both an elementary and a high school education to residents.[21] This change, too, involved a series of laws structured by the state legislature. Under the structure of these laws, Baldwin Park joined the Covina Union High School District in the early 1910s before separating from it again at the end of the 1950s.[22]

Beverly Hills—an exclusionary subdivision planned for white and affluent families by the Rodeo Land and Water Company—had its borders defined by state action, plus an additional layer of state lawmaking governing municipal governments and their connection to school districts. Finding the rural one-room district school that would have served the planned subdivision unacceptable, the company and the district's first residents requested from the state the power to form their own separate school district. It was created, with approval from state officials, in 1913. The following year, Beverly Hills incorporated as a city, in the process being granted special privileges from the state and, under state law at the time, making the newly incorporated city a school district with coterminous boundaries.[23] State laws regulating high school district annexation and incorporation permitted Beverly Hills voters to hold an election and send their children to the Los Angeles City School District for high school in 1921. A similar state law allowed Beverly Hills to withdraw in 1936 and create a unified elementary and high school district, Beverly Hills Unified. Between 1936 and the late 1950s, the state added territory to Beverly Hills Unified eight times and removed territory from it twice.[24]

It was not just the physical boundaries of the districts that were constituted by the state. State lawmakers also structured the extent to which the boundaries of Baldwin Park and Beverly Hills—and all the boundaries within Los Angeles County and the state writ large—were relevant to how schools were funded. Only upon their creation as school districts could communities such as Baldwin Park and Beverly Hills practice the purportedly timeless tradition of raising a local tax for their schools, always on terms and within strict limits set by the state.[25] The state first authorized districts the power to raise such a tax in 1858, several years after it had already started providing funds directly to common schools and regulating who could attend them by classifying children by race.

More important for the story told in this book, this system of localized funding was not passively enabled by the state. It was encouraged and discouraged by state policy makers at crucial moments over time. Before the 1910s and 1920s, ample state support and a commitment to county-level funding allowed most districts to operate without raising local taxes, even as they spent more on schools per pupil than districts in nearly any other state. This changed during the early twentieth century when a coalition of self-appointed educational experts, state policy makers, and public service corporations aiming to limit their tax burden abolished the statewide property tax. At the time, the general property tax had technically been a tax on all forms of wealth across the state. This coalition replaced it with a district-level property tax on a narrower definition of wealth, limiting the redistributive character of school funding in the state. These efforts went against past precedent and popular ideas at the time. In sum, localized funding was constituted by the state, and it, along with the inequities it produced, was no accident.

In the years before this shift, California had been a regional leader in alternatives to district-level financing and an increasingly important model for eastern states. Lawmakers in other western states similarly replicated the funding system developed in California in the 1850s and 1860s, and, even after the Civil War, resisted adopting the district property tax. Although some scholars have used historical funding data to claim that centralized funding systems depress overall investments in education, those same scholars have missed this pattern in the West. The pattern itself, moreover, contradicts their thesis. Funding was far more centralized in western states than in other parts of the nation after the Civil War, and it was higher, too.

Before this deliberate shift toward district-level school funding, dollars for public education had flowed freely across the boundaries of school districts, both statewide and within individual counties. Supplementing statewide funding were county-wide taxes. These county school taxes are classified as "local" in analyses of historical funding data, helping partially explain why historians have missed the Progressive Era shift described in this book. Yet, conflating a district-level tax with a county-level tax distorts the nature of education funding in the geographically expansive and economically diverse counties of California and other western states. Historical descriptions of localism in school funding do not apply neatly to places like San Bernardino County in California, for example, which alone is nearly twice as large as the state of Massachusetts. A county tax in San Bernardino meant neighbors who were separated by more land mass than separated residents on opposite ends of Massachusetts shared in raising and spending money for schools.[26]

The purposeful shift toward district-level financing dismantled this earlier system. Figure 0.1 illustrates the broad scope of this shift. The shift is visible at the state level. In 1870, not a single school district in forty-four counties raised a district-level tax; dollars flowed freely across the boundaries of districts in the unshaded counties. In 1910, on the eve of the abolition of the state property tax, only 4 percent of the funds for elementary schools in Los Angeles County came

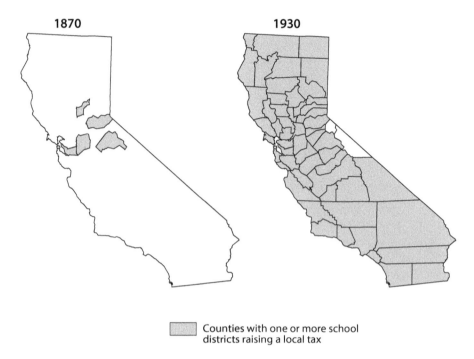

FIGURE 0.1. Counties where at least one school district raised a local tax, circa 1870 (*left*) and 1930 (*right*). Data from biennial reports of the superintendent of public instruction discussed in the appendix. Cartography by Bill Nelson.

from district-level taxes. But by 1930, every county but two had at least one district raising a local tax, effectively constricting the flow of dollars.

The localization of school funding within counties was equally clear, with the rise of district-level funding further dividing space. Figure 0.2 illustrates these patterns among the school districts in eight northern California counties between 1870 and 1940. In 1870, a growing number of districts were raising a property tax to generate revenue: approximately 17 percent. This figure then declined throughout the rest of the nineteenth century. In 1900, approximately 6 percent of the districts in these counties raised a property tax. District property taxation spread rapidly after 1910. By 1920, slightly more than half the school districts raised a property tax to obtain money for schools. By 1939–40, 85 percent of districts were raising a local tax. This shift in funding runs contrary to ahistorical narratives claiming localism was baked into US public schools from the start.

The major consequence of this reliance on unequal tax bases for funding was reflected in a widening chasm in education spending that both reflected, and helped drive, racial and economic segregation between school districts. The

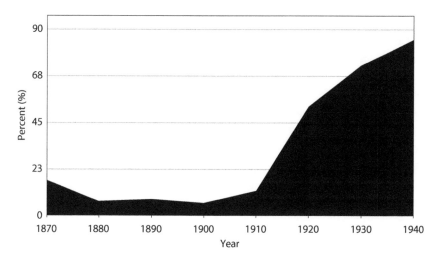

FIGURE 0.2. Percentage of all school districts raising a district-level tax for elementary schools in Alameda, Contra Costa, Marin, Napa, San Mateo, Santa Clara, Solano, and Sonoma Counties combined, 1870 to 1940. Adapted from data in annual reports (Common School Reports), Department of Education Records (F3601:326–784), California State Archives, Sacramento. Graph by Bill Nelson.

coefficient of variation is a measure of inequality. It represents the ratio of the standard deviation to the mean. In school finance analyses, decreases in the measure indicate that school funding is becoming more equal. Increases in the coefficient of variation indicate that school funding is becoming less equal. Along this measure, school funding became much more unequal. The coefficient of variation jumped from 2.2 to 3.7 in just the ten years from 1920 to 1930, a 68 percent increase. Put simply, the spread of the local school tax meant the entrenchment of inequality in education funding.

On top of these policies, a host of more familiar instances of state action enabling, encouraging, and shaping racialized boundary making were enacted by state lawmakers in the early twentieth century, further fragmenting the state into unequal and competing local governments divided by race and class. State support and enforcement of racially restrictive covenants, alongside zoning requirements that permitted the construction of large homes only, helped make Beverly Hills one of the most economically and racially exclusive communities in the country.[27] Later, a federally constituted mortgage market that made federal subsidies for homeownership available only to whites stifled development and suppressed the growth of the taxable wealth of Baldwin Park. One mortgage security map that redlined Baldwin Park by giving it the lowest security grade in 1938 explained the rationale for the grade by noting, "Mexicans are scattered throughout area."[28] In combination with increasingly localized funding for schools, these policies were the infrastructure for a world of stark inequality and the diminishment of a sense of shared citizenship long considered one of the central purposes of public education.

It was upon this already divided world that the postwar metropolis was built. The well-known geographic transformations of the era—the Great Migration, suburbanization, and the national shift of economic growth toward the Sun Belt—are ultimately what brought the inequality of postwar California into its fullest form, but the mechanism of unequal school funding and the policies that facilitated it helped set the spatial terms of how postwar inequality unfolded.

Contributions

By bringing to light the world of state policy making that is minimized by fictive narratives about the localist origins of school funding, this book shows how public policies regarding education funding during the Progressive Era helped structure the division of California by race and class via school district boundaries. In doing so, the book uses a longer chronological frame, wider geographic scale, and sharper focus on the relevant laws to situate postwar structural inequalities in education within a broader history of the state's hand in creating unequal places over time.

In centering public policy choices made during the early twentieth century, this book sets the scene for the well-known synthesis that historians have produced to tell the story of inequality in metropolitan regions after World War II. Three dynamics central to that postwar synthesis are important for situating the contribution offered by this book. First, histories of metropolitan regions after World War II reveal the deeply spatial nature of inequality.[29] Second, these histories bring to light the significance of governmental action, especially federal policy making, in producing the racial and economic inequality assuming spatial form during this period.[30] Federal policies across a number of domains—from transportation, defense, and urban renewal to the now well-known policies shaping the mortgage market and subsidizing white homeownership—helped segregate the postwar metropolitan landscape, a point the United States Supreme Court glossed over in declaring patterns of residential segregation "de facto" creations that the state was not responsible for correcting.[31] Third, scholars have explored in detail the consequences that the racially and economically divided metropolitan landscape held for ideas about community and the sharing of the costs and benefits of postwar affluence.[32]

California looms large in accounts of the postwar metropolis. The state's multiracial composition and long history of decentralized development made it regionally distinctive and, at the same time, key to the story of the United States writ large after World War II. Historians such as Mark Brilliant and Shana Bernstein, for example, have retold the history of the civil rights movement from the vantage of multiracial California, noting how the state was a leader in both civil rights advancements and actions to limit and reverse those advancements.[33] As Brilliant notes, the status of California as "national bellwether" makes its history of multiracial civil rights activism key to "America's increasingly multiracial civil rights present and future."[34] Historians have long noted as well how development in California was decentralized and dispersed, making it both initially distinct from eastern locales and also anticipatory of national trends in the postwar era. As early as 1967, Robert Fogelson declared that Los Angeles by 1930 represented "the fragmented metropolis par excellence, the archetype for better or for worse of the contemporary American metropolis."[35] A number of other historians have reiterated how California's early patterns of decentralized development, design, and construction of full-scale planned communities, along with its tradition of competitive boosterism, placed it in the vanguard of city planning and land-use controls.[36] It is for this reason that Robert Self has declared California and the metropolitan West "the archetypal postwar region." Los Angeles, Self has also pointed out, was particularly important in these histories; it was to the twentieth century what Chicago was to the nineteenth century—"a paradigmatic city on western soil."[37] These patterns have made California a key site for locating the early roots, and telling the subsequent national story, of what Kevin Kruse and Thomas Sugrue have called "the most salient feature of metropolitan America: the fragmentation and proliferation of local governments."[38]

The broader story of postwar politics, too, has been told repeatedly through the story of metropolitan California. Lisa McGirr, for example, has located the development of the New Right in the suburbs of Orange County.[39] Similarly, Becky Nicolaides has disrupted early histories of monolithic, affluent suburbs while showing how whites in federally subsidized homes in the working-class suburb of South Gate in Los Angeles County developed a political ideology and mobilized in opposition to civil rights using a language of homeowner and property rights.[40] Self has brought together the story of uneven metropolitan development, civil rights, and national political movements in his history of Oakland and its surrounding suburbs. Analyzing the unequal places of Alameda County—of competing "industrial gardens"—Self has shown how white suburbanites worked to monopolize economic growth, tax revenue, and public goods at the expense of both Oakland's Black residents and other nearby suburban and urban communities. From this fractured world of competing places rooted in western city building, Self has traced the rise of Black nationalism in Oakland and the rise of antitax conservatism in the suburbs surrounding the city.[41]

The public school was a critical site in making these competing and unequal metropolitan places, in California and across the nation. Historians have noted, for example, how white resistance to desegregation was crucial to the development of white suburban conservatism during these years. Nicolaides has shown how struggles over desegregation in South Gate—a part of the Los Angeles Unified School District—became part of a broader political transformation, culminating in "a defining moment in the development of white working-class politics" as whites "began formulating the ideological and organizational bases of a conservative countermovement."[42]

Early accounts, however, missed or understated the place of the public school in this history of metropolitan inequality.[43] The relationship between schools and postwar racial and economic inequality runs deeper than overt battles over desegregation, as a growing body of work makes clear. In recent years, historians have examined the connections between education and development, uncovering how the public school was not simply transmitting racist and classist patterns in housing and uneven development but, critically, helped create these patterns. Several historians have illustrated how housing and schooling were mutually constitutive, tracing the role of the public school in the development of racially divided landscapes.[44] The contributions of schools to place making were central to the creation of the fragmented, competing industrial gardens of postwar California. Historian Emily Straus persuasively illustrated the educational problems confronting the schools of Compton, and how an "education crisis" was not "at heart a crisis of schooling" but a "long-term crisis of suburban development" that trapped the district in a vicious cycle of underdevelopment. Saddled with debt since the Great Depression, the district repeatedly tried, and was unable, to cobble together the basic resources it needed to function, and ultimately the district's schools "both inherited and perpetuated" the broader political economic environment in which it was situated.[45]

As valuable as these accounts are, they are incomplete without a wider frame. The disparities in funding for public schools, the role of the state in promoting segregation—these are well documented and well known.[46] But *how* policy mechanisms link education funding with local wealth is peripheral to most of the stories told in the postwar synthesis.[47] More importantly, *why* those policy mechanisms were implemented in the first place is largely left unexplored as well. Tracing how options other than localized funding were dismantled in the Progressive Era reveals a broader world of policy making that stitched together residential segregation, local disparities in wealth, and funding for education—structuring the spatial and fiscal terms of postwar educational inequality. Policy makers helped cement and expand early patterns of uneven development across California through lawmaking connected to school funding, compounding advantage and disadvantage over time.

When the inability of school districts like Compton to get ahead, which historian Emily Strauss details with clarity and force, is viewed in relation to this earlier history, state lawmakers' use of schools to create unequal places comes into even starker view. Compton's problems were not only problems of suburban development in the postwar era. This book argues that they were also problems of policy making rooted in much earlier and even more deliberate lawmaking than historians have addressed. Such a system simultaneously created an advantage for affluent white school districts. Compton's high tax rates and low levels of school funding subsidized more affluent districts nearby. If they simply shared in a county- or statewide property tax system—as they had for decades before the 1920s—they would have shared in the costs of running the schools of Compton.

Above all else, this book shows how Compton's postwar problems were ultimately rooted in how education was, and still is, imagined as only a semipublic good. In the postwar era, this was clearest in the diminishment of wealthy white suburbanites' collective sense of obligation to children who did not live in their state-subsidized, racially segregated communities. That way of thinking, the book argues, was cultivated in part by school funding policies, and—in ways big and small, day in and day out—it led to the idea that problems facing the public schools of Compton were solely "Compton's problems" with *its* schools, and not Los Angeles County's problems with its schools, California's problems with its schools, or the United States' problems with its schools.

In making the deeper history of these policies and ideas visible, this book illuminates the deliberateness with which educational inequality has been structured, sustained, and rationalized over time. The way that historians have pushed education funding to the periphery of most accounts has obscured these dynamics. It is not just a neglect of how policies structuring the financing of an institution purportedly designed to serve the common good actually funded that institution in practice. It is also a neglect of where the bulk of the money raised by state and local governments went in the postwar era. How those dollars were raised and why those dollars went where they did is the story of a massive policy infrastructure with enormous consequences for spatial inequalities in education, housing, and economic development. This book argues that the story of postwar educational inequality cannot be told in full without attending to the earlier world of lawmaking that helped order it.[48]

The (perverse) logic of localized funding is so ingrained in policy and culture that it can be difficult to recognize how intentionally it was adopted to benefit some communities over others, and how much its adoption contradicted earlier ways of imagining the nature of state responsibility for education. Moreover, localized funding was considered notoriously impractical and expensive in the nineteenth century. Observers often lamented the fact that it cost more to levy these taxes than they produced in revenue. District-level taxes also produced a series of seemingly unending wars over school district boundaries that became wars over resources for public schooling. Lawmakers in California and other western states initially lacked the language to describe district-level taxation in the 1860s and 1870s, calling the property tax a "special tax." Some state legislators even struggled to untangle whether use of any district-level tax would convert a "general," "common," or "state" system of schools into a "local" or "municipal" one. Still others wondered if schools financed with district-level taxes were even technically public. Indeed, the district school tax was at times discussed as a private funding source like a tuition charge.

Reckoning with the longer history of these policies and the deliberateness with which school funding was localized also offers an important corrective to the way some scholars have written about the history of public school funding. Some historical accounts describe resource inequities as the product of abstract, economic forces that determine property values. In these accounts, the free market, not the state constituting and structuring it, becomes the source of inequality. In some instances, inequality itself even becomes something to celebrate, a reflection of how a market system efficiently distributes public goods by creating the market-based "local public good."[49] State policies shaping property values and deliberately connecting them with school funding are absent from these accounts.

While this book locates the roots of structural inequalities in state lawmaking, it also argues that a deeper understanding of those inequalities and how they become *structural* requires reckoning with both the ideas undergirding the initial making of laws and the ideas that take root as a consequence of that lawmaking. These ideas are about the fundamental goals and meaning of education, the nature of state responsibility for it, and the place of markets in educational provision. Decisions about school finance forced lawmakers to translate those ideas into material form. School finance policies, once implemented, shaped how education, state responsibility in education, and the limits of private markets were imagined and conceived.

This contest crystallized around what it meant to have schools that were "public." Debates often involved conflicting interpretations of the literal meaning of the word, but always reflected more fundamental clashes over ideas than definitional wrangling on its own may suggest. This book focuses on three overlapping dimensions of these debates over the meaning of "public." On the first level, they centered on whether public education was a state and national project, or a local and geographically bounded one. Deciding about the place of local financing in education meant deciding whether schools served a national and statewide public or a geographically narrow public contained within the boundaries of particular school districts. The history of school finance in California brings into view how this question was far more contested than previously imagined.[50] From these debates, it becomes clear that localism was both constituted by the state—much later than scholars have realized—and that inequality was in part the point of devolving funding to localized and competing school districts.

On another level, the debates over the public traced in this book were inextricably connected to questions about what constituted a public good in the United States and where the boundary between the public world of the state and the private world of the market should be drawn. A localist vision of education calling for the use of district taxes was a quasi-privatized way of conceptualizing public schools and was criticized as such by some early school officials. In the early years of public schooling, state officials even excluded dollars raised through local taxes from the "public" category. At least in California, localized funding was about treating the public school as something that could be bought and sold with land, that impacted the value of that land, and to which access should be conditioned to some degree on wealth. This quasi-privatized view of education emerged as the victor in these struggles, as today's designation of district-level property taxes for schools as a public form of funding attests.

In still a third sense, these debates over the public concerned how unevenly and unequally the educational system could be structured. These debates centered on whether education should be egalitarian, or, conversely, how inegalitarian it could be allowed to become along racial, economic, and geographic lines. In the end, localized funding fostered racial exclusion that could be described in a color-blind policy language of market forces and local control. The net result was a system of educational apartheid that survived repeated challenges to exclusion on racial grounds. Segregating the state by race and income via school district boundaries—and linking those boundaries to funding—policy makers enacted, and still enact, laws with unambiguously racist outcomes without being labeled racists.

These struggles over the meaning of the public often took shape in relation to the physical landscape—school funding policies both reflected and influenced how land was ascribed an economic value, given racial meaning, and divided into private property. Writing this story from a specifically western perspective shows how ideas about place that entwined public schools, development, property values, and race were reflected in and encouraged by early school funding policies. As early as the 1850s, the creation of common schools funded by the state shaped patterns of residential segregation as well as ideas about the racial and economic character of the land around schools, together marking the conquest of "civilization" in the expanding nation's racial imaginary. Real estate's status as a commodity was itself shaped by the creation of educational institutions. This way of thinking about schools was, moreover, structured and encouraged by federal and state land policies. Those policies and their approach to granting expropriated Indigenous land to finance schools helped circulate and spread popular narratives describing how state-supported schools would attract permanent and "respectable" white settlement, create economic value, and ascribe racial meaning to the lands around public school buildings by making them appear like permanent parts of the United States, home to white families.

Even before unequal land values were explicitly connected with school funding, governmental policies related to educational land grants, taxation, school construction, municipal incorporation, and school districting, among others, helped direct uneven development. This was reflected most clearly in the hardening of the school district boundary. California created the legal framework for school districting during the early 1850s, but boundaries were poorly defined and rarely used to regulate school admissions. As late as 1912, San José permitted children living outside of it to freely attend San José schools.[51] School district boundaries were of such little consequence in some places that no one even thought to write them down. When the Sonoma County superintendent was asked to create a map of his school district boundaries in 1895, he refused. The boundaries had previously mattered so little that no one had kept a precise record, and he insisted in a letter to the county board of supervisors that the task was "absolutely impossible."[52] At the same time, the legal framework existed for communities to make district residence a prerequisite for school admissions by the late 1860s, which supported efforts to connect schooling with local development. Residency requirements gradually spread, often in response to other public policy changes that helped local actors use claims of educational distinction as a strategy to promote development. When communities began limiting access to their schools based on residence, they increased the significance of school district boundaries. But this did not emerge organically: the transformation of school district lines into fortified borders was enabled, structured, and encouraged by state action that localized school funding, structured access to the high school, empowered local governance through municipal home rule, enforced racially restrictive covenants, permitted racialized zoning, and directed school district and municipal unification, consolidation, annexation, and secession.

State policy makers chose inequality—especially racial inequality—again and again, redistributing wealth upward to wealthy and white Californians. Policy makers used school funding policies to expropriate Indigenous and Mexican land in the 1850s, and extract wealth from that land as it was distributed to white settlers and a nascent class of white land monopolists. State lawmakers capitulated to wealthy districts and land developers by devolving education funding more and more to local sources. They structured a connection between segregated housing and educational resources, guaranteeing that racial and economic apartheid would translate into educational apartheid—while helping to further segregate housing in the process. Finally, in the 1930s and 1940s, they consolidated a localized funding regime even as they claimed to be pursuing equal educational opportunity. Through the local property tax for schools, a sprawling system of redistribution was created—and hidden in plain sight. The tax served as not only a strategy for conditioning the distribution of funding on race amid successful civil rights challenges. It was also a subsidy for segregated development, a tax burden shifted onto renters of color by predatory landlords, and a way for banks and corporations to minimize their tax liabilities and push the cost of government onto private citizens. From this vantage point, postwar school funding disparities were never simply the product of postwar development patterns. Postwar school funding disparities were instead creations of the state, creations rooted in legal mechanisms, ideas about the degree to which education was a public good, and what a public good even was. The state set the terms upon which the more familiar forces detailed in postwar histories—public and private—operated.

Plan and Scope of the Book

This book is organized roughly chronologically. Chapter 1 considers the place of national and state policy in structuring the development of school funding in California and the uncertain and contested meanings of the world "public" that were circulating at the time. Contesting the myth of localism in the early history of public education by retelling the story of the common school from the perspective of the West, chapter 1 also brings into view what most historical narratives conceal: the role of racial violence and colonial conquest in the creation and funding of early state school systems by state and national governments. Taking that role seriously, the chapter argues, requires reckoning with how 7 percent of the contiguous United States was composed of dispossessed Indigenous land set aside to try to finance early elementary and secondary schools. Covering a similar period, chapter 2 traces the idea that schools marked the spread of "civilization" in California and how this shaped a process of racialized and uneven development. In tracing this process, this chapter also illustrates how federal and state policies were premised on the idea that schools increased the value of land by marking an area as "civilized" and attracting white settlers. Moving forward in time, chapter 3 details debates over local funding after the Civil War and how such debates became entangled with efforts to constrain the rise of heavily subsidized and increasingly powerful railroad corporations. During these years, groups of sometimes conflicting and sometimes overlapping reformers in California resisted local taxation for schooling, calling for the creation of the first need-adjusted school funding formulas and the implementation of Reconstruction's promise of racial equality in schooling. While these efforts succeeded in temporarily blocking the use of local taxes in school funding, they failed to create fully integrated schools or make corporations pay a higher share of taxes, culminating in the creation of a new state constitution that enabled localized financing.

The heart of the book's narrative are the changes to school funding enacted in California during the Progressive Era, the subject of chapters 4 and 5. Chapter 4 examines district-level campaigns to fund school reforms during the early years of the Progressive Era. While there is no shortage of scholarship detailing the transformation of schooling during this period, scholars have often glossed over the mechanics of how these reforms were financed. They required unprecedented and massive investments in school infrastructure, but annual state and county apportionments did little to help districts finance them, and local financing was contingent on voter approval in most states. Working within the legal framework established by the state, thousands of election campaigns to generate support for Progressive Era reforms deployed a language of competitive boosterism and local interest. Rather than remedy existing inequities in the distribution of wealth, reformers of the era used state policies to exacerbate and create new wealth disparities between districts.

Chapter 5 considers how state-level reforms and new forms of expertise helped narrow the vision of social responsibility. At the same time that state policies helped create new wealth disparities between school districts, a new class of experts in the emerging disciplines of public finance and school finance began advocating for the dissolution of the statewide property tax and extolling the virtues of district-level taxation for schools. Illustrating the effect of experts such as Carl Plehn and Ellwood Cubberley on state legislation during these years, the chapter explores the rise of district-level taxation in California following the abolition of the statewide property tax in 1910 and the new forms of expertise that emerged to support the practice. Indeed, expert narratives cast school funding disparities as inevitable and, in some cases, desirable features of state education systems. These narratives helped limit alternatives to district taxation in states such as California following World War I and contributed to a growing national conversation, led by emerging experts in economics and public finance, about schools spending more than they produced in outcomes.

Chapter 6 considers the consequences of local taxation and how it became even more entrenched in state law and popular discourse during the 1930s and 1940s. Even as Californians were willing to expand the reach of state government into other areas of public policy during the Great Depression and World War II, a narrative casting school funding disparities as a local problem was cemented by reforms that California lawmakers claimed would support equal opportunity. Tracing how school funding policies intersected with the expansion of federal, state, and local policies to underwrite white suburban affluence, the chapter makes the case that localized funding contributed to the racialization of the costs and benefits of education, helping establish, reinforce, and exacerbate racialized patterns of suburban, urban, and rural affluence and poverty that became even more pronounced after World War II. Indeed, the chapter contends that the effects of localized funding on postwar inequality went well beyond the decision made by policy makers to tie funding to the unequal wealth of districts. Although that connection was a requirement for postwar inequality, other aspects of the localization of school funding also contributed to the material, intellectual, and physical makeup of unequal development.

It is important to clarify several points before proceeding. The first is that the story told here is one among many that remain to be told. Given the limited amount of work on school funding, it has been necessary to rely on developments in places such as state legislative chambers to write this history. This has meant, in turn, giving considerable attention—albeit with a critical gaze—to historical actors who were positioned by their whiteness, maleness, and wealth to exercise formal power over public policies. Throughout the book, I am critical of many state and local policy makers, emphasizing the negative intent and impact of their decisions for children of color and children from poor communities attending public schools. I have also tried to push back against the language of universal opportunity that has plagued too much historical writing on the evolution of American public education. I do not wish to imply, however, just because of my focus here, that communities of color and low-income communities were not able to exercise agency and transcend the effects of these policies at various points. Furthermore, this history is not isolated to formal state politics, and I also examine sources such as popular newspaper accounts, intellectual treatises, and local school district boundary changes. Nonetheless, it remains a view from the top told primarily from the perspective of a single state. Studies of different places and periods told from different vantage points are also needed, in order to supplement the story told here.

Further clarification about my use of quantitative data is also needed. Some chapters draw on funding data. These references are based on a detailed dataset of district-level revenue and expenditure data I manually reconstructed from files in the California State Archives, supplemented with data from reports printed by the California superintendent of public instruction and the US commissioner of education. I discuss these data sources in greater detail in the appendix, but for now it is important to emphasize their limits. Scholars often misuse and misinterpret school funding data, including contemporary studies that use data from the National Center for Educational Statistics to study present-day patterns. Historical data is no better, and decontextualized analyses of school funding are more likely to create a distorted reality than reflect a reality that already existed. For this reason, I have striven to give far more analytic and narrative weight to archival sources than funding data in the pages that follow.

A note on language is also in order. I use the term "funding disparities" to describe differences in educational resources between school districts based on the way revenues and expenditures for education were distributed by state and local policy makers. For clarity and consistency with the historical scholarship engaged in this book, I have decided to use the terms "unequal" and "inequality" when discussing public school funding and its relationship to racial, economic, and spatial disparities. It is important to emphasize at the outset, however, that my use of these terms does not mean school funding systems that provide every student or school with the same amount of money—past or present—are fair. For a variety of reasons that have nothing to do with the innate abilities of children, some schools cost more to run than others. Differences in educational costs need to be taken into account when assessing the fairness of state funding systems, a point that some policy makers in California were already articulating by the 1870s.

At times, I also reference "educational opportunity" to describe access to tangible elements of schooling, including everything from a schoolhouse with indoor plumbing to a high school building. But the use of this term in a discussion of school funding requires additional clarification. I do not intend to suggest that the quality of children's education during this period depended solely on how much money their school district had. I also do not want to imply that equalizing funding is a panacea for the many other educational, racial, and economic inequalities at play.

With that said, the need to provide stipulations such as these demonstrates how widely the inaccurate claim that money does not matter for student outcomes has spread. This claim is false. The evidence shows clearly that money does in fact matter. Yet the fiction has a fierce following. Perhaps as a result, reformers have pursued numerous other strategies for making schools a place where children of all backgrounds could purportedly come together to become citizens and forge a fair shot in life. There is a radical collective decision hidden among all of this supposed common sense: for all the reforms the United States pursues or has pursued to make the institution of schooling more equitable, states have never tried—for any sustained duration—simply equitably and adequately funding it. For the short times when they have, it is clear it has positively shaped the life trajectories of children.[53] The central theme of this book is that the state has always had a heavy hand in the development of inequitable school funding, even when it has concealed it. Without taking care, present-day educational researchers can have a hand in it, too. They have a hand in concealing the state's role in funding in the questions they ask (or rather, do not ask) about how funding is made contingent on race, class, and residence. They cover the state's tracks in the stories they tell and believe (or rather, not) about the importance of addressing policies with clearly racist and classist outcomes. They absolve the state in the kinds of questions they create space for, in the voices they elevate, and in the worlds they build—be they departments, journals, or reference lists.

If there is any hope of imagining new choices in contemporary policy debates about education finance, we first must discover the choices already made—now so deeply sedimented they have become largely forgotten—that brought US schools to this juncture. For all people who believe in the possibilities of schools to support equality of opportunity, it is long past time to return to the historical roots of American school funding.

1

FUNDING FOR EDUCATION, SETTLER COLONIALISM, AND THE "CALIFORNIA EXPERIMENT" IN COMMON SCHOOL CENTRALIZATION, 1848–1865

Federal and state governments sought to extract value from about 138.9 million acres of expropriated Indigenous land to finance US common schools—that supposed "great equalizer of the conditions of man."[1] This stunning figure represents about 7 percent of the contiguous United States, yet it has been largely ignored or minimized in accounts of the public school and its early history. Even as historians have documented in detail the 11 million acres of expropriated land that financed US higher educational institutions after the Civil War, this earlier and much larger project (more than twelve times larger when measured in acres of expropriated Native American land) has received very little scholarly attention.[2] This chapter argues that the scant attention paid to the connections between the creation of a US continental empire and the creation of public education systems for white children in part reflects a foundational problem with how historians of education have imagined the origins of public education systems in the United States—conceptually, chronologically, and geographically.

Most historians locate the origins of public education systems in the United States in the Northeast during the three decades before the Civil War. It was during this period—the era of the common school—that journalist John O'Sullivan authored the article for which he is typically credited with coining the phrase "manifest destiny."[3] In the article, O'Sullivan suggested the deep links between schooling and the stories commentators in the United States told themselves to justify the creation of a continental empire in the 1840s. O'Sullivan predicted California would simply "fall away" from "imbecile and distracted" Mexico as an "irresistible army of Anglo-Saxon emigration" would take over, "marking its trail with schools and colleges." All of this would happen, O'Sullivan insisted, "without agency of our government, without responsibility of our people—in the natural flow of events."[4] Neither governments nor people are culpable of theft or violence in O'Sullivan's account.

The image conjured by O'Sullivan is of a weak national government not responsible for the expansion of its borders. The state he represented to rationalize colonial expansion parallels a mythic vision of a laissez-faire US government in the nineteenth century whose defining feature was its absence. Historians of the pre–Civil War United States have challenged that representation of governmental power across a number of domains, upending what William Novak has termed the "myth of the 'weak' American state."[5] Historians of education have also brought the "state back into" their accounts of public schooling during the Progressive Era and Greater Reconstruction.[6]

Yet the history of public education in the United States before the Civil War is often still told in a way that has more in common with the vision of the state offered by O'Sullivan than the image of strong governance documented in histories of state power in other domains before the Civil War. In large measure, this is because of where historians have decided to focus their attention in telling the history of public schooling in the United States and what that has meant for how the public school, its funding, and the state's role in education have been imagined. In the conventional narrative, the origins of public education systems in the United States did not coincide with the origins of national or state funding for education, the creation of school districts by state legislatures, the moment state legislatures granted school districts power to raise funds for schools with local taxes, or when state courts first permitted school districts to own property, sue, and be sued.[7] Nor did it coincide with the years in which students were no longer charged tuition to attend schools and schools actually became free.[8] It did not coincide, either, with the period when districts were first required to raise local tax dollars as a condition for receiving state funding.[9] It does not overlap substantially with the period when students started attending schools funded and organized under terms structured in state law at high rates, or when students were required under state compulsory school laws to attend them.[10] Some of these milestones occurred after the three-decade span during which most narratives position the beginnings of public education systems in the United States. Most preceded it.

Rather, the standard narrative of when state common school systems were created centers antebellum educational legislation in areas such as teacher training. This conventional historical narrative connects the origins of public education with a moment of widespread commentary in the Northeast criticizing state funding for schools and how reforms such as teacher training and school district consolidation could improve schools without expanding a preexisting pattern of direct state funding.[11]

Moreover, in the standard narrative, the public education systems that purportedly emerged in states such as Massachusetts during the three decades before the Civil War were ostensibly carried westward unchanged. Historians telling the history of Massachusetts have expressed few reservations about letting that provincial and partial story stand in for the history of the nation.[12] Historians have not only neglected the development of state-sponsored education outside a handful of states such as Massachusetts, Connecticut, and New York; they have occasionally included scant details about states such as Ohio to support the claim that what unfolded in the northeastern United States unfolded everywhere. Perhaps such claims make sense if one imagines that North America was unoccupied or that its original inhabitants tended, as O'Sullivan suggested in the 1840s, to simply "fall away."

This chapter retells the history of funding for education, lawmaking concerning education, and the development of public school systems before the Civil War from the perspective of the Pacific Coast. Before turning to California, it begins by tracing how historians have narrated the origins of public education systems in the United States. It argues that historians have tended to conceptualize public school systems in a way that minimizes the essential role state lawmaking played in early school funding and overstates the extent to which localism in educational finance operated independent of state action before the Civil War. One major consequence of how historians have located the beginnings of public school systems in the United States has been the obfuscation, and at times complete erasure, of the history of racial violence and Indigenous dispossession at the core of the early American state, its schools, and ideas about how schools should be funded—East and West.

After tracing that conventional history and what it misses, this chapter then uses the history of school funding in California during the 1850s and 1860s to detail the scope of alternatives to localized funding before the Civil War. Unearthing the story of these forgotten alternatives reveals the extent to which localism was constituted by state action, and how racial exclusion and white supremacy were at the heart of the way Anglo-Americans talked about the organization and financing of schools during these years. A history of public schooling from the perspective of California emphasizes how early education funding policies were connected to settler colonialism. The growing body of historical work examining the settler colonial project in the American West has started to explore its varied manifestations. Historians have long noted the role of schooling in white American efforts to eliminate Indigenous peoples through forced assimilation.[13] However, few have considered the role schooling was expected to play in efforts to repopulate Indigenous lands. In many nineteenth-century American policy makers' minds, the promise of well-funded schools would induce white families to move westward. This chapter illustrates how the expansion of public schooling was discussed as a strategy for re-creating a system of white supremacy on the Pacific Coast. At the same time, that system was resisted and complicated by the contradictions of US racial ideology in multiracial California. Many Anglo-Americans insisted that the exclusion of Black children from California's schools was central to the colonization of California. The chapter concludes by illustrating how this exclusion was challenged by Black activists in California and, to a degree, upended during the Civil War.

Conceptualizing the Origins of the Public School and Minimizing the State

Retelling the history of the common school from the perspective of the far West requires first outlining the conventional story of public education systems, their funding, and their early history. That story has often been difficult to tell because the term "public school" has long been imprecise. As a result, deciding where the story should start is no simple matter. Historians of education have long noted the unclear boundary between public and private.[14] At the same time, historians have largely left intact a long-standing consensus about the origins of public school systems—conceptually, chronologically, and geographically.[15] This section explores how that consensus has also minimized the role of state lawmaking in early school funding and overstated the extent to which localism in educational finance operated independently of state action.

Conceptually, the difference between public and private schools was unclear throughout much of the nineteenth century. Historians often make this point clear in their accounts of early public education in the United States. Before the Civil War, the meaning of the word "public" was fluid. The question of what it meant to talk about a "public" school hinged on a distinction between public and private forms of governmental activity that did not exist during the early national period. Even in the antebellum era, as Anglo-American elites worked to create a new kind of state school system in California, the term "public" did not carry the meaning it does today. As historian Michael Katz explains, the term initially "implied a performance of broad social functions."[16] An entity or project serving the common good was assumed to have a public character during these years, even if it took forms that might today be considered private. Policy makers claimed schooling of white citizens was an instrument of the common good. A range of institutions that provided schooling were, in turn, cast as public during the late eighteenth and early nineteenth centuries. Even as those institutions were financed by what we today consider "private" means, they existed in the American imagination as "public" agents of the state.[17] At various points, these schools received subsidies from state legislatures, but they were largely funded through tuition payments known as "rate bills." Yet these schools were understood to have a public dimension all the same.[18] A teacher opening a school that charged tuition, historian William Reese points out, was assumed to perform "a 'public' function" since that teacher was "offering a 'public' education in the sense that anyone who could afford the tuition could presumably attend."[19]

Chronologically, historians usually locate the origins of the public school in antebellum legislative activity in the Northeast between the 1830s and 1860s. In the process, they have created a way of talking about antebellum education reform that minimizes the role federal and state governments played in shaping education before this period and, to an extent, during it. Moreover, even as they acknowledge the unclear boundaries between public and private, they have tended to suggest that public education as an idea was largely settled by the antebellum school legislation passed during this same period. While the three decades before the Civil War certainly involved new kinds of state-level policy making in education, the period did not represent the beginning of state involvement in education in general or school funding in particular.

On the one hand, historians of education before the Civil War have tended to qualify their studies by noting both the unclear boundaries between public and private and by stipulating how their primary analytic focus is the development of *systems* of public education rather than the origins of state involvement in education. On the other hand, many of these same accounts reinforce the notion that state governments did not play a role before lawmakers such as Horace Mann became interested in education. One group of historians, for example, notes state action that preceded the so-called common school reformers, but also places substantial emphasis throughout their analyses on the idea that state involvement in education before 1840 was practically nonexistent. Drawing on data illustrating large enrollments before 1840, they emphasize how those enrollments "preceded substantial state intervention in schooling." Throughout their analysis, they repeatedly frame the period before the 1830s and 1840s as a period before state intervention. They provide a political analysis of the Massachusetts legislature in 1840, for example, and frame that analysis as a way to examine the beginnings of "state intervention" in education.[20] The importance of the 1830s and 1840s for increased state regulations of education notwithstanding, casting these years as the beginnings of "state intervention" in education minimizes earlier patterns in state lawmaking. Economic historians make similar claims about a completely absent state, emphasizing "grassroots action rather than top-down campaigns" while glossing over the substance of state lawmaking structuring such grassroots actions.[21] Another economic historian, for example, calls the use of local taxes to fund education—an unambiguous product of state laws enabling local taxation and required by legislatures in some states in the nineteenth century—the product of "spontaneous political will to levy local taxes in thousands of school districts."[22]

In placing undue emphasis on antebellum common school reformers in this manner, historians have minimized state involvement in schooling before 1840 in three notable ways. First, they largely neglect the extent to which local taxation was a product of state law and thus a conscious political choice among state lawmakers. Local communities could not legally raise a tax for schools without authorization from the state. Enrollments during this period that preceded "state intervention" were nonetheless within school districts authorized under state law and financed with local taxes structured by earlier legislation. Historian Nancy Beadie makes clear the significance of state action during this period before 1840 in her work on New York. For example, she notes how New York State's 1815 school law created and structured a decentralized pattern of localized funding. The 1815 law, she explains, "detailed procedures for dividing towns into districts, electing school officials, assessing local taxes and distributing state and local funds. In effect, state law established the structure of local governance for schools."[23]

Second, even as local communities engaged in grassroots activity that some scholars cast as separate from the state, they often used state law and privileges granted by the state through incorporation to engage in that work. Nancy Beadie finds that "access to corporate legal power" was one of the most important ingredients in the early formation of schools, blurring the boundaries between public and private in New York State during the early national period.[24] The broader history of academies illustrated a similar pattern where state governments shaped education through incorporation, mixing what are now considered public and private means. Supporters of academies considered them public institutions. Connecticut author Theodore Dwight, for example, declared academies in Massachusetts part of that state's "great machinery of public education."[25] As other commentators wondered "whether academies could ever benefit the public good since they served an exclusive clientele," they critiqued direct government financial support for them.[26] Common schools in most states, like academies, charged tuition.[27] Incorporation was critical for the ability of common school districts to operate, too. Even after state legislatures authorized school districts to raise local tax dollars, uncertainty continued to surround their legal status. In Massachusetts, the ability of school districts to enter and enforce contracts was initially unclear. When state courts ruled that districts had sufficient legal status to enter a contract, jurists drew on and applied corporate law.[28]

States pursued a range of projects by chartering corporations. As entities created by state legislatures, these early corporations had a public character—in exchange for the privileges conferred by incorporation, they performed functions for the state. Such corporations were, as historian Eric Hilt explains, "instrumentalities of the state."[29] They built infrastructure, administered early welfare programs for the poor, provided urban services, and administered criminal justice.[30] Corporate charters granted to what are now considered municipal corporations, such as the Corporation of the City of New York, had a clear public character.[31] Business corporations, too, displayed what historian William Novak calls a "curious mixture of public-private forms and functions." In the early American republic, incorporation served "as a peculiar instrument of statecraft."[32] Such corporations were created by state legislatures and had an obligation to support the common good as a condition for receiving privileges conferred by their charter. US Supreme Court justice Joseph Story's concurring opinion in *Dartmouth College v. Woodward* established two types of corporations—one public and one private—in 1819, but the public/private distinction remained fluid both before and after the ruling. With the rise of general incorporation laws, the nature of the business corporation changed. The first general incorporation laws were for manufacturing firms, spreading to most states by 1860.[33] Sociologist William Roy has described large-scale business corporations as moving from "quasi government agencies" in the early republic to "the institutional basis of private accumulation" at the end of the nineteenth century.[34]

Third, national and state governments engaged in direct funding for schools that has been minimized in many accounts, even though that direct state funding provided an alternative to district-level taxation authorized by the state and considered by policy makers. Indeed, the range of governmental sources for school support circulating in the antebellum Northeast created a fiscal framework for reformers to expand as they sought to create state common school systems. The amount of revenue produced by both direct state subsidies and state-enabled local taxes was generally small and varied by state. Still, most states had created school funds by 1830. Connecticut's school fund was famously large and among the best known, with annual disbursements supplemented with revenue from state taxes. Throughout the 1820s and 1830s, a series of proposals that would have provided federal funds to expand state school funds and finance the expansion of American education circulated Congress.

In states like Massachusetts, localized funding was not simply structured by the state. It was also a choice with alternatives. Those alternatives were revealed, for example, in the debates over the creation of a permanent school fund in the state. Massachusetts did not create a school fund until 1834, and throughout the 1820s proposals to create a fund were criticized by lawmakers who called instead for better teacher training.[35] As one commentator pointed out in the *Common School Journal*, for example, localized funding meant that children "on one side of a boundary line" were disadvantaged even though "there is room enough to spare" on the other side. The same commentator in the *Common School Journal* critical of localized funding in Massachusetts declared "it would be difficult to say why one child does not need education as much as another, and why every child has not a right to claim an education as good as the best that is furnished to any other children."[36] The residents of Savoy, Massachusetts, raised a similar question more subtly when they requested state funding to support their ambitious reforms, pleading that "on account of our poverty, we are denied justice."[37] While some common school reformers advocated changes to prevent districts within each town from being funded in such an egregiously unequal manner, they had little to say about differences between towns themselves.

The impact that federal "donations" of expropriated land had on how Anglo-Americans imagined the role of state governments in schools was reflected in the regional differences that emerged regarding funding during the antebellum era. Midwestern and western states had a distinct pattern of centralized funding, in clear contrast to New England states. English official James Fraser remarked on these differences in his comparative analysis of schools in Scotland, Canada, and the United States. Fraser noted how the "sum required by local taxation is considerably diminished in the Western States, as compared, at least, with Massachusetts." Western and midwestern states became more likely to adopt state-level taxes to supplement their school funds, while states in New England, Fraser noted in his report, did not adopt state-level taxes for schooling at all.[38]

The various ways the state was involved in education and the range of alternatives to local financing that existed are critical because what it meant for a school to be public remained uncertain into the 1850s. Even as Anglo-Americans were beginning to construct California's school system in ways that would attract national attention, commentators and state lawmakers in Massachusetts continued to feel the meaning of "public school" was sufficiently unclear to require elaborate explanation. Consider how slippery George Boutwell found the phrase "public school" during his tenure as secretary of the Massachusetts Board of Education in the 1850s. He found it too ambiguous to share without an explicit definition: "A *public school* [italics in the original] I understand to be a school established by the public, supported chiefly or entirely by the public, controlled by the public, and accessible to the public upon terms of equality without special charge for tuition."[39] Still, this definition must have seemed incomplete to Secretary Boutwell, as he followed it up with extensive elaboration. Boutwell's need to create an elaborate definition in part reflected the fuzziness of the distinction between "public" and "private" governance during the nineteenth century.

The conflicting decisions that early state school officials made when designating which sources of funding were labeled "public" are illustrative of the competing ideas about the meaning of public and private that circulated in the nineteenth century, as well as about the appropriate role of the state in education. In their reports, school officials regularly created a category for the "public funds" or "public monies" spent on schools in a state, with an increase in the share of funding from these sources signaling progress. In multiple states, these "public funds" and "public monies" categories excluded district-level tax revenue before the Civil War, implicitly casting this funding mechanism as something other than public. Iowa superintendent of public instruction Maturin Fisher summarized how this category was constructed in his state when he added revenue from Iowa's permanent school fund to dollars raised by county taxes to generate "the total amount of public money apportioned in the State." But he excluded the district tax from the category.[40] Wisconsin officials compiled their data in a similar manner. The Wisconsin superintendent of public instruction's 1851 report recorded a category for "amount of public money" that included various sources but none of the subcategories of "district tax."[41] The same was true in Indiana, where the state superintendent worried about how money for school construction was being derived from "public funds." He considered a local tax, a "special township tax," the appropriate source of funding for schoolhouse construction, much like a construction bond would be used today, because "the use of the public money for such a purpose" would prevent the public fund from being able to cover teacher salaries.[42]

As district-level funding was placed outside the "public funds" or "public monies" category, it was considered private, like tuition payments charged to students through rate bills. Both supplemented "public funds," with school officials usually favoring the district tax option, though not always. In an early report from Illinois during the same period, for example, officials noted how districts were running out of "public money" and collecting "the money from the patrons of a school," something one official from Stephenson County thought should be raised by a tax on "the property holders of the district" instead.[43] Even in northeastern states that relied heavily on localized funding, there was a similar logic of tuition and local taxes being two different avenues for supplementing "public money." In New York, for example, officials reflected this way of thinking by categorizing funding into "public money" and two additional categories: money "raised on rate bills from those sending to school" and money "raised by district tax to supply deficiencies in the collection of such rate bills."[44] Even in Connecticut, school officials sometimes described rate bills and district taxes as two funding mechanisms separate from public funds that communities could use to demonstrate their commitment to schools. One official complained in an 1861 report, for example, about small districts that received "from the public funds more than pro rata share of school money" but did not contribute "a single dollar, voluntarily, either in rate-bills or in district taxes, for the support of schools."[45]

In minimizing the hand of the state in early funding, historians have also tended to erase the range of alternatives to localized funding that existed in these years. Historians have essentially selected one particular conceptualization of public school systems—state-authorized districts funded with local taxes—and elevated that conception in their accounts while obscuring both its predecessors and its alternatives. The next section further considers the broader impact of this historical narrative by highlighting the history of racial violence and Indigenous dispossession that it erases as well.

Indigenous Expropriation and the Public School

Locating the origins of public education in the Northeast during the 1840s has served to obscure the centrality of the connections between Indigenous dispossession, education, and school funding. Erasing the history of state action in school funding thus has consequences that extend far beyond how historians understand the early public school. Indeed, minimizing the early history of state action in education funding obfuscates acts of racial violence and Indigenous dispossession that were fundamental to both territorial and educational expansion in the early national and antebellum eras.

The links between dispossession and governmental support for public elementary and secondary education have escaped the level of scrutiny applied to the Morrill Land-Grant Acts after the Civil War. The best-known example of such links began in the 1780s with the insertion of educational provisions into the Northwest Ordinance of 1785. The ordinance established the procedure that the United States would follow—the public land survey system—to orchestrate the settlement and sale of the Indigenous land it seized. Federal officials used the public land survey system to divide up new land claims into a grid of rectangular townships, a grid that today covers much of the continental United States outside the original thirteen states. Each township in this grid was to contain thirty-six square miles, with one square mile in each of these townships reserved for public use as a donation to support early public schools. This figure increased to two square miles after 1850 and four square miles in the late 1890s.[46] White settlers could extract value from these "donations" by selling the land and creating an endowment, leasing it and collecting rent, or in some cases extracting and selling commodities like timber from it.

The history of these land grants is often treated separately from historical accounts of the public school and its origins in the United States, if examined at all. Some historians cast the origins of federal land donations as little more than a land speculation scheme, given the role that a land development group called the Ohio Company of Associates played in shaping the educational provisions of the Northwest Ordinance. To interpret the Northwest Ordinance in these simple terms, however, misses the broader mission that the architects of the ordinance imagined that the lands donated for education would fulfill. As historian Carl Kaestle has explained, the Ohio Company's founders' "commercial motives [were] woven together with concerns about how to recreate republican society on the frontier."[47] The re-creation of this society was only possible if white settlers could be persuaded to move west and educated to become loyal American citizens once there. Enticed in part by subsidies for schools, these settlers would help kill, relocate, or forcibly assimilate tribal residents of the Northwest Territory. These donated school lands were therefore part of the broader framework for a territorial system created by the Northwest Ordinance. The schoolhouse itself became a rich symbol of "civilization" conquering the "wilderness" in American representations of the frontier and its conquest.

Even beyond the states receiving federal "donations" of township school sections, lawmakers on the Atlantic Coast developed early forms of support for education by expropriating land from their Indigenous neighbors. Many of the original thirteen colonies assumed ownership of Native American lands beyond their western borders at the conclusion of the American Revolution, lands that they eventually transferred to the federal government. Connecticut, however, maintained its claim to Indigenous lands in present-day Ohio, a parcel called the Connecticut Western Reserve. In 1795, Connecticut created a large permanent school fund with the revenue from the sale and rental of these lands. Other states claimed that their borders encompassed territory that Indigenous people had not ceded and of which they had not yet been dispossessed. New York, for example, used land it derived from its encroachments into the territory of the Haudenosaunee Confederacy that it claimed were within its borders to experiment with state-supported schooling during the same period.[48] Maine, New Hampshire, Massachusetts, New Jersey, Pennsylvania, North Carolina, and Georgia dedicated dispossessed Indigenous lands that they claimed ownership over to subsidize different kinds of educational activity during the late eighteenth and early nineteenth centuries as well.[49] The history of these efforts to finance common schools and the far-reaching racial violence upon which they were founded vanishes from historical narratives that locate the origins of the public school in the legislative activity of antebellum lawmakers.

Dispossession and educational provisioning were also linked in repeated proposals to expand the role of the federal government in education during the 1820s and 1830s. These proposals centered on the claim that the dispossessed Native American lands that made up the "public domain" were the shared property of all white Americans and that states east of the Mississippi River ought to benefit more from them. The language of the proposals themselves exemplifies the racialized, colonial logic behind the use of dispossessed Indigenous land to fund education. For example, the notion that the shared work of conquest made its fruits the shared property of whites was at the center of Maryland lawmaker Virgil Maxcy's proposal for federal education funding in the 1820s. Maxcy's proposal was premised on the argument that "extinguishment of the Indian title" was accomplished "by the common sword, purse, and blood of all the States, united in a common effort."[50] Proponents and opponents of Maxcy's proposal disagreed about which region of the American nation should benefit from conquered lands. Both sides agreed, however, that the lands belonged to white citizens of the United States and represented a fund that ought to be used in part for schools educating white settlers. Although Maxcy's proposal did not come to fruition amid the national politics of the 1820s, proposals to provide federal support for state school funds continued to circulate in Congress in 1826, 1827, 1832, and 1838.[51]

Even early instances of governmental support for education that seem disconnected from Native American dispossession can be traced back to the massive transfer of wealth from Indigenous people to white settlers. That system helped constitute what historian Michael Witgen has termed a "political economy of plunder."[52] For example, sixteen states dedicated at least a portion of the funds they received from Congress after the passage of the Surplus Revenue Act of 1836 to the support of common schools.[53] The dollars distributed by that act can be traced to increased revenue in the federal budget from public land sales accompanying the expansion of white settlement in the 1830s.

Figure 1.1 illustrates an estimate of the total acres of expropriated Native American land used to support early elementary and secondary schooling. All told, thirty of the thirty-four states admitted before the Civil War dedicated such dispossessed land to support early public school systems. Across all forty-eight contiguous states admitted both before and after the Civil War, I estimate about 138.9 million acres of expropriated land were set aside, in total, for early school funding. This represents about 7 percent of the total acreage of the contiguous United States—but even this is likely an underestimate.[54] Two of the four states without a value displayed in figure 1.1—Tennessee and New

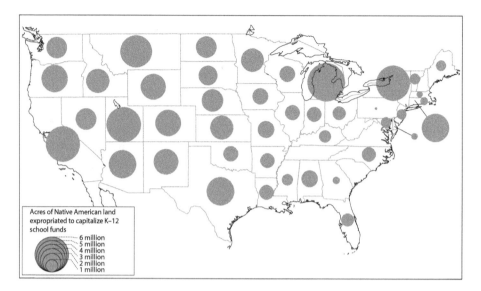

FIGURE 1.1. Estimated acres of expropriated Native American land used to capitalize K–12 school funds. Data adapted from multiple sources. See appendix for details. Cartography by Bill Nelson.

Hampshire—committed the revenue from land sales to education, but the acreage cannot be traced. The estimate also excludes the "donations" of expropriated land allocated for higher education from the 1860s onward.

Common Schools and Continental Empire in the Far West

Retelling the history of the antebellum public school from the Pacific Coast brings to light the continued uncertainty of the public/private distinction into the 1850s and 1860s, the range of alternatives to district-level funding circulating in these years, and how fundamentally entangled ideas about schools and their funding were with ideas about race.

California became a part of the United States in 1848 and a state in 1850. By the end of the 1860s, lawmakers in the state developed a centralized system of education funding that constituted an alternative to the localized model structured by state governments in places such as Massachusetts. This model was reflected in three areas. First, the state created a large centralized school fund at its constitutional convention. The federal government promised half a million acres of expropriated lands for "internal improvements" to the state. Delegates at California's constitutional convention decided to place revenue from these lands into a centralized state school fund, in addition to money received from the estates of persons who died without heirs and the payment of criminal fines. Second, state lawmakers decided to centralize the revenue derived from the sale or rental of the sixteenth and thirty-sixth sections of each township into a single fund so that differences in the value of the land surveyed in each township would not shape funding. The delegates at California's constitutional convention initially left township school lands under the control of townships, resulting in a political debate over who were the rightful "owners" of revenue from dispossessed Indigenous and Mexican lands. Although wealthy townships with more valuable township lands opposed consolidation, lawmakers decided to place all revenue extracted from township school sections into the statewide school fund in 1861.[55] Third, lawmakers adopted a statewide property tax to provide direct state funding to support common schools and supplement revenue derived from expropriated lands in the school fund.

These three policies reflected a broader rejection of localized funding and an understanding of education as a public good that was connected to it. Some commentators in California claimed a district-level tax was private since inequities in taxable wealth between communities could shape how it operated. The contemporary notion that tuition payments are private funding while a district-level tax is a "public" form of funding is rooted in a widespread logic today: even when disparities in school funding are critiqued in the present, the notion is broadly accepted that schools funded with taxes drawn from fragmented, district-wide economic pools are "public." But the history of school funding in California makes this logic appear strange and inconsistent. According to some commentators at the time, a school funded with a district property tax was something other than a free public school. Calaveras County superintendent Robert Thompson insisted that only a state tax would produce "the permanent establishment of Free Schools."[56] Similarly, Henry Gaddis, the superintendent of schools for Yolo County, thought a proposed increase in state taxation—not a new rate bill, district tax, or county tax—was the only thing that could make schools in his county "*free*, in the proper sense of the term."[57] Placer County superintendent Percival Millette was a staunch opponent of the district property tax. He instead felt the 1858 law allowing for this "so-called school tax" should be "totally, absolutely, and immediately repealed."[58] Millette was unwilling even to concede that this fiscal instrument was a tax. Today, tuition is treated as the quintessential marker of a private educational institution at the elementary and secondary levels. In higher education, public institutions charge tuition and are hardly free, since some students will go into heavy debt to attend. District-level funding is criticized on various grounds, but it is never a threat to the status of an educational institution as public. When officials minimized localized funding in California, they were also lumping the rate bill and the district tax into a category of funding separate from public.

The net result of these centralized funding mechanisms and these overarching ideas about whether a district-level tax was public was a system of school finance that limited the use of district-level taxation even after the structure for it was created and enabled by the state. In 1858, the legislature technically granted school districts the power to raise property taxes; but because of these centralized funding policies, few California school districts raised district-level taxes throughout the nineteenth century. They relied instead on more redistributive taxes like the statewide property tax or allocations of school funds derived from expropriated land. By 1863, the state superintendent reported that only 17 of the state's 684 school districts, or about 2.5 percent, raised a district-level tax.[59] The trend continued into the twentieth century.

The limits placed on localized funding in California were reflected in the writing of eastern commentators at the time as well. By the late 1860s, the state was at the center of national conversations about centralization and expansive state power in education. Social reformer Charles Loring Brace encouraged New Yorkers to learn from the advantages of California's system, and the editors of the *Pennsylvania School Journal* argued that California's school system was a model for the entire nation.[60] Connecticut common school reformer Henry Barnard, while occasionally critical of state-level funding, dedicated a section of his *American Journal of Education* to praising centralization in California during the 1860s, noting how "there is nothing so liberal in the way of taxation in any other state in world."[61] Other commentators expressed apprehension regarding the school system emerging in California and the way it made schooling a state, rather than local, project. Ohioan education reformer Emerson White would later recall learning the "principle of uniformity" from Californians and state that the "California experiment" in uniformity had "inspired efforts in different sections of the country." At the same time, however, White saw California as too centralized. "The leadership of California in public education," White reasoned, was "sacrificed by the undue development of the state system and an over-organization of the principle of state uniformity."[62]

The Racial Project of Repopulation

Tracing how and why centralized finance policies were adopted illustrates how deeply rooted school funding was in efforts to promote racial exclusion. This was apparent in two ways. First, early policy discourse around centralized funding fixated on the utility of well-funded schools for attracting white families westward to colonize California. In the process, policy makers adopted a way of talking about the creation and funding of schools that centered a settler colonial project too often neglected in histories of education. Second, these same funding policies were used to regulate and restrict access to schools. State efforts to enforce restrictions on who could benefit from the state's school fund served as a way for the state, according to observers at the time, to re-create eastern racial hierarchies in multiracial California and further a racial project purportedly necessary for integrating California into the United States. These racial restrictions on access to school funding in the state worked to police the racial boundaries of citizenship and the definition of just who constituted a public benefiting from state-sponsored schools. These restrictions were forcefully challenged as well. It is useful to start with the first dynamic before addressing the second.

When Anglo-Americans began to imagine a common school system for California at the end of the Mexican-American War, there was already a pattern of linking state support for education with the seizure and sale of Indigenous lands noted above. As they formulated funding policies for common schools at California's constitutional convention, delegates established a strong and direct role for state government in financing education. In part, their thinking reflected the distinct way that access to dispossessed lands for education was structured. The process in place meant that it was only upon statehood that land "donations" were made available for education. When the United States incorporated new regions into its borders, it typically first made those places incorporated territories that would then apply for statehood after some number of years. Officials in these territories could and did levy taxes at the scale of the entire territory to finance education.[63] They could also decide, however, to levy county or district taxes, allowing localized funding to take root before state funds were organized. California, however, drafted its constitution less than two years after the end of the Mexican-American War, meaning that the revenue from the recently expropriated lands was immediately available. As a result, lawmakers were poised to think about a stronger state from the beginning.

At the same time, Anglo-Americans described California as unique in a number of ways and sought to adopt policies that would attract the largest number of white families to the Pacific Coast as quickly as possible. The sense of urgency around growing the population of white families in California was in part a reaction to the flood of miners who had rushed to the state following the discovery of gold. About 95 percent of these migrants were men. Most were there to make money, and few seemed committed to staying permanently.[64] Even worse in the eyes of Anglo-American policy makers, many of these migrants were neither white nor from the United States.[65] The gold rush did not just bring Anglo-Americans to California. It also brought Chinese, Chilean, European, and Mexican migrants. Nothing seemed to disturb Anglo-American visitors to the region more than its racial and ethnic diversity, and nothing seemed to represent a greater obstacle to the integration of California into the United States than its multiracial character. Pennsylvanian Bayard Taylor described the shock of visiting San Francisco and finding people "of as diverse and bizarre a character as the houses: Yankees of every possible variety, native Californians in *serapes* and sombreros, Chileans, Sonorians, Kanaka from Hawaii, Chinese with long [pony]tails, Malays armed with their everlasting creeses [daggers], and others in whose embrowned and bearded visages it was impossible to recognize any special nationality."[66]

Early Anglo-Americans leaders were particularly anxious about the presence of former Mexican nationals, whose place in the Anglo-American racial imagination made California seem that much further from becoming American. Former Mexican nationals deemed European were not subject to the same logic of elimination applied to Indigenous peoples in the state. With the Treaty of Guadalupe Hidalgo at the end of the Mexican-American War, the United States had granted citizenship to Mexicans living in the ceded territory. Some Anglo-Americans considered these citizens "half civilized," and they occupied an "ambiguous position" in many commentators' minds.[67] Commentators had already worried, before the war concluded, about the prospect of incorporating large numbers of Mexican citizens into the American national fabric. As these commentators debated how much of the Mexican nation the United States should annex, the racial logics that helped justify the invasion of Mexico also helped justify calls to limit imperial ambitions in the region.[68] While supporters of the "all Mexico" movement called for the United States to annex the entire nation, critics like Senator John Calhoun insisted the United States should not annex densely populated sections of Mexico like Mexico City, the largest city in North America, because the United States ought never to incorporate "any but the Caucasian race."[69] According to Calhoun, "more than half of the Mexicans are Indians, and the other is composed chiefly of mixed tribes."[70] The "all Mexico" movement did not succeed.

Within this broader context, delegates at California's constitutional convention celebrated the idea of creating a large state school fund, and they insisted such a fund was needed to help grow the white population of California. Delegates explicitly described a large school fund as an indispensable tool for colonizing California, as it would encourage white families to migrate to the state. According to delegate John McDougal, "we can create no fund too large for the purpose of education," because such a fund "will introduce families into this country." For delegate Jacob David Hoppe, a large fund was essential because it would bring "that intelligent and permanent character of population which will add wealth to our country and stability to our institutions." With such a large fund, Hoppe continued, "in place of the husband coming here to dig gold for his family and carry it home, he will not leave them, but will bring them here to reside in this country permanently." As delegate Francis Lippitt explained, "the very fact that California offers such a munificent fund" will serve as an "inducement to a most valuable class of population to come here—families having children." A large fund, Lippitt continued, "will make our population a permanent one."[71]

Delegates insisted that creating a large school fund capable of attracting a "valuable class of population" was uniquely important because of the state's existing and implicitly less valuable population. Convention president Robert Semple emphasized how a comprehensive system of public schooling was "a subject of peculiar importance here in California, from our location and the circumstance under which we are placed." Delegate M. M. McCarver made a similar assertion, contending that "nothing will have a greater tendency to secure prosperity to the State, stability to our institutions, and an enlightened state of society, than by providing for the education of our posterity."[72] In an address introducing the new constitution to the public, delegates similarly stressed the "peculiar circumstances in which California becomes a State—with an unexampled increase of a population coming from every part of the world, speaking various languages, and imbued with different feelings and prejudices."[73] The presence of "natives of Old Spain, Californians, and those who have voluntarily relinquished the rights of Mexicans to enjoy those of American citizens" made the role of public schools in attracting citizens particularly important.[74]

As Anglo-Americans discussed adopting and expanding state taxation for common schools throughout the 1850s and 1860s, they reiterated the logic connecting ample state funding for schools with attracting white settler colonials. In his regular appeals to the legislature for increased funding and centralization, for example, state superintendent Andrew Jackson Moulder referenced "the natural tendency of the heads of families to seek for a settlement in those counties which furnish the best facilities for the education of their children."[75] It was imperative to early school leaders that the citizens attracted by schools would be of the right variety. "The more numerous and the better the schools a county possesses," Moulder informed the legislature, "the greater will be its accessions of population—and the population to be most desired."[76] For California's second superintendent, Paul Hubbs, the role of common school funding in enticing white families to the West meant it was irrational to force them to fund schools with a local tax and that a state-level tax and other funding were more appropriate. According to Hubbs, forcing families to pay for schools "after parting with the last dollar on the journey to the home of their adoption" would inhibit the development of the state: "This is so well known and severely experienced by tens of thousands of devoted fathers living among us, as to require them to separate themselves from all the holy ties of the family home, and to refrain from bringing their wives and children to California, in order to educate their offspring in lands more congenial to the future prosperity of the children of their dearest hopes. No Government is worthy the name of civilization that refuses to educate, and to educate properly, the children of the State."[77]

Continued delays in increasing state contributions to public schooling, Hubbs argued, would "impoverish" the state school fund and keep "the children of our citizens" back east.[78] According to this line of thinking, the money had to precede local settlement. This logic was repeated often in various appeals for increased state school support in California during these years. State superintendent of public instruction John Swett appealed often to this logic connecting state funding with population growth. When he called for a new special state school tax in the early 1860s, for example, he cast it as both an alternative to a county or district tax and a magnet for families willing to settle in the state. He insisted schools helped drive the growth of San Francisco by attracting "hundreds of families" to the city, which increased the wealth of the place in turn by "hundreds of thousands of dollars." Elsewhere in the state, he argued, a "lack of Schools . . . has kept from our shores thousands of families which otherwise would have gladly settled here."[79] According to Swett, increased state funding and a new special state tax were needed as a result.

The assertion that state funding for education would attract white population growth became a common refrain among the Anglo-American press as well as it advocated for centralized funding policies. Within weeks of California achieving statehood, editorialists in the Anglo-American newspapers called for immediate action by the legislature to create and fund common schools. The editors of the *Marysville Herald* celebrated the "gentle influence" of new schools and their effectively "magic" powers: "Their gentle influence, as by the power of magic, would soon change the constitution of society; and from the wild chaos of our present, a well organized commonwealth would rise in beauty and glory. And all our families would soon be here."[80] The *Marysville Herald* editors insisted that this transformation was not possible until the state provided direct funds for its schools. The American commonwealth would only "rise in beauty and glory," the editors explained, "were suitable provision made for the education of our children." Until then, they insisted, families "cannot—ought not to come." The editors of the *Daily Alta California* contended that "one hundred thousand dollars expended for our school system would do more to increase the population than any other investment of capital that could be made."[81] Others featured the promise of a well-endowed school system in their promotional efforts, a plan that would not be possible without legislative action to provide revenue for the schools via a dedicated fund or taxes. The founders of the Pacific Immigrant Aid Association of California, for example, argued that sharing information about

California's "common schools and other educational privileges" would surely "encourage, aid, and facilitate emigration to our shores."[82]

In the adoption of state property taxation to supplement a centralized school fund composed of expropriated Indigenous land, school funding became entwined with the dispossession of land owned by former Mexican nationals as well. By manipulating the process to assess land values, which themselves determined the tax burdens for the state school tax, Anglo lawmakers facilitated the transfer of millions of acres owned by Mexican ranchers to Anglo-Americans. For instance, even though state taxes were purportedly uniform, they fell more heavily on Mexican than Anglo-American residents. By one account, the tax on land owned by former Mexican nationals was $1.50 per acre, while the tax on Anglo-Americans was 20 cents per acre. These Mexican Americans, many of whom were subsistence ranchers and farmers, either paid these tax bills—subsidizing state spending for white children and lower tax rates for Anglo-Americans—or they lost their property through tax delinquency, thereby subsidizing cheap land prices for Anglo-Americans, who often went on to purchase the land at auction.

When Anglo-American lawmakers and newspaper editorialists described how common schools would attract migrants to settle permanently in California, they were engaged in a broader racial project of repopulation. Sometimes they did not specify that these families ought to be white because that assumption was so deeply rooted in their thinking about who should be a citizen. In other instances, Anglo-Americans were quite explicit that white population growth would counteract the racial diversity of California. For example, the editors of the *San Francisco Call* insisted that "one of the best methods for fighting Chinese labor is to meet it with a better class—white."[83] The businessman and president of the California Immigration Union C. T. Hopkins frequently discussed how strategic population growth could counteract the presence of Chinese residents. He wondered whether anyone could "doubt that if an American or European, even of the lowest order originally, now occupied the place of each Chinaman in California our state would be commercially, industrially, morally and politically at least thirty per cent better off than it now is?"[84] Governor Henry Haight appealed to this logic, too, when he declared that "we need population—not of races inferior" but "immigrants of kindred races who will constitute a congenial element and locate themselves and their families permanently upon the soil."[85]

Racial Boundaries of the Public

The direct role of state government in education funding allowed lawmakers to exercise substantive control over who was deemed eligible for funding and thus who was a member of the imagined "public" served by state-supported educational institutions. Even in discussions that emphasized an egalitarian vision of schooling for "all," the children included in "all" were determined by the broader ideology and legal architecture of racial exclusion. To white lawmakers, "all" meant citizens, and citizens were necessarily white in the minds of those same lawmakers. Consider an example from Georgia. While the South did not have a system of state-supported schools until formerly enslaved people created these systems after the Civil War, southern state officials like Governor Joseph Brown adopted the idiom of common school reformers. When he declared in 1858 that lawmakers should "let the children of the richest and poorest parents in the State, meet in the schoolroom on the terms of perfect equality of right," he also declared that in the schoolroom there should be "no aristocracy . . . but an aristocracy of color and conduct."[86]

Ideologically, deciding who a public school system would serve was easy for Anglo-American lawmakers for whom racial exclusion was a central, foundational element of their common school system. As established previously, common schools were intended to transform California into an American place by attracting white settlers; crucially, this transformation was also contingent on preventing nonwhite children from benefiting from these schools. Through the rigid segregation of schooling and restriction of state funding for nonwhite students, advocates of the expansion of common schools imagined the state's school system would help define the racial boundaries of citizenship.[87] In the words of one commentator, segregated schooling would allow California to practice the "secret of Britain's success as a colonizing power," preventing the creation of a "mongrel race of moral and mental hybrids" and ensuring the success of American state-building along the Pacific Coast.[88] As historian Barbara Berglund has pointed out, re-creating American racial hierarchies in the region was essential to "an ongoing process of incorporation and hierarchy-building with its genesis in the imperial impulse."[89]

Yet linking whiteness and citizenship in California required policing the boundaries of an abstract racial category that Anglo-Americans had made contradictory in California's multiracial environment. The children of former Mexican nationals were legal citizens under the terms of the Treaty of Guadalupe Hidalgo and usually, though not always, deemed white in the racial ideology of the day. Yet in the buildup to the Mexican-American War, white racial ideology had cast Mexican nationals as nonwhite. Efforts to exclude nonwhite children from California's common schools therefore quickly fell apart, also because a community of Black activists challenged the imprecise boundaries of the "public" by successfully convincing some school boards to admit children of color who "appeared white." One of the earliest cases came in 1855, when school officials in Grass Valley asked the state superintendent if permitting "colored and white children mix as scholars" would jeopardize state funding.[90] Hubbs had assumed that local officials were excluding children considered nonwhite and was outraged to learn that common schools in Grass Valley were integrated. "I had not supposed it necessary to give any instruction upon this subject," Hubbs wrote. While Hubbs claimed to "have no antagonism to the education of the negro, the mongrel, and all other races of man," he also insisted that integrated schooling would threaten "the success of our public school system" and the "present and future good of our country." For Hubbs, the problem with integration centered on the role of common schools in creating citizens. "I maintain the opinion that the law in relation to public schools applies to those only who are capacitated (as the Californians and the Americans are)," he explained in an open letter, "to become citizens of the republic."[91] Members of the legislature responded to the controversy in Grass Valley by leveraging the state's funding policies to promote segregation. In 1855, state lawmaker Wilson W. Jones proposed inserting the word "white" into the state's school code so that only white students qualified for a share of state education funding. While the bill received strong support from most lawmakers, a handful of assembly members voting against the bill expressed concern that many Californio and Mexican children technically had native ancestry and were therefore not white, even though Californios were classified as white by the Treaty of Guadalupe Hidalgo. Politicians such as Timothy Guy Phelps were concerned that the bill would unfairly harm Californio communities.[92] But despite this opposition, the change passed.[93] The state's census marshals would now identify and count each child living within the region and classify the child's race.

The confusion regarding Californio children shows how adding the word "white" into the law did little to clarify who should have access to California's common schools. Indeed, the situation in Grass Valley hinged similarly on the definition of whiteness during this period. According to some observers, in Grass Valley the issue was not that schools were integrated. Instead, it centered on the meaning of whiteness and its boundaries. In Grass Valley, school officials discovered that "three of the white children had colored parents," but, since the children themselves were "white," they had been allowed to attend the schools.[94] E. A. Tompkins, one of the Grass Valley school trustees, expelled the children who were "suspected of being tainted with Indian or negro blood," but he maintained the children were "as white as many others not suspected of any such taint."[95] Perhaps the ambiguous racial classification of the students helps explain why the trustees may have initially ignored Hubbs and not expelled the students in question.[96]

Throughout the 1850s and 1860s, Black Californians used the ambiguity of the state's racial categories to support their challenges to racial exclusion. At four conventions between 1855 and 1865, Black Californians focused their activism on the state's ban on court testimony from nonwhite people and racial restriction in the state's schools.

Civil rights activist Peter Lester successfully enrolled his daughter in all-white public schools in San Francisco.[97] In 1858, she was even attending San Francisco High School. The editors of the *San Francisco Herald* exposed Lester's attendance and agitated for the San Francisco School Board to expel her from the school. Some members of the board, however, wanted Lester to stay at the school because of her academic success and because she "so closely resembles a white person." According to one board member, there should be exceptions in "cases where the white blood predominates."[98] In contrast, opponents insisted that allowing Lester into San Francisco's public schools was dangerous because it created a precedent for other Black families and California's other "inferior races" to seek access to the public schools. The editors of the *San Francisco Bulletin* viewed the violation as evidence of the need for greater vigilance in segregating "white and inferior races in our State." The editors of the *Daily Alta California* contended that allowing Lester to remain enrolled would "open the door to additional trouble of a like nature."[99] Other commentators connected "amalgamation" in schools with the potential failure of an American colonial project in California: "While the colonies planted by France and Spain languish and decay, those planted by England flourish and grow into vast empires and nationalities. But few writers attribute this to the real cause, which is, the preservation in its integrity of the white race."[100] For those educational leaders worried about integration, the state role in school funding provided the most powerful tool for challenging local resistance to segregation. During the debate over Sarah Lester's attendance and status, Moulder, the state superintendent at the time, subscribed to the ideas of the editors of the *San Francisco Bulletin* about the maintenance of racial order through schooling. According to Moulder, the state's nascent school system would collapse if the school were integrated because white parents would withdraw from the schools rather than "permit their daughters—fifteen, sixteen, and seventeen years of age—to affiliate with the sons of Negroes."[101] Like other observers, Moulder saw the mixing of Black and white students as part of a broader integration of all of California's "inferior races," insisting that allowing Black, Indigenous, or Chinese children in "our white Schools" would "result in the ruin of our Schools."[102] Moulder argued that these controversies over integration in Grass Valley and San Francisco were part of a much broader pattern. He worried that too many local districts were admitting nonwhite students even though those students did not qualify for state aid. To respond, he sought greater control over the distribution of state aid, requesting the power to "withhold the public moneys from any District that permits the admission of the children of the inferior races."[103]

Moulder and his supporters contended that "inferior races" should be educated in California, but that education should take place in segregated schools. In the wake of the Sarah Lester incident, for example, most newspaper editors conceded that nonwhites in California also required education. The editors of the *San Francisco Bulletin* contended that "if we must have negroes and Chinamen among us it is better, of course, if they are educated." That education should also be segregated, they contended, to "preserve our Caucasian blood pure."[104] Moulder insisted segregated schools should be available to students of color since "it is not desirable" students of color "be brought up in ignorance and heathenism."[105]

In the early 1860s, local school admission practices continued to undermine state-mandated segregation and shape educational politics. As the start of the Civil War shattered the California Democratic Party's control over state politics, the 1862 campaign for superintendent of public instruction became highly contested. California Democrats accused Union Fusion Party candidate John Swett, a former San Francisco principal, of admitting nonwhite children into the Rincon School. Democrats circulated handbills depicting "a Yankee schoolmaster teaching a mixed class of whites and blacks, with a little Negro boy at the head of the class."[106] Swett insisted the claims were untrue, contending a separate official had accidentally admitted some "very light mulatto girls" that Swett had removed when he learned they were not white.[107] Both Union Fusion Party leaders and Democrats released public messages affirming their commitment to racially segregated schools.

The controversy over segregation notwithstanding, voters elected Swett. Swett called for the creation of an education system that would address California's diversity thorough a mixture of Americanization to educate all children and maintaining racial exclusion and racial hierarchies. The diversity of California, he continued, made the creation of this system particularly important. "Her population is drawn from all nations," Swett explained, and "the next generation will be a composite one, made up of the heterogeneous atoms of all nationalities. Nothing can Americanize these chaotic elements and breathe into them the spirit of our institutions but the public schools." According to Swett, for schooling to Americanize the region, it had to occupy a careful balance: maintaining American racial hierarchies through the segregation of schooling while ensuring, simultaneously, that children of color were not a threat to the social order because they did not receive an education. In the same report, Swett asserted that "children of all classes, whether white, black, tawney, or copper-colored," must be educated. This education, however, had to take place in "separate schools." Swett imagined the common school re-creating a Euro-American social order in California through a mix of compulsion, exclusion, and segregation.

During the final months of the Civil War, California's Black community—well-organized politically and already successful at upending the state's racial restrictions on court testimony—focused on amending the school law. Since 1855, California's school law made racial exclusion from the public schools legal. The law gave districts the option to create separate schools for nonwhite children and admit them into those separate schools. Yet it also prohibited districts from allowing children of color to attend white schools, and it permitted districts to exclude nonwhite children from schools altogether. In 1865, Black civil rights activists at California's Black Convention resolved to "present a petition to the Legislature to so amend the School Law that colored children, by its provisions, shall receive the benefit of its advantages in common with others."[108] The following year, the effort succeeded, and the school law was amended to guarantee Black students an education in the state's public schools, albeit in separate schools. The new law still permitted local districts to operate separate schools for Black students, but it also mandated that Black students be permitted to attend all-white schools if a separate school was not created.[109]

Important exceptions notwithstanding, historians have tended to tell the early history of state-sponsored education in a way that minimizes the place of government action in the development of state school systems. In the process, historians have overstated the place of localism in education and its character as "grassroots" and "spontaneous." As the state fades from education and its funding before the Civil War in historical narratives, the deep links between the racial project at the heart of US colonial expansion and the education project that developed alongside it tend to fade as well. A history of education in California before the end of the Civil War makes clear the range of alternatives to the localized approach adopted by lawmakers in the Northeast during these years. It also demonstrates how far-reaching the impact of a racial project of US colonial expansion was to the formulation of early ideas about public schools.

The role of dispossession in early state funding for common schools is one of the fundamental links between schooling and the creation of a continental empire. Anglo-American policy makers imagined much of the land in North America as a potential fund for government-sponsored projects, and the sale of dispossessed land was one of the largest sources of revenue in the federal budget for decades. Still, the connection between education and Native American dispossession ran much deeper, in both practical and ideological terms. Examples include nineteenth-century representations of western, frontier spaces where the schoolhouse itself became a rich symbol of "civilization" conquering the "wilderness," of the American empire dispossessing Indigenous people of their lands. Anglo-American policy makers insisted there was no place more in need of settlement by white families than California, that settlement would transform California into an American place, and that well-funded schools could accomplish these objectives by enticing white families westward and making citizens of white children—and white children only—residing in the state. This association between ideas about race, "civilization," and schools had a far-reaching impact on how Anglo-Americans thought about community building and what it meant to treat education as a public good. The next chapter traces the spread of schools at the granular level of the neighborhood and school district to examine how funding policies structured ideas about education, race, and land.

2

BUYING AND SELLING SCHOOLS AND RACIALIZING SPACE IN A WESTERN STATE

A single-room structure composed of rough-hewn redwood lumber, Eden Vale was one of the first American common schools created in Alameda County, California. Located on the north side of the San Lorenzo Creek, it was a simple structure that, by 1855, was receiving state and county funds for 115 children—all white, under the terms of state law.[1] While the building was crude, nineteenth-century Anglo-Americans believed buildings like Eden Vale would accomplish astonishing things. As chapter 1 discussed, in formulating the policies that provided funding to Eden Vale, Anglo-American policy makers encouraged a particular way of thinking about the relationship between common school buildings, race, and the physical landscape. Indeed, school buildings like Eden Vale told an elaborate story to nineteenth-century observers about the north side of the San Lorenzo Creek. Moreover, buildings like Eden Vale helped conceal other stories that could be told about the area: how it was recently Mexican territory, a part of the Spanish Empire before that, and how it remained what it had always been, the land of the Muwekma Ohlone people.

When the trustees of the Eden Vale School gathered for their regular meeting at the end of May 1864, they discovered that the schoolhouse could no longer tell a story about race and place, at least not on the north side of the San Lorenzo Creek. Under the cover of darkness, a trustee lamented in the district's minutes, the building had been stolen.[2] The thieves were promoters from Hayward's Addition, a rival community on the other side of the creek. Around midnight, the group had surreptitiously ventured into the canyon where Eden Vale was located, hoisted the structure onto their wagon, and carefully wheeled it several miles. When they finally arrived in the area that would eventually become downtown Hayward, they deposited the building on a lot donated by the biggest land speculator in the area, Faxon Atherton. Within a few years, real estate advertisements would boast about this high-quality, albeit stolen, common school.[3] More than that, residents of the area used state school districting policies to separate Eden Vale and Hayward. With legal support from the state, Hayward residents excluded children from the other side of the San Lorenzo Creek from their stolen school. Although school district boundaries remained fluid in many parts of California during these years, an emerging localist ideology and mechanism of exclusion through districting began to take root. The policing of school district boundaries was less dramatic than stealing a schoolhouse, but it operated in a similar fashion—and with legitimacy from the state's own law—to divide the landscape and further promote exclusion.

This chapter considers how the policies discussed in chapter 1 encouraged a cultural narrative about education that linked schools, race, and land values in the middle of the nineteenth century. It then explores, in turn, how policies governing school districting and construction helped divide and segregate Anglo-American communities as well. As early as the 1850s, schools—by virtue of their purported function as magnets for white colonials—were described as tools for driving population growth and for extracting new forms of value from dispossessed Indigenous and Mexican homelands. After examining the spread of these ideas about schools and property values, this chapter illustrates how the imagined connection between whiteness, educational institutions, and land encouraged a localist political ideology with a narrow sense of shared responsibility for the education of other people's children—racially, economically, and geographically. In short, the tangled connections between schools, race, and land value had far-reaching consequences for conceptualization(s) of the public.

The connections between schools, race, and development explored in this chapter make clear the centrality of public education to early patterns of uneven development and segregation. The use of schools to mark, divide, and extract value from dispossessed land is one of the many ways that spaces have been racialized. Land does not have a race, of course, but observers regularly ascribe elaborate racial meanings to different areas. Schools have been central to this process since the creation of public school systems. This point is largely missed in histories of spatial and educational inequality, which tend to focus much more on the second half of the twentieth century. Yet these nineteenth-century precedents are critical for historians of the twentieth century to consider because they unfolded while basic structures of public education were still being created. They shaped basic institutional features of state public education systems we often take for granted today, and they reveal the degree to which the state, racialization, and schooling have long been entwined.

Tracing the place of schools in the racialization of space is critical, too, for understanding the history of the idea that public schools are commodities, or, said another way, the notion that educational quality is something to be bought and sold with land. This chapter illustrates how ideas linking schools and property values are also rooted in the nineteenth century, something historians can miss without a longer chronological frame and wider geographic focus.

Some economic historians suggest Anglo-Americans have imagined a relationship between schools and property values since the late eighteenth century.[4] These accounts have been largely premised on the idea that eighteenth-, nineteenth-, and twentieth-century Anglo-Americans had the same ideas about education and real estate as Americans in the twenty-first century. This chapter illustrates how problematic those economic histories are by emphasizing the centrality of what they almost completely ignore—the state, white supremacy, racial inequality, and dispossession. In the nineteenth century, Anglo-American elites used the link between education, property values, and race to divide landscapes, harden boundaries separating communities, and build fortunes for themselves at the expense of others. The land markets structuring those links were constituted by the state, part of the broader legal framework through which the United States government was actively redistributing wealth from Indigenous and Mexican people to white settlers through land and education policies. Historical accounts about school funding that are rooted in claims about neutral market forces shaping public schools during these years—claims that recast inequalities as efficiencies—are not just incomplete but fundamentally misleading when they obscure the strong hand of the state and its racial project.[5]

Value

Before tracing the history of the links between race and the idea that public schools are commodities—that educational quality is something bought and sold with land—it is helpful to consider how nineteenth-century Anglo-Americans migrating to California thought about land and its economic value. The occupation of California by the United States brought thousands of Anglo-Americans determined to extract value from dispossessed Indigenous and Mexican land. They did so through a variety of means, the simplest of which involved extracting and harvesting things from the land that could be exchanged for profit. When they mined for gold, ranched cattle, or farmed wheat, Anglo-American migrants to California extracted value from the land and benefited from a massive redistribution of wealth to white settlers underwritten by the United States government.

Anglo-Americans also extracted value by turning the land itself into a commodity that could be bought and sold. This could be a simple task when a parcel of land offered for sale promised buyers access to some other commodity already deemed valuable—minerals beneath the surface of the land, crops that could be grown in its fertile soil. However, value could also be abstract. Indeed, the value ascribed to land was never a product of its physical geography alone. Consider how little the physical geography of two sections of Ohlone Territory explained their divergent economic values by the 1860s—the competing cities of Yerba Buena and Francesca or, as they were later rebranded, San Francisco and Benicia. San Francisco, of course, was the more successful of the two. Its growth occurred so fast that one historian of the West has dubbed it an "instant city." But the site of Benicia was a far more logical place for a large commercial city—it was flatter, its soil was less sandy, lumber resources were more accessible, it had better access to trade in both the Pacific and gold region, and it lacked the extensive mudflats that made the development of San Francisco's port so costly. Famed Civil War general William Tecumseh Sherman insisted in 1875 that Benicia was "the best natural site for a commercial city."[6] Benicia also, observers at the time insisted, had much better weather. Although the chronicler of California history Hubert Howe Bancroft had been a San Franciscan since the 1850s, he was still convinced Benicia would have been a better site for a city. In 1888, he lamented how the "cold, bleak, circumscribed, sand-blown and fog-soaked peninsula on which the city of San Francisco is actually placed, was about as ill-chosen as possible."[7]

In the end, land in Benicia was worth a lot less than land in San Francisco. This was true even when that land and its resources were physically indistinguishable. The difference in value between the two places was instead a reflection of the different ways they came to be perceived by Anglo-Americans, what kind of places they were. Bancroft pointed this out in the 1880s, noting the reason San Francisco grew faster than Benicia was that eastern migrants perceived it as the place to do business in the region in 1848 and 1849.

The differences in perceptions of Benicia and San Francisco were rooted in culture and ideology, reflecting abstract ideas about place. But these perceptions of place were shaped by the state in clear ways. It was a series of decisions by the national government that ultimately entrenched the idea that San Francisco was the commercial center of the region, the place with more valuable land. It began when the US Army made Yerba Buena the base of its operations during the Mexican-American War, establishing the quartermaster's store, customhouse, and troop quarters there. Federal spending on San Francisco expanded throughout the 1850s. As Roger Lotchin explained in his classic history of the city, "the federal government built a mint, a marine hospital, and a customs house in the city; fortified Fort Point and Alcatraz Island; established a navy yard at Mare Island; subsidized the Pacific Mail Steamship Company with a mail contract; built lighthouses on the coast; and purchased supplies for Indian wars in the state—all of which significantly helped San Francisco."[8] It was clear enough to land developers that federal subsidies would make or break a city. Benicia's developers worked hard to secure federal investment, even bribing high-level US military officials by gifting them Benicia city lots in an effort to lure federal military operations from San Francisco to Benicia. Benicia, though, never caught up with San Francisco.

The State and Narratives about Race, Schools, and Land Values

As the case of Benicia and San Francisco suggests, public policy impacted how nineteenth-century Americans thought about and valued different geographic locations. Through the land-based education funding models discussed in chapter 1, national and state governments shaped abstract ideas about place and value at an even broader geographic scale. Anglo-Americans said again and again that school buildings were potent symbols of colonization and dispossession, marking particular areas as conquered and settled for white families. The logic undergirding these narratives was simple—educational institutions made western land more desirable to white residents of the Atlantic Coast, increasing their willingness to move westward and increasing the value of land as a result. That logic was rooted in public policy.

The way various governmental officials talked about township school sections reflected the role of federal policies structuring this connection between land values, white population growth, and state-supported education. For example, according to a committee of the Illinois General Assembly discussing federal land policy in the 1820s, schools made lands across the Northwest more appealing to settlers from the East; these land-based subsidies for education made the region more desirable for families "of the Atlantic States," functioning as "encouragement to emigration and purchase."[9] Lawmakers also assumed that schools would increase the value of land. The idea that establishing schools was a mechanism for creating value and extracting revenue was reiterated routinely, at every level of government. Members of Congress argued that land donations for education did not cost anything for the federal government, since schools increased the value of nearby land that the federal government sought to sell. As one congressional committee explained, "the donation of section sixteen for the support of the township was an inducement to purchasers, the sale of which indemnified the government for the donation which it made."[10] President Franklin Pierce framed federal subsidies for education in terms of the impact that schools had on the value of land.

Schools as Commodities

Anglo-American migrants' embrace of the notion that schools, whiteness, and the economic value of land were entwined impacted ideas about the public and private character of educational institutions, making the value created by common schools not revenue for a government, but wealth for individuals. Even before the end of the Mexican-American War, Anglo-Americans sought to use schools to profit from dispossession. For example, both Robert Semple and Thomas Larkin were born in the United States and arrived in California before the gold rush. They persuaded Mexican general Mariano Vallejo to donate land on the north side of the Carquinez Strait for them to market and sell lots from, for a proposed city. The venture's success was contingent on rapid population growth, and Semple believed one of the best ways to attract growth was to create a school and advertise it. The original deed for the city was published in the *Californian*, promising readers that a school fund would support "the establishment of public schools for the benefit of the families who colonize said city."[11] After donating land for schools in the city and recruiting a teacher, Semple made "best of schools" a prominent feature of his advertisements for city lots. Provisions for public schools, Semple promised prospective migrants, would be among the chief advantages of living in the community. "Another incalculable advantage," he explained, "is that ample provisions have already been made for an adequate SCHOOL FUND, which will fully secure the citizens in the best of schools."[12]

In a letter to Larkin in 1849, Semple explained the logic shaping their efforts to bring American schools to the area. Hoping to "settle the death warrant" of San Francisco, Semple described to Larkin his efforts to make Benicia "*the City*" (emphasis in the original). As part of those efforts, Semple hired a teacher "of high respectability" to run the schools and explained the school would "secure a class of population far above the other towns in California, and before the first of the next year we shall be ahead of this place in point of numbers and wealth."[13]

Leveraging the long-standing association between schools and permanent white settlement, other migrants from the United States also constructed educational institutions on expropriated lands that they sought to sell during the earliest years of American occupation. These Anglo-Americans bound together schools, whiteness, and property values through their efforts. They also created new ways of talking about public schools as commodities that could be bought and sold with land. For example, Charles Weber, an Anglo-American who sought to market the city of Stockton, financed the city's first public school and promoted it in advertisements to prospective settlers.[14]

For Anglo-Americans, creating and marketing schools was a way to extract value from expropriated land through city building. That process began with taking the land, often under dubious circumstances. In the years immediately preceding the gold rush, Vicente Peralta and his family owned the land that was the future site of Oakland. The Peraltas, like most Mexican and Spanish land-grant families, lost title to their land through the combined prevarications of American squatters, businessmen, and lawyers. In the summer of 1850, three recent arrivals from the East—Horace W. Carpentier, Edson Adams, and Alexander Moon—began squatting on Peralta's land and subdividing and selling lots for a town site even though the land was not theirs to sell. Peralta tried, unsuccessfully, to have the men removed. Reflecting the dubious means through which most speculators obtained their land, Carpentier, Adams, and Moon had visited Peralta at his home with a gang of other Americans and "persuaded" Peralta to lease the men a portion of his land.[15] The men then subdivided lots for a town site and funded an elegant school building.[16] As the first elected mayor, Carpentier was clear that investment in education was intended to attract white migrants to the community. "Of all the duties devolved upon you," Carpentier explained in his first address to the town council, "that of fostering common schools is perhaps the most important." He argued that the council must "anticipate the wants of the citizens rather than follow after them."[17] While we often imagine that schools were created in communities to serve children who were already present, a different process unfolded amid town site speculation schemes in nineteenth-century California. In constructing a schoolhouse before there were residents and imploring the newly formed council to do the same, Carpentier invoked a logic that was pervasive in the region: if you build a schoolhouse, children will come.

Carpentier, Semple, and Weber were not alone in using the schoolhouse and all it seemed to represent about permanent white settlement to sell land. Anglo-American lawmakers encouraged the use of schools in such private development schemes through the policies they adopted governing how school facilities could be funded. Throughout the 1850s and 1860s, communities could operate well-funded schools without levying a local tax, but they could not finance a school building as easily.[18] Only half of the revenue from county property taxes could be applied to school construction. The ability of counties to levy property taxes, moreover, was constrained by state policies.[19] Initially, the requirement that school funds raised in a given year must be used during that year complicated matters further, making it impossible for communities to save money to finance school construction gradually.[20] New districts, too, had to have students enrolled to receive a state or county apportionment, which required a building. As a result, the construction of school buildings was privately financed in some communities, and in others, schools first operated in crude and temporary multiuse structures. This dynamic made the presence of dedicated and elaborate school structures even more of an indicator that a place was permanently settled and more "civilized" than other nearby places.

In a context where educational institutions were believed to increase land values but where the state constrained how their construction could be financed, it is unsurprising that we can trace the initial financing of the earliest common school buildings to Anglo-Americans with stakes in nearby development. We can see this pattern clearly in the San Francisco Bay area. J. G. Clark, a farmer and large landowner, funded the Decoto School. In Cambrian, the first school was constructed in 1863 on property donated by Lewis Casey, a farmer from Ohio who had a substantial stake in local real estate. The first public school in Alviso, a section of Washington Township, had an almost identical origin story.[21] It happened again and again and again. Sparse historical records make it impossible to trace the origins of every schoolhouse in the San Francisco Bay area. However, remaining records—records that in their own way are a sort of random sample produced by two hundred years of fires, floods, and poor recordkeeping—tell a remarkably similar story. Searsville School, Horner School, and Lincoln School. Centerville School, Whisman School, and Woodside School. Summit School, Rio Vista School, and Cotati School. Irvington School, Ocean View School, and Pleasanton School. Niles School, Dixie School, and Franklin School. All were created by large landholders with huge financial stakes in nearby development.[22]

Common schools became further entwined with Anglo-American efforts to extract personal fortunes from dispossessed lands as white population growth became the centerpiece of how Anglo-Americans talked about economic development. As mining collapsed and the gold fields emptied, commentators increasingly described a combination of land speculation and population growth as the new path to California riches. "The palmy days of mining are on the wane," one writer claimed. "For our future prosperity, we must have population."[23] Many nineteenth-century Californians came to view population growth as an economic panacea. "The financial depression would be entirely removed by immigration on a large scale," one San Franciscan noted in 1869.[24] Some even tried to quantify the exact amount of money that each additional migrant would bring: between

$1,000 and $2,000 for a man or woman in the prime of their life.[25] Schooling, as chapter 1 makes clear, seemed to be the key to facilitating the "right kind" of white migration that was needed to cure economic ills. Superintendent of San Francisco schools Thomas Nevins was clear about the connection between education, population, and profit. "Without a doubt," Nevins told the San Francisco City Council, the creation of an elaborate school system was in the "pecuniary interest of the city" since "the influx of population would be greater for having the system completed."[26] People and profit, not state building, became seen as the primary benefit of creating schools. This way of thinking about the relationship between schools and population growth also led to an early iteration of growth liberalism. Stockton's L. M. Hickman pointed out how the growth in population and land values produced through educational investments would both increase "our revenue" and "lessen our taxation."[27] The editors of the *Weekly Colusa Sun* appealed to the same logic when they called on trustees in the district to not just build a new schoolhouse but one "that will be an ornament and a credit to the town" because "good school accommodation would give at least three hundred additional inhabitants."[28]

This logic centered on a narrative connecting a school at a given location with increased property values for nearby landowners. In turn, this narrative produced a way of seeing public education as a quasi-privatized good with a geographic character, something that produced monetary benefits for landowners in a bounded area as much or more than any broader benefit for the state or nation. The editors of the *Los Angeles Daily News* cited this way of thinking when they commented on the "influence of good institutions" on "demand for land in the immediate neighborhood."[29] In one case, they noted how land values went from "twenty dollars per acre" to "about five hundred dollars per acre."[30] The idea that the establishment and endowment of educational institutions could benefit property owners became so pronounced that newspaper editors began to comment on, and in some cases criticize, the logic. In 1870, the editors of the *San Francisco Bulletin* pointed out that the object in these liberal endowments of institutions of learning was largely speculative, landowners giving their land more as an investment than a gift, as the transfer would add many times more value to their remaining lands than the amount donated.[31] Furthermore, the logic was flawed, the editor maintained. Commerce, not educational advancement, distinguished successful from unsuccessful cities. "The calculation is exaggerated," the writer complained. "What is Ann Arbor to Chicago?" The former had a university but had not become a metropolis. Nevertheless, such doubts seemed to have little impact as proponents of educational expansion continued to promise the pecuniary benefits of school expansion.

Common Schools as Amenities: Real Estate Advertisements, Exclusivity, and the Nature of the Public

Given that Anglo-Americans treated public schools as instruments for increasing land values via white settlement, educational institutions occupied a prominent role in promotional materials created to market and sell land in the 1860s. That material took the form of booster tracts and advertisements for family farms in local California newspapers. Exploring the content of this narrative in more detail illustrates how ideas about the public school symbolizing permanent white settlement developed into ideas about high-quality public schools marking an elite residential enclave settled by a racially and economically exclusive group of Anglo-Americans.

The language of real estate advertisements and their emphasis on "school privileges" that accompanied land purchase entrenched a cultural narrative casting access to public schooling not in terms of citizenship, but as a pseudo-amenity. Offering payment through installments, one group noted the unique advantages of several properties for sale: "fertile soil, genial climate, facility of access, the surpassing beauty of its location on the beautiful San Lorenzo Creek, with a full view of the Bay, its Church and School privileges, and the low price and easy terms of payment."[32] Boosterish descriptions of Santa Clara claimed it was "spoken of far and near as a very desirable place of residence" because of its well known "school privileges."[33] This logic was repeated constantly. One property was marketed for its proximity to a "good school" within "six hundred yards of the house."[34] Julius Wetzlar—a Sacramento businessman who fashioned himself a "real estate agent, and negotiator of loans"—used similar language in real estate advertisements. In one advertisement, for example, he promised prospective buyers that lands were "well improved" and "in the vicinity of the best schools in the State."[35]

Local political elites reinforced the logic of treating schools like a commodity in their discussions of local financing and growth, claiming that investments in local school construction would pay for themselves. In his inaugural address as mayor of Stockton, L. M. Hickman emphasized this logic as he noted that "providing good schools in our city" meant "many will be attracted here merely on account of the educational advantages they will be entitled to enjoy—advantages of which they cannot avail themselves in many of the rural districts."

Increasingly, the promise of "good schools" was about marketing places as more than simply "settled" by white colonials, but as racially and economically exclusive residential enclaves. Advertisers and boosters were careful to ensure this distinction was not lost on readers. Purchasing land in a place with good schools, commentators explained, meant acquiring residence in a white, middle-class, and elite community. Drawing on racially and economically resonant promises of "good society" and the "best," most "respectable," and "refined" populations, this literature crafted a narrative connecting "good" public schools with segregated, white residence. As one writer explained while trying to convince readers that Santa Clara schools were superior to those of other places, "good schools and churches, well attended, are pretty sure indications that a people's heart is in the right place, and pervaded by a high moral tone."[36] One promoter from Gilroy drew on the same logic in 1860 as he detailed the "wealthy and thriving" population in the "clean, quiet, new-looking little village" of Gilroy.[37] Since "the number of school houses and churches in this little village" was an indicator of "a people zealous in the cause of education and morality," the booster concluded that no "better location for permanent settlement could be found in the State for families desirous of enjoying the advantages of good schools and good society."[38] Anglo-American community leaders in San José crafted a story of a place where schools were attracting "people looking for pleasant homes" and where educational excellence was bringing "a large and constantly increasing immigration" of the "very best class of citizens."[39]

Campaigns using schools to indicate how an area was an exclusive residential enclave also shaped how properties for sale in homestead associations were described in the 1860s. Conceptually similar to the twentieth-century subdivision, homestead associations were planned, subdivided residential areas for sale on the installment plan. In the 1860s, they offered lots with or without houses in both existing cities and on former *ranchos* not yet incorporated as towns or cities. These homestead associations were also the basis of rural farming communities clustered around central villages with institutions like schools. Hayward's Park Homestead Union, for example, aspired to sell small, affordable homes along the San Lorenzo Creek. In the advertisement, promoters focused on how the place was a good fit for those who "desire good Society." The indicators for that "good society" featured in their market materials were the "two fine Churches" and a "two-storied Public School Building." Inside that building, they also noted, was "an excellent school now in progress."[40] Schools were cast as both a benefit to prospective buyers and an indicator of what kind of "society" characterized a place.

The narrative casting "excellent" public schools as something that could be purchased alongside an elite residence accompanied early invocations of the suburban ideal and the importance of education for that ideal within the context of the West. While in the East the countryside could evoke images of a romanticized pastoral landscape, in the West those same landscapes could easily conjure images of a frontier not yet home to white families. The promise of quality schools helped advertisers promote an area as settled, but also free from the crowding, racial mixing, and public health concerns of the nineteenth-century city. Real estate agent G. E. Smith, for example, offered twenty-, fifty-, and hundred-acre lots for sale near San Leandro, emphasizing the "beautiful" location in the county only one hour from San Francisco. In advertisements for the lots, he emphasized in capital letters "GOOD SCHOOLS" along with two other amenities that made it an appropriate place for farming: "GOOD WATER" and "BEST OF SOIL."[41]

Homestead associations and other developers also used appeals to climate to illustrate how the purchase of a property could shield families from the diseases and other ills linked to urban life in the middle decades of the nineteenth century. A booster tract describing Sebastopol made all these advantages of rurality explicit, emphasizing how "good society and good schools" characterized the place "away from vice and all of its alluring attractions." The same account emphasized how the rural location made it ideal for escaping the spread of disease linked to the concentration of people in nineteenth-century cities: "Parents who have children to educate cannot find a more delightful climate or a more desirable country to build a rural cottage home, away from malaria and contagion."[42] F. A. Hihn planned a subdivision that would form large parts of early Santa Cruz and Soquel. As a trustee and active promoter of Santa Cruz schools, he geared advertisements for his subdivided lands toward "families" and emphasized the lands' "best climate in the world," "beauty of natural scenery," and "good schools."[43]

Racialization of Space

The racial logic connecting public schools with exclusive residential enclaves in promotional literature was both reflected in, and entrenched by, local policy making on school construction and siting. Indeed, tracing the spread of early common schools at the neighborhood level in what were two very different places in the 1850s and 1860s—San Francisco and Los Angeles—reveals the far-reaching impact that narratives connecting schools, value, and race had on the way nineteenth-century Americans thought about urban space and the role schools played in place making.

Despite the many differences between San Francisco and Los Angeles in the 1850s and 1860s, constructing and locating American school buildings in both places shaped how urban space was imagined and attributed racial meaning. Through education policies developed at the municipal level, an emerging Anglo-American elite used school siting and construction to organize and divide space along racial, ethnic, and economic lines. This process used the common school to segregate neighborhoods economically and racially, as well as creating racialized ways of thinking about the unique physical features of each city. For instance, schools helped shape the way San Francisco's hills were marked as desirable places to live. Ultimately, the use of schools to mark and divide the landscape facilitated the racialization of space. As sociologist George Lipsitz notes, the racialization of space constitutes a way that people are taught "about who belongs where and about what makes certain spaces desirable," and, crucially, it serves to "produce and sustain racial meanings."[44]

San Francisco

By constructing schools to attract the "right kind of immigrants," real estate developers and an emerging elite demonstrated the power of public education to help create, rather than simply reflect, residential segregation. The creation of schools had helped shape the expansion of San Francisco since the late 1840s. Located south of the original village of Yerba Buena, along what would eventually become Mission Street, Happy Valley was home to thousands of miners living in canvas tents during the early years of the gold rush. One recent arrival from the East recalled "a large collection of tents pitched in a valley near the beach which may contain some 2,000 inhabitants, mostly newcomers waiting for a chance to go to the mines" in September 1849. He noted how miners "locate in Happy Valley wherever they see fit, and any attempt to collect rent of them (there have been several such attempts made) is rejected as absurd."[45] Large landowners in Happy Valley, especially W. D. M. Howard, Henry Mellus, and Joseph L. Folsom, had more profitable ideas in mind. The men cleared squatters from the area with the help of the new San Francisco Police Department.[46] Then they leveled the hills surrounding the valley and imported prefabricated cottages from Boston and China.[47] Next, Howard and Mellus donated a school building christened the "Happy Valley Public School."[48] In creating the school, these speculators were attempting to use it to transform space, to convert an area of squatting miners into a desirable, economically segregated neighborhood. For a short window of time, the move seemed to pay off. San Francisco's elite residents all constructed homes in Happy Valley, including many of the early political and business leaders of the city such as William Howard, Edwin Bryant, Rodman Price, Thomas Larkin, James Lick, J. H. Poett, Sam Brannan, and John C. Frémont. San Francisco's first mansion was reportedly constructed in the area. By 1851, the *Daily Alta California* editors were marveling at the transformation of the area from a land "whitened with the canvas tents" to a place of "large and elegant structures." "A school house," the editors continued to boast, was present and "well filled with scholars."[49] Another observer said that as he first witnessed the "pleasant sight of the rows of pretty cottages," he found that "here was civilization again."[50] School construction helped drive the expansion of the city toward the south.[51]

By the late 1850s, distinct middle- and working-class sections of the city had developed. Drawing on land-use maps from the United States Coast Survey and a 10 percent sample of city directories, historian Roger Lotchin found a clear area of middle-class "preponderance" bounded by Montgomery Street to the west, Greenwich Street to the north, Sutter Street to the south, and Gough Street to the east (figure 2.1).[52] Within this area, middle-class residents were in the clear majority—ranging from 60 to 75 percent of the residents in each block—even though only 39 percent of San Franciscans were middle class. Moreover, the working-class residents living in this section were rarely laborers; most were artisans and skilled workers.[53] An additional elite area also developed south of Market Street on Rincon Hill, a neighborhood bounded by Spear Street to the east, Second Street to the west, Folsom Street to the north, and Bryant Street to

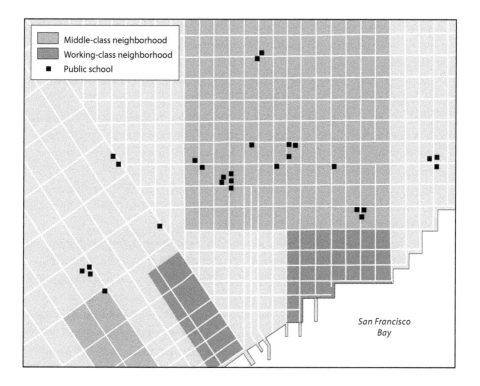

FIGURE 2.1. Map of San Francisco public school buildings and residential patterns circa 1856. Adapted from *San Francisco City Directory ... Compiled and Published by Harris, Bogardus, and Labatt* (San Francisco: Whitton, Towne, 1856), 135–36; and Roger Lotchin, *San Francisco, 1846–1848: From Hamlet to City* (New York: Oxford University Press, 1974), 22–25, 353, notes 28–30. Cartography by Bill Nelson.

the south.[54] By the 1860s, this neighborhood was considered the most elite section of the city, described by author Gertrude Atherton, the daughter-in-law of land baron Faxon Atherton, as one of "the only places in those days where one could be born respectably."[55]

Working-class San Franciscans increasingly had their own spaces within the city as well. From Montgomery Street to the waterfront, the ratio of working-class to middle-class residents was two to one. South of Market Street, the clearest working-class neighborhood developed. In the area bounded by Market Street to the north, Mission Street to the south, Second Street to the west, and Steuart Street to the east, 89 percent of residents had occupations considered working class.[56]

Mapping San Francisco's schools reveals an important pattern: almost all public schools during the late 1850s were in the middle-class sections of the city. While histories on the growth of urban school bureaucracies in the nineteenth century have at times concentrated on the importance of school expansion for efforts to discipline an emerging working class, the sites of schools were consistently within the middle-class sections of San Francisco in the 1850s.[57]

In 1856, thirty-three public schools were listed in San Francisco city directories, some of which shared a building.[58] Of these, all but nine buildings were within the area of middle-class dominance between Montgomery, Greenwich, Sutter, and Gough Streets. Of the nine schools not located in this middle-class section of the city, five were in middle-class neighborhoods north and south of the city. Three were in the wealthiest section of the city at the time, Rincon Hill. Two more were in North Beach, which was a developing middle-class neighborhood in the late 1850s.[59] Perhaps more tellingly, there were no schools within the sections of the city dominated by the working class.

The fact that common schools clustered around the middle-class sections of San Francisco was intentional. As the different parts of the city became increasingly differentiated, city officials deliberately moved schools out of working-class areas and pockets where racial and ethnic minorities were forming distinct neighborhoods. As Happy Valley became an area associated with working-class residences and manufacturing, the city relocated the Happy Valley School to a newly constructed building at the center of San Francisco's middle-class district, with 67 percent of the residents on the block having middle-class occupations. In the same year, Schoolhouse #4 was moved from the corner of Broadway and Montgomery Streets, which at that time was the border of a predominantly working-class section of the city, to a predominantly middle-class residential area along Dupont Street. In 1854, Schoolhouses #3 and #5 became a source of embarrassment for Superintendent William O'Grady. Schoolhouse #3 was moved because, according to O'Grady, it was "in a locality of physical and moral impurity." The area corresponded to the city's emerging Chinese neighborhood. Schoolhouse #5 had raw sewage from Powell Street running underneath it, though Grady's biggest concern seemed to be how "in the upper part of the building families of different nations resided, who—not understanding or appreciating Public Schools,—were a constant source of annoyance."[60]

Common schools were not simply moved to middle-class neighborhoods in the 1850s, however. They also helped create middle-class neighborhoods where they had not existed before. Indeed, school expansion in San Francisco helped transform the city from a demographically mixed to an economically segregated city. In the 1850s, San Franciscans constructed an elaborate brick schoolhouse in North Beach, at the time an emerging middle-class neighborhood. The school preceded the development of the area. In 1856, the school only had fifty students, even though it was designed to house six hundred.[61] The construction of schools in neighborhoods like this one preceded, rather than followed, population growth and helped create new, middle-class sections of the city.[62]

Rincon Hill's development provides another example of how common school expansion encouraged residential segregation in the city. Rincon Hill was what historian Albert Shumate called San Francisco's "early fashionable neighborhood."[63] In a speculative venture, developers again sought to use school construction in their development schemes, leasing a building for free to the newly formed school board to ensure the creation of what eventually became the Rincon Point Grammar School.[64] Again, developers emphasized schools when they advertised lots, boasting about "some of the best residences in the city, as well as churches and schools."[65] And the move again helped transform a previously undeveloped area into an elite enclave. The school opened in 1852, and by 1854 five elite San Franciscans had moved to the hill: bankers Edward Church and Peder Sather, future mayor Thomas Selby, future army chief of staff Henry Halleck, and President Zachary Taylor's cousin John Wilson. By the 1860s, newspaper editors noted how Rincon Hill was "covered with elegant homes" and that it represented "unquestionably the most elegant part of the city." School construction helped create this economically segregated space.

Common school expansion was fundamental to the development of residential segregation within the city because it helped to lead San Franciscans to think differently about urban space. In the late 1850s, elite San Franciscans were increasingly moving to the periphery of what would become the downtown area, segregating the city by class, and embracing new residential developments, like Rincon Hill, on top of the city's hills. San Francisco's hilly terrain suddenly became an asset for developers, offering a way for elites to separate themselves physically from working-class residents while also providing a separation between home and work. By building their homes on hills that only carriages could easily reach, as historical geographer James Vance pointed out, elite San Franciscans "stratified residence in a very literal sense."[66]

Before San Franciscans would willingly head for the hills, however, they had to change the way they thought about the city's terrain. Lotchin notes that most San Franciscans initially showed a "preference for low ground."[67] As the editors of the *Daily Alta California* explained, real estate on top of San Francisco's hilly terrain was "almost worthless"—"It was hardly supposed that anyone would travel up there to live so long as there were any level places left."[68] But then San Francisco's educational leaders developed an ideology about the importance of constructing schools at high elevations. "Elevated and commanding sites should always be selected for schools," the superintendent explained to the city council in 1854. He insisted that schools "should never—if possible to avoid it—be placed in the heavy air of hollows and low places." Placing schools on top of hills would cure many of the problems endemic to common schooling, the city's early educational leaders reasoned. The top of hills, Superintendent O'Grady wrote, provided "pure air." This would, in turn, cure "much of that sluggishness and drowsiness found in many schoolrooms." In the same vein, school construction at a high elevation would even, the superintendent argued, end "bad lessons," "idleness," and "want of interest."[69] Given the difficulty that children would have in reaching these sites, as most of San Francisco's hills remained undeveloped, many objected, but hilltop locations for schools were nonetheless privileged by city leaders in the early 1950s, including the construction of a new school on Rincon Hill in 1852. In these ways, San Francisco's early educational leaders worked together with the city's real estate speculators not only to spread the American common school but to convince elites that they should embrace living at higher elevations. While educational policy by itself did not cause elite San Franciscans to segregate themselves, it was an important part of the process.

Los Angeles

In Los Angeles as well, decisions regarding school construction and location by local policy makers facilitated a transformation in how space was organized and imagined, helping drive residential segregation. Los Angeles had a reputation among Anglo-Americans for being rough and tumble in the early 1850s. One early chronicler of the city's history called it "undoubtedly the toughest town of the nation."[70] But by the end of the 1870s, the city had acquired a reputation as a settled place and a good investment for Anglo-Americans looking to profit from development in the far West. The *New York Times* noted the city's "progress of improvement" and that "many buildings are going up ... and the land is still rising in value."[71]

The change in Los Angeles's reputation was part of a demographic and geographic transformation marking it as a town with a distinct, white Anglo-American residential area. In 1850, the *pueblo* of Los Angeles was home to about fifteen hundred people. The buildings, mostly adobe, were clustered around a central plaza that served as a political, economic, and cultural center. Architecturally, they reflected the town's history, first as a Spanish *pueblo*, then a Mexican one. As the pueblo became a US town, and then a US city, developing in multiple directions out from the historic Plaza, residential segregation along lines of race and class emerged. Schools helped shape this pattern.

North of the Plaza, the construction of adobe structures that matched the original Mexican architecture continued. Spanish-speaking Angelenos—made up of both recent arrivals from Mexico and former Mexican nationals who became US citizens when the border shifted—built their homes in this section of Los Angeles. By 1870, a majority of Angelenos with Spanish surnames were concentrated in this ten-block section north of the Plaza.[72] Many of the new arrivals living in this area were from Sonora, and the area was disparagingly called "Sonoratown" by Anglo-Americans who saw the residents as "racially mixed outsiders."[73] In contrast, southwest of the plaza, a distinctly Anglo-American residential area developed by the middle of the 1860s. Here, new houses were constructed with wood frame and brick, rather than adobe. These building mirrored eastern architectural styles.

This partitioning of Los Angeles into racialized residential districts was hardly organic. Instead, the construction and placement of public buildings by Anglo-Americans helped mark newly subdivided spaces south of the Plaza as white. For instance, Anglo-American Jonathan Temple built a theater, city hall, and courthouse in an Anglo style south of the historic Plaza. By the 1870s, a new common space called Pershing Square was created. Originally called Central Park, it served as "a kind of Anglo replacement for the Plaza."[74]

The construction of the city's first schoolhouses was central to the creation of this Anglo-American area. The first public school building opened in 1855 south of the Plaza, near the corner of Second and Spring. Made not of adobe but brick, the structure followed an architectural design familiar back east, including two classrooms and two recitation rooms. When the school opened, the area had not yet been divided into smaller residential lots, and much of the city's population remained concentrated around the Plaza. One account described the location as "suburban"[75] and emphasized the logistical problems that accompanied the school's remote location.[76] The editors of the *Los Angeles Star* celebrated the new building but called for modifications that would make it seems less disconnected from the houses that remained concentrated near the Plaza. They called for changes that could make the building "an ornament to the city." "It should be finished in good style," the editors suggested, and additional improvements should be made to the land around it to "give [it] an air of permanence and finish that all such houses ought to present."[77]

As the land south of the Plaza was subdivided into residential tracts, more new school buildings helped further drive the formation of economically and racially homogeneous sections of the city. Anglo-American leaders in the city began an ambitious school building program in what were then the outskirts of the city. The newest and most valuable schools were clustered away from Sonoratown and an emerging Chinatown and in the Anglo and increasingly middle-class residential tracts emerging south of the Plaza. Figure 2.2 illustrates the ways in which

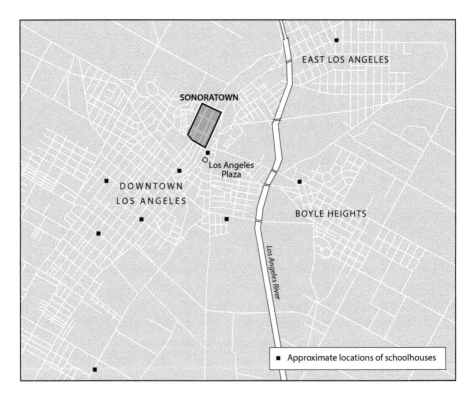

FIGURE 2.2. Map of Los Angeles public school buildings circa 1880. Data adapted from the *Annual Report of the Board of Education and City Superintendent of Schools, 1883–1884* (Los Angeles: Marley & Freeman, 1885), 18, and David Samuel Torres-Rouff, *Before L.A.: Race, Space, and Municipal Power in Los Angeles, 1781–1894* (New Haven, CT: Yale University Press, 2013), 137–46. Cartography by Bill Nelson.

schools helped to shape the segregated, outward growth of the city away from the Plaza and the Spanish and Mexican past it represented.

Many of the new neighborhoods in these Anglo-American sections of the city were planned subdivisions with schools constructed with public funds. In some cases, school buildings were constructed before the size of the population itself warranted it. The promoters of Brooklyn Heights, a residential tract marketed by the Brooklyn Land and Building Company, sought to convince prospective settlers that the area was destined to become "one of the most delightful residence portions" of the city. As late as May 1875, the promoters of the tract were still trying to convince potential buyers that there would be soon a "rush for this property" once water was actually made available, insisting that the subdivision was destined to become a place where "men of means" would "build their villas and fine residences."[78] Before the land around it was fully developed into residences—and even as the city struggled to accommodate all students in existing school buildings—officials dedicated a new schoolhouse to the tract.[79]

Quasi-privatized Impulses, Funding Policies, and the Early Politics of Localism

In casting the benefits of public education—and public goods themselves—as something that families could purchase alongside a house, narratives framing public schools as commodities helped produce an early politics of localism. This politics of localism was rooted in an understanding of "public" that was not simply quasi-privatized and focused on private gain, but also increasingly based on a (geographically) narrow view of the degree to which responsibility for educating other people's children was shared. It was not enough to buy and sell schools with land: the emerging Anglo-American elite increasingly cast the development of schools in *other* communities across California as a threat to their own.

The idea that schools drove population growth and shaped its demographics made private development and public school expansion inseparable in the minds of some commentators. This shaped how those commentators imagined their responsibility for the education of children in different parts of the state. As the belief grew that there was a finite number of "valuable" migrants, the intensity of competitive boosterism grew with it. This pattern was clearest in the way that the wealthiest districts increasingly talked about the importance of making sure that they had a better system of public education than those being created elsewhere. Boosters in San Francisco pursued a series of reforms that they described not so much as a way to improve San Francisco's schools or the preparation of San Franciscans for citizenship, but as a way to make sure children in San Francisco went to better schools than children in Benicia and San José. Superintendent Thomas Nevins embraced this logic in his appeals to the city council: if San Franciscans did not create the best school system in the region, he warned, families would relocate to "Benicia, San Jose, or some other places," harming San Francisco's prospects.[80] Similarly, the editors of the *Californian* used the threat of development in Benicia to spur enthusiasm for common schools in San Francisco. Describing, in 1847, the "considerable anxiety" among citizens for the creation of schools, the editors warned that "our neighboring town on the sea board is in this respect far surpassing us."[81] Benicia's boosters were not to be outdone. In his correspondences with Thomas Larkin, Robert Semple was clear that he wanted to create a school to "secure a class of population far above the other towns in California," so that, "before the first of the next year we shall be ahead of this place [San Francisco] in point of numbers and wealth."[82] In Sacramento, elites also justified educational expansion not in terms of its imagined benefits for the nation, but for the misfortune of San Francisco. Each development in San Francisco schools seemed to represent an ominous development for Sacramento's future. Local editors wrote, "San Francisco is greatly in advance of Sacramento in her system of common schools. Hers has been established some two years, and by the attention and labor of those to whom its infancy was entrusted, is now a firmly established and well managed system.... Turn we to our own city and ask what has she done for the cause of education? The mortifying answer is—*nothing!*"[83] For local boosters, that another city provided better schools and their own city's reputation would be harmed as a result were the primary reasons further investments in schools were needed. It was not the importance of schools for creating citizens or promoting social order that was foremost in civic boosters' minds, but the prospect that inaction would "be a stigma upon the good name of our fair city."[84]

The more Californians talked about schools in terms of population growth and increased land values, the more they reflected the decoupling of communities across different parts of the state. This narrowing of their conception of shared responsibility was increasingly clear in efforts to use residence to monopolize common schooling for one community at the expense of places nearby. The theft of the Eden Vale School discussed at the beginning of this chapter reflected this pattern in a particularly extreme manner.

The drawing and policing of school district boundaries restricted enrollment, a less drastic but arguably more effective tactic than physically taking school buildings. Indeed, county authorities refused to intervene in the Eden Vale incident and even allowed the residents of Hayward to create a new school district, including the relocated school, which Eden Vale's children were excluded from attending. During the early years of American public education, however, residence and schooling were not clearly linked. In San Francisco, there were initially no attendance zones.[85] If white students showed up, they were given a seat. Oakland schools were also open. Scattered throughout school district records housed in county archives are references to children crossing district boundaries to attend the schools of a neighboring village or town. As late as 1872, editors of the *Oakland News* were inviting children from the neighboring town of Brooklyn to attend the city's excellent schools,[86] and children in Oakland schools were explicitly invited to cross municipal boundaries and attend Temescal's schools.[87] As late as 1875, the children in Belmont were trekking to Redwood City for school, instead of attending the supposedly inferior one in Belmont.[88] Some children regularly walked several miles each day, even fording the San Lorenzo Creek, to attend out-of-district schools in Alameda County.[89]

In the 1860s, some California school boards instituted policies that made district residence a requisite for public school admission. The process was uneven, usually only applying to children from wealthy families. Still, these decisions reflected how a particularistic and locally bounded way of imagining education was slowly taking shape. In large part, the changes were a response to the challenge of financing infrastructure. In Sacramento, local elites took measures to address "non-resident pupils" in 1861. After identifying several students who lived outside the city but were attending Sacramento schools, board members decided that the poor ones could continue to attend for free but that wealthier children should pay tuition. Many smaller communities initially only raised a local tax once to finance construction of a new school building, and often it was only around the years of levying such a tax that local officials guarded district boundaries with care. In Santa Cruz, after a new schoolhouse was constructed, the local paper tried to persuade the school department to exclude children who lived outside the district from attending, though it is not clear if the trustees actually did begin to police their boundaries. When editors of the *Santa Cruz Weekly Sentinel* visited the school in January 1865, they commented on the presence of "several children from the adjoining Districts" and insisted they "ought not, in our opinion, to be allowed" because it was "robbing the children of this District of their real rights in the Teacher's time and attention."[90] Other places were far more committed to using the boundaries for exclusion. In San Mateo County, for example, the first requests for clear district lines were made in 1862, when a group of local boosters from the Laguna District petitioned the Santa Mateo County Board of Supervisors to clearly demarcate the district boundaries of their community. Having "erected a schoolhouse at very considerable expense," the citizens requested that the district line "be so *definitely* specified by *naming and including us* in the *Laguna District*" (emphasis in original).[91]

This localized, narrow conceptualization of the "public" shaped the politics of school finance, particularly in debates over the role of state governments. The idea that access to schools could be bought and sold fostered a sense of entitlement to school funds derived from land and property values, a way of thinking that gave shape to a language of local rights. This localist language crystallized in opposition to two proposals that were described by their supporters as making funding more "public" for white children by severing the link between variation in land values and the amount of money raised for education and, in so doing, promoting universal access to public school for white children. While both policies were implemented, wealthier districts did mount a staunch opposition to both. The first policy centralized revenues from the sixteenth and thirty-sixth sections of land that townships set aside for financing education (described in chapter 1) into the state-level school fund (called centralization), and the second increased the rate of the state property tax.

Opponents to centralization introduced a new way of talking about school finance that reflected their geographically based and quasi-private conceptualization of a public good. Newspaper editors and political representatives from communities benefiting the most from the unevenness in California's school funding system were the staunchest opponents of policies that severed the connection between land values and funding. Their claims were rooted in a logic that ignored how they benefited directly from state action, neglecting the degree to which state-sponsored acts of racial violence drove the dispossession of Indigenous and Mexican land that benefited most Anglo-American landowners in California. Without that state action, no Anglo-American would have been able to acquire land and use value derived from that land to educate their children. Nonetheless, opponents of centralizing township school funds erased the existence of this state subsidy to claim that all the wealth generated from land—whether "donated" by the federal government in school sections—belonged only to the white children who resided inside the boundaries of the township or city where those lands were located.

Proponents of this localist ideology claimed that residents in a given township or city had an exclusive right to the value derived from dispossessed lands because of their role in improving those lands, just as Anglo-Americans, in US legal discourse more broadly, were often said to own lands that they had improved. They believed that white residents, by virtue of their labor, had been the ones to create the value of the lands they had colonized, making them the rightful owners. The same logic supported the dubious claim that Indigenous peoples had never acquired ownership rights over their homelands, as they had not labored to improve them. The editors of the *Sacramento Daily Union* used this logic when they opposed the centralization of townships based on the purported effort that rural districts had put into settlement and how that effort had created, in turn, a right to the value extracted from those lands. Insisting that a consolidated school fund would benefit larger towns and cities at the expense of rural areas, the editors emphasized how families in these "sparsely settled" districts had "suffered many more inconveniences" in settling and creating schools in these places. As a result, the editors insisted, those families "have a right to the interest in the land."[92]

Other commentators opposed to centralization emphasized that the quasi-private rights acquired through purchase were violated by efforts to equalize school funding. The argument was simple. If access to particular schools had been bought with land, then access to the local school fund attached to that school had been purchased as well. Thomas Laspeyre, a state representative from San Joaquin County, made this claim in a speech on the floor of California State Assembly opposing centralization. He insisted that centralization would violate "a vested right the people of the townships acquired in obtaining this land."[93] The residents of the township were "reaping their just rewards" by "applying the proceeds of their lands to educating their children," he insisted. Centralization, by contrast, would purportedly take away a permanent source of local funding for schools, something that he insisted was "their heritage."[94]

A language of possession and ownership permeated this political rhetoric. Under the logic of commentators like Laspeyre, the value derived from dispossession had become the private property of all white individuals living within the boundaries of a given township or city. This fact of their possession and ownership of that land meant, in turn, that redistribution of the taxes derived from property values by the state would be an act of theft. The editors of the *San Joaquin Republican*, for example, described centralization as "attempted legislative robbery." The editors of the *Placer Herald* insisted centralization meant that the current and future residents of those townships with the most valuable parcels of land designated to be school sections would effectively be "defrauded."[95] When John Conness ran for governor, the editors of the *San Jose Tribune* reminded readers that as a member of the state legislature, he had introduced the legislation consolidating congressional school lands into the state's permanent fund, "taking from the children of the agricultural counties the sixteenth and thirty-sixth sections of land given them."[96] This language of theft also helped reinforce a diminishing of the responsibility for educating other people's children, as "our" children and "their" children varied by region, never including all children, or even all white children, in the state. For instance, for the editors of the *Sacramento Bee*, centralization had meant "the children of the mining counties got what was not intended for them," and "our children are robbed."[97]

The second policy where this localist ideology began to take form was in opposition to the levy of a state property tax to grow state funding for public schools. Representatives from the wealthiest communities in the state at the time also resisted those state tax levies. In doing so they also invoked the same logic of ownership and theft by insisting the money raised for schooling did not belong to the entire state, but to the community where that money was raised, like membership dues. Legislators representing San Francisco insisted that state school taxes were "redistributing" money from wealthy to poorer communities—an act of theft. The substantive opposition to the school bills passed in the 1860s and discussed in chapter 1 emerged from representatives of the state's largest towns and cities, all sharing in the logic that if money for schools in one place went to schools in another, something was not right. Efforts to increase the state school tax in 1864 were opposed in the assembly by representatives from San Francisco, who framed the tax as "unjust" to San Francisco since city residents would likely pay more than they would receive in benefits.[98] When the 1864 bill reached the state senate, it was similarly opposed by representatives from San Francisco.[99] When the bill finally passed, it was without support from any San Francisco representatives.[100]

When Anglo-Americans used common school funding policies to convert conquered lands into American ones, they encouraged a particular way of thinking about the relationship between school buildings and the physical landscape. Henry Whitney Bellows reflected this way of thinking in a speech at the dedication of the Denman Grammar School in San Francisco. A Unitarian minister from New York who had worked closely with reformer Horace Mann to found Antioch College, Bellows used his speech to reflect on how the sight of common school buildings in California made him feel as if he was back east:[101] "I feel as if that long voyage that lies between me and the Atlantic States were abolished, for I find myself in the midst of this assembly, as it were, in old Boston again—a copy of one of her beautiful school-houses before me."[102]

Even before lawmakers codified into law the connection between wealth, racial segregation, and educational provision during the early years of the twentieth century, land and education policies encouraged nineteenth-century Americans to imagine a deep connection between schools, the character of a place, and the racial composition of its inhabitants. Some commentators expressed this association in an overwrought language of "civilization." In the words of one commentator, schools produced value through the "softening and refining influences" they purportedly had on the people who attended them and the places where they stood.[103] Other commentators expressed this way of thinking in economic terms. As they softened and refined a place, the commentators insisted, schools increased the economic value of land. In both instances, schools such as the Denman Grammar School in San Francisco signified Anglo-American settlement and, in the process, the ideas about race and nation that went along with it.

State funding policies and these related ideas about race and place encouraged nineteenth-century Americans to treat schools like a magnet for white settlement and a tool for increasing land values. They also encouraged Anglo-Americans to use the state's own policies regarding school districting to hoard wealth, exclude children, and create early patterns of racial and economic segregation. As developers, politicians, and others cast the common school as a local institution in defense of those efforts, they also created a new language for challenging the organization of school funding.

Yet the impact of state policies in areas such as school districting and the success of a language framing the common school as a quasi-private good remained limited. The state's funding policies and the continued reliance of those policies on funding sources that crossed district boundaries placed limits on the salience of district boundaries, even when those boundaries were drawn with precision and policed by local officials. Moreover, the end of the Civil War brought new challenges to the premise of racial exclusion in public schools. Reconstruction raised new questions about how capaciously lawmakers would imagine education as a public good provided to all children on universalistic and egalitarian terms. Competing visions of the public school project, whom it should serve, and whom it should benefit, were circulating in the state by the end of the 1860s. Those competing visions and their interactions with—and impact on—state lawmaking are the subject of chapter 3.

3

FINANCE REFORM AND THE CONTESTED MEANING OF "PUBLIC" IN THE 1870S AND 1880S

San José's newly constructed Santa Clara Street School was an impressive structure. The elegant building, like most Second Empire–inspired architecture in the United States, was reminiscent of the Louvre in Paris. Complete with a rectangular tower, steep mansard roof, and molded cornices, the "magnificent edifice" was full of modern conveniences: water and gas, an exhibition room in the attic, and eight commodious classrooms.[1] Several miles west of Santa Clara Street School, on the top of a hill, sat Alpine School, a much more modest structure. The school's poor insulation was a concern for the editors of the *San Mateo County Gazette*. "Every breeze that blows," the editors lamented, "has full sweep through the open, rattletrap of a building." There was no water available at the school's site, and toilet facilities were crude. The biggest problem confronting the school, however, was a snake infestation outside the structure. The problem was so bad, one county superintendent recalled, that it took two people to enter the schoolhouse, "one to watch for snakes."[2]

The physical differences between Santa Clara Street School and Alpine School reflected the contrast between wealthy and poor school districts across the nation in the 1870s and 1880s. These differences raised existential questions for some Americans. If state or territorial governments provided some school districts more resources than others, were those schools still common? Were they still public? Did the money raised for schooling through taxation belong to a public that encompassed an entire state and nation, or a public contained within the boundaries of individual school districts?

These questions about the differences between schools like Santa Clara Street and Alpine, moreover, were raised at a moment when the questions of who had a right to access public schools and who constituted the public the schools served were hotly debated. The passage of the Thirteenth, Fourteenth, and Fifteenth Amendments to the US Constitution after the Civil War—abolishing chattel slavery, guaranteeing citizenship to formerly enslaved people, and extending the right to vote to men regardless of race or former enslavement—held the potential to transform the meaning of public schooling by expanding who had access to it. In the South, formerly enslaved Black Americans transformed the geographic reach of the public school during and immediately after the Civil War. Black Americans funded, built, and taught in a system of free schools in the region. They lobbied for, legislated, and embedded in state constitutions a legal framework for universal education that had not existed for children in the South, Black or white, before the Civil War.

In multiracial California, the relationships among race, citizenship, and the universality of the public school was no less fluid in the years immediately after the Civil War. There, Black Americans continued to fight for a more expansive conception of who was included in the public school project and on what terms. They brought Reconstruction to California, drawing on the passage of the Fourteenth and Fifteenth Amendments to challenge segregated schooling. They organized and secured support from white politicians like Newton Booth and members of the legislature. After a test case on school segregation and the Fourteenth Amendment established a "separate but equal" doctrine (two decades before *Plessy v. Ferguson*), they succeeded in having lawmakers codify in state law the right of Black Americans to the same schools as white Americans. During these same years, the Tape family successfully secured a right to state-sponsored education for Chinese Americans at a time when they were almost universally excluded from public schools, albeit in segregated schools quickly codified into law by state lawmakers after the Tape family's court victory. Meanwhile, Indigenous people faced the continued invasion of their lands and expropriation of those lands to finance the growth of white schooling in the West. They were also facing a new system of residential boarding schools created by the US government that, in the words of the founder of the Carlisle Indian Industrial School, aimed to "kill the Indian in him and save the man."[3]

Within this context of changing ideas about who should have access to the public school, the questions of how those schools should be funded and on what terms also arose. These questions were different on the surface but conceptually similar, ultimately centering on the question of how universal and egalitarian the public school should be in California. District-level taxation for school funding remained rare in California and several other western states, but its spread was alarming some observers. This alarm was part of a broader concern raised by a new species—the modern business corporation. Corporations like the railroad were creatures of the state that were once thought to have a quasi-public function. Their leaders continued to promise that their companies were contributing to a rising tide that would lift all boats. While they consumed massive subsidies based on that premise, they increasingly seemed to be privatizing the public good instead. Further, the leaders and backers of modern corporations aggressively sought to avoid the state and local taxes that funded public schools.

To observers critical of this new economic order, resource disparities between schools like Santa Clara Street and Alpine seemed to illustrate the consequences of the way wealthy entities and people were monopolizing resources, refusing to pay their taxes, and undermining the common good. If such resource disparities between schools were permitted to continue, rural lawmakers in California maintained, the state would no longer have schools that were common, public, or part of a state system, by definition. Rural lawmaker B. F. Tuttle put the matter in stark terms on the floor of the state legislature. Any form of school funding that did not share wealth across the entire state equally, he insisted, meant that California no longer had "a common or general school system at all, but a local one."[4] In response, a coalition of rural politicians and educational reformers sought to increase state support for schools, reform the tax system by ensuring taxation of property like stocks and bonds and not just real estate, and equalizing the way revenue was apportioned to school districts. Efforts to increase state school support were not isolated to California. Across the West, a number of territorial and state officials followed California and resisted district property taxation. Even in places where these taxes eventually became the norm, commentators nonetheless viewed the growth of the "special tax" among districts with alarm. Further east, some reformers began to argue for fiscal centralization beyond the township. In several states, they succeeded in creating new state taxes designed to limit local financing in public education systems. Although later reformers would either misrepresent these reforms or ignore them completely, thirty-one state or territorial education taxes were being levied by the fall of 1876. As a result, local taxes played a smaller role in school funding than they would for the entirety of the Progressive Era. Only in the years following World War II would local taxes again play as small a role in education funding as they had during these years.[5]

Moreover, definitions of a "statewide public education system" were also contested throughout the 1870s and 1880s, and what it meant to have schools that were "public" was unsettled as lawmakers debated the place of district taxation in school funding. While some western reformers insisted that district-level taxation was antithetical to the idea of having a statewide public education system, others were quite comfortable with local financing and the inequities it produced. Representatives from larger towns and cities were particularly open to district financing, and they increasingly opposed efforts to expand state school support by emphasizing their frustrations that their public schools might receive less education funding than they paid in state or county taxes.

While the story of education funding in the postbellum South is well known, scholars have tended to overlook western and northern debates over district property taxation during the 1870s and 1880s.[6] As a result, historians often overstate the extent to which district property taxation was accepted and actually used to fund educational expansion after the Civil War, further casting the inequities produced by local financing as inevitable, even natural, features of US schooling. This chapter reconstructs debates over the district property tax and shows what they reveal about the contested and unsettled meaning of the word "public" in the 1870s and 1880s. Contemporary understandings of public education—and the extent to which inequality thrives in state school systems without raising existential questions about whether in fact public schools have been abolished—owe much to the outcome of these debates.

The Common School and Greater Reconstruction

Education, citizenship, and race were bound together in particular ways before the Civil War.[7] The collective that was brought together within the walls of the common school—which in some formulations constituted the nation itself—was synonymous with whiteness in the writing and lawmaking of white Californians, as it was across the antebellum nation. As chapter 1 made clear, defining what that meant in multiracial California was never simple. More important still, Black Californians successfully challenged elements of this racial order by the end of the Civil War, obligating the state to educate Black Americans, albeit in separate schools.

The end of the Civil War brought the terms of this relationship between education, citizenship, and race—across the North, South, and West—into question. The public school quickly became a central object of political discourse on what a reconstructed United States would look like. It was fundamental to writing, lawmaking, and other actions focused on creating a new world in the wake of chattel slavery, as well as counterefforts to narrow that world and carry into it the racial hierarchies of chattel slavery.

For Black Americans, education had always been liberatory. Historian Jarvis Givens uses a language of "fugitivity" to capture the far-reaching power of Black education, noting continuities in how "Black education was a school project set against the entire order of things."[8] In the South, formerly enslaved Black

Americans engaged in just such a project as they rapidly established and funded schools, building on a tradition of Black education that had operated surreptitiously under chattel slavery.[9] In the process, they brought public education itself to the South. As historian James Anderson has observed, Black Americans "played a central role in etching the idea of universal public education into southern state constitutional law."[10]

In national politics, education represented a tool for rebuilding and reconstituting the nation, as articulated by Republicans in Congress. In the optimistic words of Senator Henry Wilson of Massachusetts, education would become the "centerpiece of a new Reconstruction of all of American society."[11] Pennsylvania educator James P. Wickersham expressed a vision shared by others, of a new nation created by the public school, casting education as a way of "making homogenous our social as well as our political institutions. . . . Without it, there may be reconstruction, but there can be no true union."[12] A series of bills were proposed to create a national system that could integrate the North, South, and West, part of what some historians have come to call "Greater Reconstruction."[13] As historian Nancy Beadie has shown, efforts to create a national education system in the 1870s and 1880s reflected the importance of education for Greater Reconstruction; the effort's failure helped entrench and expand the existing racialized and decentralized structure of US education. Throughout the 1870s and 1880s, Congress considered approximately twenty different bills to create a national education system. The most influential was the so-called Blair Bill, which would have provided federal funding to states in direct proportion to their literacy rate.

None of the bills passed.[14] Black education in the South remained liberatory and subversive, but also became a target for whites conspiring to limit Black citizenship by limiting Black education. Most overtly, Black teachers, students, and schoolhouses were regular targets of violence by white southerners seeking to maintain their system of racial domination. With more subtlety, northern philanthropists and southern whites worked to limit the resources and narrow the curriculum for Black schools in an effort to turn the public school into a site for maintaining a racial caste system and limited, second-class citizenship for Black students. White southerners systematically underfunded and denied Black schools resources, even as they taxed Black communities at high rates to finance white school systems.[15] Southern schools, in the words of one historian, were intended by some to "bind, not to liberate."[16]

But in California and across the West, education occupied a different place in Reconstruction and unfolded differently. For Black Americans in California, Reconstruction brought setbacks but also civil rights milestones, even as its fate was still uncertain back east. In San Francisco, activists were in the middle of a battle with the school board over the closure of the city's Black school on Broadway and its relocation to a series of inconvenient sites and substandard buildings when the Fourteenth and Fifteenth Amendments were ratified in 1868 and 1870. Initially, San Francisco's Black community demanded equal school facilities.[17] But by the fall of 1871, Black Californians had gathered at an education convention in Stockton and called for not just equal school facilities but the abolition of segregated schools. Delegates at the convention concluded that "proscriptive schools are contrary to pure principles of Democracy" and, under the new amendments to the Constitution, were illegal. They called for "full educational privileges which we cannot obtain in the caste schools as now organized" and determined that the best way to secure such privileges was through legislation and a "test case" in state courts.[18]

In the legislative session that began the month after the education convention, Republican lawmakers expressed strong support for integrating the state's schools. The newly elected Republican governor of California, Newton Booth, included in his inaugural address a call for lawmakers to ensure the "right to education independent of color," insisting that "the doors of our schools should be open to all with no prejudice of caste."[19] Although the initial bill to integrate the state's schools introduced by Representative J. F. Cowdery stalled in the legislature, similar bills were introduced during successive sessions, with one eventually passing in the early 1880s.

Simultaneously, Black activists leveraged the passage of the Fourteenth and Fifteenth Amendments to bring their planned test case challenging segregation through the courts. The resulting decision in 1874 did not prohibit segregation, but it did require the state to provide all Black Californians with an equal education, ruling that if a Black school were not equal to the school provided to whites, Black children were entitled to attend the white school. This was described in the Black press as a major victory.[20] Activists at the local level were even more successful, convincing individual school boards to abolish segregated schooling despite court rulings affirming the principle of separate but equal. By 1875, African American children were admitted to integrated schools in San Francisco, Vallejo, and Oakland.[21] By 1880, the legislature formally removed the word "white" from the California school code.[22]

Reconstruction in California was also multiracial, and the civil rights successes of Black Californians stood in contrast to a series of setbacks for Chinese Americans. In 1875, Sacramento admitted Chinese students into the city's public school system.[23] But San Francisco refused to, even after closing its separate school for Chinese students in the early 1870s and as the number of Chinese American children in the city climbed to one thousand by the early 1880s. In the fall of 1884, a Chinese American named Mamie Tape tried to enroll in the city's school system. While no legal mechanism clearly excluded her, both the city and the state superintendent insisted that neither she nor any other Chinese child could be admitted to the public schools. The Tape family sued, and succeeded. The legislature responded by amending the school law to permit the creation of segregated schools for Asian and Native American children. San Francisco quickly opened segregated Chinese schools, and Mamie Tape, despite her vindication in court, was never admitted into a nonsegregated school in the city.[24]

Across the West, education was also part of a reconstruction of a different sort rooted in continued dispossession and conquest. As the Union Army withdrew from the South, it was deployed in the West. On maps created immediately after the Civil War, the United States claimed control over all lands between Canada and Mexico west of the Missouri River. All lands outside reservations and Indian Territory were, in theory, contained within US states or territories. But the army was overextended. In practice, land west of the Missouri River in the 1870s and 1880s was not actually under the control of federal, state, or territorial governments, especially on the Great Plains. Indigenous nations continued to resist US expansion. While many of these tribes were later defeated by the US military, they remained in control of their lands immediately following the Civil War. The Ute continued to claim lands in the Great Basin, and the Apache maintained a formidable presence in the Southwest. On the Great Plains, it was far from clear that Comanche, Arapaho, Cheyenne, and Lakota lands would eventually be ceded to the federal government, surveyed into townships, and sold or rented to finance US common schools. Even in areas technically contained within the boundaries of US states, the Nez Perce, Bannock, and Modoc resisted efforts by the US military to force their relocation.[25] Even after land was ceded to the United States by tribes, it had to be surveyed and then sold or rented to produce revenue upon statehood.[26]

The drive to create common schools in western states and territories remained inextricably connected to the notion that educational expansion would transform the region by spreading "civilization," converting the West into an "American" place and its lands into increasingly valuable commodities. John Gast's lithograph "American Progress" suggested how the process would unfold. According to the publisher who commissioned the lithograph in 1872, the image was designed to illustrate "the grand drama" of US expansion. In the foreground, a floating figure "bearing on her forehead the Star of Empire" carries "a book representing the common school." In retreat in the image are bison and Indigenous people, vanishing with the advance of "manufactories, schools and churches" that are "indicative of civilization."[27] Most Anglo-American westerners believed that investments in common schools would help to lure white families in their direction, increasing land values to such an extent that revenue from federal school lands would eventually cover the costs of operating a public school system.

Over the course of the next decade, territorial and state governments in the West created an astonishing number of common schools. On average, they created just over three public schools each day between 1870 and 1880.[28] The proportion of school-age children attending schools in most western states and territories was among the highest in the nation. California, Colorado, Idaho, Kansas, Nebraska, Nevada, Oregon, and Wyoming all enrolled a larger share of their school-age population in public schools by 1880 than did Massachusetts.[29] There were also more schools per capita than in any other region, prompting historian Elliott West to conclude that "public education was more accessible in the West than in any other part of the nation."[30]

Business Corporations, District Taxes, and the Menace of Privatization

Within a broader context where ideas about citizenship, education, and race were shifting who was considered part of the public poised to benefit from, and access on equal terms, state-sponsored schooling, the nature of the line separating public governance and private markets was being redrawn. And according to an increasingly vocal group of rural critics and urban laborers, a monstrous new creature was doing much of the redrawing. That creature was the large business corporation. It had existed long before the Civil War, but it had grown unrecognizable and seemed to assume its most hideous form, according to its critics in California, as the railroad corporation. As Californians reckoned with the emerging world of corporate capitalism, many state leaders developed a sharp critique of how the common good was being privatized, hoarded, and corrupted by a selfish few trying to get rich—and succeeding. That critique further prompted residents of the state to articulate a vision of education as a public good that should not be subject to the inequities of localized funding.

During the 1870s and 1880s, a coalition of reformers and politicians in California grew increasingly concerned that district-level taxation was expanding in rural areas and that, more broadly, the public education system was being dismantled and privatized. According to these critics, rural districts were being forced to raise a local tax to supplement their state appropriations, and this tax was private, like tuition, rather than public. The nature of this critique and the understanding of the boundary between public and private that sustained it must be understood in relation to the transformations of the economy, wealth, and taxation during the 1870s and 1880s.

As noted in chapter 1, business corporations were originally thought to have a public character. In exchange for supporting the common good, they received special privileges from the state. The leaders of railroad corporations talked a lot about how they deserved such privileges, as well as various subsidies, because of their support for the common good. Edward Tompkins, an adviser to California governor Henry Haight, similarly justified corporations' public purpose in California, explaining that the railroads would "add immensely to the prosperity and wealth of the State." He reasoned that "the People having the benefit, ought to bear a reasonable proportion of the cost."[31] Critics of the railroad corporation insisted, on the contrary, that it was hoarding wealth and privatizing the public good for private gain. This view was rooted in a populist critique and in language chastising monopolies and the threat they posed.

The critique of the increasingly large business corporation was rooted in a concern that the state itself had been converted into a mere appendage of private entities seeking to extract profit for themselves at the expense of the common good. In the now-iconic representation by Frank Norris several decades later, the Southern Pacific Railroad was an octopus with its tentacles reaching far and wide. In the early 1870s, three areas of government finance in particular became sites of an emerging critique of corporate capitalism, shaping how reformers sought to retool and reorganize the financing of the public school.

The first such area concerned how the state was distributing resources that critics considered the collective property of the public. This meant, most obviously, how the state spent the dollars it raised in taxes. Reflecting the clear racial boundaries of how the public was imagined, it also meant how the government distributed expropriated land, including unceded Indigenous land. Such land was cast in political discourse as a resource for the collective, akin to tax dollars, and critics pointed out how much had been given to railroad corporations and how little they seemed to provide to the common good despite those subsidies. From the federal government, the railroads received over one hundred million acres.[32] Much of it was still unceded and contested Indigenous territory on the plains. In California, the state also passed legislation in 1859 that permitted counties to purchase stock in railroad companies and thus contribute public tax dollars to private businesses. Counties invested about $4.6 million of taxpayer dollars in rail lines. The state government invested, too. In 1861 and 1864, it gave large subsidies to the Central Pacific line in exchange for free transportation of some state services.[33] By the early 1870s, Californians were increasingly critical of how such subsidies were being funneled to wealthy individuals. Rural farmers felt particularly exploited by the rates railroads charged them to ship their harvest to market. In the 1870 election, voters elected leaders who promised to rein in subsidies for railroads in a language that pointed to how they were plundering the public for private gain. Henry Haight defied his adviser and came out against rail subsidies during his reelection campaign. He told voters he valued corporations in their "proper sphere" but objected to their transformation into "agencies for public plunder." He lost to Newton Booth, who had been even more vocal in his opposition to the railroad.[34]

The assertion that government subsidies to railroads reflected the privatization of common resources for personal gain was connected, too, to the concentration of landownership in the hands of an ever-smaller number of people in California. A language of "land monopolism" emerged among rural residents of the state, and it evolved rather seamlessly into a broader critique of the large business corporation.[35] Concerns over the concentration of landownership started early. Anglo-Americans considered all of California theirs for the taking, including the large Mexican-and Spanish-held lands before the Mexican-American War that the United States had promised to honor, which soon became the target of squatters. The legally dubious methods that Anglo-Americans used to dispossess former Mexican nationals of their land flowed into a series of similarly questionable strategies for manipulating the public land sale process. For example, purchasers could use "dummy" entry persons to work around limits on how much public land a single person could purchase. In 1872, the California State Board of Agriculture issued a report showing that one hundred people owned over five million acres of land—a figure that was likely an underestimate.[36] The railroads were not the only corporate culprits; entities involved in large-scale, industrial farming or ranching operations like Miller & Lux also owned vast amounts of land in the state.

The second area of government finance subject to critique was related to what sorts of property were actually being taxed. California's state school tax, like most state taxes across the nation, was a general property tax. As late as 1890, such taxes accounted for 72 percent of all state revenue in the United States.[37] It was a universal tax on wealth: from the stocks of a corporation to the land owned by a small farmer, all forms of wealth considered property were ostensibly taxed. California's $1 millage rate for the state school tax meant every person or entity was responsible for paying $1 in school tax for every $1,000 of property that person or entity owned. The owner of a farm worth $100 would have paid ten cents toward the state's common schools, while the owner of $500,000 worth of property would pay $500.[38] The general property tax, however, was rarely a universal tax on wealth, because not all forms of property were assessed at their actual value. Stocks, bonds, and cash were the embodiment of the emerging pattern of extreme wealth owned by a select few that the modern business corporation seemed to represent. In theory, these intangible forms of wealth were taxed alongside everything else, including tangible forms of wealth like land. In practice, they were not. As the character of wealth itself shifted, assessments of intangible assets like bonds, stocks, bank deposits, and other financial instruments became increasingly undervalued. As one historian of the general property tax explained, "where officials were disposed to tax it, the new wealth proved difficult to assess or, more generally, impossible to locate."[39] Between 1860 and 1880, the national gross domestic product almost tripled. While the assessed value of real estate had increased 87 percent, assessed value on personal, movable property had fallen 24 percent.[40] Wealth in the form of land owned by corporate entities often escaped taxation. Railroad land grants were not taxed until they were surveyed and the companies took formal title, a process they drew out in some cases to escape taxation.[41] Industrial farm operators could keep their taxes low through bribery; at one point Miller & Lux paid the Merced County assessor to limit their property tax liability by underassessing their wealth.[42]

The third problematical area in government finance made the first two areas even more objectionable. For critics, it was bad enough that corporations like the Southern Pacific received massive public subsidies to turn a private profit and that, in the form of intangible wealth, such profit seemed to escape the taxes that everyone else had to pay. But railroads, as well as banks, worked hard to avoid paying taxes, often through extensive litigation. Sometimes they lost. In the 1860s, for example, the San Francisco and San José railroad (later acquired by the Southern Pacific) received about a third of its funding to build a rail line from the City of San Francisco, the County of San Mateo, and the County of Santa Clara. When one of the school districts it crossed in San Mateo County voted for a district-level tax, the railroad refused to pay, arguing in court that the school districts did not have the right to levy a tax of that sort. The railroad eventually lost the case in the state supreme court, but the suit reflected a broader, often effective tactic for avoiding tax payments.[43] Such cases, successful or not, clearly reflected a disconnect between the quasi-public good that the companies purported to promote and the rather thin commitment they exhibited to the common good when it was time to pay their taxes. In Placer County, for instance, the county superintendent of schools had to sue the auditor to place the revenue from the county's school tax into the school fund. The auditor claimed that a law granting the county permission to purchase stock in the Central Pacific had been passed by the legislature more recently than the bill authorizing the financing of common schools, and the county school tax revenue actually needed to be used to purchase railroad stock.[44]

Litigation to avoid taxation was often successful as well. In the early 1870s, California lawmakers instituted a series of reforms to address unequal taxation and prevent intangible forms of wealth from avoiding taxation. The legislature created a State Board of Equalization and passed a law increasing the power of officials to collect taxes on wealth that had been systematically underassessed. In a single year, the board nearly tripled the assessed valuation of personal property in the state. In a series of court cases in the 1870s, however, both banks and a group of wealthy San Franciscans challenged the taxation of intangible forms of wealth. A cycle emerged where the legislature would try to tax intangible wealth, lose a lawsuit, pass a new law, and get sued again. By the end of the 1870s, the state's constitutional definition of property had essentially been narrowed to the point that it was not possible to tax intangible wealth.[45]

These dimensions of public finance all became focal points for a broader critique of inequality and corporate capitalism. The issue of unequal taxation and railroad greed was particularly important for farmers during the 1870s. Across the nation, this critique was clearest among members of the National Grange of the Order of Patrons of Husbandry, the organization typically associated with the beginning of antimonopoly politics. In California, a central concern of the "farmers' great awakening" was the "inequality of taxation" rampant in the state.[46] Farmers, one California member of the National Grange explained in 1875, "pay nearly all the taxes that are required for the machinery of the Government" as a result of the "burdens of taxation from which the wealthy manage to escape." Recalling an early meeting of the organization, future state superintendent of public instruction Ezra Carr recounted how members would use "language more forcible than elegant" to express the "outrage" Americans would feel when they realized that "they have been compelled to pay tribute to capitalists."[47] This theme was often repeated by critics of the way tax burdens were distributed. The ability of the wealthy to escape taxation was most common, critics reasoned, in the large towns and cities where intangible forms of property were concentrated. As historian Nicholas Parrillo put it, the assumption was that "the escape of intangibles was particularly widespread in cities, where most intangible property owners lived."[48] This resentment over wealth and taxation, alongside deep frustration with railroad rate setting and commodity prices, helped to fuel the rural radicalism that developed over the decade.

Rural critics framed school district taxation as a further injustice of the tax system, yet another way that the common good was being subverted and government itself privatized. The criticism was rooted in the notion that an equal per pupil disbursement of state funding did not account for the costs of operating a rural school. Owing to rising teacher salaries and low enrollments, the most sparsely populated districts were unable to operate without levying a local property tax to supplement the money sent to communities on a per pupil basis. As the editors of the *California Teacher* explained, granting each community a set amount per pupil discriminated "most unjustly against the thinly populated districts of the state" as capital and salary expenses were disproportionate to the number of pupils. As one reformer wrote, "One district may have fifteen census children, another fifty; still the same amount is needed by each district to maintain a school for a definite length of time."[49] The superintendent of Butte County similarly complained that "it costs as much to support a school of fifteen scholars as it does to support one of forty scholars."[50]

For critics of local financing, the problem was that it was simply incompatible with the basic premise of having a state school system. "Our whole State school system," editors of the *California Teacher* argued, "is based upon the theory that the richer and more populous counties may be taxed for the benefit of the poorer and more thinly settled counties."[51] According to the calculus of rural Californians and state school reformers, the district property tax was abominable. "In a State system of public instruction should not all the children be treated alike?" the editors of the *California Teacher* asked. "As a good mother," they continued, "she should dispense the blessing of education with an equal hand. . . . Let all the property of the State be taxed to educate all the children of the State."[52] For this coalition of rural educational leaders, lawmakers, and state school officials, local taxation was antithetical to the idea of having an education system that was statewide and public.

The precise meaning of the phrase "state public education system" seemed increasingly unsettled in debates over local taxation and the distribution of state funds. When referring to district property taxation, many lacked the language to describe the practice. The *San Francisco Chronicle* discussed controversies surrounding the need for rural communities to levy district taxes as a "private expense."[53] Editors of the *California Teacher* insisted that "a state system is worthy of universal support only, insofar as it gives as much as possible, the same educational facilities to all districts."[54] Unless the resources across districts were equalized, editors of the *California Teacher* proclaimed, "our system fails in the object by reason of which alone it can claim our recognition and support." The editors insisted that the basis of this claim for support relied on the ability of the state to provide "the free and equal education of *all* the children of the State irrespective of the standing in society, or the residence of their parents."[55] Indeed, unequally sharing the costs of public education was so detestable to state reformers that some feared it would make the entire enterprise of state schooling collapse. "It is a duty of the state," one reformer explained, "not only to tax alike but also to furnish equal educational facilities to all districts—rich or poor—in the centers of wealth or on the borders."[56] State educational leaders reasoned that it was impossible for the state to fulfill this duty if state schools were funded through sources that could not be redistributed.

Did California even have a state education system if there were clear disparities between school districts? Some critics said no. If school expenditures were based on the notion that "the apportionments must be in proportion to the proceeds of local taxation," one reformer reasoned, "a state school system then becomes impossible."[57] "As it now is, it is not a common or general school system at all, but a local one," State Senator B. F. Tuttle argued. "If a common school system is desirable," Tuttle continued, "if it is of sufficient importance to call it a State system, let us make it so in fact as well as in name."[58]

Concern over the spread of district property taxation and all the ways it seemed to undermine the purposes of public schooling prompted lawmakers to create one of the first need-adjusted funding formulas in the nation. Expecting increased revenues from taxes on banks, railroads, and land monopolists under reforms implemented in 1872, Senator Tuttle introduced a new law to provide "justice" to "the children of these poor sparsely settled districts."[59] This law, referred to as Tuttle's School Bill at the time, passed the legislature and was signed into law after an antimonopolist majority obtained control of the state legislature in 1874.[60] Tuttle's School Bill was designed to increase state funding for common schools and distribute these increased funds according to need. It was justified with the language of antimonopolism and framed as part of a broader effort to address "unequal taxation." Drawing on the distinction between the "producers" of wealth who farmed the land, and the capitalists who collected rent on it, Tuttle characterized rural districts as "constantly creating and adding new wealth to the world," wealth that was "constantly being concentrated at the large cities."[61] The law substantially increased state financial support. Between 1874 and 1875 state contributions to districts more than doubled, from $427,157 to $1,210,808.[62] The new law also ensured that each district, regardless of size, could afford a teacher.

Under the provisions of the new law, state leaders would distribute state funds to districts based on "teacher units." The idea of apportioning funds in this manner was new in California, and the concept of "teacher units" later became a popular principle in school finance, borrowed by other western states in the 1870s and codified by administrative progressives at the turn of the century. The concept was simple. Each district was entitled to $500 for each "teacher unit." One hundred children on the census qualified a district for one teacher, and any district with fewer than one hundred children received a fraction thereof from the school fund. Districts with between ten and fifteen children would receive $300 to guarantee they had the funds needed to hire a teacher without a local tax. Smaller districts with fewer than ten children would be forced to close.

The new legislation was bold. According to its leading proponents, it would ensure that the school fund was "apportioned according to the needs of the several districts" and would equalize funding.[63] The bill also further inserted California into conversations about centralization in school funding. Its approach also spread during these years. Nevada lawmakers adopted the "teacher unit" in the 1880s, while North Dakota officials incorporated it into state law in the 1890s. When Progressive Era education professor Ellwood Cubberley surveyed the apportionment of school funds in the first decade of the twentieth century, he considered the "teacher unit" an innovation and an improvement over the per pupil basis. He found what he called the "teacher basis" also being used in New York, New Jersey, Pennsylvania, Delaware, and Vermont.[64]

Redistributive Funding in the 1870s and 1880s

During the 1870s, not only B. F. Tuttle was describing district-level taxation for education funding as incompatible with the idea of a statewide public education system. As western officials made investments in education, many did not consider a district-level property tax an appropriate or viable source of revenue. Even in the many western states and territories where district taxes were technically permitted, officials usually considered them supplemental and temporary. These taxes were expected to serve the role that bonds tend to play in contemporary school finance—an appropriate way to periodically fund a new schoolhouse, perhaps, but not a way to sustain a system of common schools. Observers sometimes described taxes raised at the district level with names that reflected an expectation they would remain rare, labeling them a "special tax" or a "special district tax" in some cases.[65] The first superintendent of public instruction in Colorado simply called it the "vexatious special tax."[66]

The district tax remained rare in several states and territories. In California in 1870 there was not a single school district raising a local tax in forty-four of the state's fifty counties.[67] This pattern was mirrored across the region. In Nevada, only 6 percent of school districts reported a local tax at the conclusion of the 1870–71 school year.[68] In Nebraska, only 10.4 percent of the money spent on public schools was derived from local property taxes in 1870.[69] In Washington Territory, a majority of the school districts operating in 1879 were located in counties without a single district raising a "special tax."[70] Out of the 103 school districts across nine counties in the Montana Territory in 1877, only 32 were in a county with district property taxes.[71] North Dakota generated less than 1 percent of its total school revenues from district taxes when it became a state at the end of the decade.[72]

The principle that the wealth of a school district should shape the ability of that district to fund its schools was anathema to some observers, and they viewed with alarm the prospect of district property taxation becoming a normal feature of public school funding. School officials insisted that land in general, and school lands in particular, would rapidly increase in value. Some claimed that this increase would eventually render taxation for common schools unnecessary. The first superintendent of public instruction in Montana, for example, asserted that "it is but a question of time" before "the interest on the school funds of the State and rents accruing from the leasing of school lands will be sufficient to maintain every common school."[73] Still, most officials also recognized that taxes needed to be levied before school lands could be surveyed, sold, or rented, as that was not even possible until statehood. In the meantime, taxes needed to be raised for schools, and officials preferred the kind of taxes that would redistribute wealth between school districts. Sometimes this meant taxes that could redistribute wealth within the large counties of the region, many of which were geographically larger than the small states of New England.

Whether redistribution occurred at the state, territorial, or county level, these officials were typically quite clear that a tax that only redistributed wealth within school districts must be limited or avoided entirely. Indeed, officials often expressed grave concern if they felt district taxation was spreading. The first state superintendent of Colorado worried that the "selfish impulses of the rich" were leading to a growth in district taxes. These wealthy communities were the largest in their counties, dictating the outcome of special tax elections. They kept county taxes low while supporting their own schools liberally through a special district tax, leaving "their poor neighbors to struggle on as they may."[74] In Dakota Territory, W. H. H. Beadle praised the territorial tax levied for schools. He worried, however, that the territorial legislature would encourage district taxation and "subdivide sovereignty among unequal local parts." This move seemed antithetical to the premise of the general tax for schools, since "the educational system is a state (territorial) institution... authorized by the commonwealth for the equal, uniform, common advantage and general public benefit."[75]

Instead of local taxation, officials in California and other western states and territories emphasized the importance of creating or expanding state or territorial taxes for public schooling. Throughout the 1870s and 1880s, they proposed county or territorial taxes as an alternative to district-level taxes while waiting for revenue from school lands. The superintendent of Dakota Territory, for instance, argued for a "general school tax."[76] The territorial superintendent of Utah proposed a "light state tax" that could go along with the eventual "munificent grants of land from the national domain."[77] Reformers in western states, too, advocated for the creation of new state school taxes modeled after those of California. The Nevada state superintendent of public instruction advocated a state tax to supplement Nevada's permanent school fund, contending that the tax could promote uniformity in taxation and education. Describing the California state school tax, he pointed out that the "Hon. John Swett, ex-Superintendent of Public Instruction of that State, said that he regarded this [the state school tax] the very best feature of their State school system." This state school tax, he further explained, was growing the state school fund and allowing schools to flourish. "By reason of this large State Fund thus annually accumulating," he stated, California was able to "provide handsomely for each and every one of her school districts."[78] Increased state school support was among the most commonly proposed reforms contained in the annual reports of state school officials during the 1870s.[79]

This focus on redistributive funding sources did not mean schools were underfunded in western states and territories. Per capita spending in the West was above the national average as early as 1870, and by 1880 westerners were spending more per capita on their schools than any other region.[80] The gap in spending between western states and territories and the rest of the nation in part reflected the higher salaries teachers earned in the region. Table 3.1 illustrates these patterns for western states and territories and illustrative states from other regions. In 1880, the highest-spending states east of the Missouri River were Massachusetts and Rhode Island. On average, a teacher in Rhode Island earned less per month than teachers did in Arizona, California, Idaho, Montana, and Nevada. Teachers in California were earning $15.88 more per month than the average teacher in Rhode Island and $23.43 more per month than the average teacher in Massachusetts. The salary gap was largest between teachers in Nevada and the highest-spending eastern states. Nevada teachers earned $32.62 more per month than the average Rhode Island teacher and $40.17 more per month than the average Massachusetts teacher. If just the gap between teachers' pay in Nevada and Massachusetts had been an average monthly teacher salary, it would have been higher than the average salary of teachers in twenty-nine other states and territories.

Reformers in eastern states also called for the creation and expansion of state taxes to support public education. On both sides of the Missouri River, these efforts to create and expand state taxation for public schools placed limits on the role of local taxation in school funding that have too often gone unnoticed by historians. By 1879, twenty-nine of the forty-seven states and territories that reported fiscal data to the US commissioner of education were generating revenue through a state or territorial tax. As a result, public schools at the end of the 1870s were less reliant on local taxes for revenue than they would be for much of the twentieth century. Table 3.2 summarizes these patterns. Since the share of school funding nationally that came from local taxes varied by year, the table reports the highest and lowest annual percentage for each decade. As the table illustrates, it was not until the 1940s and 1950s that schools were, in aggregate,

TABLE 3.1 Spending per student and average teacher salaries in 1880 by state or territory

	EXPENDITURES PER STUDENT ($)	AVERAGE TEACHER SALARIES ($)
West		
Arizona Territory	14.52	76.50
California	18.04	72.50
Colorado	17.88	41.86
Dakota Territory	15.48	24.30
Kansas	7.86	29.23
Montana Territory	14.98	64.03
Nebraska	12.30	34.02
Nevada	12.63	89.24
Oregon	8.37	38.79
Utah Territory	5.43	28.50
Washington Territory	8.15	37.24
Wyoming Territory	10.58	55.94
Idaho Territory	5.74	85.00
Northeast		
Massachusetts	16.81	49.07
Rhode Island	12.15	56.62
Midwest		
Michigan	8.58	31.51
Wisconsin	7.45	31.03
South		
Alabama	2.09	20.96
North Carolina	1.56	21.75
National average	**8.13**	**39.11**

Source: Report of the Commissioner of Education for the Year 1880 (Washington, DC: Government Printing Office, 1882), table 1, 406–12. Expenditures per student based on students counts in column 12 and total annual expenditures in column 43. Some states reported monthly salaries for men and women separately. For those states, the average was used to create comparison. Data for New Mexico Territory was incomplete.

less reliant on local taxes for educational revenues than they had been at the end of the 1870s.[81]

Of course, variation between states remained a defining feature of school funding policy during the period. Some eastern states remained staunchly opposed to state taxation. Although Massachusetts distributed its meager school funding in relation to need starting in the 1870s, lawmakers in the state resisted the use of state taxation to finance education far longer than other northeastern states.[82] As late as 1895, Massachusetts still was not raising any additional revenue for schools through state taxes. In contrast, in New Jersey the state superintendent emphasized

CHAPTER 3

TABLE 3.2 Percentage of school funding nationally from local taxes, by decade

	LOWEST ANNUAL % TOTAL REVENUE FROM LOCAL TAXES IN DECADE (SCHOOL YEAR)	HIGHEST ANNUAL % TOTAL REVENUE FROM LOCAL TAXES IN DECADE (SCHOOL YEAR)
1870s	57 (1875–76)	66 (1873–74)
1880s	65 (1881–82)	69 (1887–88)
1890s	76 (1892–93)	80 (1898–99)
1900s	80 (1899–1900)	84 (1906–7)
1910s	82 (1911–12)	84 (1915–16)
1920s	83 (1919–20, 1923–24, 1927–28)	84 (1921–22, 1925–26)
1930s	69 (1937–38)	83 (1929–30)
1940s	58 (1947–48)	68 (1939–40)
1950s	56 (1955–56)	58 (1951–52, 1953–54)

Source: See "National Percent Distribution of Public School Revenue by Source, 1872–1990" section of the appendix for further details.

Note: Decade based on end of school year (for example, 1909–10 is included in 1910s).

TABLE 3.3 State share of funding in New Jersey in 1870s and recent years

YEAR	% TOTAL REVENUE FROM STATE
1872–73	71
1969–70	27
1974–75	31
1979–80	36
1984–85	41
1989–90	39
1994–95	38
1999–2000	41
2004–5	44
2009–10	36
2014–15	42

Source: 1872–73 figure based on *Report of the [New Jersey] State Board of Education and the State Superintendent of Public Instruction for 1873* (Trenton: State Gazette, 1873), 11. Percentage excludes taxes for construction from total to enable comparison. If including funds from interest on state school fund, figure is 73 percent. Figures for later years from *State Comparisons of Education Statistics: 1969–70 to 1996–97* (Washington, DC: US Department of Education, 1998), table 33; *Digest of Educational Statistics 2008*, table 173; *Digest of Educational Statistics 2013*, table 235.30; *Digest of Educational Statistics 2018*, table 235.30.

that "the cause of public-school education is regarded as a State and not a local interest." This state interest, in turn, required a "uniform State tax." In 1873, the tax provided 71 percent of the funding for schools in New Jersey. As table 3.3 illustrates, this figure has not been matched by the state of New Jersey in recent years.[83]

Localism and Opposition to State Aid for Public Schools

Advocates of increased state support for common schools spoke about the grandeur of the public school's mission and the need to spread its costs and benefits widely. Still, what exactly it meant to have a public education system remained an open question after the Civil War. Residents of wealthier urban communities embraced an alternative view, albeit one that was imprecisely defined. Among those who imagined their common schools as a source of local pride and urban growth, it was not always clear that the costs and benefits of schooling had to be shared equally. Commentators and lawmakers from the communities that tended to benefit the most from local financing began articulating a quasi-privatized view of the public school—one where any dollars raised for schooling belonged to the residents of that community. This approach to funding was based on the belief that the benefits of schooling were contained within the boundaries of their individual districts, rather than everyone benefiting from a collective investment in education and the future.

In California, this alternate view prompted politicians from larger towns and cities to oppose Tuttle's School Bill. Lawmakers from San Francisco concentrated on whether their communities would receive more or less in "benefits" than they paid in state taxes under the terms of the proposed law. On the floor of the California Senate, they expressed dismay that their communities would pay "by tax very much more money than would be returned by apportionment."[84] San Franciscans, they argued, would annually pay $150,000 more than they would receive, to "aid the school districts of the interior."[85] Another urban representative complained that "under this bill, San Francisco would pay that much more than her share of the school tax, and the State would receive the benefit of it."[86] For residents of the region's larger towns and cities, changes to the distribution of funds were seen as an effort to take wealth from urban communities and redistribute it to rural districts.

Other commentators agreed to the premise of increased funding but also insisted that wealthier communities should receive a higher proportion of the benefits from the state's school system. A San Franciscan, State Superintendent Henry Bolander found the idea that "the State alone should contribute the means to educate all the children of the State... just and desirable in theory." But "when a county like San Francisco must contribute forty per cent toward the State School Fund, and receives in return only twenty-four per cent from all State apportionments," he argued, "there must certainly be a limit beyond which San Francisco ought not to be expected to support the schools of other counties."[87] Bolander's logic made sense to Californians who imagined San Francisco's schools serving a public contained, at least in part, within the boundaries of the city.

As more and more states and territories considered raising additional revenue for public schools through state taxes, the assertion that school districts should not pay more toward education than they received in funding became a staple of urban resistance to increased state support.[88] The *Chicago Daily Tribune* was particularly vocal in its critique of the state school tax adopted in Illinois in the 1870s. The editors repeatedly argued that the "unjust and inequitable school-tax" forced Cook County residents to pay more in school taxes than they received in school funding. For rhetorical effect, the paper often calculated the exact gap between the amount the county paid in taxes and the amount it received in revenue: $145,556 in March 1875, for example.[89] This calculation was a district-level articulation of the "benefits theory of taxation" that political economists and tax reformers later aimed to dismantle in other areas of public finance in the Progressive Era.[90] The argument did not completely abandon the idea that tax dollars should be raised and redistributed to educate children that were part of a "public." That "public," however, was not a state or national one. Instead, it was contained within the boundaries of school districts.

The claims by urban communities that their residents—and the new forms of intangible wealth increasingly concentrated inside their borders among a small number of those residents—need not share in a statewide or national public school project resonated with a localized vision first articulated by some northeastern common school reformers before the Civil War. These critics of state support for schooling argued that too much state funding harms every school district, rich and poor. They rarely used a language of local choice or control, instead emphasizing the dangers of excessive charity and dependence. The loudest voices making this claim remained northeastern politicians who identified as school reformers and who tended to dominate policy making in Pennsylvania, Massachusetts, and Connecticut. In his first report as US commissioner of education, William T. Harris summarized this view when explaining that some states "regard State aid as an auxiliary agency" that should be "within restricted bounds." These states, Harris said, recognized the "truth" that "in education, as in the other departments of human activity, it is self-help that stimulates the healthiest and most vigorous growth and leads to the most enduring results."[91]

Birdsey Northrop, secretary of Connecticut's Board of Education, believed that charity did indeed have the potential to "pauperize" a person by providing "alms that no man could accept without impairing his manliness and self-respect." He insisted, however, that education was not a charity when it was funded in a way that made "help in school" become "help towards doing without help."[92] He advocated for a state school tax in the early 1870s to address a decline in the already small share of funding coming from Connecticut's permanent school fund. J. P. Wickersham embraced this same logic. One of the founders of the National

Education Association and Pennsylvania's state superintendent of public instruction from 1866 to 1881, Wickersham believed that too much state aid had the potential to destroy the state's common school system.[93] When the editors of the *Bedford Inquirer* called on the state to raise "all the money necessary to carry on our schools by a general, uniform State tax," he acknowledged the inequities of taxation in the state and called for some relief, but ultimately believed it would be a "fatal mistake" to "depend entirely upon State taxation to support our schools."[94]

The notion that education funding not generated locally would promote dependency among an undeserving poor and "pauperize" was invoked frequently in editorials arguing against a national education system.[95] Opponents of federal legislation often recycled the language of antebellum common school reformers who had opposed the expansion of permanent state school funds, emphasizing "dependence," its affront to "self-reliance," and the way individual "character" would be "demoralized" by it.[96] Exaggerated tales of Connecticut's generous support for its schools before the 1820s made the rounds. The editors of the *Saturday Evening Post* said Connecticut's experience showed that too much state or federal funding was a "curse," as it had produced the "darkest period" of Connecticut's educational history.[97] The deleterious effects that state aid had purportedly had in Connecticut supposedly showed that such aid would produce "a permanent loss in character vastly more important—the loss of self-reliance and self-respect." Local funding, in contrast, would leave the people of the South—both "black and white"—"more manly, more self-reliant—yes, and more intelligent too, in the long run—if they are left to work out their own salvation."[98] The argument that federal education funding would undermine the principle of self-help, however, does less to explain the failure of federal funding proposals after the Civil War than do reactions against the vision of racial equity contained within some of the proposals, even though that argument was made more commonly.

The Legibility of School District Boundaries and the Inefficiency of District Property Taxes

School district boundaries continued to reflect contrasting ideas about who did and did not share in the public school project; their drawing and redrawing were where such debates played out on the ground. In the absence of localized funding, legible school districts were not very important. Only when a community wanted to exclude children did it become essential to locate such boundaries with precision. As late as 1895, in rural sections of California, district lines did not exist. When Sonoma County superintendent E. W. Davis was asked that year to create a map of school district boundaries, he refused. The boundaries had previously mattered so little that no one kept a precise record, and he insisted in a letter to the Sonoma County Board of Supervisors that the task could not be completed as a result.[99]

At the same time, when communities worked to have the state relocate, redraw, or clarify boundaries, they used an instrument of the state—school districting—to hoard wealth, divide the populace, and withdraw from a public school project shared with taxpayers and schoolchildren. As wealthier cities raised local taxes to fund ambitious school construction programs in the 1870s and were critical of using state taxes to fund public schools, they started charging tuition to students from outside of town and created a new species: the "nonresident pupil." As noted in chapter 2, the process of linking residence with common school access was uneven. As it spread, it reflected a powerful reconceptualization of the public school. These new "nonresident pupil" policies were often connected to rivalries between communities and a broader context of one group seeking to withdraw from a shared public school project with other people and places. After Alameda voted down consolidation with Oakland in 1873, for example, Oakland's school board revised its open admissions policy, deciding that they would charge tuition to any children considered to be "outside pupils."[100] San José implemented a similar policy in February 1874, directing the superintendent to collect "tuition fees from all non-resident pupils." Residency itself, though, was insufficient for some officials. Even if the pupils "board within the city limits" for school purposes and their family lived elsewhere, the San José Board of Education concluded, "they shall be regarded as non-resident pupils, and must pay."[101]

The use of local taxes to fund schools—even when limited to raising funds for a school building—often encouraged bitter fights over the location of school district boundaries. Those battles, too, provided clear examples of how narrow, divided, and exclusionary a localist vision of the public school was in practice. Sacramento County created an official map of school district boundaries in 1871, but by 1872 local communities were demanding even more precise boundaries separating specific districts that seemed engaged in battles over territory with one another. The Union School District and the Pleasant Grove School District requested "a more definite description" of their boundary. The Elk Grove School District and the San Joaquin School District pleaded for the line separating them to be "more clearly defined."[102] Residents of Mount Dell raised a tax to construct a new schoolhouse. "The district was organized, census taken, trustees elected and schoolhouse built, and all things went well," one resident wrote to the Santa Clara County Supervisors, "but during the month of February we were informed that the school house, all the trustees, and nearly all the children are out of district."[103]

These cases do not reflect an efficient sorting of families based on tax preferences, as some accounts have suggested. Nor do they suggest a harmonious process of Americans neatly sorting themselves into school districts independent of the state.[104] Instead, they tended to center on efforts to use districting policies to promote deliberate exclusion. Maurice Woodhams, for example, had constructed a school for the community in the vicinity of his property in a rural section of San Mateo County. In 1871, however, a group of families living in the same district managed to gain control of the board of trustees and relocated the school to their far eastern part of the district, away from where the original school had been located. After carrying away the furniture to the eastern school, residents of the district petitioned the county for the creation of their own separate district.

Even in states where the district property tax was regularly used to finance public education, school district boundaries were sometimes unclear and very often an object of contestation. Historians have tended to reserve their criticisms of nineteenth-century taxation for the supposed impracticality of the statewide general property tax, sometimes echoing the same Progressive Era commentators who insisted an income tax was equally impossible to implement. Ultimately, though, issues with assessment and avoidance were sometimes even worse when the school district was the taxing unit.[105] John Eaton lamented this pattern during his tenure as US commissioner of education. The regular problem of "ill surveyed and ill marked district boundaries," he noted, produced "uncertainty as to which district is to collect the tax and educate the children." The debates over the boundaries also undermined the notion that communities and their residents shared in a communal educational project since they produced, Eaton also pointed out, regular "disputes and bickerings."[106] Even when boundaries were clarified, constant manipulation meant they did not stay clear for very long. One New York official reported how land was "continually changing hands, passing from one district to another, many times greatly to the injury of a weaker one." The official proposed a simple solution by prohibiting boundary changes, so that "all the land within the bounds of a school district could remain there."[107] This uncertainty regarding boundaries likely contributed to the problem that it sometimes cost more to collect a district property tax than what it produced in revenue. As one exasperated Connecticut official reported, it "costs as much or more to make out the tax and collect it, as the whole amount required."[108] This more granular account of district property taxes shows how they worked to promote both exclusion and a narrowed sense of shared obligation.

High Schools and a New Constitution

The core questions raised by competing conceptions of "public" as it applied to school funding—as well as the broader problem of finding a way to tax corporations as they consumed public resources for private profit in unprecedented ways—were addressed in tandem in 1879 when Californians rewrote their state constitution. Tuttle's School Bill, after it was passed in 1874, had succeeded in slowing the spread of the district property tax. The success of broader efforts to equalize taxation was, however, much shorter lived. Efforts to guarantee corporate taxation through the state's Board of Equalization fell apart when a group of San Francisco banks simply refused to pay their new tax bill. When county officials moved to auction bank property in response, a court issued an injunction to prevent them from doing so. The litigation that ensued culminated in a state supreme court case declaring the Board of Equalization illegal under the California State Constitution. Frustrated citizens responded by declaring the need to write a new state constitution that could equalize assessments and tax corporate wealth. A majority of voters agreed in 1876, and delegates gathered to rewrite the state's constitution two years later.[109]

Voters supported the convention for a number of reasons. The 1870s were difficult years for many. No state was spared from the economic crises that followed the Panic of 1873, and Californians had been particularly hard hit. Throughout the decade, farmers experienced persistent drought and falling prices for their commodities. Migration from the East slowed. Unemployment was rampant in the region's developing cities. Corporate corruption, especially on the part of the Central Pacific Railroad and its subsidiaries, was widespread. California historian Kevin Starr described the period as an "unmitigated disaster of drought, crop failure, urban rioting, squatter wars, harassment and murder of the Chinese, cynical manipulation of politics by the railroad, depression, price fixing, bank failure, and stock swindles."[110] Urban workers, organizing the Workingmen's Party of California in cities like San Francisco and San José, and rural farmers, organizing the People's Independent Party, became increasingly critical of centralized state authority, corporate power, and political corruption. They were also quick to blame economic inequality on Chinese immigration, often physically attacking Chinese Americans as scapegoats for the excesses of the railroads.

Californians were particularly determined, when they gathered in Sacramento, to tax corporations and intangible forms of wealth and ensure those corporations did not continue to turn the state itself into an agent for the accumulation of private wealth. The convention, historian Arthur Rolston has written, "reflected the understanding of a majority of the delegates that only constitutional remedies could remedy the imbalance and limit the power of corporate interests in the halls of government."[111] Historian David Igler has described the convention in a similar way, summarizing it as a "fledgling attempt to curtail the worst aspects of modern corporate capitalism."[112]

As delegates considered how to rein in corporate corruption, the question of how the high school fit into the state's common school system revealed just how ambiguous and imprecise the meaning of the phrase "public education" was. As convention delegates and voters wrangled over whether or not equity between communities was required for California to have a statewide public education system, they also had to contend with a vexing problem of the time: the nature of the high school. The uncertainty that surrounded the question of what it meant to have a public education system was particularly clear in debates over high schools after the Civil War. Even as more and more Americans came to believe high schools were necessary, whether or not these schools should receive a share of state education funding raised controversial questions. Many of these questions again centered on the basic definition of terms and concepts that have since become far more settled. First, there was the question of how high schools should be defined, as there was a wide variability of what high schools looked like across communities. As historian William Reese observed, "Whenever educators requested state aid, legislators naturally demanded a clear definition of a high school, which educators could not provide." Some advocates made simply defining what a high school is an object of reform. One Indiana reformer encouraged members of the Indiana State Teachers Association to "define what a High School is, and then suggest the same to our law-makers."[113]

Equally contested was whether or not high schools were or should be considered public. Some commentators insisted that they were not. High schools, where they existed, rarely served the entire population of a community. The schools themselves were also concentrated in more prosperous communities with enough property wealth to create them. If these schools received state aid, there would be less funding for common schools. Full state funding for high schools was rarely on the table. Since few poor communities could afford a high school, and few children statewide attended these schools, this meant state aid for secondary education would simply divert state funds from common schools that served all white children in a state. These funds would be redirected toward high schools that served very few children in comparison to common schools. This prompted some officials and lawmakers to argue that these were not, in fact, public schools but something better described as "local." The superintendent of public schools in Missouri reflected how uncertain the high school was as an institutional category when discussing how these schools related to elementary schools and state-supported universities: "The university is for the whole State. High schools are for particular localities. If it is found that high schools are absolutely needed as feeders for the university, then it may be proper for the State, with public funds, to place here and there these 'stepping stones' to its highest educational privileges. In this case all such high schools should be free and open to all the State, or be everywhere distributed. But this scheme is scarcely practicable."[114]

The insistence of many nineteenth-century Americans that a high school would increase the value of nearby land provided even more fuel to the claim that these were not public institutions serving a state or nation, but local ones. This was the logic of the superintendent of public instruction in Illinois in his appeal for a new law that would allow rural districts to unite with one another to create a tax base large enough to fund a high school with local taxes. "Every good township high school," he explained, "will prove a good investment to the farmers and other property owners and tax payers of the neighborhood, by enhancing the value of all lands and other property in the vicinity." The reason for this, he continued, was that "such institutions invite the coming and settlement of people of means and character, people who value educational privileges for themselves and their neighbors, and who give tone and dignity to a community."[115]

The role of public school expansion in boosterism and regional rivalries in California raised questions about how the state should distribute funding for an institution that seemed to primarily benefit a narrow group of land speculators or wealthy urbanites who rural delegates felt had worked to avoid the property tax. The tendency for many Californians to focus on how creating a school could help one town surpass its rivals seemed incongruent with claims that state-funded schools supported a broader mission for a statewide and national public. But in the 1870s, the high school was the booster institution par excellence. Californians were accustomed to the booster's pitch: high school creation was an excellent source of population growth and increased property values. Boosters from San Rafael contended that the high school had been what allowed Oakland to grow.[116] Proponents supporting the creation of a high school in Marysville made a related appeal: "It is for the interest of the city that such a school should be established, reasoning from a selfish view." "Where the best facilities for education are furnished," they continued, "there is where the refined and intelligent heads of families locate." Not only would the attraction of a "superior class of citizens" add "wealth and good society," but money invested in a high school "enhances the value of all the property surrounding it, and we might add, the whole of the property of the city is affected in a greater or less degree."[117] Under this logic, high school served a private purpose for a publicly defined locality.

At the constitutional convention, many observers viewed the connection between boosterism and school expansion as evidence that an overly aggressive state role in education was inappropriate and potentially biased. Why should the state provide funding and try to create uniformity, some delegates wondered, if the advantages of public education were destined to help some communities more than others? The emphasis on the benefits of high schools for nearby property owners made state support for the institution seem antithetical to the egalitarian goals of public schooling. The fact that the high school was not accessible to smaller communities lacking a critical mass of older students, even though it would be supported through universally collected state taxes, made it a clear example of inequity for convention delegates. "There should be no royal road to education for one half of the children of the State, and none for the other," one convention member argued. "Not a dollar," delegate Henry Larkin explained, "will I allow to any school in this State that each and every child in the State has not got access to."[118]

Supporters of high schools reinforced the logic of their critics by accepting the premise that high schools did not benefit the larger state or nation. Instead, supporters reasoned that given these localized benefits, communities should have the right to create and pay for them themselves. The high school should exist if communities wanted to create and pay for them, these delegates reasoned. While delegate Peter Joyce from San Francisco was "opposed to any such extravagance," he conceded that it should not be outlawed. "If the county wants to pay that way," he explained, "let them pay."[119] The proposed constitutional provision, San Franciscan delegate John Hager explained, grants "each locality the right to have these schools when they want them."[120] Since high schools would be funded at the district level, their resources could be determined completely by the wealth of a given community, and they would not be universally available. Nevertheless, these institutions would be considered part of the state's public school system. This arrangement promised to mollify those who believed that California did not have a statewide public system if it was not funded equally. Inequality and public systems did not have to be incompatible.

Supporters of high schools wanted them to be defined as part of the state public school system but paid for exclusively by local communities. "This scheme only proposes that these institutions, such as high schools and evening schools[,] shall exist in those localities where the people desire their existence, and provide means for their support," one convention delegate explained. "It studiously exempts them from the reception of public moneys.... It only gives to each locality a right to have these schools when they want them," he continued. According to delegate Eli Blackmer, "They [communities] should have the right to establish any school that they see fit to establish, and . . . that school shall be a part of the public school system of this State," he reasoned.[121]

Opponents worried about the implications of the shift for the meaning of public education in the state. Delegate Thomas Laine, for example, did not understand how locally financed high schools could be part of the state system. "When it comes to the organization of municipal schools, matters of that kind, within local jurisdiction, let them do as they please," Laine said. "But when they say the public school system what do they mean? Do they mean the public school system of the State or of the municipalities of the State? I think it should begin and end with the State."[122] For detractors, it did not make sense to embed within the "state system" something that was not available to every student in the state. The distinction between public and private seemed to collapse.

In the end, a compromise was reached among delegates. Article 6 of the new constitution defined the high school as part of the state's public school system but required local communities to fund high schools exclusively through district property taxes. As a result, the new constitution effectively granted legitimacy to a principle that reformers had sought to challenge with Tuttle's School Bill: the notion that the wealth of a local district, not the wealth of the entire state, could determine the resources for some aspects of the state's education system. The final document created a legal precedent for the idea that elements of a public system can, in fact, vary with the wealth of individual communities. This helped to both legitimize emerging inequities between school districts and create new ones, especially in relation to high schools. By 1880, state policy resolved some of the tensions that animated the writing of reformers like Tuttle: California would have a public education system, and that system would remain "public," even if it distributed the costs and benefits of public schooling unevenly, inconsistently, and unequally.

San Franciscans and the residents of other large towns and cities framed their opposition to the new constitution in terms of its implications for their high schools. In public meetings and editorials in the *Pacific School and Home Journal*, they encouraged teachers to "cooperate vigorously with us to aid in securing its [the new constitution's] defeat."[123] They emphasized how localized high schools would undermine what they considered a statewide public system. "No intelligent man can for an instant doubt that the destruction of the entire system is effected by the new instrument," one commentator warned.[124] "Here truly is local government run mad!" another observer exclaimed. "Why not at once disintegrate this State of California, and establish as many separate sovereignties as there are counties?"[125] The constitution is "altogether in the interests of the rich, and calculated to deprive the poor of the greatest boon of a free land—the means of giving a thorough English education to their children," editors of the *Pacific School and Home Journal* lamented.[126] Despite their pleas, the new constitution was approved by voters.

Consequences

The new constitution held far-reaching consequences for how the public purposes of schools were defined in state law and how widely tax burdens for government in general were felt across the state. With the cutting off of state funds for the state's existing high schools, some communities were forced to close their high schools. Santa Rosa, for example, closed its high school after the new constitution was adopted.[127] High school closures and other changes, in turn, further transformed the meaning of the school district, expanded disparities between communities, and increased competition between districts. Some communities that had been receiving state funding for their high schools had not required pupils to be district residents for free attendance. By forcing communities to completely fund high schools with their own taxes, however, the new constitution encouraged communities that had not yet restricted outsiders' access to their schools to do so. This was the case in San Francisco. Before 1879, qualified students from outside the city were permitted to freely attend San Francisco's high school. Numerous students from Marin County had taken advantage of the privilege. After the passage of the new constitution, the *Marin Journal* reported that "pupils from San Rafael expect to be debarred from the school hereafter, because, under the new law, it will receive no state money, and will therefore exclude non-residents."[128] Former state superintendent Ezra Carr insisted that the high school had been "a barrier against the establishment of class distinctions in American society."[129] Would that remain the case?

In an irony for the critics of high schools who rooted their opposition in egalitarian claims, the limits on funding for schools also limited access to the state's newly empowered state university.[130] Since a high school education was a prerequisite for admission to the university during the 1880s, Californians outside of the handful of urban communities with high schools could not access the university without purchasing a private high school education. The impact of this shift was evident in enrollment trends at the University of California. Four years after the new constitution was adopted, enrollment dropped by 30 percent. Moreover, students from the wealthy communities of San Francisco and Oakland monopolized access. In 1889, two-thirds of the students enrolled at the University of California were from San Francisco and Alameda Counties.[131] Some school districts now offered easy access to a publicly funded secondary and university education, while others did not provide anything beyond the basics of a primary school education.

The new constitution halted the expansion of the institution of high schools outside the wealthiest communities. In the ten years after the passage of the new constitution, as the number of high schools across the country was growing rapidly, only six new high schools opened in California.[132] Scarcity only increased the significance of these high schools for local communities as a tool to attract residents and increase land values. While few students had had access to a high school or university education before the constitution, the pattern of disparate access was now fully established.

Yet while the new constitution helped produce, in the long run, new legitimacy for a fractured, narrower vision of the public school project, critics of the way intangible wealth had formerly escaped the general property tax watched the proceedings and eventual adoption of the new constitution with glee. The clause on corporate taxation had created a legal framework that would permit state and local governments to tax corporate entities previously avoiding taxation. For some observers, the corporate tax provision fulfilled a promise that the Workingmen's Party of California had made on the eve of the convention to "destroy the great money power of the rich by a system of taxation that will make great wealth impossible in the future."[133] The new constitution sparked global attention because of the provision. The *London Times* saw in the constitution's "menacing" provisions the "Paris Commune." Karl Marx saw in it an attempt to address the fact that "nowhere else has the upheaval most shamelessly caused by capitalist centralization taken place with such speed. . . . California [is] very important to me."[134]

The fate of the new corporate taxation clause in the 1880s, however, showed how difficult it was to translate the property tax into a broader levy on all forms of wealth, especially when the national government was prepared to function more as an instrument of tax avoidance for the wealthy than as an instrument for spreading tax burdens fairly. Instead of producing additional revenue for schools, efforts to enforce the new corporate taxation clause produced a series of fiscal crises that shuttered schools across the state and culminated in a decision by the US Supreme Court that extended Fourteenth Amendment protections from discrimination to corporations themselves.

The trouble began when officials across the state attempted to collect school taxes from corporate entities. The Southern Pacific refused to pay and instead initiated litigation, hiring one of the authors of the Fourteenth Amendment as their lawyer. School officials found themselves in a fiscal crisis without the new revenue they had expected. Since the railroad refused to pay any school taxes whatsoever, school officials could not even count on the tax revenue they were able to collect before the new constitution. As the state controller bluntly put it, "The ordinary obligations of the counties could not be fully met, and in many of the counties the public schools were closed for want of funds."[135] San Diego was forced to close its schools and hold a special election to raise new taxes that would allow county schools to finish their term. "It is, no doubt, an unpleasant thing to have to resort to special taxation, even for so small a matter as one-fifth of one per cent," editors of the *San Diego Union and Daily Bee* lamented.[136]

Placer County had a $33,000 deficit caused by the "refusal of railroads to pay their taxes," as noted by local officials. They were only able to keep the schools open by shortening the term and "by an increased rate on the property of the people who cannot afford to fee an army of lawyers and go to courts."[137] Editors of the San José–based *Daily Morning Times* thought "the practice of the corporations in refusing to pay their taxes" proved that "the railroad magnates and their prominent employees" were "opposed to popular education."[138] Since the railroad had exploited its debt to avoid taxes in the past, the new state constitution aimed to tax corporate debt, but not the debt of individuals. From the ensuing legal battle came *County of San Mateo v. Southern Pacific Railroad Company* (1882) and *County of Santa Clara v. Southern Pacific Railroad Company* (1883), cases in which the US Supreme Court invalidated tax bills because the state of California had included fences alongside railroad tracks when assessing railroad property. This ruling was then cited in future cases to assert corporate "personhood" under the Fourteenth Amendment.[139] It was thus by way of the railroad's tax avoidance and the related shuttering of common schools that the promise of Reconstruction, embodied in the Fourteenth Amendment, and with its hope for universal schools, was further broken.

The debate over the precise meaning of "public" as it applied to state school systems reflected the degree to which resource disparities were contested after the Civil War and raised existential questions about the meaning and purposes of education. District property taxation for elementary schooling remained rare, especially as new state and territorial taxes also dramatically decreased the role of local taxation in education funding nationally. Yet plenty of Americans still associated funding derived from anything but a district-level tax with charity and the threat of pauperism. In the end, the state's new constitution offered a definition of "public" that flummoxed reformers like B. F. Tuttle. High schools were public, but they had to be funded with local money. Only children from wealthy communities, it seemed, were permitted access to certain parts of the state's system. Residents of the nation's expanding towns and cities, moreover, became increasingly comfortable with the idea that state public education systems can and should distribute a degree of educational opportunity unevenly. This view of education funding and its centrality to district-level Progressive Era school reforms is the subject of chapter 4.

4

STATE-SPONSORED INEQUALITIES, BOOSTERISM, AND THE RACE FOR PROGRESSIVE ERA SCHOOL REFORM, 1890–1910

Across the United States, Americans remade their schools during the Progressive Era. Enrollments exploded, school systems grew more complex, and the modern public school as we know it was born. Control over district governance was centralized, and superintendents were empowered. The average size of school boards shrank from 21.5 in 1893 to 10.2 in 1914.[1] To meet the needs of expanded curriculums, new pedagogical methods were implemented and new vocational training programs and courses in subjects like domestic sciences were introduced. Children spent a larger portion of their lives in school than ever before. More and more schools added kindergartens. The high school expanded rapidly to become a mass institution. New forms of equipment that we associate with schools today could now be found in many large districts—playgrounds, sanitary drinking fountains, and cafeterias where students could be served hot meals for a low cost.

Historians have told in great detail the story of why, when, and where these transformations occurred. They have typically focused on—and fought about—who was responsible for these education reforms, what motivated their efforts, and whether or not it makes sense to call them "progressives."[2] Yet most of this work glosses over the mechanics of how the transformations of the Progressive Era school were financed. Many of the period's variegated reforms were united by the massive financial investment in school infrastructure they required. Progressive Era education reforms were costly: age grading required new, centrally located buildings; courses in vocational education and domestic science required new kinds of classrooms with shops and kitchens; playgrounds and sports fields required the purchase of additional real estate for large school lots. The passage and enforcement of compulsory school laws, a shift that increased the power of schools as state-building institutions, required the rapid construction of new classrooms to accommodate increased enrollments.

Even where local financing for general operating expenses was rare, annual state and county apportionments did little to help districts finance the massive infrastructure investments required to implement Progressive Era education reforms. This chapter examines how state policies structured local efforts to increase revenue for school district infrastructure through the incorporation of new cities and suburbs, annexation of lands outside municipal borders, approval of school district bonds, and formation of new kinds of school districts to expand access to high schools. Moreover, officials used new legal powers granted to municipalities to divide and segregate neighborhoods, schools, and school districts in new ways. Working within the legal framework established by the state, reformers often deployed a language of competitive boosterism and local interest in the thousands of election campaigns needed to generate support for financing Progressive Era school reform. This language added ambiguity to the scope of the "public" to be served by the Progressive Era school, emphasizing how costs and benefits of public schooling can and should be contained—at least in part—within the geographic boundaries of the local, racially segregated school district. This vision shifted the meaning of education itself, offering a version of its aims and purposes that was quasi-privatized.

This chapter also illustrates how the state structured and encouraged changes in school district and municipal boundaries that made the distribution of property between school districts increasingly unequal. Accounting for these state and local dynamics provides an important window into the way educational expansion unfolded unequally during the Progressive Era. Since most accounts of the period focus on developments within individual cities or rural schools separately, they often miss the ways in which the new wealth of urban districts and the growing poverty of rural districts were created in tandem. Working within the legal framework established by the state, some districts quite literally became rich by making others poor as they relocated their boundaries. Rather than reflecting existing inequities in the distribution of local wealth, reformers of the era used state policies to both exacerbate and create new wealth disparities between school districts.

Moving Boundaries and Redistributing Wealth

The number of cities with more than one hundred thousand inhabitants more than doubled between 1870 and 1910, while the number of residents in the fifty largest cities more than tripled.[3] Rapid urbanization brought a host of logistical challenges for city governments. Across the nation, urban residents responded to these challenges by enacting a series of reforms that transformed the organization and reach of municipal governments. They restructured local government, experimenting with new ways to distribute power through commission and city manager plans advocated by "good government" reformers. American city dwellers also expanded the functions of their local governments. They advocated for municipal ownership of water, power, and gas. They constructed parks, libraries, and sewage facilities, and they introduced new municipal services like street cleaning, garbage collection, and water filtration. "The city," historian Daniel Rodgers explains, "stood at the vital center of transatlantic progressive imaginations."[4]

Although state governments are sometimes peripheral to accounts of Progressive Era urban reform, few of these reforms would have been possible without state-level changes that granted a degree of "home rule" to municipalities. Local governments are creatures of the state. At the end of the nineteenth century, these local governments could only expand their functions as far as they were given explicit permission to do so under state law.[5] As legal scholar Richard Briffault explains, "Dillon's Rule" required that all local governmental activity be "traced back to a specific delegation." When explicit state permission for municipal corporations to expand their functions could not be identified, courts were to "assume that the *locality* lacks that power."[6] State legislatures were often opposed to providing this permission, prompting Robert Wiebe to conclude that "state governments rejected urban reforms almost as a matter of policy."[7] Through state constitutional changes enabling home rule, municipal governments could be granted the power to write their own charter. Organizations like the National Municipal League were strong proponents of legal changes that could enable municipal home rule. Clifford Patton observed that home rule made "its greatest gains in the West" and that the "bitterest contest for home rule was waged in the East."[8] The first home-rule charter was granted to Saint Louis by the state of Missouri in 1875. California's 1879 constitution created a constitutional framework that granted home rule to municipalities of certain sizes, and it was quickly followed by Washington State in 1889 and Minnesota in 1896. This reform spread throughout the Progressive Era, reaching about one-third of states by 1930.[9]

Home rule provisions granted Progressive Era reformers the legal authority to expand the power and functions of municipal governments. This included the power of city officials to promote and enforce racial segregation. Indeed, the home rule provisions contained in California's 1879 constitution created a legal architecture that white Californians used to harass and segregate people of color. Starting in the 1870s, white lawmakers in Californian passed a series of ordinances targeting Chinese Californians. Alongside overt and extralegal acts of racial violence perpetuated against Chinese Californians, these local ordinances sought to restrict where Chinese residents could live and work. The ordinances with overtly racial language were overturned by courts. San Francisco's Bingham Ordinance, for example, was overturned in 1890. If implemented, it would have required Chinatown residents to relocate to a small strip of land.[10] Before the Bingham Ordinance, white lawmakers also enacted implicitly racial ordinances targeting Chinese residents by regulating land use. Even when draped in a raceless language of public health and safety, the racist intent of these ordinances was unambiguous.[11] Some ordinances were overturned by courts. A San Francisco ordinance regulating laundries run by Chinese San Franciscans, for example, was overturned by the US Supreme Court. The blatantly prejudicial way city officials administered the ordinance, the court ruled, violated the Fourteenth Amendment.[12] At the same time, other ordinances targeting Chinese residents through restrictions on land use were upheld by courts citing the broad power granted to municipalities to regulate "local, police, sanitary, and other regulations as are not in conflict with general laws" under California's new constitution.[13] The power of California municipalities affirmed in these cases created important legal precedents for zoning. The "germ of the zoning idea," according to one legal scholar, originated in these California cases.[14] Similarly, the historian of city planning Sonia Hirt labels cases involving anti-Chinese ordinances enacted in California during these years among the "building blocks for municipal proto-zoning regulation efforts in the United States."[15]

Home rule provisions also afforded local governments the requisite autonomy and authority to offer new municipal services. Alongside the promise of racial segregation, the municipal services enabled by home rule helped persuade white residents of outlying areas to merge with nearby cities. Throughout the nineteenth century, urbanization was as much about cities coming to people as it was about people coming to cities. Chicago added 133 square miles in 1889. In 1898, New York annexed Brooklyn, Queens, Staten Island, and the Bronx, increasing its size from forty-four to three hundred square miles. Baltimore more than doubled in size through an 1888 annexation. "Without exception," Kenneth Jackson explains, "the adjustment of local boundaries has been the dominant method of population growth in every American city of consequence."[16] As David Freund explains, since outlying communities "lacked the resources and administrative capacity to provide capital-intensive services and improvements (such as sewer systems, electrical grids, paved roads, and parks), their residents usually promoted annexation by richer and bureaucratically established central cities."[17]

Drawing on the autonomy granted to municipalities by the state under its new constitution, cities across California used the promise of increased municipal services and the prospect of racial segregation to grow their borders. Municipal and school district boundaries were coterminous under state law. As cities redrew their boundaries, they redrew the boundaries of local school systems as a result. The expansion of Los Angeles and its coterminous school system was perhaps the most dramatic, with the politics of water access facilitating the rapid growth of the city. In 1890, the incorporated city of Los Angeles was 29 square miles. By 1920, the city had increased its territory to 364 square miles.[18] The territorial expansion of municipalities was not isolated to familiar large cities. Across California, municipalities big and small engaged in expansionist policies. The city of Ventura gobbled up the territory on its periphery, more than doubling in size in 1906. Redwood City increased its territory by reincorporating with larger borders in 1897. Several cities expanded their borders by annexing new suburban housing tracts. San José acquired East San José, Gardner, Hester, Hanchett, and College Park. Oakland annexed communities like Temescal, Golden Gate, Bushrod, Elmhurst, Fruitvale, Melrose, Fitchburg, and Claremont.

The promise of access to innovative—and racially segregated—schools played a prominent role in generating voter support for annexation proposals as well. Proponents of annexation would frequently describe access to larger, centralized school systems as one of the potential benefits for outlying suburban communities. The educational "innovations" of the era were often concentrated in larger districts. As historian David Gamson notes, commentators on American education increasingly claimed that "large school districts offered advantages unavailable to students in individual schools or even in small school districts."[19] Access to better schools, especially high schools, was a common theme in arguments describing the benefits smaller communities would receive by voting for annexation to larger municipalities. Attempts by Gardner and Sunol to join San José were described as an effort to obtain "fire protection, sewer, lower fire insurance rates, high school privileges, etc."[20] San Leandro's boosters promised outlying communities that unification would grant them a new school building.[21] Supporters of Alameda's expansion similarly boasted that the annexation of surrounding communities would bring tremendous "school advantages."[22]

Through economies of scale, larger schools were cheaper to operate. They made the expanded functions of schooling easier to finance as a result, allowing districts to do more with state and county apportionments than they could in a smaller community. Advocates of annexation and consolidation often appealed to this fact in their efforts to persuade voters to support changing their municipal boundaries. Members of the Oakland Chamber of Commerce sought to convince Berkeley residents that "the great burden of school expenditures in Berkeley, growing heavier and heavier, would be lessened in the larger community" if the city consolidated with Oakland. Since "the bearing of such burdens, covering a larger area, would be felt less by the individual," boosters promised that Berkeley's schools would decrease in cost.[23] The prospect of several East Bay cities uniting to form a single city and county government was also discussed in terms of its potential benefits to the schools. "Federation will permit of One Uniform School system.... One school board and one superintendent will have charge instead of FIVE or SIX as at present," advocates of city and county consolidation argued.[24] Residents of Alameda noted, "If we did join, we could maintain the school system at less cost and with much greater efficiency."[25] "City extension," proponents of a Greater San José argued, would produce "greater economy" in the "management and maintenance" of city services like schools.[26]

The incentives to join a community were not simply the benefits that would accrue to voters, however. Real estate developers and related economic interests also had much to gain. The home rule provisions of California's 1879 constitution provided a legal structure that allowed new communities to incorporate easily and offer their own municipal services. Through projected growth and emerging suburban land-use patterns, these new communities could provide the housing density needed to create a large and progressive school system. Even in rural areas far from larger population centers, real estate promoters began incorporating communities with suburban land-use patterns. These communities, as Paul Sandul explains, were promoted as the "perfect mix" of "agrarian virtue" and the amenities representing "salient nineteenth-century symbols of modernity and progress."[27] When California's 1879 constitution was adopted, there were 55 incorporated municipalities in the state. By 1920, this figure increased to 246. Similar patterns unfolded across the nation. In 1868, there were 419 municipal corporations in Ohio. By 1910, the number reached 784. Illinois had 1,066 municipalities by 1910.[28]

Together, both annexation and incorporation allowed officials to maintain racial segregation in schools. The authority that home rule granted municipalities to implement land-use restrictions was critical for maintaining racially segregated schools during the Progressive Era. School officials already had the authority to operate segregated schools for Indigenous and Chinese American students; officials in San Francisco and Sacramento maintained separate schools for Chinese American children using their authority under the state school code to maintain separate schools for "Indian, Chinese, or Mongolian" children.[29] As a result of the Tape family's activism discussed in chapter 3, local officials were not permitted to completely exclude Chinese American students from public schools. In San Francisco, this meant officials needed to expand the number of segregated schools they operated in order to maintain segregation. When the segregated "Oriental" school near Chinatown only offered a primary education, officials were required to admit Chinese American students advancing beyond a primary education into an integrated secondary school until they created a separate "Oriental" secondary school.[30]

The state school code, however, limited the ability of white officials to consistently maintain de jure, separate schools for children of color within school districts. Local officials in Stockton, Los Angeles, and San José permitted Chinese American students to attend integrated schools, probably because it would have been too costly to create a separate school for the smaller Chinese American student populations in those districts at the time.[31] Moreover, local school boards were not permitted to operate formally segregated schools for Japanese or Black children under the school code. Following an influx of Japanese immigration to California and growing animosity among white residents to Japanese people, local officials in San Francisco tried to segregate Japanese American students and require they attend the city's segregated "Oriental school" in 1906. However, the decision created an international incident that culminated with the US government agreeing to permit Japanese children to attend integrated schools in exchange for new limits on immigration with the so-called 1907 Gentlemen's Agreement.[32] The success of civil rights activists in outlawing separate schools for Black children in the early 1880s also prevented school officials from operating separate schools for Black Californians. As Black people left the South and headed to Californian cities with the start of the Great Migration in the 1910s, Black migrants initially found integrated housing and relatively integrated schools in cities such as Los Angeles. These patterns of integration in Los Angeles prompted W. E. B. Du Bois to celebrate the city and its inclusivity in that era.[33]

The power granted to municipal corporations to regulate land use allowed municipalities to create and maintain racially segregated neighborhoods. Through the manipulation of district policies determining which children attended which schools in the district, officials could then translate early patterns of residential segregation into school segregation. Two mechanisms through which lawmakers across the nation created patterns of racial segregation were developed in California during the Progressive Era. The first was the racially restrictive covenant, first created in 1905 by subdividers in Berkeley, California, and Kansas City, Missouri.[34] Covenants are restrictions on how a property can be used that are written into the deed. Through racially restrictive covenants, men like Duncan McDuffie in Berkeley created entire subdivisions where the sale or occupancy of properties was restricted to "Caucasians." Black Americans, Mexican Americans, and Asian Americans were all prohibited by such restrictions from purchasing housing. In some cases, restrictions would also exclude "Jews, Italians, Greeks, Slavs, and Turks."[35] In conjunction with homeowners' associations and restrictive covenants, residential subdivisions across California became the exclusive enclaves of whites.[36] In 1913, one housing study noted how Mexican

Americans could not find housing in Los Angeles because racial restrictions were placed "upon every new tract of land where lots are sold."[37] One survey found that 90 percent of subdivisions in California were covered by racially restrictive covenants by the 1920s.[38] The second mechanism used to accomplish racial segregation consisted of land-use restrictions that could reinforce racially restrictive covenants. Early zoning practices effectively helped enforce covenants by prohibiting families from residing in areas not zoned for residential purposes and thus restricting where people could live to properties with racial restrictions. Los Angeles and Berkeley adopted some of the earliest restrictions on land use. Los Angeles officials adopted an ordinance dividing the city into strictly residential and industrial areas in 1908.[39] In the 1910s, Berkeley officials adopted land-use restrictions to prevent Chinese and Japanese businesses, as well as a "negro dance hall," from opening near white residences.[40]

In enabling both municipal annexation and incorporation, the state helped spur a fiercely competitive land race between communities that combined racial segregation and an uneven geography of taxable wealth carved up by municipal boundaries. In the twentieth century, incorporation replaced annexation in much of the nation. Historians often discuss how the rise and fall of municipal annexation that was necessary for suburbanization rested on the legal framework of home rule. The transition from annexation to incorporation was uneven and far from linear. As a result, annexation and incorporation could unfold in opposition to one another in a struggle over land. This process has been noted in Southern California, but it also unfolded across the state. Communities near each other often had designs on the same territory. After they incorporated in 1906 and 1910 respectively, Burlingame and Hillsborough in San Mateo County, for example, each aspired to become the largest community in the area, and they both sought to annex the same residential tracts that other boosters also hoped to add to their city.[41] In the end, each community absorbed enough additional territory that by 1910 they shared borders with one another. In the early 1910s, San José and Santa Clara engaged in what one commentator called an "annexation race to the water front of South San Francisco Bay."[42] In the northern portion of Alameda County, things were particularly heated as San Leandro, Alameda, and Oakland all fought to annex the communities of Fruitvale, Elmhurst, and Melrose.[43] This contested territory is illustrated in figure 4.1. Oakland eventually won the prize, frustrating boosters from Alameda and San Leandro.

Incorporation could stop a proposed expansion dead in its tracks, further positioning communities in opposition to one another. At one point, Hayward's boosters imagined their city gobbling up all of the land between them and Oakland, completely writing San Leandro out of the equation.[44] When communities incorporated, it was often interpreted as an attempt to counter the expansionist

CHAPTER 4

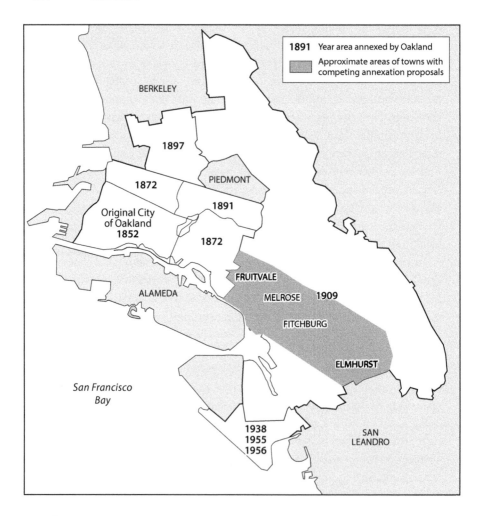

FIGURE 4.1. Territorial growth of Oakland and competing annexation proposals from nearby communities. Cartography by Bill Nelson.

ambitions of other large communities in the area. Piedmont resisted annexation by Oakland through incorporation in 1907.[45] Residents from San José interpreted Sunnyvale's incorporation as a direct attack on their own city's growth. According to one San José merchant, Sunnyvale's incorporation was "merely a plan to checkmate the proposed annexation by this city of a portion of the South Bay Shore for harbor purposes."[46] Reporters in San Francisco described San José's opposition to the incorporation of Sunnyvale as a "war over annexation."

As proponents of various municipal annexation and incorporation plans used the state's legal structure to relocate political boundaries, they redistributed taxable wealth. More than anything else, struggles over annexation and incorporation were struggles over taxable wealth and the Progressive Era innovations it could finance. Alamedans embraced the idea that annexation could increase municipal revenue. The former president of the city of Alameda's Chamber of Commerce insisted that annexation was necessary for the city to maintain municipal improvements while also decreasing local taxes. "If Alameda does not take outside territory, the tax rate is bound to increase," he said.[47] The prospect of annexation, another representative from the city of Alameda's Chamber of Commerce explained, is ultimately about "a whole lot of money."[48] Another annexationist from Alameda framed the issue in similar terms, noting how "our territory is limited. Property is assessed at its reasonable value. The rate was increased. But there were many things for which we were unable to provide." Only by increasing tax revenue through annexation could communities like Alameda provide more municipal services to residents without increasing the tax rate.[49] Boosters from San José made similar assumptions and expressed a similar rationale for annexation. When making their case for a "Greater San Jose," representatives from the city's Chamber of Commerce and Merchants' Association made taxation-based arguments. "Taxation [per resident] will be less in dollars and cents," they argued.[50] Annexationists in San Leandro explained the logic of annexation for that city. With annexation, they argued, "our tax rate can be greatly reduced thereby saving to the tax payers a great deal of money."[51] When the city succeeded in annexing territory in 1908, editors of the *San Leandro Reporter* expressed their excitement in terms of taxable wealth. Boasting a "magnificent victory" and "new era of San Leandro," they emphasized how the new territory would add "between $700,000 and $1,000,000 of taxable property to our assessment rolls."[52] In their move to generate support for the incorporation of South San Francisco, boosters focused on drawing the boundaries of the community to maximize assessed valuations, hoping to create a community worth $592,000.[53]

The arguments for and against consolidation in Alameda County were typical, illuminating the extent to which public discussion of annexation and incorporation centered on taxation. The debates over whether or not Berkeley should be annexed to Oakland revolved around taxes, with each side making the case that annexation would either increase or decrease the tax rate and therefore Berkeley's ability to fund reform. Proponents of Oakland's annexation of Berkeley claimed that Berkeley was on a dangerous path. "In twenty-five years the rate of tax would be so heavy that all residence lots in Berkeley would have to be subdivided," boosters from Oakland warned residents.[54] In order to maintain municipal services at the same level of quality to which the community had become accustomed, boosters insisted, unification with Oakland was key. In a pamphlet designed by the Oakland Chamber of Commerce and Merchants' Exchange, annexationists emphasized how the union of the two cities would reduce costs for local government and local schools.[55] With annexation, they argued, residents of Berkeley could expect an increase in property values and a reduction of taxation.[56] Without consolidation, boosters from Oakland argued, Berkeley would experience stagnation and population flight. Berkeley's high tax rate, they said, would create a downward spiral of flight and depressed property values. Annexationists from Oakland argued, "It is a fact that high taxes drive enterprise and capital from a city. The average citizen will be driven from his present home in Berkeley because of high taxes."[57] Opponents made the opposite case: consolidation with Oakland would decrease property values.[58] Other residents opposed to annexation cast doubt on claims that consolidation, based on the success of New York's borough model, would reduce taxes and promote efficiency.

It was not just by creating the legal framework for annexation and incorporation that state law enabled the new inequities in taxable wealth produced by this zero-sum struggle over territory. By making municipal and school district boundaries coterminous, the state connected the redistribution of wealth wrought by boundary changes with the resources available for public schools. Even before Californians embraced the district property tax en masse, they created pockets of wealth and poverty. The two often went together. When Hollywood City incorporated in 1903, the voters created a wealthy new school district for themselves and a poor school district for nearby residents whom they deliberately excluded from their new boundaries. As the *Los Angeles Herald* explained, Hollywood City School District "sliced off a chunk right from the middle" of two school districts. One of these districts was "so cut down" that it was now "little more" than the poor sections of the nearby community of Coslegrove, with "the best part of the little burg" of Coslegrove having been placed inside the border of the Hollywood City district. Incorporation immediately created a wealthy and a poor district.[59]

Through the drawing and redrawing of municipal boundaries, one district could make itself rich by making another one poor. In Orange County, the *La Habra Star* detailed the precise impact Fullerton's incorporation had on the wealth of the Placentia, Orangethorpe, and Brea school districts. After a "legal tangle" that lasted for years, the Orange County Board of Supervisors finally settled the boundaries of the four districts. Fullerton was immediately made richer by the ruling, at the direct expense of neighboring districts. "Under this ruling," the paper reported, "the Placentia district loses approximately $2,000,000 of its assessed valuation and the Orangethorpe district loses about $6,000,000." Brea district was harmed the least, with the lost property "amounting to not more than $100,000."[60] Although few statewide valuations of school districts during the Progressive Era have survived, Los Angeles County published district-level valuations starting in the 1910s. One of the earliest records showed the wide gap in wealth between Santa Monica and neighboring Sawtelle, with the county reporting that Santa Monica had over six times more wealth than Sawtelle. The wealth of Santa Monica was in a sense a product of Sawtelle's comparative poverty. Santa Monica was first incorporated in 1886. Although it served to check the growth of Los Angeles, the city grew its borders at Sawtelle's expense.[61] In 1906, Los Angeles county supervisors voted to move a section of Sawtelle into the Santa Monica school district. The decision divided "the town of Sawtelle almost in two" and added fifteen hundred acres to Santa Monica. These acres came, in turn, from an area that was home "to many wealthy families" called Westgate.[62]

The creation of new municipal boundaries connected all of these patterns in unequal taxable wealth with race. Incorporation created entire municipalities that were exclusively white and armed with legal mechanisms from the state permitting them to police and enforce racial apartheid over time. As new communities incorporated, local voters, developers, and elected officials could use racially restrictive covenants and zoning to ensure the new municipalities were homogeneous. Glendale, Culver City, Seal Beach, Beverly Hills, and Hawthorne were all incorporated during the Progressive Era, for example, with nearly every residential property in these municipalities covered by racially restrictive covenants.[63] When a real estate agent in the incorporated city of Redlands in San Bernardino County was asked about racial segregation in that community, he responded by explaining how they used city zoning and racial covenants in each new subdivision. In Alhambra, another real estate agent responded to the same survey by emphasizing the same mechanism for segregation. An agent from Montebello, meanwhile, noted how the creation of new subdivisions would not be permitted by the city without racially restrictive covenants.[64]

Annexation and incorporation were used to exclude people of color, creating a clear pattern where Mexican and Japanese Americans, for example, often resided in unincorporated areas just outside incorporated towns and cities. Many Mexican Americans connected to the agricultural labor market resided in *colonias* in the Santa Clara Valley. These communities were bypassed by the movement of municipal boundaries as cities with restrictive covenants such as San José grew through annexation and cities like Sunnyvale were created through incorporation. One study of *colonias* in the region found most were just outside the municipal boundaries.[65] Similarly, Japanese farming communities were concentrated in unincorporated areas as well. The state's alien land law created in 1913 and expanded in 1920 and 1923 added additional layers of exclusion by prohibiting Asian immigrants from owning land.

Municipal annexation and incorporation could also have an immediate effect on the state and county funding distributed to nearby racially segregated school districts. When unincorporated territories were incorporated into new municipalities or annexed into existing ones, they removed pupils along with land. Since state and county apportionments were tied to these enrollments, this change sometimes had an immediate, negative impact on districts serving unincorporated communities. The impact Mill Valley's incorporation had on the Eastland School District illustrates how the formation of new municipalities could create small rural schools. Located in Marin County, Eastland District had 247 students before Mill Valley incorporated. Financially, educating a student body of this size allowed districts like Eastland to save money through economies of scale. The hiring of multiple teachers both enabled the perceived advancements of age grading and created the cost savings that made it possible for districts to afford other signs of "progress" in education, like the newest books and supplies. With Mill Valley's incorporation, the bulk of Eastland's students were now concentered in a new district. Overnight, Eastland District was transformed from a flourishing school of 247 to a rural school of 15.[66]

As municipal school systems grew in population and territory in the Progressive Era, they helped create smaller schools that educators would consider part of the "rural school problem." State school officials and other educators connected to organizations like the National Education Association began discussing disparities between rural and urban schools in the early twentieth century as part of a broader problem with rural schools. As Tracy Steffes observed, "As city schools expanded their aims and activities to offer a new education for modern life," educators discussed how "rural children were being left behind."[67] The new offerings of urban schools and the financial struggles of rural schools often went hand in hand. Consider four counties near San Francisco. The number of incorporated municipalities grew from thirteen in 1890 to thirty-four in 1920. Most of the growth occurred between 1890 and 1910 as the number of municipalities in these counties more than doubled. During these same years, existing municipalities annexed surrounding territories. Through both annexation and incorporation, school districts throughout these counties were carved up into larger municipal school systems and smaller rural ones. As a result, enrollments in rural districts declined even as a handful of districts grew larger. Between 1880 and 1910, the percentage of districts with fewer than thirty students increased from 9 percent to 28 percent in Alameda County, 3 percent to 44 percent in Contra Costa County, 26 percent to 54 percent in San Mateo County, and 12 percent to 37 percent in Santa Clara County. The number of even smaller districts increased at similar rates. The percentage of districts with fewer than fifteen students increased from 2 percent to 11 percent in Alameda County, 0 to 11 percent in Contra Costa County, 0 to 25 percent in San Mateo County, and 2 percent to 20 percent in Santa Clara County.[68]

The increase in smaller rural districts could sometimes reflect the consequences of migration patterns as Americans across the country moved from farms to towns and cities. At the same time, it could also reflect the fragmentation and subdivision of school districts produced by the transformation of political boundaries accompanying municipal annexation and incorporation. The impact of shifting municipal boundaries on educational resources in San Mateo County illuminates how this process unfolded. In 1890, the only incorporated municipality in the county was Redwood City, the county seat. By 1914, the number of incorporated municipalities in the county increased from one to seven, and Redwood City reincorporated with larger boundaries and new charters in 1897 and 1903.[69] With the newly incorporated communities clustered in the northeastern corner of county, the school districts they formed removed portions of land and enrollments from a single district named Millbrae. Figure 4.2 illustrates the territory taken from Millbrae, leaving it with a one-teacher rural school. Each incorporation had an immediate impact, reducing the number of students attending the district and, in a single year, shifting the state and county aid attached to those pupils to the districts of the newly incorporated municipalities. Incorporated Burlingame, South San Francisco, San Bruno, San Mateo, and Hillsborough all removed pupils from Millbrae, alongside the state and county funds that came with them.[70]

As the Millbrae district was locked out of development and the growing wealth that accompanied it, the innovations of Progressive Era schooling became slow to arrive. Each of the districts in incorporated municipalities had a kindergarten by 1920, along with new buildings and supervised instruction under the guidance of a principal. When a school survey of the county was conducted in 1916 by J. Harold Williams, he described the schools of the newly incorporated municipalities in glowing terms: "Buildings, in all cases, are large and substantial.... The teachers, in general, are well selected and well paid, and the equipment is complete and modern. The principals are mature school men, and presence at the county institutes is very beneficial to the rural teachers."[71] For small rural schools like Millbrae, the account provided by Williams was far less cheery. The old building and those of the other rural districts in the county were deemed "insanitary, poorly lighted and ventilated, and difficult to keep at the right temperature." He continued, noting that the "economy idea in modern sanitation has not as yet found its way into many schools" and that "feather dusters, straw brooms, tin water buckets" abound. These schools were almost exclusively "taught by 42 women teachers, wholly without supervision."[72]

Dividing school districts also allowed the new, larger districts to implement age grading, often at the expense of the smaller districts they left in their wake. After the incorporation of Palo Alto, for example, the new municipality and the adjacent town of Mayfield disputed their boundary line. The disputed section was home to seventeen children, and the county census marshal was unsure

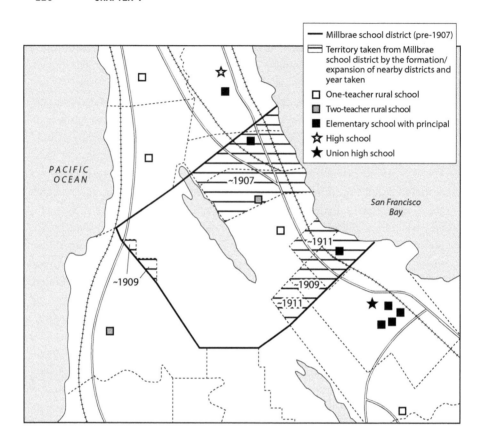

FIGURE 4.2. Removal of territory from Millbrae school district, circa 1907–16. Data adapted from Byron C. Curry, "History of San Mateo County Public School Districts" (EdD diss., Stanford University, 1950); J. Harold Williams, *Reorganizing a County System of Rural Schools: Reports of a Study of the Schools of San Mateo County, California*, United States Bulletin of Education No. 16 (Washington, DC: Government Printing Office, 1916), 20. Cartography by Bill Nelson.

which district should receive the associated funding. The settling of the boundary moved the children into Palo Alto, which in turn cost the Mayfield district a teacher.[73] This movement of school district boundaries could have a particularly negative impact on rural districts experiencing outmigration to larger towns and cities. In Sacramento County, residents of the Galt School District were worried that their "glory of population" was dwindling. A proposal to remove land and pupils from the district for a new one that could be connected to an emerging population center would have meant the district "would lose a teacher and might have to revert to the old ungraded school."[74] In rural Tehama County in northern California, this dynamic shaped the controversy that surrounded an effort to remove land from the Moon District. "We have a good school," one of Moon's school trustees argued in opposition to the proposal. "Now we have the benefits of a graded school" but will "be burdened with a greater tax and get no advantages" if the change was implemented.[75]

As annexation and incorporation campaigns transformed the organization of taxable wealth, voting to remain separate from a larger community could be costly. A larger community contained a threat as much as a promise. Joining a larger city would provide a greater tax base with better educational services, while remaining separate would provide few services, a low tax base, and limited growth. In shaping the contests over municipal space embodied in annexation and incorporation schemes, schooling clearly played a dominant role.

School Bonds and the Expansion of the Progressive Era Public School

As municipal reformers in the nation's cities expanded their borders, they also increased their school districts' tax base. Even in cities that grew their populations without expanding their territory, swelling school enrollments made a number of education reforms cheaper to implement in large districts than in small rural districts. From a financial standpoint, it is hardly surprising that urban school systems became, as historian William Reese put it, "the most important arena for school reform in the first half of the twentieth century."[76] Yet the innovations of the Progressive Era school's expanded social and economic functions were costly. Not only did more schools need to be built, but those schools also needed a host of new features. From a woodshop to support vocational education to sanitary water fountains to promote public health, most reforms of the era required investments in school infrastructure. Across the nation, even the wealthiest school districts could not pay for new buildings, facilities, or equipment with their yearly tax revenue on a "pay as you go" basis. Increasingly, they issued bonds to pay for these new investments in public schooling. As one Philadelphia school official, Theodore MacDowell, explained in 1915, borrowing was necessary so that schools could fund "the introduction and maintenance of the superior educational advantages which a large number of the more progressive localities desire."[77] In aggregate, the debt of school districts increased 576 percent between 1880 and 1913.[78]

Behind the indebtedness of American school districts was a range of state policies and public finance changes that both enabled and incentivized the use of bond issues to finance the new functions of the Progressive Era school. When

Theodore MacDowell surveyed state laws for the United States Bureau of Education in 1915, he found that most states had permitted local districts to sell bonds. The only states that did not allow districts to sell bonds to finance new school construction, for example, were the states of New England—only New Hampshire permitted the practice universally—along with Alabama and Maryland.[79] In aggregate, the debt of school districts nationally increased dramatically as a result. Expressed on a per capita basis after adjusting for inflation, the growth of debt held by school districts was spectacular, increasing 260 percent between 1880 and 1913.[80]

In California, bonds quickly became an attractive option, since the new constitution expanded bond financing provisions. The legal structure enabling debt financing also linked district-level wealth and the ability of districts to borrow money. Although by 1893 the legislature granted all school districts the legal right to call an election to issue bonds, in practice poorer rural districts had only limited access to debt financing. The ability of a district to borrow was limited by its assessed valuation, and no district was permitted to borrow any sum that exceeded 5 percent of its assessed valuation. For school districts with the lowest valuations, the amount they could actually raise through bond sales was consequently limited. Furthermore, the poorest districts could only produce revenue from bonds if they could actually sell the bonds they issued. Even with an emerging national bond market, bonds from rural school districts were not considered a sound investment. In his 1911 guide to bond investment, for example, Lawrence Chamberlain warned potential investors against investing in rural districts because hardly any information could be obtained about them.[81] Even with the advent of bond rating, only the largest and wealthiest districts were reported by bond raters like Moody's.[82] Access to debt financing was therefore concentrated in the wealthiest districts. In aggregate, school districts in California, like those across the nation, borrowed large amounts of money to finance the expanded scope of Progressive Era schooling. This debt, however, was unevenly distributed across districts.

New school bonds and the reforms they enabled required support among voters.[83] Under California state law, even a simple majority would not suffice; the successful passage of school bonds required a two-thirds majority. In this way, increased investments in capital expenditures were often tied to publicity campaigns that crafted and spread popular narratives about the purposes of Progressive Era schooling and reform. Proponents of new bond issues often reinforced narratives connecting the fruits of Progressive Era school reform with a "public" contained within the borders of the school district. The language used in these campaigns often included appeals to invest in education. At the same time, they explicitly framed their arguments by connecting the benefits of new educational reform with local economic development and justifying spending by giving one district advantages at the expense of another.

In wealthier districts where bond measures were feasible, residents developed spirited campaigns supported by a broad coalition of local reformers. Booster groups often helped initiate these campaigns, but they were never alone in their efforts. The movement for a new high school in San José originated with the San José Board of Trade in 1893.[84] In 1912, the campaign for another new high school again originated with a local commercial body, the Chamber of Commerce.[85] Nevertheless, to succeed, school bond campaigns usually had to draw support from an array of different groups and reformers. For example, San José's Board of Education thanked a long list of clubs and organizations for their support of a successful 1916 school bond campaign. According to school leaders, the Chamber of Commerce, the Merchants' Exchange, labor organizations, student clubs, women's groups, and parent groups all deserved praise for their tireless efforts on behalf of increased school spending.[86] The story was the same across the region. In cities like San Leandro, Mayfield, Hayward, Berkeley, and Pacific Grove, proposals for new school construction were often spearheaded by boards of trade and chambers of commerce, but crucial support was also derived from a broad coalition of residents.[87] Labor organizations were important supporters of Oakland's 1906 bond campaign, and women's clubs were essential to the success of school bond campaigns throughout the region.[88] Some commentators even emphasized how women's suffrage would enable new levels of school spending, providing a strategic advantage to local bond efforts.[89] Despite several failed attempts to pass bonds for a new high school, residents in Hayward were certain that the 1911 campaign would succeed because of the expanded electorate. "Four hundred ladies registered who can be depended on to vote for the bonds," one resident boasted.[90]

The supporters of school bond campaigns often deployed a rhetoric connecting their investments in school reform and local economic development, reframing the public school itself as a quasi-privatized good. Mill Valley's tremendous growth, according to the editors of the *Marin Journal*, related to the willingness of residents to approve bonds for new schools and street improvements. "The towns that grow and prosper are the towns that are not afraid to issue bonds and make public improvements," they concluded.[91] "Nothing will make a town," A. L. Graham declared, "like good schools and good buildings."[92] This logic was pervasive. Oakland resident F. K. Shattuck celebrated the impact of bonds on "growth and prosperity."[93] "Voting bonds for the schools," another Oakland resident insisted, "is the first step in a comprehensive scheme of advancement."[94] William Augus, the head of the Hayward Chamber of Commerce, made similar arguments in his appeal for school bonds in the *Hayward Review*: "This district MUST have a new high school building if this community wants to grow."[95] That newer and more elaborate schools would facilitate economic development became one of the most common arguments proffered to prospective voters. Resident Thomas Calkins featured this reasoning in his plea for the passage of new school bonds, contending that they "will assist materially in the upbuilding of this community."[96] "Nothing could be more beneficial to a community than a new school," another booster claimed. Not voting for bonds would be a disaster for development, boosters warned citizens. The failure of a bond measure in Berkeley, supporters claimed, would certainly "retard the progress of the city."[97] "Let us not deceive ourselves," supporters of school bonds in Oakland warned. The failure of school bond measures "cannot be otherwise than disastrous."[98] Through a seemingly unending collection of speeches, advertisements, and newspaper editorials, reformers spread and reinforced the notion that the expansion of local schools would spur economic growth.

In connecting school reform to development, the promoters of new bond issues reinforced the idea that prospective migrants were attracted to communities with high-quality schools. The superintendent of Alameda city schools Fred Wonds, for example, tried to garner support for new school bonds by emphasizing that "to get a large population, you must have good schools."[99] D. W. Kirkland seemed to have faith in the same principle, contending that new bonds for school improvements in Oakland would "stir things up so that people would be attracted here by the thousands."[100] The failure of school bond elections, many argued, would be bad publicity. W. W. Garthwaite from the Oakland Bank of Savings warned that the defeat of school bonds would represent "a bad advertisement for the city, and would retard if not actually arrest our municipal development."[101] "It would be the worst sort of black eye for Gilroy," one resident of that city argued, "to have it go to the world that bonds for a new school house had failed to pass."[102]

As school bond promoters spread popular narratives connecting new construction with economic development and population growth, they reinforced a vision of the "public" that was neither statewide nor national, but contained within the boundaries of racially segregated school districts. One of the primary beneficiaries within this narrow public was the local property owner, invariably white in racially restrictive subdivisions and a state where Asian immigrants were prohibited from owning property in land. Indeed, proponents of school bonds rarely discussed how school reform might benefit children, their families, or the state. Even rarer were references to the value of educational credentials for job success. Instead, school bond promoters concentrated their rhetoric almost exclusively on the various ways school reform could enrich the private fortunes of a select group of district residents, regardless of whether or not they had children.

According to reformers, local school reform would serve business leaders by increasing the volume of trade and increasing profits. "Everything that draws people to the city makes business of all sorts better," Oakland merchant Hugo Abrahamson said.[103] With the passage of new bonds, Oakland attorney Victor Metcalf argued, "people will come here . . . and the effects of that growth and prosperity will be felt in all lines of business."[104] Former Oakland mayor John Glascock told prospective voters that bonds were "a business question submitted to a business community."[105] "It would be interesting to get the figures," an advocate for new school construction in San José contended, "as to the amount of trade brought to San Jose because of her High School. It would certainly be considerable." The bonds proponent concluded, "It pays San Jose."[106]

Property owners would also supposedly benefit from the expansion of schooling in the Progressive Era. Washburn Andrus, a former mayor of Oakland, used this reasoning in his appeal to potential voters on a bond issue. "As a small property owner," he explained, "I feel that the taxes which I would be required to pay would simply be adding so much to the value of my property on the installment plan, for I know that the small home which I own will be worth much more than I will have to pay, as my pro rata of the bond indebtedness."[107] Charles Crocker, an executive with the Southern Pacific Company, was even more direct in his appeal for the same bond measure: "Property values will be increased."[108] The editors of the *Alameda Daily Argus* made the same appeal to voters. Public improvements like new school buildings, they argued, "tend to attract population and so increase the value of holdings and the income from those holdings."[109] "San Jose as an educational center attracts many people," one city resident agreed. This population growth, he continued, "sends up the general level of realty values."[110] The idea that new school construction would increase the value of real estate was often invoked to justify the cost cities might incur. "This increase in the value of property more than compensates for any extra taxation which may be levied on the poor man's property," one bond supporter argued.[111] Boosters in San José wrote, "Good schools pay a community in dollars and cents."[112] Some supporters of new school bonds even attempted to quantify the amount of money new bond measures would produce for local property holders. As the merchant M. J. Keller calculated it, "The small property holder who owns $2000 worth of real estate and improvements, assessed for $1000, would the first year have to pay 5 cents on the $100, or 50 cents. That would be his contribution and his property would, meanwhile, have increased in value, $80."[113]

The logic of debt financing itself seemed to reinforce the connection between education, population growth, and property values. Bonds made sense to many communities because backers assumed that increased population and property values would mitigate future costs. In a plea for school bonds in Gilroy, editors of the *Gilroy Advocate* explained to readers that growth in population and property values would allow new school construction to practically pay for itself. Each year "the assessment rolls would be greater," the editors wrote. In addition, they continued, "the amount to be raised would be $50 less" as "property grew more valuable."[114] Hayward's boosters asked voters to accept the same principle: every year paying back the bonds will be "lighter," they assured, "as the district becomes more densely populated and subdivided."[115] "As the city increases in population and wealth," an Oakland booster echoed, "the cost of paying for the bonds will become relatively lighter."[116] "It will take lots of money," Mayor Frank Mott conceded, "but every dollar that is raised by the tax levy will bring more than a dollar's worth of value in return."[117]

As they translated into American currency the benefits that would accompany the growth and construction of new schools with expanded functions, these bond campaigns added ambiguity to the "public" character of state-sponsored educational institutions. Increased property values and business were public in the sense that they would accrue to all the property owners and businessmen within a community. That public, however, seemed to have very little to do with the learning that children obtained within school buildings or the credentials they carried with them to the labor market. This public, moreover, could never extend beyond the boundaries of the school district. Families that did not own property or businesses within a community, even if they had children, were marginal beneficiaries in the rhetoric of school bond campaigns. At the same time that Americans were increasingly discussing schools in terms of democratic opportunity and equality, the rhetoric of school bond campaigns suggested that you needed to own a business or property to really benefit from state-sponsored schools. This vision of education cast schools as quasi-privatized goods. The local school functioned like an amenity attracting prospective residents who were prepared to pay a user fee in exchange for access.

By entangling reform in intercity rivalries, school bond campaigns also spread narratives valorizing education funding that purposefully excluded other districts. This complicated the public character of state-sponsored schools even further. Consider, for example, the language that drove the campaign for the passage of new school bonds in the small community of Gilroy, near San José. In their appeals to voters, Gilroy's boosters were careful to list communities that had better school facilities. "Are our school buildings as good as those of Morgan Hill, Hollister, Watsonville, or any neighboring towns of similar size?" they asked readers of the *Gilroy Advocate*. "All who have definite knowledge say No."[118] "During the last ten years San Jose, Palo Alto, Santa Clara, Mountain View, Los Gatos, Campbell, and Morgan Hill have built new high school buildings entirely away from their Grammar Schools," boosters from Gilroy argued in another editorial.[119] To garner support for a new high school in Hayward, one commentator drew on a mixture of competition and shame: "There is not a community in California with half your wealth that has such a poor high school building."[120] Speaking before the Hayward Chamber of Commerce, high school trustee J. B. Parsons emphasized how the proposed bonds were necessary if the community wanted to "keep pace with the rest of the state."[121] Residents in Oakland were too pretentious to compare themselves to their immediate neighbors, and they instead focused on the upstart cities of the Middle and Mountain Wests: "In 1880 Kansas City, Omaha, Minneapolis and Denver were in the same rank with Oakland. There was but a slight difference between the taxable wealth and population of those cities and the city of Oakland. How have we fared since then? In 1890 Oakland had about 50,000 inhabitants while Omaha had 139,000, Minneapolis 164,000, Kansas City 132,000 and Denver 106,000. In value of property those cities have still further outstripped us. What has been the reason of this? Those cities were not afraid to issue bonds and improve."[122] Whether the competing community was a distant city with equal urban aspirations or an adjacent town of similar size, these efforts to outdo one another limited the geographic scope of the imagined public to be served by new school bonds.

Narratives of spirited competition and boosterism can seem quite innocuous when regarding the provision of municipal services such as roads. The implication that the benefits of schools should be limited by the boundaries of the school district was far more problematic. At the same time that Progressive Era reformers across the nation emphasized the broad national public served by expanding the role of public schools, local communities used a language of creating and monopolizing opportunities to generate support for reforms that would make their individual schools "progressive." As districts considered financing, the prospect of equalizing educational opportunity across these competing school systems seemed increasingly absurd to local residents. Instead, progressive boosterism created a system of competing publics. Boosters would usually identify by name the communities they hoped to surpass. In Hayward, the passage of new school bonds was aimed at outdoing San Leandro. The prospect of students in San Leandro receiving a quality education that equaled that offered in Hayward scared local boosters: "San Leandro will get the plum."[123] The editors of the *Marin Journal* opposed any attempt to equalize the schools of San Rafael, Oakland, and San José, since they already worried that Oakland and San José would steal San Rafael's population if they did not provide a high school.[124] The advocates of school bonds in San Mateo also seemed to embrace the idea of competing publics. They worried that schools on the bay side of San Mateo County would equal San Mateo by constructing new buildings and providing playgrounds. "If we would keep to the front we must provide these things," they argued. If they did not, proponents of a new school bond measure warned, "it is to such communities that the most desirable citizens will go."[125] Boosters in San José imagined themselves at war with Berkeley and Oakland for residents, a war that could only be won through public schools.[126] The prospect of equal educational facilities across the largest towns of the Pacific Coast seemed to terrify Oakland's boosters. The goal of passing bonds, as one resident noted, was to emulate "these municipalities that have gone ahead of their neighbors." Towns with "one-tenth of the advantages we have are springing up," another Oakland booster warned, and they were "gradually becoming important" while Oakland was "jogging along at the same tortoise like pace."[127] Even state officials responsible for formulating policies that would shape a supposed state system embraced this line of thinking. Hayward needed to have "as good or better schools" as competing communities in Southern California, State Senator Edward Strobridge asserted to an audience at a meeting of the Hayward Chamber of Commerce.[128] Having a better school system than regional rivals was a serious proposition to the school bond campaigners in the Bay Area during the Progressive Era. Failure to pursue such a course, former Oakland mayor John Glascock warned, would represent a deliberate forfeiture of the "race for municipal honors"; giving up on that race was "not simply picayunish," but "suicidal."[129]

As they sought to persuade residents across the region to back their campaigns, school bond supporters reinforced a narrative about the purposes of reform and the scope of the public to be served by state-sponsored schooling that seemingly contradicted the more ambitious visions of Progressive Era education reformers. These campaigns rarely discussed a national community that would benefit from investments in schooling or a collective that extended beyond the boundaries of local school districts. Instead, school bond campaigns spread popular narratives concentrating on the relationship between school expansion and educational advantages that could reap benefits that were exclusively local. In the rhetoric of local reformers, even the children scheduled to attend new schools seemed like marginal beneficiaries. As these campaigns exposed more and more Californians to the idea that disparities between school systems were unproblematic and desirable, they helped justify a series of additional reforms that transformed schooling in the era: efforts to relocate municipal and school district boundaries through annexation and incorporation.

High School for Some

State educational policy regulating high school creation encouraged even more communities to relocate their boundaries while connecting Progressive Era reform with a language of competition and local advantage. Although the high school was made an official part of California's public education system after 1879, the restrictions of the new constitution made it an exclusively locally financed institution. Throughout the 1880s and 1890s, the office of the state superintendent of public instruction remained dominated by former school superintendents from San Francisco and Oakland. These state superintendents remained convinced that high schools should be locally financed. At the same time, they were not satisfied with the slow growth of the institution and confronted regular complaints from county superintendents about inequities in access to the high school. Instead, state superintendents Frederick Campbell and Ira Hoitt both proposed that state educational policies facilitate and encourage local financing for secondary education. Two laws to this effect were first proposed by Campbell and then subsequently passed by the legislature during Hoitt's administration. Called the County High School Act and Union High School Act, the legislation permitted groups of districts—by unifying with their neighbors or at the county level—to unite in order to increase their tax bases to pay for high schools. The unification policies would work, Campbell and Hoitt argued, because connections between education and property values would encourage competition and thus spread secondary schooling without state funding.

In proposals for creating county high schools and union high school districts, the state's education leaders were clear that they had no intention of providing universal access to secondary schooling or the prospect of financing it with a state tax. It did not matter that these county and union high schools would be considered a part of the state system, or that they would provide the necessary link between the state's common schools and a publicly funded university. While some state education leaders argued that the new constitution should be amended to allow state-supported universal access to high school, Campbell disagreed. Instead, he proposed a solution to the high school problem that centered on empowering local communities to vote for, and fully fund, secondary schools. While Campbell acknowledged that limited access to high school prevented most residents from obtaining entry to the state university, he believed the state should simply encourage communities to pay for high schools themselves. "The people of every considerable community," Campbell argued, "should be encouraged and stimulated to organize such schools or classes as shall bring to their children the advantages and benefits of *their own* University" (emphasis in original).[130] Not every community was of the "considerable" variety, of course, and Campbell's proposal would never make high school and the state university equitably available to all Californians. Nevertheless, Campbell's proposal formed the basis of the reforms passed by the legislature in 1891.

From the inception of the County High School Act and the Union High School Act, the bills' advocates not only acknowledged but celebrated the fact that the legislation might inspire competition between communities. According to state educational leaders, competition was productive, and the state's appropriate role was to inspire and structure it. "Doubtless," Campbell wrote, "localities would compete for the location" of the new high schools. This competition, in turn, would produce "liberal donations of land for a site," along with "other assistance."[131] Since the establishment of a high school would make a community "a more attractive home for families with children," Hoitt imagined that most communities would, on their own, create the institution if given appropriate encouragement by the state.[132] The entire proposal was premised on the idea that communities would create high schools when competing with each other for prospective residents. "A large increase in the number of desirable residents, with all its attendant benefits, will inevitably follow the establishment of a good High School in any community," the editors of the *Pacific Educational Journal* wrote following the passage of the laws. Given this connection, the editors assumed that the new laws would lead to dramatic growth: "It is safe to say that within two years after the general establishment of the new system of schools the number of High School pupils will quadruple itself."[133] The point of the reform was not to make high school universally available, but to help communities help themselves. "The establishment of even an ordinary high school is generally recognized to be of inestimable benefit to a community," educator John Clarke explained in the *Pacific Educational Journal*. Given this fact, Clarke expected high schools to spread quickly.[134] For state reformers, the benefit of competition as an engine of bottom-up expansion outweighed its inherent downside. The editors of the *Pacific Educational Journal* did not acknowledge the limits of this approach, instead stating, "In wealthy communities that appreciate educational advantages, these schools should prosper."[135] The fact that less wealthy communities would not share in the prosperity did not register concern.

State leaders seemed increasingly willing to accept a vision of "public" that cast local property owners as important beneficiaries of public schooling. Since the creation of high schools would increase the value of land, state leaders thought it only made sense to fund the institution through local property taxes. They imagined that, in the long term, the high school would pay for itself. After the establishment of a high school in an area, one commentator estimated, local tax revenues would "increase from year to year as property values increase, and they will certainly and rapidly increase with the improvement of school facilities."[136] Invoking a logic embraced by early school promoters and community boosters during the first three decades of statehood, the same commentator explained that "the phenomenal growth of those progressive communities which have been most active and liberal in providing excellent school facilities, in which growth these facilities have formed a most potent factor, shows that within ten years after its establishment a high school of the broad, liberal and modern type before described would return to the community in dollars and cents alone a hundred times its cost."[137] In short, high schools meant land values would increase and property owners would benefit.

The high school legislation reflected a core contradiction: leaders imagined increased educational investment as indispensable for equalizing opportunity and supporting national goals, but they also framed the particular details about how it should be financed in ways that suggested a much narrower view. While the architects of California's new high school laws emphasized the pecuniary benefits of high school creation for local property owners, they also framed the high school as an indispensable institution for social mobility. Most state education leaders were unconcerned by the contradiction of a site supposedly enabling social mobility being unavailable to many. At the same time that John Clarke emphasized how high school creation would increase property values, he also insisted that the institution was "the laboring man's friend and should and will be his pride, for he is coming to know that this is the institution which will level the distinction between the rich and the poor."[138] One commentator framed the high school as an institution necessary for economic advancement: "Competition is keener; opportunities are fewer; the common school has made the general educational equipment of the masses of the people better. . . . He who would outstrip his fellows in the race must make special preparation for special work."[139] The state's superintendent of public instruction Frederick Campbell insisted that the state had an obligation and "should give the poor lad whose only fortune is in his arm and brain . . . every generous chance we can offer him to make a thoroughly educated man of himself."[140] The contradictions embedded in these writers' ideas are striking: the state has an obligation to provide equal educational opportunity, but the state need not make the high school universally and uniformly available. Many reformers seemed to have settled on a definition of public education that held that all schools in the state were equal, but that some schools were more equal than others.

High School Expansion, State-Sponsored Competition, and New Disparities in Educational Access

The policy makers expecting that California's new high school laws would encourage competition between communities were not mistaken. Regional competition between communities shaped the laws' implementation, and the new provisions certainly encouraged some communities to create high schools. The problem was that competition was as likely to prevent as it was to encourage high school expansion in the state. In the end, California's new high school laws ensured that the benefits of the state's public system would be unevenly distributed. The history of high school expansion in the area around the San Francisco Bay during the 1890s reflects how deliberate state policy created new forms of spatial inequality in California, which continued to raise questions about the precise meaning of "public" to some observers but ultimately seemed reconcilable with dominant definitions of public education since the revision of California's constitution in 1879.

The implementation of the County High School Law makes clear how state law structured and encouraged a process of fragmentation that brought educational opportunities to some communities while taking them away from others. The state's new high school provisions created new forms of spatialized inequality in the region. The legislation stipulated that an entire county could elect to create a high school funded through a county tax. If the community said yes, the new high school would be automatically located at the county seat. It was not an issue in counties where the county seat was the community most fairly positioned to reap the benefits in property values that would ostensibly accompany high school creation. Unfortunately, however, these counties were few and far between. When the state superintendent of public instruction James W. Anderson surveyed the expansion of high schools in the state following the passage of the County High School Law, only five of the fifty-seven counties surveyed decided to create county high schools—Del Norte, Kern, Mendocino, San Benito, and Siskiyou Counties.[141] The problem perhaps related to size. California's counties were large. Surely many communities did not want to fund a high school that would be impractical for students to regularly attend. If the distance to the school was too far for students to travel, it was also unlikely that the promised benefits for property values would materialize. Comments by Superintendent Armstrong of San Luis Obispo County explained how uneven benefits stymied high school decision making: "A county high school is out of the question here. The county seat would like one, but other sections of the county, through motives of self-interest, would defeat it."[142] The competition envisioned by former superintendent Campbell was indeed in play across the state, but it often made the idea of a county high school a difficult pill to swallow.

The Union High School Law structured and enabled a similar process. Unlike the County High School Law, the Union High School Law stipulated that after districts decided to unite to pay for a high school, they would elect a board of trustees to determine the location of the new school. While doing so would unchain the siting of the new institution from the county seat, it didn't make the location any less contested. Community rivalries and competition between districts only increased with the formation of union high schools. In Alameda County, for instance, most residents of Washington Township embraced the notion of uniting to form a high school, but trouble started when they had to pick a location. The editors of the *Oakland Daily Tribune* succinctly summarized the brewing tensions:

> It looked for a time as if there was going to be trouble in Washington township over the proposed Union High School—each town has commenced scratching for the location of the High School building. It will be a fight to the finish. Niles wants the school and so does Irvington. Mission San Jose people claim that they are entitled to it and Decoto makes a bid for it. Alvarado demands it and Centerville will claim it. So it would appear that there is bound to be a little ill feeling for the location of the proposed new school.[143]

The "scratching" for the location created even more "ill feeling" when Centerville residents rigged the election for the trustees who would select the site. By advertising the election only in Centerville, town boosters sought to push the siting process in their favor.[144] The editors of the *California Teacher*, summarizing the tensions, described how "the ambition of rival villages was manifested" by the election process. Following an "amicable understanding" between communities, another election was held. The contest was "waxing warmer every week," according to the *Oakland Tribune*. The elected trustees eventually selected Centerville, perhaps because of the community's central location, the number of residents it was able to bring to the polls, or the town's standing threat that if the school was not located in Centerville, it would join with the Alviso, Newark, and Lincoln districts instead and locate the school at Centerville.[145]

Across the state, town rivalries and the notion that high school creation would increase property values made siting the institution within an existing community improbable. In Marin County, the towns of Sausalito and Mill Valley united to form a high school. As the editors of the *Marin Journal* explained, "There is apt to be considerable difficulty over selecting a suitable location. Both towns naturally want the building and both will undoubtedly put up a strong fight to get it. As the county between both places is rapidly growing up, those who believe that it should be located midway between the towns will have the best of the argument and probably win."[146] The editors were correct. The decision to locate the new school in an undeveloped section midway between the towns was indeed the only workable solution to the contention surrounding the location of the new school.

The tensions between communities did not always resolve themselves, however. The fate of the first union high school in Contra Costa County demonstrated how the ferocity of local rivalries could undermine high school arrangements between districts. In the summer of 1891, voters in twelve districts elected to unite in order to form a high school district. When the elected trustees selected Antioch as the site of the institution, however, residents outside of Antioch claimed that they were "grossly deceived" by the process and that it was "under a misapprehension" that they voted for the new school. Locating the institution at Antioch made it "of no benefit to them," according to outlying districts.[147] The rival districts refused to send their children to the school and worked with the county superintendent to ensure that the district be declared lapsed because of low attendance. While the *Contra Costa County Gazette* insisted that the institution's closure was lawful and caused by the "sins of its progenitors," the editors of the *Antioch Ledger* insisted that the institution "was strangled and laid low by foul means."[148] The feelings surrounding the fate of the Antioch High School were so bitter that politicians from Antioch had difficulty gaining support in other parts of the county. C. M. Belshaw, a candidate for the State Assembly, complained that members of his own party were refusing to support his candidacy because he was from Antioch. "We have nothing against you Mr. Belshaw," he recounted hearing from voters, "and if you lived here with us, we would probably all vote for you, BUT you live in Antioch."[149] While Belshaw insisted that the high school was "not a political issue," prospective voters interpreted the situation differently.

The Union High School Law did not just encourage competition over where to locate a high school. It also created new tensions around which districts would unite and which districts would be left out of unification efforts. When Washington Township created its union high school in Centerville, high school promoters attempted to deliberately exclude three districts that wanted to join the union.[150] Similarly, residents of Mill Valley and Sausalito decided to drop Corte Madera from their proposed union high school district.[151] In many cases, the decision of which district to exclude was based on ideas about undesirable people. The decision to leave out the Parks district from a proposed unification in Woodland, for example, stemmed from concerns that one of the leading residents of the district was, in fact, an immoral man. He was, in the words of one commentator, "now being in the penitentiary, in a felon's cell."[152]

As the Union High School Law encouraged new forms of competition between school districts, it helped to reinforce the idea that the primary benefits of educational expansion accrue to property owners within a geographically bounded area, rather than the larger state or nation. Throughout their discussions of high school creation, local communities extended a vision of the purposes of public education first articulated by early town site promoters and real estate developers:

that one of the primary benefits of educational expansion is increased property values for a geographically bounded group of people. The idea that the high school was a municipal rather than statewide good was not just built into the school legislation of the 1880s and 1890s. It was repeated over and over in local discussions about whether or not to create a high school. When discussing the prospect of creating a high school for Sausalito and Mill Valley, newspaper editors claimed that no one was opposed to the idea because "the people of both places seem to realize that nothing builds a place up like schools."[153] When residents of Sebastopol started discussing high school creation, editors of the *San Francisco Call* wrote, "The people of Sebastopol are discussing the question of joining with the neighboring school district to maintain a union High School in that town. If they succeed in this it will prove the most profitable investment they have ever made."[154] "Educational institutions have the same effect in increasing the values of property in the country that good roads and other improvements have," one writer in Ukiah asserted. "The high school proposition," the writer continued, "is one that is worthy of the consideration of every business man and property holder—especially those having families."[155]

Boosters who took advantage of the state's new high school legislation emphasized how, in addition to increased property values, high school creation would attract the "right kinds of people," helping to create economically and racially segregated communities. The editors of the *Sausalito News* insisted that a high school not only gives a "community and its people a certain prestige," but it also shapes "the number and class of people who immigrate there."[156] The editors of the *Oakland Tribune* marveled at the effect of high school creation on the demographic composition of Hayward. The presence of a high school, editors argued, "is bringing a most desirable class of people here who prefer [Hayward] to any other place to educate their children."[157] Frank Coates, a representative from the Southern Pacific Railroad, made the same point in a speech delivered at the dedication of a new union high school in Woodland. "Education centers," Coates told the audience, have always helped "the settling up of countries with the best class of citizens."[158] The *Ukiah Republic Press* agreed: "People, especially those of brains and money, when looking for a home will be attracted, other things being equal, to that locality which has the best educational facilities. Isn't that the class of people we want to induce to settle here?"[159] People of brains and money were sure to follow high school creation, boosters reasoned.

The new high school legislation of the 1890s reflected the ways in which competition exacerbated inequality between districts. When Superintendent Anderson surveyed the effects of the new laws in 1894, he found that most school districts in the state continued to lack access to a public high school. The development of the institution in the Bay Area makes this pattern particularly clear.

Community boosterism and local enthusiasm for a high school encouraged the creation of new high schools in several communities. Overall, however, the growth was extremely uneven. By 1894, there were 489 school districts organized in the counties surrounding the San Francisco Bay. Only 86 of those districts had access to a high school following the implementation of the law. The innovation unleashed by the combination of boosterism and competition did not reach 82 percent of the school districts in the region.[160] While the number of high schools increased from 48 to 120 during the first ten years of the law, progress remained uneven. Only one-third of the school districts within the state had a connection to a high school in 1900.[161] As late as 1936, a survey from the Works Progress Administration identified several Bay Area districts that continued to lack access to high school.

Accounting for how the state structured efforts to generate additional revenue for schooling during the Progressive Era reveals how much state policies helped to create new disparities in the tax bases and the educational opportunities offered by different school districts. It also highlights the often-overlooked discourse about how the costs and benefits of the Progressive Era school should be distributed. This conception of the public school was brought into view clearly in the growing city of Oakland in the fall of 1892. School officials expended considerable effort assessing the physical development of their students. They carefully manipulated children's bodies to gather their statistics. The pupils were poked and prodded, measured and weighed. The results were graphed and publicized.[162] Nothing seemed to exemplify the expanding power of state-sponsored schools during the Progressive Era more than the privileges officials now exercised over the bodies of other people's children.

Historians have created numerous interpretive frameworks to help us understand this data-collection project and the broader transformation of American schooling during the Progressive Era. Most have neglected the minutia of how the particular school system collecting this data was funded and what commentators said about how the project and the various education reforms of the era ought to be financed. And even the most sophisticated accounts leave little room to explain what Oakland officials did with the information they gathered: Superintendent John McClymonds had this data graphed in order to make a boisterous point about the irrefutable superiority of Oakland. The children in Oakland, according to McClymonds's careful calculations, were in fact physically superior to the children in other communities of urban pretention and national repute. None other than Franz Boas confirmed the fact that children in Oakland were taller and heavier than the children of Boston, Worcester, Toronto, Saint Louis, and Milwaukee. This fact, the superintendent explained to the city's Board of Education in his annual report, was most definitely flattering.[163]

In celebrating the way Oakland's schools and pupils were better than those of other cities, McClymonds underscored a particular way of thinking about how the costs and benefits of the Progressive Era school ought to be distributed. While many reformers hoped that schools could mitigate the effects of urbanization and growth during the Progressive Era, some also hoped that schools could encourage such urban growth. The expectation that school reform could grow one community at the expense of its neighbors did more than simply add an additional function to an overburdened institution: it articulated a conception of the "public" served by schools that historians have failed to consider. The reformers who roam existing histories ascribed new purposes to schools during the Progressive Era that were often contradictory, but they tended to share an imagined public that transcended the narrow geographic boundaries of the school district. Whether they were hoping to promote democracy for all or provide new skills to a narrow class of workers, these reformers imagined a public that was broad and diffuse. Even the most private rationales for reform, to provide individual children with the skills and credentials that could earn them money, were connected to a rhetoric of opportunity and meritocracy that did ideological work for a broader, national public. At the very least, reformers did not imagine the benefits of public schooling as contained within the geographic confines of the school district. Yet the expansion of the Progressive Era school itself was bounded with the idea that its benefits should be distributed unequally. This idea would come to define state taxation policies in California after 1910 as well, helping to narrow what forms of wealth were taxed, at what rate, and to what ends in both the Golden State and across the nation.

5
THE RISE OF THE DISTRICT PROPERTY TAX, EDUCATIONAL EXPERTISE, AND RATIONALIZED INEQUALITY, 1910–1928

Writing in the spring of 1918, C. L. Phelps expressed grave concern for the future of public schooling in California. Lawmakers, he worried, were dismantling the state's public education system and replacing it with something different. "We have a state system of schools in only a very limited sense," Phelps bluntly concluded in the *Sierra Educational News*.[1] For Phelps, the trouble related to money. State lawmakers, following the abolition of the statewide property tax, were now forcing communities to increasingly fund their schools with a local tax on real estate. "The burden of supporting the common schools is being shifted from the State and county to the district," Phelps worried.

The pattern that concerned Phelps was reflected in the spread of district property taxation across the state between 1890 and 1920. In 1890, more than half of the revenue California school districts received was from the state (53 percent). By 1920, this figure had dropped to less than a quarter of their total funds (22 percent). In many communities, this meant school districts were raising a permanent, district-level tax for the first time. In the nine counties around the San Francisco Bay in 1890, for example, only 8 percent of school districts even raised a district-level tax to help pay for elementary schools; 92 percent of the school districts in the region were funded through sources completely unrelated to the wealth of that local district, and dollars flowed freely across school district boundaries. By 1920, school funding in the state was dramatically transformed. Sixty percent of the districts in the region were regularly collecting a district-level tax to help fund their schools. Only 40 percent of districts were exclusively funded through sources that continued to redistribute wealth across school district lines.[2]

This chapter traces the spread of district property taxation for schooling in California and its implications for disparities in education funding. Phelps was disturbed by the growth of local property taxation because he knew state policy was responsible. Through the abolition of California's statewide property tax in 1910, a purportedly progressive reform separating state and local revenue sources manufactured a fiscal crisis for schools. As more and more districts were forced to use local taxes to generate revenue, the amount of "property" they could tax was narrowed considerably as well. Under the terms of the reform, intangible forms of wealth were removed from the tax bases of school districts and counties. Now local governments could only tax real estate, even though many districts had assumed massive amounts of debt to finance Progressive Era educational expansion—with the understanding that their taxable property had included this wealth. Advocates of tax reform had insisted that by separating sources of state and local revenue, corporations would pay a higher share of taxes because they would be more efficiently taxed by the state. But when it came time for the state to increase corporate tax rates to generate funding to keep pace with growing educational costs, such revenue never materialized. Instead, the architect of the state's new tax law helped lobby the legislature on behalf of the state's corporations to not increase taxes on his clients' entities, arguing that schools were too expensive and wasting money. More and more lawmakers began to buy into this argument that schools were wasting money, especially after World War I.

The transformation of taxation and school funding institutionalized the narrowly conceived vision of public education embodied in the popular narratives discussed in chapter 4. New experts in public finance and school administration, groups like the Taxpayers Association of California, a new breed of corporate lobbyists, and state politicians from wealthy communities embraced this vision and worked together to shape state law accordingly.

Activists like Phelps resisted the rise of local property taxation and the vision of public education it implied. Ultimately, however, this resistance was unsuccessful. New and increasingly powerful university experts, organizations like the Taxpayers Association of California, and powerful state politicians not only embraced public policies that expanded and exacerbated disparities between school districts, but they also reframed inequality in school funding itself as an inevitable and thus unchangeable feature of public education systems. As they recast district inequality in ways that concealed the role of local reformers and state policy in creating it, these experts, activists, and politicians empowered inequality. The rise of school finance as a discipline, in particular, did profound ideological work to make school funding disparities seem both natural and desirable. Developing new ideas about how local funding was connected to democratic local control, reformers like Ellwood Cubberley transformed not only the organization of educational funding during this period, but shaped the stories we continue to tell about school finance today.

The Science of Public Finance, Tax Reform, and the Local Benefits of Public Schooling

In the same years that Americans expanded the social and economic functions of their schools, they also increased their critiques of the general property tax systems that sustained those schools. Whether levied by state or local government, the general property tax was theoretically a levy on all forms of wealth. In practice, critics of the general property tax insisted, it only taxed real estate, leaving intangible forms of wealth like stocks and bonds free from assessment. As Ajay Mehrotra observed, "nearly every economic commentator and political activist in the late 1800s singled out state and local general property taxes as abject failures of American law and public policy."[3] Of course, many critics of the general property tax said the same exact thing about state income taxes—they were inherently flawed, impossible to enforce, and simply unworkable.[4] The ability of governments to eventually prove that they could in fact enforce an income tax suggests that the general property tax could have been enforced as well. This is exactly what political activists in California tried to do until 1910.

As noted in chapter 3, one of the major challenges confronting policy makers when it came to taxation in the state was actually implementing corporate taxation. Another challenge for the operation of the general property tax was the manipulation of tax assessments by both corporate entities and individual taxpayers. Across the nation, businesses and individuals could evade taxation thanks to locally elected assessors who could be cultivated for their ability to underassess property at tax time. "Before the enactment of prohibition," historian Clifton K. Yearley argues, "nothing in American life entailed more calculated and premeditated lying than the general property tax."[5] California's State Board of Equalization was designed to curb these abuses and did intervene, as needed, to overturn the assessed valuations in some counties.[6] Between 1895 and 1910, the assessed valuation of California increased enough that lawmakers were able to lower the state's tax rate while increasing the size of appropriations for common schools, which *increased* from $2,195,459 to $3,199,335 between 1895 and 1910, while at the same time the state common school tax rate *decreased* from 20.4 to 14.2 cents per $100 of assessed valuation.[7]

Although the State Board of Equalization helped prevent the total assessed valuation of the state from declining, corporate entities nonetheless continued to find new ways to avoid the general property tax. For example, consider the taxation of banks. In theory, under California's general statewide property tax, banks were liable not just for their real estate holdings, but their stocks, bonds, solvent credits, and money they had on hand on assessment day. Under federal law, however, national banks could only be taxed on their real estate. To avoid taxation by the state, a number of banks converted to national banks in the years after the new constitution was created. In the year it was created, there were only eight national banks in the state. By 1910, there were 185.[8] In 1899, lawmakers succeeded in passing a law that taxed shares of stock in national banks, but banks took the state to federal court, and in 1905 California's taxation scheme was overturned. Other banks simply converted all their assets to tax-exempt bonds right before assessment day or, in some cases, moved all their assets into a different jurisdiction until assessment was complete.

If the behavior of their lawyers and political representatives was any indication, the largest corporations in California were staunchly opposed to reforming the general property tax. Consider the stance of the entity most identified with the corporation: the Southern Pacific Railroad. The company's political machine managed to get one of its former lawyers—Henry Gage—elected governor in 1899. During his tenure, members of the legislature worked to reform the way businesses in the state were taxed. State representative Anthony Caminetti insisted that "there is a vast amount of property such as personal property, money in bank, bonds, gross receipts of corporations, franchise and licenses, that could be taxed and should be taxed."[9] He called for state support of high schools, junior colleges, and a new tax system to provide funding.[10] While his call for high school and junior college support succeeded, his tax reform plan did not. Other lawmakers shared Caminetti's concerns, however, and called for an investigation before any bill was passed. When three state senators released the results of an investigation in 1901, they described how "wealthy holders" of "intangible securities" were evading taxation. Given the "gross injustices" of this evasion, the committee recommended "a radical change be made in the present system of obtaining support for the Government" so that "a large part of the burden be shifted to business."[11] Gage ignored the report and instead insisted that the state's expenses were too high, rather than the wealthy were evading their tax obligations. He made his mission cutting "waste in the expenditure of state funds."[12]

Companies like the Southern Pacific did not support reforming the general property tax, though they would eventually support the abolition of the tax altogether through a state constitutional amendment in 1910. This meant they had much in common with university experts in the emerging fields of economics and public finance. Progressive public finance experts like Columbia University's Joseph Seligman and the University of Wisconsin's Richard T. Ely insisted that the general property tax was beyond redemption. Instead, they argued that it needed to be replaced. Through "separation of sources" reforms, the general property tax would be replaced with taxes on specific forms of property. The kind of property that state and local governments could tax would be separated as well. Local governments would only tax real estate. State governments would tax corporations. The reform was supposed to increase the tax burden of corporations by, ostensibly, making it easier for state governments to locate and tax corporate wealth. Henry Carter Adams, a professor of political economy at the University of Michigan, comprehensively outlined the idea for a separation of sources in 1894.[13] In California, its champion was University of California political economist Carl Plehn. When former Oakland mayor George C. Pardee assumed the governor's office in 1903, he lamented the way California was "growing in wealth more rapidly than in population [while] assessors have been able to find very little of this newly-created wealth."[14] To execute reform, the legislature appointed a committee of four elected officials, chaired by Plehn, to comprehensively study the state's taxation system and create specific proposals for its reorganization.

The tax reform supported by Pardee and Plehn was far less progressive than historians have sometimes suggested. Even as Pardee called for increased taxation on new wealth, he also called for a curtailment of state spending. Education spending in particular seemed too high for him. "State government already contributes to the support of the schools in larger proportion than other States," he said in his inaugural address. Making a powerful appeal for the use of local rather than state taxes to fund schools, Pardee emphasized the need for localities to assume a "fair share" of the cost for education:

> The policy has been adopted by all the States of dividing the cost of maintaining public schools between State and local governments. But while the average of all the States shows that sixteen per cent of the total is borne by the State governments, the proportion so borne in California is forty-five per cent, or nearly three times as great. While the State is interested in having good, even the best, schools, still, it would be well, I think, to have a fair portion of their cost assessed upon the localities where they are situated.[15]

Of course, an increase in local contributions would only ensure that disparities between school districts increased, since different communities had radically different abilities, depending on local property values, to fund themselves.

In making California's foremost political economist chair of the Committee on Taxation and Revenue, lawmakers deferred to Plehn's expertise on how the state's tax system ought to operate. As he designed his reform proposal, Plehn in turn deferred to corporations on how they should be taxed—and at what rate. Soon after the committee was formed, Plehn addressed the Bankers' Association of California and promised "this movement contains nothing that is hostile or dangerous to capital or to the corporations."[16] He and the committee organized a series of "hearings" that were simply informal meetings where different companies could explain their point of view on how they should be taxed. The first meeting was with bankers, followed by insurance company representatives, railroad executives, and officials from public utility companies.[17] Each of these "hearings" began with gatherings Sunday night, followed by meetings with Governor Pardee in his office on Monday morning. Plehn explained to the secretary of the California Bankers' Association that the committee's goal was to be "rather informal so that there may be the freest possible interchange of opinion."[18] At the conclusion of the committee's work, Plehn was pleased to report strong support for his proposal that seemed rooted, at least in part, in the role companies had played in shaping the proposal. For example, Plehn concluded his meeting with insurance company representatives by modifying the committee's proposal. He also allowed attorneys from light, heat, and power companies to prepare "modifications" to the final amendment proposed by the committee.[19]

Representatives from organizations that would be subject to a new tax on corporate earnings seemed to assume that the largest companies in the state would pay less under the system Plehn proposed than they had with the general property tax. One banker, for example, believed the rate on corporate earnings Plehn proposed in lieu of the general property tax appeared high, but that it would in practice be at least "partially offset" by the savings it would produce.[20] Plehn promised the Pullman Company, for example, that any increase in tax rates "would be more nominal than real as the expense of the tax attorney's department would be greatly reduced by the change."[21] While Plehn described the "adequate and non-political taxation of public-service corporations and banks" as a primary objective of reform, this did not necessarily mean he thought the taxes on the entities should go up. In some instances, he seemed to believe they should go down.[22] When one member of the legislature pointed out that his plan would lower the tax rate for a railroad in his jurisdiction, Plehn replied that it "was overtaxed and was entitled to the decrease."[23]

In their official report, Plehn and his colleagues crafted an expert narrative that justified the inequities produced by the local financing of education by connecting schools to the benefit theory of taxation. In the process, they weaved into the emerging science of public finance—and eventually state policy—the narrowly conceived vision of public education embraced by community boosters and municipal reformers who proclaimed a link between educational expansion and real estate values. According to Plehn's committee, the separation of state and local revenue was founded on the notion that schools primarily benefit local communities and, as such, should be funded locally. "The theoretical principle for the separation of State from local taxation is found in part in the natural distribution of functions between State and local governments," Plehn wrote in the Commission on Revenue and Taxation's report.[24] This natural distribution, he continued, clearly defined the appropriate beneficiaries of schooling in narrow terms:

> The activities of the local governments, such as the protection of property by the police, the fire departments, the local courts, the construction and maintenance of roads, streets, bridges, and the like; the provision for schools, the care of the sick and of the poor, redound distinctly, directly, and peculiarly to the benefit of local real estate owners, or local industries and enhance and sustain the value of real estate and of other tangible property in the localities. This has always been the ground for the making local governmental expenses a local charge.[25]

In their emphasis on how the "provision for schools . . . redound distinctly, directly, and peculiarly to the benefit of local real estate owners [and] enhance and sustain the value of local real estate," the report's authors recast the purposes of schooling in the familiar terms of boosters and real estate developers. The vision of schooling contained within the report seemed fundamentally at odds with much of the Progressive Era writing on schools. Whether they were defined as valuable institutions for Americanizing immigrants or providing economic opportunity to individual children, schools were often discussed in terms of a broad national project, one that transcended the boundaries of the school district. Plehn and his colleagues, with the weight of their expertise, recast the purposes of schooling and the public it served, fully enclosing them within the boundaries of the local school district. Plehn and his colleagues also expanded on the local character of schools by casting doubt on the state's role in funding them, extending the notion that schools were local rather than state institutions: "The $4,000,000 collected by the State for the support of the common schools is only nominally State revenue—it is in reality local revenue. Save for the supervision exercised by the State Superintendent of Public Instruction and the State Board of Education, the control and management of the schools is a matter of local government solely. The State collects, apportions, and disburses the school monies as an agent for the districts."[26] In framing the state's role in collecting and disbursing money for schools as a matter of "local revenue," the authors of the report rendered the idea of redistribution problematic. How could it make sense for a wealthy community to provide financial assistance to the schools of a poorer community if the money collected by the state for these purposes was only "nominally State revenue"? If the State was only "an agent for the districts," as Plehn and his colleagues argued, the use of anything other than a district's property tax seemed to make little sense, despite the massive inequalities that such reliance would create.

In casting the scope of the public to be served by public schools in these narrow terms, Plehn and his colleagues suggested that the "ability to pay" principle so central to progressive tax reformers did not fully apply to education. Public finance experts like Adams, Seligman, and Ely were fierce advocates for the "ability to pay" theory of taxation. In contrast to the idea that individuals should pay in taxes the amount they received in benefits from the state, the "ability to pay" theory assumed that individuals should pay tax rates that corresponded to their wealth. Plehn seemed to take an opposite view regarding schools and also seemed to contradict the writings of other progressive public finance experts. Adams articulated a systematic "blueprint" for the separation of revenue sources in an 1894 essay, and he elaborated on the idea in his influential *Science of Finance: An Investigation of Public Expenditures and Public Revenues*.[27]

While Adams may have served as a partial model for Plehn in thinking about the need for a separation of state and local revenues, their respective conceptions about how schooling connected to this separation were radically different. For Adams, schooling was undeniably and inescapably a statewide public good. "In every instance an analysis of the social results shows that the benefit of education to the individual is proportionally less than its advantage to the other members of the community," he insisted to readers.[28] While Plehn and his colleagues reveled in the idea that local real estate owners benefit from schooling and should thus pay for it, Adams was adamant that any application of the benefit theory to schooling would threaten the very notion of public education. "If taxes for the support of schools . . . should be levied to citizens in proportion to the value to them respectively of the public-school system," he argued, "no sound reason could be urged why the State should undertake to provide public schools at all. . . . It would cause the schools to disappear, yet this is what the benefit theory of taxation logically applied would logically lead to."[29] For Adams, schools served a larger social purpose that demanded broad state support—equally applied. It was California's native political economist who transformed Adams's idea into a justification for a disparate system of school funding.

The Commission on Revenue and Taxation's approach to tax reform was narrow enough that some voters reacted against it. The state legislature responded to the commission's report by crafting a constitutional amendment implementing the commission's recommendations for voters to consider. In the buildup to the vote, critics of the amendment said that it was too friendly to public service corporations. Some of these critics pointed out instances where such corporations would be able to lower their tax bill under the terms of the proposed tax plan. Others, including the Commonwealth Club of California, argued that the amendment rendered the prospect of increasing the tax rate on corporations in the future impossible. The amendment would not allow a majority vote of the legislature to increase the rate of taxation on corporations. Instead, a constitutional amendment was needed to increase rates. "With all the corporations banded together, as they will all of necessity be to protect themselves in this new favored class created by the proposed amendment, it will be almost impossible to increase the rates embodied in the proposed amendment," members of the Commonwealth Club warned in a summary of their objections.[30]

When a modified version of the amendment that empowered the legislature to increase tax rates and created at-large elections for the Board of Equalization was reintroduced to voters as Amendment No. 1 in 1910, it passed with broad support from business, real estate, and farming organizations. While they were ultimately unsuccessful, critics of "the Plehn plan" pointed to the work of large corporations in the state as evidence that the plan was not what it seemed. "In vain did a handful of men," one journalist noted, "point out the incongruity of the corporations spending their good money in a publicity campaign to have their taxes 'increase.'"[31] San Francisco attorney Matt Sullivan accused business interests, in their publicity campaigns, of misleading voters about the amendment. "The corporations, whose taxes are supposed to be increased by the Amendment," Sullivan explained, "[created] a fund, which is now being used to *convince the people that the taxes of the masses will be reduced if the Amendment goes into effect, and that the taxes of the corporations will be correspondingly increased*" (emphasis in original).[32]

State Senator A. E. Boynton was concerned by the fact that "the largest street railway system in the State are in favor of the measure. . . . No one would accuse these two corporations of not looking out for their own welfare."[33] A number of critics also worried that the reform would allow corporations in the state to evade their responsibilities to fund schools. The editors of the *Los Angeles Herald*, for instance, opposed the amendment for its potential impact on state school support, expressing dismay that "the adoption of the amendment will upset the present legislative provisions for raising a state fund to support the public schools and the state university."[34] Boynton provided a similar justification for his opposition to the amendment, citing his belief that the amendment would "impair the school fund."[35] These arguments seemed to have little impact on the final success of the measure.

The writings of Plehn and the Commission on Revenue and Taxation appeared to grant scientific legitimacy to the notion that the scope of the public served by state schools was contained within the boundaries of the local school district. He and his colleagues created theoretical justification for the idea that schools served a local, rather than statewide, public. In accepting the logic of the Commission on Revenue and Taxation, voters translated into state policy these ideas about the nature of the state's role in education. It was a move that would dramatically alter the nature of school funding in California.

Spread of the District Property Tax

As the passage of Amendment No. 1 in California transformed into policy, state support for schools became more precarious. Reform had removed an important source of revenue for schools from the state's budget. Plehn had been well aware of the negative impact the change would have, explaining to Governor Pardee that the corporate earnings tax would not produce enough revenue and that it would be "absolutely necessary" to find another revenue source if the state was to maintain its funding to schools.[36] The policy shift also generated a new political dynamic around the idea of what "tax rate" was needed to replace the missing revenue. Under the general property tax regime, the legislature did not specify a tax rate in advance, but rather the amount of revenue to be derived from taxation. Depending on aggregate assessed valuations, the tax rate was then set to produce the amount of specified revenue. As a result, the tax rate varied from year to year. In contrast, California's new tax regime saw the tax rate set by lawmakers in advance; appropriations no longer determined the tax rate. The tax rate now seemed to determine appropriations, and corporations worked hard to set that rate as low as possible.

Of course, efforts by business interests to shape state policy were hardly new. Representatives from the Southern Pacific Railroad were fixtures representing corporate interests to the state legislature. Yet observers of state politics during the 1910s and early 1920s insisted that a "new breed" of corporate lobbyist had emerged in response to the "Plehn plan." Journalist Franklin Hichborn observed this surge of large corporations shaping state fiscal policy throughout the 1910s and early 1920s: "The corporation managers," he observed, "[have] very adroitly been shifting the State tax burden away from themselves."[37] According to historian R. Rudy Higgens-Evenson, "once corporation tax rates became the subject of legislative fiat . . . corporations took an even more intense interest in what went on in the state capitol."[38] With each session of the legislature, wrote George Mowry in his classic account of state politics *The California Progressives*, "the influence of the state's great corporations seemed to grow."[39]

Efforts to limit corporate tax rates succeeded in transforming the way the state—and its schools—were funded. Almost immediately, the revenue produced under the new tax system was insufficient. In the first year, the chairman of the Senate Finance Committee warned, "Under the present rates the annual deficit will increase rather than diminish, as the needs of the State are increasing faster than the revenues of public service corporations."[40] The senator proved to be prescient. With control of the governorship and the statehouse, Hiram Johnson and his allies managed to increase the corporate tax rate in 1913 and 1915. Both increases, however, were insufficient. After the 1913 increase, the state school fund was still left with a deficit of $3 million. San Francisco's school system was short $104,000 in 1915 and $130,000 in 1916.[41] Each district in the state lost approximately $1 per pupil in 1915 dollars.[42] Some communities responded by withholding teacher salaries.[43] Others simply closed their school systems early.[44] The 1915 increase in the corporate tax was insufficient as well. Educational costs expanded as school districts created high schools, evening schools, kindergartens, and other ancillary institutions. While overall state tax revenue from corporations grew, the increase did not keep pace with the growth of the state's population and its growing educational costs. Even excluding expenses like construction and funding for new high schools, kindergartens, and evening schools, state contributions per elementary school student decreased from $29.34 per pupil in 1890 to $14.31 per pupil in 1920.

These shifts in school funding were justified theoretically by experts like Plehn with popular narratives that framed school reform as a competitive-development strategy designed to serve a local, rather than statewide, public. The idea that the benefits of public schooling "redound distinctly" to local property owners made the broader notion of statewide school support seem dubious. If local property owners were the primary beneficiaries of schools, why would the state use anything other than local property taxes to support education? Nevertheless, these changes were not without controversy. A small but vocal opposition criticized the transformation in California's school financing structure that had been initiated by the work of the Commission on Revenue and Taxation. For critics, the trouble related to the district property tax. While present-day scholars assume that the district property tax was a universal and inevitable feature of American public schooling, some Californians considered it strange and highly problematic. Critics worried that the state was retreating from its responsibilities and, in the process, redefining the very nature of schooling in the state. "For several years in California," a commentator wrote in the *Sierra Educational News*, "protests have been repeatedly voiced at the increase being put upon the locality, either the county or city, and at the diminishing help from the state in the support of schools."[45]

The critics were right. As the state abolished existing sources of school funding, district and county property taxes became increasingly important for school financing. While per-pupil state contributions for elementary schools decreased between 1890 and 1920, per-pupil contributions from counties and school

THE RISE OF THE DISTRICT PROPERTY TAX

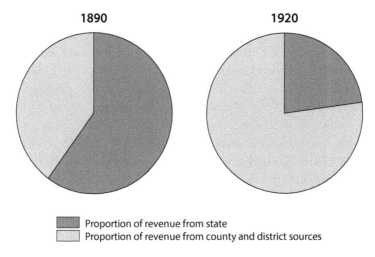

FIGURE 5.1. Declining proportion of elementary school revenue from state sources in Alameda, Contra Costa, Marin, Napa, San Mateo, Santa Clara, Solano, and Sonoma Counties in 1890 (*left*) and 1920 (*right*). Adapted from data in annual reports (Common School Reports), Department of Education Records (F3601:326–784), California State Archives, Sacramento. Graphic by Bill Nelson.

districts increased. Figure 5.1 illustrates these patterns for a sample of school districts in eight counties in northern California. The state was responsible for 60 percent of the total expenditures for elementary schools in 1890. By 1920, it was providing only 23 percent of the money spent on elementary schools in the region.

According to critics, the problem with this shift was not simply that the wealthiest residents in the state were shirking their responsibilities, but that the transformation of school funding was redefining what it meant to have a public education system. Since schools were increasingly funded through taxes that did not redistribute wealth between communities, some critics wondered how anyone could claim that California continued to have a state system of schooling at all. The legislature "is not doing its duty towards the public schools, which are State institutions—not county institutions," one newspaper editor lamented. "The matter of providing for the public schools should not be passed to the counties ... for the schools are not county institutions. Public education is for the benefit of the State. ... Education knows nothing of county lines."[46]

The real trouble with declining state contributions to public schooling was not that it increased the salience of county lines, however. Many counties were close to the legal maximum in their ability to generate revenue through property taxes. The state stipulated that counties could only raise a certain percentage of their assessed valuations in property taxes to support schools. For poorer communities, or communities that purposely kept their assessed valuations low, this meant that they were going to have trouble raising enough money to cover the state's declining share of school expenditures. County taxes, moreover, seemed to make less and less sense to Californians who were opposed to the idea that wealth should be redistributed between communities in order to pay for schools. As a result, it was the local school district that came to assume an increasingly important role in California school funding. This fact terrified critics of the narrow public imagined by boosters and experts like Plehn. "California has shifted the burden of Education from the State to the counties and the districts; and many of the counties are forcing the districts to carry an undue burden," one writer observed in 1918.[47]

This shift in state funding translated into an increasingly important role for local school districts in educational finance. Indeed, local district taxes played a minimal role in school finance in 1890 but a profoundly different role by 1920. While 40 percent of the money spent on schools in the San Francisco Bay Area was derived from county and district taxes in 1890, most of that money came from countywide taxes, a revenue source that could redistribute tremendous amounts of wealth between school districts. Indeed, only 13 percent of total school expenditures were derived from district property taxes in 1890.[48] In Alameda County, wealth from Oakland was redistributed to fund rural districts like Eden Vale, a small district in a poor farming area with low property values. In Sonoma County, Santa Rosa's wealth was applied to isolated rural schools like Alder Glen. The wealth of cities like San José and the increasingly wealthy suburbs like Mayfield was redistributed to help poor districts in underdeveloped and impoverished areas in Santa Clara and San Mateo Counties. The story was the same in Napa, Marin, and Solano Counties. In fact, so much wealth was being redistributed through county taxes in 1890 that fewer than 10 percent of the school districts in the San Francisco Bay Area even raised a district property tax that year. In other words, over 90 percent of the school districts in 1890 were being funded by revenue sources that did not limit educational resources to local wealth. All of this changed dramatically after the passage of Amendment No. 1. By 1915, almost 30 percent of the school districts in the region were raising a district property tax and thus relying on revenue sources that could not redistribute wealth across school district boundaries. By 1920, this same figure jumped to 61 percent.

Even as more and more Americans described how their schools equalized economic opportunities, tax reformers like Plehn helped facilitate a profound shift in how those opportunities and their attendant costs were distributed.

Increased reliance on district-level property taxes allowed wealthy residents to hoard opportunities for their own children while limiting their responsibilities for the education of children who resided elsewhere in California. Increased reliance on district-level taxes also decreased the financial contributions of the state's wealthy corporations toward the operation of public schools. According to Hichborn, one of the key ways the "billion dollar" lobby helped corporate interests shift "the State tax burden away from themselves" was by transferring the cost of state services to smaller governmental entities like school districts. "Here," Hichborn observed, "the subtle influence of the corporations has been amazingly effective." State officials estimated that the burden of all state taxes had shifted by 1921 so that "the tax rates of the banks and corporations on the *ad valorem* basis were 35 per cent lower than the rates paid by the general tax payer." Hichborn calculated the precise terms of this shift for schools, estimating that "there had been an increase in the plain citizen's annual tax for the schools of $748 a year per teacher." The equivalent tax for state corporations, Hichborn estimated, "had *decreased* $7."[49]

This financial shift only made school district boundaries more contested and the idea that schools served the entirety of the California public more precarious. As the wealth within each district came to play a greater role in determining how much money a community would have available for school spending, the drawing and policing of district lines became more important. Even a small amount raised in district property taxes could have an impact on how local communities imagined their school district boundaries. Figure 5.2 illustrates this for Santa Clara and San Mateo Counties, where in 1890 school district boundaries were fairly insignificant for elementary school funding. Every school district, with the exception of five, within the two counties was funded exclusively through county and state sources. As a result, the local wealth of each district did not impact how much money the state spent on elementary schools. Funds flowed easily between the borders of these districts. But by 1920, the funding of elementary schools had been transformed; the wealth of local communities now determined the amount of money available for elementary schooling in thirty districts.

The growing number of districts raising a local property tax increased the number of communities unwilling to allow children to attend school across district boundaries. County and district officials, reacting to changes in the state's approach to school funding, helped enforce school district boundaries in the Bay Area. For example, as late as 1911, Santa Clara County school officials were distributing state and county aid to the schools that children actually attended, rather than to the schools in the district where their families resided. Changes in the state's approach to school finance, however, prompted the superintendent of Santa Clara County to rethink this practice, interpreting the bevy of public

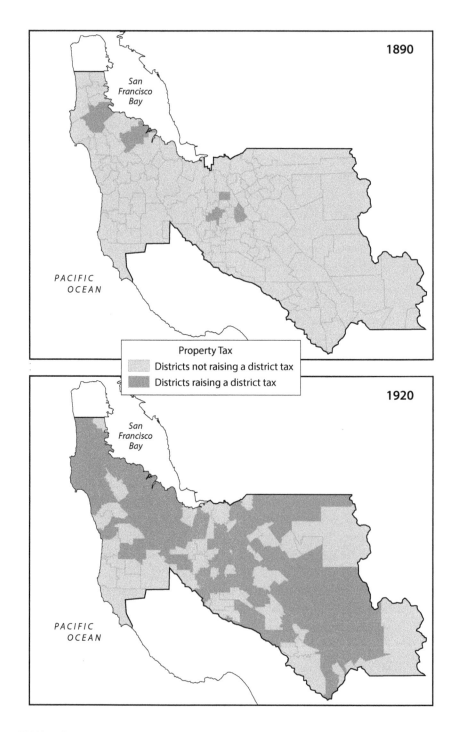

FIGURE 5.2. School districts in Santa Clara and San Mateo Counties raising a district-level tax for elementary schools in 1890 (*top*) and 1920 (*bottom*). Adapted from data in annual reports (Common School Reports), Department of Education Records (F3601:326–784), California State Archives, Sacramento. Cartography by Bill Nelson.

finance legislation as a clear mandate to stop allowing county school funds to follow children across district lines. The change upset the San José superintendent, who interpreted the shift as "manifestly unfair," since the city had educated "147 such outside children" the previous year.[50]

The spread of district property taxation solidified the link between residence and educational access. In the 1910s and 1920s, residents inundated county officials with petitions to move district boundaries to reflect attendance patterns on the ground. A careful examination of the requests in Santa Clara County reflects both the early disconnect between the first recorded school district boundaries and actual attendance patterns, as well as the repeated attempts by local districts to reverse the pattern as communities increasingly relied on local taxes to pay for schools.

For example, George A. Smith requested his land be moved into the Coyote School District because, he explained in the petition, his "children have always attended the Coyote School." Another group of residents petitioned for a change to the Franklin School District's boundaries so that the section of the Oak Grove District where they lived could be included in the Franklin district. The families felt "compelled to patronize Franklin School on account of inconvenience to attend school in the district where they reside at present." Another proposal to expand the boundaries of the Meridian School District was again based on the assertion that children from outside the district, who also "mix socially" with the Meridian students, "have and are at present attending the Meridian School." The Meridian School, the petitioners insisted, should be the one to benefit from the presence of these children. Residents made a similar appeal in a request to change the boundaries of the Gardner District. A change to the boundaries between the Alviso and Midway Districts transferred the land of J. P. Nilson from Alviso to Midway. Nilson, in requesting the change, explained, "My children have attended the Midway school to my entire satisfaction for the past two years."[51]

Los Gatos and Campbell, Doyle and Meridian, Machado and Morgan Hill:[52] over and over again, district lines were changed to accommodate and reflect where families were choosing to send their children. The fact that so many children regularly crossed district boundaries to attend school reflected the continued fluidity of district lines in rural areas. That so many communities sought to change these boundaries with increased local taxation demonstrates the social transformation that accompanied increased local taxation.

As it became more and more difficult for children and money to freely cross school district boundaries, disparities between districts became ever more pronounced. The Los Angeles County superintendent of schools Mark Keppel recognized the increasing inequality and discussed its implications for both educational opportunity and the meaning of California's state system: "Certain of the counties are forcing the districts to carry an undue burden," he worried, explaining that this trend was producing a situation where "there is no such thing as reasonable equality of educational opportunity," since many district communities were "rich in children and poor in assessed valuation."[53] The California Teachers Association adopted a resolution in 1918 critiquing this trend in financing while also making clear its implications for the very meaning of education in the state: "The burden of supporting the common schools is being shifted steadily from the state and county to the district, and more and more our state common school system is becoming a district system with ever-increasing inequality of educational opportunity for the children of the elementary schools. Wealthy districts can do all things for their children, while poor districts can do almost nothing."[54] According to the logic of these critics, California's state system was being dismantled, and a fractured district system was being built in its place.[55]

Within an environment where school districts were competing with each other for resources, the political discourse surrounding funding policy shifted as well, even when the legislature moved to increase state school contributions. The editors of the *San Francisco Call* dismissed one school-funding bill as "an effort to favor Los Angeles in school apportionment. . . . Los Angeles would be the greatest gainer, and the two largest losers would be San Francisco, $28,084, and Alameda, $6,487."[56] The legislature was eventually able to reach a compromise after delegates from San Francisco secured an amendment to the bill, prompting the editors of the *Los Angeles Times* to exclaim to readers, "South Is Beaten in School Fight."[57] Although some education leaders attempted to remind state politicians that "money paid in school taxes belongs to the schools of the state" and not the individual communities, their exhortations were ignored.[58] According to one observer, the entire discussion of school finance produced "a lengthy debate in which each member of the assembly appeared to consider it his bounden duty to discuss in detail just how the proposed new law would affect the school districts of his own particular county."[59]

From Tax Evasion to Excessive Spending: Reframing the Problem of School Finance

As the district property tax spread, critics asserted that California was dismantling its "state system" of public education and replacing it with a "district system." Public finance scholars like Plehn, however, helped to further justify the change by redefining the problem confronting California's schools as one of growing costs, not declining state contributions. In the process, these experts helped change the meaning of "tax reform" while also helping entrench and justify the inequities of the expanding district property tax.

Across the United States, popular commentators insisted that the nation's schools were plagued by a funding problem in the early twentieth century. How that problem was defined profoundly shaped the way its solution was imagined. For radical political activists and rural school administrators in California, the funding problem was rooted in taxation. State contributions to education had declined, and school districts were being forced to raise local tax revenue to compensate. Critics maintained that this shift created an injustice, and the state needed to generate more tax revenue to address it. Hichborn, for example, described the "shifting of the State's part of the cost of the maintenance of the public schools" as an effort by banks and public service corporations to shift "the State tax burden away from themselves.... Here, the subtle influence of the corporations has been amazingly effective."[60]

In contrast, economy-minded commentators insisted that the problem with school funding was not a decline in the state's share of education funding but how much money schools seemed to waste. Concern over public school costs expanded in the 1910s. The increased social and economic functions imposed on the public school made its costs liable to new forms of scrutiny. So, too, did the shift in the way it was financed in states like California. Popular publications began criticizing public school expenditures during these years, insisting that the amount of money spent on education no longer produced the returns public school advocates had supposedly promised. The *Ladies' Home Journal* ran a series of articles in 1912 criticizing almost every aspect of the American public school system. Insisting that Americans have "invested nearly a billion dollars in the public school-system [and that] each year they contribute over four hundred million dollars more toward the same end," the editors of the popular magazine framed their entire critique around increasing costs and diminishing returns. "Surely for so huge an outlay the returns should be stupendous," the editors stated before methodically seeking to demonstrate that American public schools were, in fact, an "utter failure."[61]

Education spending became more visible in the years surrounding World War I. Across the nation, unprecedentedly high inflation produced a dramatic increase in the costs of operating schools. In combination with the growing number of functions assigned to schools and the increase in the nation's school population, commentators like journalist Robert Crawford began to question "whether or not" these "great expenditures can be justified" by "the returns in greater efficiency in society."[62] National statistics on draft rejections during the war revealed a shocking number of illiterate and physically unfit rural Americans, suggesting that these "returns" did not exist.[63]

"The common schools of our country cost, in mere maintenance, $500,000,000," H. E. Miles insisted. "They use in addition, plants of the value of billion dollars, and far the greater part of this expenditure is for only half the children. It is far too great an outlay for a deficient return."[64] William P. White received applause from the membership of the National Association of Manufacturers when he described "the expenditure that is being now made [for public schools], and the laws that are being passed for its expenditure are as absolutely a waste as though it were thrown into the gutter."[65]

Henry Pritchett was one of the most vocal critics. President of the Carnegie Foundation for the Advancement of Teaching, he insisted that Americans had grown "critical as to whether the system of education for which they are paying is justifying itself in the results which it brings forth."[66] Pritchett himself insisted that Americans "were wasting millions on educational fads and frills." John Butler, a faculty member at San Francisco State Teachers College, lamented the power of this rhetoric, criticizing the "panic over school expenditures" that he felt was creating a "nation-wide wave of retrenchment in school expenditures."[67]

Increasingly, influential experts at American universities provided scientific legitimacy to the argument that the nation's schools were spending more than they produced in value to society during the 1910s and 1920s. According to Plehn, the problem with school funding was not the decreasing role of state governments in education financing, but the way state contributions were being spent unwisely.[68] In addition to viewing schools as a local rather than state responsibility, Plehn questioned the logic of observers who called for increased state support to education. He complained to a national audience of fellow economists gathered in California, "School expenditures went up so that we wondered whether the people would have breath left to say, 'Ah!' when the rocket burst." He viewed practically every innovation of the Progressive Era regarding schools as an unwarranted and extravagant "frill": "It seems the height of luxury and extravagance for a school department to furnish automobiles to bring the children to school, and to feed them at the public expense.... Then come the health nurses, dental inspection, special 'gym' suits, and so on. How much further it will go, who can say? Free text books is another large and growing item." According to Plehn, this extravagance was particularly troublesome because increased spending did not translate into increased outcomes. "I fear that the schools have not improved in like measure as their costs have risen," he concluded. Since schools had not, in fact, managed to accomplish the long list of expectations Americans projected onto them, Plehn called for increased economy, not increased spending from states: "The only remedy is that these vast and complicated expenditures shall be carefully scrutinized, and justified, item by item. . . . That is the essence of all economy, and under present conditions economy is a necessity."[69] Policy makers, according to his work on public finance, should focus on rearranging a shrinking pie, rather than increasing its size.

For experts like Plehn, embedded within this critique of educational costs and outcomes was a broader shift in the discourse surrounding what it meant to reform public finance after World War I. The tax problem that he had previously described in terms of intangible forms of wealth escaping taxation became a problem of governmental excess in the 1920s. "It's spending not taxing that counts," Plehn summarized in an article describing what he imagined as the next step in tax reform. Taxpayer associations created the space for experts like Plehn to frame the problem confronting schools as one of increased costs while also working to change tax policy across the nation. The most prominent organization for public finance scholars was the National Tax Association, founded in 1907; the organization's bulletin reflected an emerging consensus on the excessive nature of school spending in the 1920s.[70]

Members of the Taxpayers Association of California became connoisseurs of educational policy, helping to spread Plehn's expert narrative that cast the problems facing education in the state in terms of growing costs, not declining state contributions. In 1917, the organization created a Bureau of Educational Investigation. The director of the group, Wilford Talbert, explained the purpose of the special bureau in terms highlighting the need to "get better educational results for the money spent."[71] Indeed, the organization shared Plehn's assumption that the problem confronting schools in the state was not the increasing reliance on revenue sources that exacerbated educational disparities between districts, but the way too many districts mishandled existing revenue. The criticism that the state was pushing its burden onto local districts was misguided, according to Talbert and his colleagues. The educator "who continually cries for 'more money for the public schools' is only inviting disaster for the institution he cherishes," Talbert insisted. The entire premise that increased expenditures could produce anything positive for the schools was fatally flawed to Talbert: "The problem of the efficient and economical administration of the schools is one which calls for at least as serious study as the raising of the maximum corn crop per acre. In neither case does the amount of money spent have very much to do with the results. Efficiency comes rather from using the right methods."[72] The evidence connecting increased funding with increased equality of opportunity was perhaps tenuous, but the consequences of the growing reliance on the district property tax were clear. The more the state refused to increase its contribution and the more it refused to redistribute wealth to support schools meant the more it accepted disparities between school districts.

The Science of Education and the Art of Changing the Subject

The rise of the district property tax received a degree of respectability from economic-minded experts like Plehn. It also became increasingly acceptable to some of the most engaged and influential writers on education: the new university-based experts of school administration. Scholars of educational administration challenged inequities in education funding, but they also reinforced the notion that local taxation should play a critical role in state school financing systems. As schools in California became increasingly reliant on the district-level property tax, experts like Ellwood Cubberley framed the state's reduced financial role in education as a model for the nation. While scholars in the emerging fields of public finance and educational administration did not always agree, both disciplines wielded their new forms of expert authority to reinforce and naturalize the inequities of local financing.

Cubberley was one of the most influential of these early scholars, helping to create Stanford University's Education Department and eventual school of education in 1898. He was one of the first scholars to advocate the systematic study of school finance. Starting with the 1905 publication of *School Funds and Their Apportionment*, Cubberley spent much of his career articulating an underlying theory of school finance and using it to inform proposed policies. Unlike Plehn, Cubberley insisted that education was a statewide public good and that consequentially schools must receive funding from the state. Cubberley also insisted that this funding should be used to equalize educational opportunities between communities. In developing his theory of state school support, he contrasted his view of education with growing popular narratives connecting education to local development, contending that "the maintenance of good schools is not, like the maintenance of sewers or streets, a matter of local interest." Instead, Cubberley insisted that education was a "common good."[73] Cubberley's formulation of state school support became influential nationally, prompting one historian to assert that "the theory of state school support began with Cubberley."[74]

Yet while Cubberley was a proponent of state funding and a critic of disparities in education funding, his vision of state funding was also limited, and his work helped create a new theoretical justification for the use of local property taxes to fund education. Even as he called for reformers to challenge the most extreme disparities created by local property taxes, he also created a new theoretical justification for their continued use. In theorizing the need for state support, Cubberley consistently emphasized the importance of local taxes in education, framing the local district tax as an indispensable and essential component of any effective state education system. Throughout his writing, he stressed the need for the state to equalize some educational opportunity by apportioning funds according to need. Need alone, however, should not determine state apportionments, he argued. Instead, he insisted that "local effort" must also be taken into account and rewarded by the state. Indeed, for Cubberley an "equitable division" of state school funds required "reference to local needs and local effort."[75] It was a "wise and generally accepted educational principle," he argued, "[to] distribute aid in such a manner as will not destroy the local taxing instinct." Although he insisted that this principle should not be used to deny help to poor schools, he also viewed the disparities that might develop because of local effort in often-celebratory terms. Cubberley discussed the need for state finance systems to ensure that local communities essentially paid their own way, describing the value of "baits" to encourage local expenditures and concern with any funding scheme that might "place local effort at a discount."[76]

This emphasis on the centrality of local taxes and the value of local efforts to support school finances allowed Cubberley to theorize a public education system that was a "public" and "state system" but financed in ways that nevertheless ensured drastic resource disparities between communities. For critics, the growing use of local property taxes compromised the status of education in California as a public, state system. For Cubberley, public state systems could be truly public and statewide even when they were unequal between districts. This view led him to more broadly dismiss equity as an impossible goal in school finance and education across districts. "Theoretically all the children of the state are equally important and entitled to have the same advantages," Cubberley wrote in a 1920 publication on the history of education, but continued, "Practically this can never be quite true." In case there was any confusion, he insisted that a system redistributing wealth across the entire state to support schooling was totally undesirable:

> If all the cost of education in California were borne by the state as a whole, and paid from the permanent funds, from federal grants, and from a state tax laid on the entire wealth of the state, inequality of maintenance burden could be removed. With such a provision, however, would almost surely go complete control of the schools by the state and so the disappearance of all local responsibility. This has not been accepted as sound social and educational theory in the democratic form of political organization.[77]

Cubberley resolved the contradiction cited by critics, who contended that a system was not statewide nor public if it allowed massive district inequalities to persist, by developing an argument about the way in which the use of local property taxes was a necessary form of democratic, local control.

In his historical scholarship, Cubberley reinforced the notion that reformers should not challenge the underlying source of school funding disparities—local taxation. In 1919, he published a history of education textbook—*Public Education in the United States*—that would shape the way generations of university-trained teachers and school administrators thought about the organization of American schooling. The book itself was designed as a "very practical" guide that could help readers "see the problems of the twentieth century in the light of their historic evolution and the probable lines of their future development."[78] In turn, one of the lessons his history offered readers was that systems of education funding that do not include local taxes are destructive. Reviving Henry Barnard's interpretation of Connecticut's school fund, Cubberley told his readers that once the fund began to produce enough income to cover the costs of education it had "made the people negligent as to taxation" and produced, as a result, "a decline in interest in education in Connecticut." Cubberley warned readers, "From probably the best schools of any State at the end of the colonial period, the Connecticut schools had fallen to a very inferior position."[79] His book became a staple of education courses across the country, selling eighty thousand copies by 1934. Lawrence Cremin observed in 1965 that it remained a popular textbook.

Other early researchers in school finance repeated the notion that the history of Connecticut's school funding illustrated the danger of providing too much equalization aid to schools. Fletcher Harper Swift, an education professor at the University of Minnesota who would eventually join Plehn at the University of California, critiqued the national decline in the share of education funding derived from state governments between 1890 and 1920. He called for the use of state or national revenues to address the "inequalities and ills" produced by local taxation. Still, even as Swift provided a trenchant critique of "the fetish of local support," he assumed the continuance of local financing and called for states or the federal government to provide funding "sufficient to pay large, perhaps indeed the major, portion of school costs."[80] Swift accepted, in turn, the assumption that completely abandoning local financing posed dangers reflected in the history of Connecticut's education system and claimed the state had "nearly ruined her schools (1801–40) by attempting to support them entirely from the process of her permanent school fund."[81]

Cubberley illustrated the limited view of equalization developed by these new experts in school finance with his analysis of California's school funding system, which he wrote with Stanford colleague Jesse Sears for the finance inquiry commission. Cubberley never criticized the growing importance of district property taxes in the state, and as the state's contributions reached historic lows in the 1920s, he praised the California's finance system as a model for the nation. As Cubberley and Sears pointed out in the report, "the costs for education in

California are better equalized than in most states of the Union."[82] At the same time, the authors went out of their way to celebrate the tax reform measures that had initiated the process of declining state support. They praised the separation of sources, insisting that the "segregation of operative property from non-operative property for taxing purposes ... has, in certain respects, been a good thing for the support of education in the state."[83] After considering other alternative methods of support, moreover, they used the report to conclude that California had the best system in place. In the same year that California's proportional share of school revenue across the state dropped to 12 percent—and the share of individual school districts rose to 64 percent—they insisted that there was no better alternative approach to financing the state's schools.[84]

"The present laws for equalizing the burdens of support have been an important contributing element in making long terms and adequate support possible," Sears and Cubberley concluded. The inequality that did exist within the system, they argued, had nothing to do with declining state contributions but was a result of the small size of rural districts. "The chief inequalities still existing are due to the retention of the little school district as a taxing unit."[85] Increasing the size of the poorest districts, rather than challenging the rise of the district property tax, represented the appropriate course of action under their logic.

In discussing school finance in California, experts like Cubberley and Sears directly challenged critics who questioned the state's increasing reliance on the district property tax. Cubberley outright dismissed the criticism that the problem with California's schools related to declining state contributions. Despite the dramatic transformation in the nature of the state's educational finances over the previous ten years, he insisted that the "final structure" of California's financing was more than satisfactory. Larger districts, and not more wealth redistribution between them, was the appropriate course of action in his opinion: "The financial structure of the California school is and for long has been good; the important needs of the state's school system have seemed to your Committee to be rather along the lines of better administrative organization, the provision of a much better type of schools for rural people, the establishment of Junior Colleges, and the further extension of certain parts of the public school system."[86] In casting the issues with schooling in California within these terms, Cubberley directed state policy makers away from trends in declining state support that seemed to disturb more attuned critics like Mark Keppel. In defining the problem confronting the California education system in organizational rather than fiscal terms, Cubberley distracted attention from the network of state policies that had created unprecedented levels of resource inequality between school districts in the first place.

As state policy created these unprecedented forms of inequality between districts, the emerging science of school finance normalized this development. The amount of money spent on schools has never wholly determined the quality of education offered to students. Nonetheless, ideas about who should pay and how much money should be redistributed to fund schools reflected unspoken assumptions about the precise meaning of the public being served by public schools. As educational experts like Ellwood Cubberley played an increasingly important role in spreading and shaping school reform nationally, they helped justify the inequities of the district property tax in California and its persistence in other states.

Legislation

As experts in educational administration and public finance diverted attention with their theoretical justification for the district property tax, they helped ensure that reforms enacted by the California State Legislature would leave unchecked the growing disparities in school funding. By the end of the 1910s, conversations about state education spending in the California legislature were structured around the notion that the state needed to reduce expenses.

The staunchest critics of the state's increased reliance on local taxation for education viewed these calls for "economy" with suspicion. The journalist Franklin Hichborn, for one, detected publicity campaigns designed to "discourage State expenditures"—campaigns "followed by the corporations to keep the fact that they are not bearing their proportionate share of the tax burden from coming up."[87] According to Hichborn, organizations like the Taxpayers Association of California were mere proxies for "corporations that are not paying their share of the tax bill." Yet by 1918 even lawmakers who had been supporters of expanding state spending and social services during the Hiram Johnson administration began to embrace the language of economy and efficiency in state spending. Governor William Stephens called for a complete reorganization of the state government to reduce spending. Senator Herbert C. Jones of San José introduced a resolution to create a special committee to study and propose exactly how to accomplish this goal for schools in 1919.[88]

In creating a committee to study inefficiency in the organization of the state's school system, Jones and his colleagues accepted the definition of California's educational problems offered by experts like Plehn and the Taxpayers Association. The committee and its subsequent legislative proposals were premised on the idea that increasing costs, not declining state contributions, represented the most urgent area of reform for California's schools. In the legislative proposal, Jones framed the group's purpose in terms of economy, starting his proposal with a statement of the problem he wished to address. "The cost of maintenance of the educational system of this state forms the greater part of the public expense and is increasing year by year.... It is desirable that some system shall continue to be year by year within the means of the people." In order to make the system more "economical and efficient," the committee was called to "investigate the plan of education in this state and relations of schools, high schools, normal schools, colleges and universities, and the cost of education."[89] The press understood the committee in terms of an attempt to deal with soaring costs, describing it as a "legislative inquiry as to costs and needs."[90] Indeed, the underlying assumption of the committee was that California's schools were currently too expensive, an interpretation of schooling in the state that seemed to ignore the profound shift in the way the schools were funded and the rapid rise of the district property tax.

By framing the problem confronting the state's schools as one of inefficiencies, Jones was also actively rejecting calls from the California Teachers Association for increased state support. Throughout the 1919 legislative session, members of the teachers' organization offered a powerful, alternative interpretation of the state's educational problems. Calling on their membership to "rally, fight, and win," Keppel demanded that the state's poor rural schools receive increased state support during the 1919 session. Criticizing calls for economy from Governor Stephens, Keppel deplored how "the administration has tended more and more to throw the burden of expense upon the locality, and so to provide UNEQUAL opportunities for schooling among the districts." Keppel also viewed calls for reorganization by figures like Jones and Cubberley as both insufficient and misleading. The entire "rural school problem" conversation was biased, Keppel insisted, because it focused too much on questions of administrative reorganization and not "the real trouble with rural schools, namely, poverty." "The rural schools are entitled to justice," Keppel said.[91]

In organizing his Special Legislative Committee on Education, Senator Jones actively rejected the claim that the growth of district property taxation was the core problem confronting school finance in the state. When the California Teachers Association requested that Jones include a representative of their organization on the committee, he said no.[92] Dismissing the group as a "special interest," Jones instead invited Cubberley to serve as an outside member. Experts like Plehn and organizations like the Taxpayers Association of California may have influenced the way the legislature defined the problem confronting education in California, but it was Cubberley who reinforced the notion that greater economy was needed as part of the solution he proposed. In making its recommendations in its final report, the Special Legislative Committee on Education relied heavily on the emerging science of school finance and administration. In fact, the committee had Cubberley write the entire report, without receiving any oversight from the committee. No one seemed concerned that Cubberley knew very little about the committee and even less about its work. "It will be a bigger job than it appears to you," Cubberley had related in a letter to Jones in agreeing to write the report. "You see I attended no hearings, except one when I spoke, and I have no minutes and no organization for a report."[93] Cubberley persevered, producing his report in a few months and eventually relating to a friend, "The committee was delighted with the report and astounded to find how wise they were and how much they knew."[94]

In drafting the committee's report, Cubberley drew on his previous writing to critique the excesses of the district system without challenging its broader existence. Describing the "rural school problem," Cubberley used sections of the report to criticize the district system and call for the "county unit" of school administration. On the surface, Cubberley's ideas were bold. The report lamented the poverty of many districts and described in detail the ways in which the district system was "expensive, inefficient, short-sighted, and unprogressive."[95] The major problem with the district system, Cubberley explained in the report, was the way it offered better educational opportunities to children in wealthier and more densely populated communities. Under the district system, the report noted, "country girls and boys do not have equivalent advantages with the boys and girls who live in the cities."[96] As an alternative to the district system, Cubberley proposed that the state force rural districts outside of incorporated towns and cities into larger, countywide districts.

Even with this critique, however, Cubberley's recommendation for district consolidation promised to do little to challenge the growing reliance on the district property tax and the resource disparities it produced. While Cubberley's consolidation proposal would have allowed more wealth redistribution within counties, reversing some of the growing educational disparities between communities, his proposal called for only limited forms of consolidation. His reliance on the county unit would have ensured that county-level disparities between wealthy urban and poor rural communities persisted. Moreover, his insistence that incorporated towns and cities should be excluded from consolidation efforts meant that the wealthiest communities would be excluded from consolidation efforts altogether. In Santa Clara County, for example, wealth from Alviso, Gilroy, Los Gatos, Mountain View, Palo Alto, San José, Santa Clara, and Sunnyvale would remain contained within the boundaries of those school districts and not be subject to redistribution under the terms of Cubberley's proposal. Poor communities would come together, but wealthy communities could continue to live apart, hoarding their wealth.

Of course, leaving unchanged the disparities in the property values between districts only matters for district inequality when a state's educational finance system relies heavily on a district property tax. In crafting the committee's report,

Cubberley helped further entrench this approach to financing schools by ignoring the role of declining state contributions in exacerbating resource disparities between districts. He even emphasized the continued importance of the district property tax. While critics viewed any shift in funding from the state to lower governmental levels problematic, Cubberley took no issue with the arrangement of funding sources and the district property tax, skirting broader questions about how much wealth should be redistributed within a state system. "The prime purpose in educational administration," Cubberley declared in a summertime section on funding, "is to spend the money at hand in the most intelligent manner possible."[97] His continued commitment to the local property tax was made even more problematic by the fact that incorporated communities were excluded from the committee's proposal. The plan promised only to consolidate the poorest communities with the lowest property values.

As he drafted his report, Cubberley was well aware that, in the eyes of many, the issue with school funding in the state was not for schools to spend wisely, but for the state to spend more. The chairman of the State Board of Control made this point when he shared the data on taxation and education spending that Cubberley needed for his final report. After examining the history of California's school funding system, the representative from the Board of Control noted the problem that was ignored by policy makers like Jones but criticized by a handful of school administrators: "The striking thing is that the district tax which up to 1908 was only a small fraction of the total need, has mounted to where it exceeds either of the other sources of revenue." The consequences of this trend were growing inequality: "It is apparent that this all tends to an uneven school system in which the resources of certain districts enable them to pay for frills and for salaries on a scale beyond the reach of our average school districts."[98]

With the release of the Special Legislative Committee on Education's final report, even the tepid call for consolidation recommenced by Cubberley seemed to falter. The district consolidation proposal was not included in the legislation introduced by committee members during the next session of the legislature.[99] Senator Jones did introduce a bill related to school district boundaries, but it was a bill designed to help the Palo Alto high school district appropriate taxable property from the Mountain View high school district. In his correspondence with Jones, the president of the Palo Alto Chamber of Commerce called it "our bill." Members of the chamber even had the Palo Alto city attorney draft the final version of the bill that Jones introduced.[100] Of course, the bill was not what Cubberley had in mind when he called for new legislation related to district organization—although it certainly conformed to his observation about how "mistaken conceptions, real-estate ambitions, and an erroneous local pride" tended to prevent progress with school district reorganization.[101]

Two education-funding bills did succeed in the late 1910s and early 1920s, but they lent further legitimacy to the use of the district property tax. The California Teachers Association helped lawmakers pass a bill in 1919 that provided a small increase in state funding.[102] But this did little to alleviate the expansion of district-level funding and growing disparities.[103] Even with the increase, California's public schools faced a crisis by the fall of 1920. Over six hundred schools were unable to open that fall because of low property values and the difficulty of attracting teachers given the meager salaries that these poorer districts could muster. The editors of the *Marin Journal* made clear to readers the long-term trends that were responsible for the situation: "The reason for this condition lies in the fact that the state is no longer bearing its just share of the burden of school support."[104]

Other legislation increasing state support only helped to further entrench local financing—while refocusing conversations about education funding within the state. Working in collaboration with the California Teachers Association, voters introduced a funding referendum in 1920. Although it, and a subsequent legislative bill that raised the corporate tax rate to generate revenue as called for in the referendum, managed to pass, the related electoral and legislative campaigns around the referendum helped expand and consolidate the influence of groups like the Taxpayers Association of California that sought to recast the problem of education funding as one of inefficiency.

As the legislature debated a corporate tax increase for education in 1921, experts like Plehn and Cubberley again helped support the notion that schools were spending too much. As legislation to lessen the role of the district property tax in the state's school system was drafted, what one journalist called a "billion-dollar lobby" descended on the state capital.[105] This effort worked to ensure that more and more voters would see the problem of school funding not as one of insufficient state financial support to education but instead a continued need for schools to reduce spending and make local taxation more efficient. Plehn became a paid lobbyist and worked to convince lawmakers that an increase in the corporate tax rate would be a mistake because schools were spending too much money already.[106] The Taxpayers Association of California increased its publicity campaign against school spending as well. By 1920, Cubberley was listed as a delegate for the association, and its periodicals cited his work to argue against increased state support for schools.[107] By the early 1930s Cubberley would also serve as a standing adviser to the educational commission of the California Taxpayers Association, a successor organization founded in 1926.[108]

In the end, even the successful referendum to increase state school support and subsequent legislation to pay for it did little to reverse the growth of district property taxation. The increased state funding did not keep pace with inflation or population growth. By 1925, only 12 percent of the money spent on schools in the state was derived from redistributive state sources. Sixty-four percent was derived from district taxes, with the rest derived from county sources.[109] The continued growth of the district property tax itself seemed to reinforce the vocal campaigns by the California Taxpayers Association to reduce education spending. Many residents in the state were doubtless already inclined to consider education spending as being inseparable from the growth of the district property tax. Since the district tax was highly visible to voters and more likely to draw attention to local spending than other tax instruments, such as an income tax, proponents of the tax have long touted as a virtue its tendency to inspire taxpayers to revolt against it.

Public and Unequal

The rise of the district property tax in California was nationally significant, shaping the nature of school finance across the country. As an experiment in public finance, California's 1910 separation of funding sources amendment served as a national model and came to shape public finance in other states. Historians like Jon Teaford and Ajay K. Mehrotra contend that one of the reasons for the spread of finance changes designed to "separate sources" of revenue between local and state governments was their early success in California.[110] Plehn's language about how the benefits of public schooling "redound distinctly, directly, and peculiarly to the benefit of local property owners" took on a life of its own, sneaking its way into tax commission studies from states as distant as Nebraska and Arkansas.[111]

More significant, perhaps, was the way California's shift toward the district property tax developed alongside a growing national conversation about the appropriate role of state governments in school finance and the principle of equalization. California's approach to funding for elementary schools in the late nineteenth century represented an alternative to a system that was highly unequal and rarely allowed money to freely flow across school district boundaries. It was not California's alternative model that gathered the attention of other states, however. Instead, it was when the state's school districts were relying most heavily on the district property tax that figures like Cubberley touted it as a national model. Not only did emerging experts in school finance like Cubberley create a theoretical justification for the use of the district property tax by associating it with democratic local control, they also created a justification by ignoring and misrepresenting its recent vintage in California. By the time the Educational Finance Inquiry Commission reached California in 1924, the proportion of school expenditures funded by sources that could be redistributed across school district boundaries was at an unprecedented, historic low. Nevertheless, Cubberley and Sears framed the commission's final report in glowing terms, describing California's new finance structure as the best in the union and a model for other states.[112] In the end, Cubberley did not simply limit the potential for future change in California—he helped contain and prevent a more equitable approach to school financing, and a more capacious conception of what it meant to have a public education system, from gaining traction in the early twentieth century.

6
THE ART OF ADDRESSING INEQUALITY WHILE EXPANDING IT, 1928–1950

Lawmakers made a policy choice by connecting education funding with California's uneven economic and racial geography in the 1910s and 1920s. They continued to make that choice throughout the 1930s and 1940s, even as Californians expanded the role of national and state government in other areas of social policy during the New Deal and, later, the administration of Governor Earl Warren. This chapter traces the consequences those choices held for the further racial, economic, and political fragmentation of California.

As lawmakers grew the role of local financing in California's public school system during the 1930s and 1940s, they helped entrench and subsidize stark patterns of spatial inequality. Historians have already told the story of the patterns themselves and how public policy created them. Indeed, the role of federal policy makers in shaping metropolitan inequality through areas such as banking, housing, and transportation is an overarching theme in postwar historical scholarship. The importance of education policies in shaping both residential segregation and the dynamics of white homeowner politics amid battles over desegregation has been central to this work in more recent years as well.[1] Alongside older histories narrating the rise and fall of big-city school systems, more recent suburban and metropolitan histories of educational inequality in the second half of the twentieth century bring into view a host of education policies connected to growing educational inequalities along racial, economic, and spatial lines after World War II.[2]

But the place of education funding and the related world of taxation and school districting sits at the periphery of most histories discussing educational inequality. Resource disparities, to be sure, are palpable in most accounts. But why they exist and how they operate in practice are not. Instead, these clear resource inequalities are described more as accidents of biased policy making in other areas, not the symptoms of deliberate and deeply rooted lawmaking, place making, and tax avoidance traced throughout this book. This chapter argues that well-known patterns of educational inequality cannot be understood in full without also considering how the localization of school finance functioned in practice to structure inequality, or how decisions into the 1930s and 1940s embedded, rationalized, and to an extent concealed this sprawling and very much still intact world of unequal lawmaking.

This chapter places areas of state lawmaking, minimized in many postwar accounts, at the center. It is organized into two thematic sections that trace how education funding and taxation policies helped create the spatial and fiscal infrastructure upon which the patterns of the racially, economically, and spatially fragmented postwar public school were built. The first section examines the mechanics of the district-level property tax in practice. Starting in the 1930s and moving into the postwar era, the section illustrates how the tax functioned on multiple levels to structure inequality. It did more than simply connect unequal land values with educational provision. It helped create a sprawling and largely hidden welfare state for wealthy whites that allowed the state's corporations and banks to minimize the taxes they paid, provided massive benefits to suburbanites living in white-only subdivisions, and exacted punitive fiscal burdens on low-income renters, especially low-income renters of color already locked into a racially biased rental market by public and private actors. The second section of this chapter shows how these structural inequalities were rationalized in public discourse in part through narratives concealing the state's role in their creation. Reform during the Great Depression and the administration of Governor Earl Warren during the 1940s recast funding disparities as the product of uneven development and school district boundaries as having been drawn by geological processes (e.g., based on mountains or rivers) rather than by lawmakers intent on dividing people, wealth, and opportunity. This narrative sleight of hand directed attention away from the state policies that gave school district boundaries their salience. The narrow conceptualization of inequality they created was critical for cementing and sustaining structural inequalities in education in later years.

How the District-Level Tax Structured Spatial Inequality

At the most basic level, the decision by lawmakers to localize education funding was a decision to carve up the taxable wealth of California into a checkerboard of unequal tax bases. Setting aside the ways in which state action was partially responsible for some school districts having more taxable wealth than others, it was still state funding policies that linked unequal tax bases to public school funding.

Local financing, though, did much more than connect unequal tax bases with education funding. As lawmakers further expanded district-level school taxes, they created a sprawling system of redistribution that functioned in multiple, intersecting ways: as a mechanism for conditioning education funding on race; as a subsidy for segregated development; as an extractive tax on low-income renters of color; as a sprawling hidden welfare state for white suburbanites; and, finally, as a way for banks and corporations to minimize their tax liabilities and push the cost of government onto others. This section explores each of these dimensions.

Subsidizing the Segregated Subdivision

Localized funding reinforced state and federal policies facilitating segregated development. The sheer number of governmental policies that shaped suburbanization and ensured that it divided metropolitan regions by race and class is astonishing. Federal defense spending in California and across the Sun Belt facilitated suburban development.[3] State and federal investments in transportation encouraged suburban sprawl. State and federal courts allowed developers to use racially restrictive covenants, upholding and enforcing them as legal contracts through the late 1940s. Formally race-neutral land-use policies and planning practices rooted in state law supported racial and economic segregation beyond racially restrictive covenants. The federal government structured the creation of a mortgage market that made it profitable for banks to lend money to white homeowners and risky to lend money to people of color. Through Federal Housing Authority and Veterans Administration mortgage insurance programs, the federal government underwrote white homeownership on a massive scale while simultaneously defining people of color, as historian David Freund observed, "as a calculable, actuarial risk to white owned property."[4]

For white homeowners in federally subsidized suburbs, local property taxation also minimized their tax burden. They could accumulate wealth in the value of their subsidized home and protect that wealth from taxation that would have gone to support the education of children outside their district. Under the state- and county-based school finance system dismantled in the 1910s and 1920s, these suburbanites would have had to share in the cost of educating students across a much broader geographic scale. Now the concentration of taxable wealth within individual school districts permitted those districts to lower their rates. As with any tax, the total amount of money produced by property taxes depends on the amount of wealth being taxed. If the total valuation of all the real estate in a school district is $5 million, a tax rate of $1 per $100 of assessed valuation will produce $50,000. If the total valuation of that real estate is only $1 million, however, a tax rate of $1 per $100 of assessed valuation will only produce $10,000. Localized funding thus allowed white homeowners to pay a lower share of their home's value—and often their income—on property taxes. Studies of tax incidence during these years confirm this pattern. One national study from the 1950s found, for example, that the property tax rates of cities were almost universally higher than the rates of the suburbs that surrounded them.[5]

The localization of school funding also allowed white suburbanites to create high-spending schools despite their lower tax burden. For example, one Alameda County newspaper explained the mechanism behind these dynamics, which most readers knew quite well: "assessed valuation per student is the controlling factor on district [tax] rates."[6] The paper offered as an example the San Pablo Elementary School District in Richmond. As Richmond became a predominately Black city, the district began educating more and more Black students. Residents of the district found themselves paying more and more for schools, even as the incomes of Black residents were already constrained by employment discrimination. By the early 1950s, the district had a total assessed valuation of $3,129 per pupil, and a tax rate of $1.44 per $100 in assessed valuation. Nearby Briones Valley, in contrast, had $79,739 in assessed valuation per pupil, twenty-five times more than the San Pablo Elementary School District. At $0.60 per $100, Briones Valley had the lowest tax rate in the county. Yet Briones Valley spent more than double what San Pablo Elementary spent on its students.[7] This meant a home with an assessed value of $20,000 in a place like Briones Valley brought with it both a lower tax burden and access to schools spending more per pupil than a home with an assessed value of $20,000 in the San Pablo Elementary School District.

Disparate property tax rates compounded spatial advantage and disadvantage over time. White homeowners saw the value of their homes increase as a result of the money their taxes generated for nearby schools. This was particularly true as postwar Americans purchased homes "for the schools," a practice with a long history in California that further intensified in these years, just as it did elsewhere.[8] In turn, increases in the value of homes could support even lower tax rates and even higher levels of spending on education—a cycle of advantage structured by state policies.

Lower tax rates were particularly useful for attracting further development amid industrial dispersal and movement away from cities, further lowering tax burdens for white suburbanites. As historian Robert Self has detailed regarding the suburbs around Oakland in the postwar era, suburban communities sought to have their cake and eat it too, competing for taxable wealth via mixed residential and commercial development that could underwrite their tax bills.[9] The localization of school finance made the entire dynamic possible, especially since schools constituted the largest share of state and local government spending by far.

These dynamics subsidized profit for real estate developers as well, offering an additional way for them to market, sell, and profit from the entwined public investments that enabled both suburban sprawl and racially segregated housing. As noted in chapter 4, state education funding policies subsidized suburban and urban city building from the start. Through the expansion of local financing during the 1930s and 1940s, geographic variation in educational resources grew, and that variation allowed real estate developers to advertise particular school districts in their promotional material. Advertisements would emphasize how a particular subdivision was covered by racial restrictions and was contained within a particular school district, selling racial exclusion and the public school simultaneously. For example, advertisements for a subdivision called Plantation Acres in Sonoma County emphasized both racial restrictions and access to an established school district, and Vista de Vallejo in Solano County promised "protective building and racial restrictions, combined with exceptional advantages for schools and play."[10]

Promoting Racial Exclusion through District Boundaries

Together with racially segregated development, localized funding created a mechanism for conditioning the distribution of educational resources on race. To fully appreciate how this worked, it is important to first consider the various mechanisms policy makers had used to segregate children and resources by race before local financing became widespread. California's multiracial context shaped these mechanisms as well as the civil rights activism to dismantle them. Indeed, the state's multiple color lines meant that efforts to condition educational resources on race were subject to multiple, successful civil rights challenges. In response, white officials in the state explicitly pursued a color-blind language that could sustain legal challenges even as it directly led to racial inequities in education. Localized funding and school district boundary manipulation created a legal framework, financial incentive, and raceless language to rationalize such policy making.

Education officials had already experimented with a variety of strategies for distributing resources unequally within individual school systems, as described in earlier chapters. But creating separate, segregated school buildings within districts and allocating fewer resources to school buildings serving children of color had been attacked on various fronts by the early twentieth century. As noted in chapter 3, in the early 1880s, Black activists succeeded in making it illegal to segregate Black students within districts. As noted in chapter 4, after an international incident, Japanese families and the Japanese government helped make it illegal—under international treaty—for San Francisco to segregate Japanese students.[11] Starting in the 1910s, local school officials began creating separate schools for children of Mexican ancestry within individual districts and providing those schools a smaller share of state, county, and local funds.[12] The San Dimas School District, for example, built a small, crude frame building behind its elementary schools that children of Mexican ancestry were forced to attend around the First World War.[13] Santa Paula operated both a Mexican and an Anglo (white) school with vastly disparate resources.[14]

But after Mexican American residents organized and successfully challenged these segregationist practices, white officials were forced to experiment with nonracial explanations for segregation as early as the 1910s. Santa Paula in Ventura County, for example, created separate schools for Mexican American and Mexican national students around 1910. The Mexican American community enlisted the help of the Mexican government to challenge this separation, and in 1914, the Mexican government filed a formal complaint with the California governor against Santa Paula and several other school districts for discriminating against children with Mexican heritage.[15] State superintendent William Wood was instructed to complete an investigation. His report claimed that any segregation was not based on race or nationality, but because the separated Mexican American children "had no knowledge of the English language" or resided in a school district where "practically all the children are Mexicans."[16]

Similar narratives about educational differences were adopted by white school officials across the state, many of whom had probably read Wood's rationalization. As historian Gilbert Gonzalez has pointed out, "the legal justification for segregating Mexican children generally rested upon educational, not racial grounds."[17] Throughout the 1920s, local school officials, often with support from university-based educational experts also working to rationalize localized funding, claimed that Mexican American students were deficient and in need of special instruction.[18] These claims were used to justify separate, underfunded schools where Mexican American children were funneled into restrictive academic tracks, impacting their rates of high school graduation. The implications for their experiences in an already biased labor market were far-reaching, as educational credentials became increasingly central to the structure of that market.[19] These "openly racist, ethnocentric claims of inferior intelligence, language, and culture" were remarkably consistent over time.[20]

Attempts to rationalize segregation in what one commentator called a more "tactful" manner were a response to incidents like one in Santa Barbara County where a school district's attempt to segregate Mexican American students explicitly by race was followed by legal uncertainty and criticism. In 1929, officials in the Carpinteria Union School District denied Fred Montoya's children admission to their zoned school and instructed them to attend a nearby Indigenous school.[21] Montoya sued, prompting the district to request an opinion from the state attorney general. Initially, the attorney general ruled that the district had "no authority in the laws of California for the establishment of separate schools for Mexicans"—while at the same time offering a race-neutral strategy for the district to pursue instead, noting that "special class hours could be legally established for the convenience of Mexican or other children who work on farms," though "such school must not be limited to Mexicans only."[22] The district appealed the decision, pointing to the section of the state's school code still permitting separate schools for Indigenous children. The attorney general issued a revised opinion the following year, ruling that "Indians who have come to the United States from Mexico" could be segregated. Commentators estimated that the ruling covered least 85 percent of Mexican children, as they could be deemed "Indian," and suggested it could be a legal avenue for segregation given the "difficulty of Mexicans obtaining proof of their ancestry" to prove that they were not Indigenous. Still, state officials were also publicly apprehensive about the ruling. A similar case was working its way through the courts at the same time, regarding the applicability of the school segregation statute to Filipino Americans, given the state's interracial marriage ban and the classification of Filipino Americans as "Mongolian" in the same education statute. One unnamed state official felt the opinion on segregating Mexican pupils was "dynamite" that would likely produce further legal contestation while "the Filipino situation" was in its "present chaotic condition."[23] Other commentators critiqued Carpinteria Union School District officials for not using a subtler approach to segregating Mexican American children. The *Santa Paula Chronicle*, for example, critiqued Carpinteria officials by noting how in Santa Paula city "the Mexican situation is handled in a tactful manner."[24]

Justifications for segregation rooted in purported educational differences were easier to defend, but they were increasingly vulnerable to challenge by civil rights organizers as well. And claims about culture, namely that such students had cultural deficiencies or needed to be Americanized, and therefore should be separated, were successfully challenged in the early 1930s. While the ruling was narrower in scope and not as far-reaching as a subsequent ruling in the 1940s, it further shaped the terms upon which white officials had to think about creating racial inequality and the viability of inequitably distributing educational resources within school districts. In 1931, the Lemon Grove School District was forced to abandon its effort to create a new, crude school building—more barn than building—to segregate Mexican American children. The proposal would have blatantly disinvested resources that would have gone to Mexican American children, directing those resources to reduce the class sizes of white students instead. Mexican American parents organized and, with support from the Mexican consul, hired two attorneys and sued the district. The district's claim that they were intending to segregate Mexican American students based on their need to learn English and other deficiencies was rejected by the court after the testimony of Mexican American students made clear to the judge and everyone else watching the trial the dubiousness of that claim.[25]

In the 1940s, a landmark case on the segregation of Mexican American students in Orange County called *Mendez v. Westminster* ruled Mexican children to be white, further limiting how white officials could justify segregating Mexican American students and resources. To maintain separation, some districts turned toward creating separate classes within their schools; others turned toward manipulating attendance zones to link residential segregation as closely as possible to school segregation.[26] Districts were also forced to consider legal challenges after the state finally passed a law repealing the education statute that had permitted the segregation of "Indian children or children of Chinese, Japanese, or Mongolian parentage."[27] Officials became more sensitive to their legal vulnerability. Los Angeles Unified School District, for example, instructed employees not to share any information about students or make comments about race, and eventually prohibited officials from maintaining any records about student race.[28] Pasadena School District was in an older city without racial covenants in housing and had therefore used an elaborate transfer and construction policy to maintain segregated schools. Worried they might be sued by the NAACP, the district consulted the Los Angeles County Council and, out of a concern for their legal vulnerability, reversed course.[29]

Indeed, elaborate systems of student transfers, school siting decisions, and elementary school zoning used to segregate schools that served students from integrated neighborhoods were widespread.[30] But they were also increasingly challenged in court by both Mexican American and Black students, their families, and civil rights activists. Though they would receive their most far-reaching legal challenge after *Brown v. Board of Education*, the use of transfer policies to supplement segregated attendance boundaries was successfully overturned by Mexican and Black community activists in Southern California in the 1930s. The Monrovia School District, for example, had forced Black and Mexican students to attend a decrepit elementary school building condemned by the state architect while allowing white students from the same neighborhood to transfer to another school. Black and Mexican families refused to send their children to school and were eventually brought to court for truancy. Represented by the NAACP, they then sued the Monrovia district and were successful.[31] The linking of attendance zones with residential segregation were key targets for civil rights activists in the years after *Brown*. The tangible inequities created the kind of evidence civil rights attorneys could use to undermine claims about the innocence of school officials in creating such de facto patterns of segregation. Districts including Pasadena, Los Angeles, and San Francisco faced desegregation rulings. In 1963, the California Supreme Court declared individual school systems responsible for desegregation, regardless of the cause.[32]

Another strategy that allowed white officials to largely evade legal culpability for segregation was moving the actual boundaries of school systems. Given the establishment of localized funding and segregated development, boundary movement allowed those officials to shift dollars and tax burdens as well. Some districts had embraced the logic early. San José, for example, evaded the US-Japan treaty restricting segregation of Japanese American pupils by creating a separate school district.[33] Similarly, a 1920 boundary change wherein the Ontario School District annexed a white section of the Cucamonga district was successful even amid Mexican American activism against segregation. The county superintendent was explicit, however, that she approved the change because it would segregate the district. "Unless such annexation to the Ontario district is made," she explained, "the children will have to attend what is commonly termed a Mexican school in Cucamonga."[34] Such efforts were rarely challenged in court and even to this day have legal protection in the absence of blatant declarations that the intent of officials in moving the boundary is to segregate children by race.

Localized funding, then, allowed affluent white cities and suburbs to hoard educational resources, withdrawing from what would have been a shared public school project with other residents of their county and the state. It also allowed them to condition the distribution of educational resources on race, a persistent feature of public education systems in many states today. As the final section of this chapter discusses as well, much of the movement and reorganizing of districts that unfolded in California during these years was structured, encouraged, and driven by the education reform agenda of California governor Earl Warren. The state, in the name of equalizing opportunity, worked to segregate it further.

The Exploitative Nature of Local Property Tax

As lawmakers subsidized suburban city building and white affluence, school funding policies also functioned as a punitive tax on low-income renters, a growing share of them people of color locked out of federally underwritten homeownership for white suburbanites. Localized funding and economically segregated development meant lower-income homeowners paid more for less in education funding. The local property tax was most exploitative, though, as it was passed on to renters. Here people of color confronted an already biased and extractive rental market. Studies of property tax incidence of this period further show that they also faced the highest tax burdens in the state even as the schools they financed were increasingly underfunded.

The rental housing market was already notoriously exploitative and discriminatory for people of color. The US Commission on Civil Rights had concluded the rental market was more biased and exclusionary than the blatantly racist home-purchase market structured by biased lending policies such as redlining. The commission described "the rental situation for Negroes and other non-Caucasians" as worse than the home market, finding that "even owners who will sell to Negroes will not rent to them."[35]

The increased reliance of school systems on local property tax dollars to fund their operation helped create and exacerbate the exploitative and discriminatory nature of the rental housing market for people of color. While property owners were technically the party responsible for local property tax payments, studies analyzing the incidence of local property taxes during these years reveal that landlords passed those costs on to renters. One study found, for example, that over 90 percent of the property taxes levied in urban areas were paid by housing occupants, even when those occupants were renters. The author found that most families residing in cities were paying property taxes "via their rents." While homeowners and landlords could qualify for a series of federal and state tax benefits to offset property tax bills, renters could not. One study of the impact of passing property tax costs onto renters found that landlords (many of whom were already having their property tax bill effectively subsidized by the federal and state income tax code) essentially created a tax on rental housing that was so high a rate that it was comparable only to the taxes levied on alcohol and tobacco.[36] Rates on alcohol and tobacco were set intentionally high, often conceptualized as a punishment for vice and sometimes called sin taxes. The turn toward local property taxation for school funding was, then, essentially a sin tax charged to renters where the sin, for many renters, was not being white enough to receive a low-cost home underwritten by the federal government.

The property tax was also quite regressive. One study found, for example, that individuals making over $15,000 in annual income (around $150,000 in 2022 dollars) paid 1.4 percent of their income in direct or indirect (via rent) property tax payments. In contrast, individuals making less than $2,000 (around $20,355 in 2022 dollars) were paying 8.5 percent of their income in property taxes. Table 6.1 displays these patterns in 2022 dollars.

TABLE 6.1 Estimates of property tax burden passed to renters

INCOME (2022 DOLLARS)	ESTIMATE OF PROPERTY TAXES ON HOUSING AS A PERCENT OF INCOME
Less than $20,355	8.5
$20,355 to $30,533	3.9
$30,534 to $40,710	3.0
$40,711 to $50,888	2.5
$50,889 to $71,243	2.1
$71,244 to $101,776	1.8
$101,777 to $152,665	1.6
Over $152,665	1.4

Source: Data adapted from Dick Netzer, *Impact of the Property Tax: Its Economic Implications for Urban Problems* Supplied by National Commission on Urban Problems to Joint Economic Committee, Congress of the United States (Washington, DC: US Government Printing Office, 1968), 19. Expressed in 2022 dollars using Consumer Price Index (CPI-U) as of September 13, 2022, from the US Department of Labor Bureau of Labor Statistics.

A Hidden Welfare State for Homeowners

It was easy for lawmakers to conceal the ways that local taxation for public schools subsidized white suburbanites because of the indirect ways it operated. Localized funding created an additional branch in a sprawling system of subsidy. It also functioned as an underappreciated part of what political scientist Christopher Howard has aptly labeled a "hidden welfare state" created through tax benefits.[37] That welfare state comes into even clearer view, in turn, in considering who actually paid local taxes for schools and who did not.

Indeed, a portion of the property tax revenue raised by school districts each year was paid by the federal and state government through special tax benefits embedded in the state and federal income tax code. By design, this subsidy was not available to renters. Moreover, the magnitude of the benefit it offered increased with the wealth of the taxpayer it benefited. With the establishment of California's state income tax in 1935, property owners were given the ability to deduct their property tax payments from their taxable income. This provision mirrored the benefit offered to homeowners in the federal income tax code through the state and local tax deduction. For taxpayers who itemized their deductions, removing their property tax payments from their taxable income reduced the amount of state and federal income tax they were required to pay on that income. The itemization of deductions only makes sense when the deductions taken exceed the standard deduction. For this reason, these tax benefits have always skewed toward higher-income taxpayers.

This benefit cost the government in forgone revenue, effectively making it the equivalent of a direct expenditure. The chairman of the House Ways and Means

Committee explained this clearly when he described how these provisions in the tax code have "precisely the same effect on the budget as an outright expenditure. The only difference is they appear as a negative receipt rather than as an expenditure."[38] Since tax benefits like these typically escape the same level of scrutiny as direct expenditures, even though they do impact the budget, it was easier to expand them and evade critiques of government spending.

These tax benefits were also quite regressive. The higher the tax rate levied against a taxpayer, the larger the amount of revenue forgone by the reduction in a taxpayers' stated income from the deduction. For example, a $1,000 property tax bill deducted from a tax return reduces state and federal revenues by whatever amount would have been collected in income tax from that additional $1,000. Since, all else being equal, each dollar deducted would have been taxed at the marginal tax rate for a given taxpayer, a dollar deducted by the top income bracket is always subsidized at a higher rate than a dollar deducted from a lower income bracket. Consider an example of the most extreme form the subsidy for that $1,000 tax bill could have taken for a taxpayer charged the highest income tax rates in 1945: effectively 6 percent for the state income tax and 94 percent for the federal income tax, assuming the taxpayer filed as head of household. If this tax filer deducted a $1,000 tax payment to a local school district, the state of California would subsidize $60 of that district tax bill since, without the deduction, those dollars would have been treated as income and taxed accordingly. Moreover, the federal subsidy would amount to $940 because of the rate at which that income would have been taxed as well. From the perspective of this tax filer, then, this state and federal tax benefit meant the entire $1,000 paid in school taxes had been returned to the filer by the state and federal government. And from the perspective of the state and federal budgets, there was $1,000 less in revenue. Without disaggregated data on itemized deductions, it is not possible to systematically determine the magnitude of the subsidy at the time, but this subsidy's operation in later years shows that indirect federal investments in local district taxes through these tax benefits were substantially larger than direct federal spending for education.[39]

An even more direct form of this hidden welfare state emerged through a state provision exempting veterans who owned homes from local property taxes. As authorized by the GI Bill, the Veterans Administration (VA) guaranteed federally backed mortgage loans for returning veterans. The program allowed white veterans to purchase homes with a low-interest mortgage loan and without a down payment. But veterans of color, especially Black veterans, were systematically denied these benefits. As David Freund points out, the VA "rapidly expanded the government's role in creating finance capital for the purchase of privately owned homes," but the program also "guaranteed very few loans to racial minorities and refused to back loans for blacks buying homes in white neighborhoods."[40] In the region around New York City, for example, of the first sixty-seven thousand loans guaranteed by the VA, fewer than one hundred went to veterans of color.[41] The same pattern unfolded in California, where the subsidies for white veterans were compounded, in that they were exempt from property taxes. Denied access to VA- and Federal Housing Authority–backed mortgages, veterans of color were effectively precluded from taking any of these benefits and therefore more likely to rent housing and instead pay taxes via rent.

Distributing Wealth Upward

All these features of localized financing distributed wealth upward and contributed to racial and economic fragmentation in housing. It is important not to miss, however, how the rise of local financing represented a shift in tax burdens across the state, part of the continued shift in who was contributing money for schools that the state raised directly. That money came less and less from banks, corporations, and higher-income residents—and more and more from a sales tax. Reformers had long hoped that a large share of state education funding would come from taxes on banks and corporations. Local financing, however, limited how much the state taxed to support its schools and whom the state asked to pay taxes directly to it for state spending in general. Indeed, state fiscal policies lowered the relative tax burden facing banks and corporations within the state over time. In 1939, for example, banks and corporations paid 5 percent of their net income as tax in California. By 1948, this figure had declined to 3.3 percent.

Since education was the largest area of combined state and local spending, changes to how school districts were funded shaped changes in the entire tax structure of the state. Public service corporations were not subject to local property taxes until the separation of sources was abolished in 1935, so increased reliance on local property taxes for education helped shift the entire cost of state and local government away from banks and public service corporations and toward individual taxpayers. By 1932, the relative tax burden for all levels of government was higher for individuals than it was for corporations. That year, California's Tax Research Bureau found that residents across the state paid, on average, $2.14 per $100 of property valuation in taxes, while the tax burden of corporations was substantially lower. For example, taxpayers in Alameda paid $2.78 per $100 in value, while public utilities companies paid only $1.54. Oil companies and gas and electric companies in the state had particularly low tax burdens, with the average taxpayer in fourteen counties paying more than twice as much on $100 of wealth as they did.[42] Synthesizing developments in California taxation during the 1920s and early 1930s, reporter Franklin Hichborn recalled the "disproportionate rates" and "utter helplessness of the home owner, farmer and small tax payers" in confronting those rates during the lean years of the Great Depression.[43]

Changes in the rate at which banks and corporations were taxed to fund state government paralleled changes in the rate at which incomes were taxed during those years. Consider income tax rates on personal income. In the first seven years after the personal income tax was instituted in 1935, the tax rate applied to each dollar of net income above $250,000 was 15 percent. In 1943, however, that rate was reduced to 6 percent and remained there for the rest of the decade. The income tax brackets became less progressive, too. Between 1935 and 1942, income tax rates varied across fifteen tax brackets. Those with more income could afford to pay more in taxes on that income, and the rates reflected this fact. Individuals making more than $30,000 in net income were charged between 7 and 15 percent, depending on how much more than $30,000 they made. From 1943 to 1948, however, incomes above $30,000 were taxed at a single rate of 6 percent. This meant families with a net income of $30,001, $200,000, or $1 million were all taxed at the same rate. In 1949, rates were increased for two brackets—both below $30,000. The rate on net incomes between $5,000 and $10,000 were increased from 1 to 2 percent, and the rate on net incomes between $25,000 and $30,000 increased to 6 percent. This meant that for each dollar earned above $25,000, the income tax rate was 6 percent, whether those dollars were part of a net income of $25,001 or $1,000,000.[44]

These changing rates reflected a further shifting of the tax burden. Declining income tax rates were not the product of economic growth and increased absolute tax revenue alone. Indeed, the relative share of the state budget derived from income taxes declined during these years and was replaced by increases in sales tax. The Warren administration in the early 1940s found that revenues had increased because of the dramatic increase in the state's population. In response, Governor Warren worked with the legislature to decrease the upper tax rate on high incomes and modestly reduce the sales tax. The change did little to reverse the broader tax shift taking place, leading as it did to a greater fraction of revenue coming from the poorest Californians. As one critic of the change explained in a Bakersfield paper, "Governor Warren has done little to relieve the tax burden of the small taxpayer." Instead, the writer noted, he has "made very large contributions to the large taxpayers," especially because the "sales tax reduction will not mean much either."[45]

In sum, the shift toward the use of local taxation to finance public education was effectively a mechanism for the state to subsidize white affluence and redistribute wealth upward. In both a technical and theoretical sense, it was an instrument of statecraft whose magnitude and impact are misunderstood—especially when it is called a local tax, since, in the affluent, white, federally subsidized suburb, it was neither local nor a tax. As a result of a network of state and federal tax policies, far fewer white suburbanites actually paid the tax than historians have realized. In operation, it was more like a federal and state grant to white suburban schools that, unlike programs such as Title I, was subject to neither regular scrutiny nor needed to be justified by dubious claims that children of color were deficient and in need of separate, specialized programs. It was much more of a tax raised and spent locally when it was encountered by poorer Californians residing in metropolitan regions, especially renters who were, by design, people of color. As it was encountered by renters, the rate of the tax, too, was so high that simply calling it regressive does not seem to do it justice. Indeed, "regressive" is too technical a word to capture the way it operated almost like a form of punishment.

Obfuscation and Rationalization: Tax Shifting and Racist Policy as Problems of Development

White suburbanites used the localization of school finance to provide an ideological justification for the racial and economic apartheid in public schooling from which they benefited, allowing them to claim that they funded their higher-spending schools with their own money. Even today, public discussions of school finance tend to reinforce this logic by obscuring the way localized funding is structured by the state and operates in racialized ways, as a subsidy for the wealthy and a punitive tax for the poor. This is because the dollars raised and spent for education are talked about as local dollars raised for local schools, even as public commentators also insist that public schools are state institutions with a national mission to serve the common good. This narrow conceptualization of who controls the state's public schools, who furnishes the dollars that fund them, and how widely—or narrowly—the benefits of an institution with an ostensibly common purpose are shared is itself a historical creation, a way of seeing the role of state policy in school funding that was cultivated during the 1930s and 1940s. This section traces how popular narratives rationalized the inequities created by localized funding by concealing the hand of the state in structuring those inequities. The section focuses, in particular, on how these narratives shaped two moments of reform during the Great Depression and World War II where challenges to this logic were raised but ultimately served to further entrench inequity.

State Policy, or Local Problems to Be Solved by Local Taxpayers?

In the early 1930s, the early years of the New Deal, there were calls to expand the functions of state and federal governments. But representatives from the

California Taxpayers Association (CTA) worked to limit the scope of taxation and school funding reform by seeking to further embed the logic of localized funding into the way public education and taxation were discussed, building on the narratives discussed in chapter 5.[46] At the heart of this logic was a free-market narrative that rationalized funding disparities by concealing the hand of the state in their creation—a narrative that reframed inequities in educational resources as a local problem of local taxes. In shifting public conversations about school finance away from questions of overall state tax burdens, representatives of the Taxpayers Association also helped limit the tax burden of the corporations whose leaders founded, funded, and directed the organization.

The narrative promoted by the CTA centered on the claim that school funding disparities were caused by inefficiencies in district organization and were best addressed through local changes to school district boundaries via consolidation. In reframing school funding disparities as a problem of local taxes, local schools, and local development—and notably *not* stemming from the changes in tax policy in the state—representatives of the association erased the role of public policy in structuring localized funding. By extension, they worked to popularize the claim that funding was a local issue, and therefore "local taxpayers should solve local problems."[47] The ideological crux of the narrative was that funding schools through district tax bases allowed a free market in real estate to function as a rising tide lifting all boats. Such a market, members of the association claimed, would allow local residents to equalize funding on their own through district reorganization encouraged by the state but driven by local decision makers. Bradford Trenham, the group's lead education researcher, asserted that this market, on its own, "would iron out inequality."[48] Ellwood Cubberley echoed this language in the talks he delivered on behalf of the group. When he joined Trenham for a speaking tour in 1929, Cubberley told audiences how "the savings that naturally accrues" from consolidation would equalize funding since they would "more than pay for better educational opportunities."[49]

Where members of the CTA did acknowledge the state's hand in school finance, it was to criticize state funding for poorer rural districts. Indeed, members of the organization claimed that, through its aid to poorer districts, the state was encouraging waste and creating disincentives for change, preventing local taxpayers from solving "local problems." Trenham insisted the state provided millions "to pygmy schools in the form of a bonus to remain small and inefficient."[50] In other statements on state aid, Trenham repeated the claim that local districts would address inequality on their own in the absence of state intervention, while casting state aid, oddly, as a kind of punishment for efficiently organized districts that would purportedly balance out inequality on their own. He insisted that state equalization aid to districts "penalized" more "efficient counties" with a smaller number of districts.[51] Experts in educational administration and some prominent educators helped advance this framing of the state's role as well, often most clearly in speaking engagements organized by the group. In a speech delivered at the CTA annual meeting, for instance, the state superintendent of public instruction Walter Dexter repeated this framing, discussing how the current system "fostered the existence of many school districts which are too small to be effective and entirely too poor to provide adequate financing" and that new "financial inducements" might be necessary to address the issue.[52]

It was the representatives of corporations who had founded, funded, and directed the California Taxpayers Association who seemed to benefit the most from the localization of public school funding. Before the establishment of the sales and income tax in the state, corporations had generally paid for any increases in state funding needs through changes to the bank and corporation franchise tax. Pointing out that "public education costs more than any other single government function," members of the CTA used claims about the inefficiency in school districts, namely their lack of consolidation, to rationalize their opposition to proposed increases in state taxation or spending. At the height of the Depression, the CTA estimated the state could save $1.5 million by encouraging districts to redraw their boundaries.[53] Other business groups, including the California Chamber of Commerce, repeated this assertion and made it one of their recommendations for reducing state expenses and tax burdens as well.[54]

Given that the CTA clearly served special interests, it was vulnerable to sharp criticism. Harvey Lebron, secretary of the Pacific Coast Conference on Public and Private Responsibility in Welfare Work, described the CTA as a front for corporations seeking "special benefits at the expense of the plain citizen taxpayer from the present inequitable division of taxation."[55] Teacher L. S. Gerlough provided a particularly trenchant critique in one local newspaper, describing talk of the "economics of public education" as a dishonest effort by corporations—through the CTA—to mislead the public and "evade their fair payments of taxes." Leaders of corporations in the state, Gerlough warned readers, were using their "monstrous salaries" to "corrupt the public opinion of our people" so "attention will be diverted from their own activities."[56] The veteran journalist Franklin Hichborn spoke about the CTA in similar terms to how he had spoken about the Southern Pacific Railroad's political machine years earlier. He called all the talk of "waste" in education a "smoke screen behind which powerful interests evade their proportionate share of the tax burden."[57] He noted that the state budget crisis in 1932 would have been avoided if banks and public service corporations had simply "paid their just proportion of state taxes during the last half dozen years."[58]

Despite these critiques, the CTA was remarkably successful at shaping public discourse. Immediately before and during the Great Depression, the group spread its vision of taxation by embracing a new style of political communication emerging in California alongside the nation's first modern political consulting firms.[59] Journalist Carey McWilliams would later summarize this approach as a shift away from "the old-fashioned boss and lobbyist" and toward something new—"government by public relations."[60] The CTA excelled at it. The group sent representatives to give regular speeches to local community groups about how taxes were too high. They volunteered to produce cost analyses for local governments. They traveled up and down the state to help form local taxpayer groups.[61] They were particularly skilled at releasing statistical analyses in an easy-to-digest form—often featuring cartoons—and getting those analyses repeated in local papers again and again.[62] The group created and promoted a school curriculum to shape how future voters would think about taxation as well. The lessons, one member of the group offered, "should prove valuable in clarifying taxation matters in the public."[63] Rolland Vandegrift—one of the founders of the group who later became the state finance director under Governor James Rolph—was a particularly skilled communicator. He even bought and sold entire newspaper operations to assert editorial control to help communicate as needed the company view of taxation.[64]

Key to the CTA's success was its claim to technical expertise, along with its ability to persuade others to accept its analyses of state budgeting and school finance as neutral and unbiased, even as those analyses were singularly focused on "proving" that state taxes were too high. After Vandegrift's appointment to direct Governor Rolph's budget, for example, he regularly stumped alongside the CTA while couching his position in terms of his technical expertise and unique knowledge as finance director.[65] Vandegrift also advised school funding studies during the Depression, serving as one of the "finance specialists" recruited to serve on the National Survey of School Finance authorized by Congress in 1931.[66] Similarly, Bradford Trenham helped Alexander Carter compile a bibliography of educational finance in the 1930s and made sure Trenham's editorial-type publications in the CTA journal were cited repeatedly and treated like peer-reviewed, scientific publications. Trenham also contributed to studies commissioned to examine state aid and educational costs, such as A. G. Grace and G. A. More's study of funding in New York, and served on a national advisory committee on the federal role in education.[67]

The tone and tenor of discussions regarding tax reform in California during the Great Depression evince how the CTA largely succeeded in reframing school funding disparities as a local problem. Crucially, this success was at a moment, during the Depression and before the inception of the New Deal, when people began to think the state should have a bigger role in many areas. The group did not dictate the results of reform, but it was quite successful at shaping the terms of public debate and getting more and more residents of the state to discuss school funding shortfalls not as a problem of tax avoidance but one of excessive education spending. With help from Vandegrift in 1932, for example, the CTA helped persuade voters to defeat a proposition to increase state school funding by creating an income tax and a sales tax on luxury items.[68] Campaign materials identified Vandegrift as the state director of finance, not the original founder of the CTA. In the guise of an authority on taxation and budgeting, Vandegrift claimed that the proposed taxes were not viable and that the proposition would actually lead taxes to be "higher instead of lower, and education will suffer."[69]

A different tax reform proposal the following year succeeded. It was not driven by the CTA, but it reflected the group's way of talking about school finance, helped limit corporate tax rates, and further shifted tax burdens toward the poor. A coalition of state organizations put the reform, called the Riley-Stewart Amendment, on the ballot. The proposal moved the county share of education funding to the state. Framed in the language of both support for the schools and providing taxpayer relief from excessive school taxes, the reform did nothing to alleviate the actual source of growing tax burdens for education—the shift toward district-level taxation—and completely avoided the issue of corporate tax rates. With the exception of San Francisco, every county was large and economically diverse enough that shifting the county share of funding to the state would only remain redistributive if it included enough state investments to prevent district taxes from replacing the county share of funding. The increase in state support in the years immediately following the implementation of the measure seemed to suggest a profound shift in state priorities and investments. One historian, reflecting on the increase, wrote "the depression ended early for the schools."[70] In reality, the measure entrenched local taxation. Within three years of the measure's implementation, districts were more reliant on district-level revenue than they had been before it went into effect, as the percentage of funding derived from local taxes jumped from 34 percent to 41 percent.[71]

The Riley-Stewart Amendment did not specify how the additional money from the state should be generated, and the implementation of the reform ensured corporate tax rates were untouched. In the end, rather than tax wealthy entities, as reformers had hoped since the 1870s, the measure shifted the tax burden toward those who had the least. At first, the legislature and the Rolph administration—with the help of Vandegrift—created a sales tax (which is by definition regressive). This was the primary source of funds even after an income tax was adopted—against the staunch opposition of the CTA. In the 1937 fiscal year, for example, about 55 percent of all state revenue was from the sales tax: $128.8 million. Public service corporations and banks did not see their tax rates increase; that same year, taxes on banks and corporations provided only

7 percent of state revenue. The new income tax also provided only about 7 percent.[72] The reform thus did nothing to curb growing district property taxation for schools; and in making sure that state school support came primarily from sales taxes, it also asked the most of those who had the least. Historian of California John Caughey drily summarized these trends, noting how the Riley-Stewart Amendment meant that "those who paid the sales tax had the privilege of saving the schools, while taxable incomes went unscathed and corporations had their tax burdens lightened."[73] Franklin Hichborn similarly lamented that "the bulk of state taxes has been shifted to the little fellow."[74]

Finally, the Riley-Stewart Amendment limited increases in education spending, playing into the CTA's claim that education funds were not being used efficiently, a view that even state education officials and the state's teachers' union seemed to reinforce at times.[75] Stipulating that education spending could not increase at the local or the state levels by more than 5 percent of the previous year's budget, the reform cemented into law existing inequalities in school budgeting.[76] The richest districts were already a great deal richer before the passage of the amendment, and their ability to increase budgets by 5 percent helped them more easily address the rapidly expanding costs of education that accompanied inflation and population growth. The poorest districts, with already miserly budgets, found themselves even less able to make ends meet. Only months after the amendment was passed, eight hundred districts were forced to revise their school budgets because of the spending constraints. The move may have made sense in Depression-era hard times among wealthy districts, but poor rural schools found themselves, yet again, struggling to remain open.

Entrenching Inequity: District Boundary Manipulation and Reform

As governor for the decade between 1943 and 1953, Earl Warren worked with the state legislature to promote a far-reaching program of postwar planning and reform that expanded the scope and reach of state government. This program of state activism began with creation of the State Reconstruction and Reemployment Commission (SRRC) in August 1943. Originally charged with helping to ease the transition from a wartime to a peacetime economy, the commission grew increasingly ambitious during the 1940s. According to Warren's critics, the program represented the most invasive possible incarnation of the New Deal. Warren was attempting, according to one critic, to "out New Deal the New Deal."[77]

Education was a core component of the program. The SRRC, in considering the educational needs of the state, commissioned a study of California's public school system. Directed by Professor George Strayer of Teachers College,

Columbia University, the survey recommended three major reforms connected to funding, with the goal of "equalizing educational opportunity."[78] The first, at the heart of this education reform program, was school district reorganization, alongside two intentionally limited reforms intended to support reorganization: state equalization funding for districts deemed deserving and a tailored program of school construction aid. These suggestions were adopted into law during the 1940s, and all three would profoundly limit educational opportunity in the state.

All three reforms, moreover, reinforced the basic idea popularized by the CTA: that school funding was a local issue and primarily the responsibility of local taxpayers. The state could help districts, encouraging them to grow their tax bases through district consolidation. It could also provide modest assistance to help a select number of districts address their funding challenges. Ultimately, though, the premise of these reforms was that the state was not responsible for what its fiscal policies did to children and schools.

District reorganization dominated the thought of policy experts and lawmakers in the 1940s, and this focus on reorganization helped reinforce the idea that public schools were primarily local rather than state institutions. Consider how members of the SRRC discussed the purposes of state funding in their initial report: that it existed to incentivize or disincentivize local behavior and encourage districts to help themselves (by growing their tax base). Too much funding, they insisted, would interfere with this goal. "Incentives to better district organization should be encouraged," they argued. In designing an equalization program, the authors continued, "care should be taken that State aid is not so employed as to hold back district consolidation."[79] The SRRC outlined a proposal for the distribution of state aid that was intentionally limited. State funding was a last resort for districts after they grew their tax bases through consolidation and exhausted them with a local tax. Even as it claimed that redrawing district boundaries would address inequities, the SRRC also insisted that neither equal tax bases nor equal tax rates should be the goal. Such an approach, the SRRC maintained, would permit some districts to only raise as much in local taxes as required by the state's funding program. It would not be "healthy," the commission claimed, if "tax rates levied locally" were to become "identical."[80]

Following the recommendations of the SRRC, the legislature created the Special State Commission on School Districts in 1945, a group that reinforced the idea that schools were local institutions and that the state should approach how they are funded with this in mind. The commission supervised fifty-three local survey committees, each of which was instructed to study school district organization in its region and then, after receiving formal state approval, submit to local voters specific proposals to redraw school district boundaries "for the purpose of effecting feasible unifications or other reorganizations of school districts."[81]

Lawmakers sought to honor local decision making and preserve local control in boundary movement decisions; the entire approach to reorganization developed by the commission reinforced the image of the state's public schools as primarily local, rather than state, institutions. Members of the Commission on School Districts weighed in heavily on how to design a formula for distributing state funding to school districts, calling for such funding to avoid serving as an "obstacle to successful reorganization by vote of the people."[82] Providing additional aid to districts with low property valuations, according to members, could "encourage districts to remain weak."[83]

Under the direction of George Geyer and later Gilbert Jertberg, members of the Commission on School Districts shaped legislation on education funding passed in the late 1940s, making sure that it incentivized districts to grow their tax bases rather than oblige the state to address the impact of its policies. Geyer actively collaborated with members of a separate committee focused on state equalization aid to make sure "only relatively efficient school districts, from the standpoint of their organization, would receive equalization, transportation, and capital outlay aid from state funds."[84] The committee, which helped draft the state's foundation programs and model them after those proposed in the report of the SRRC, also agreed to "the principle of aiding school district reorganization through the provision of sound financial incentives."[85] This included additional funds for recently consolidated districts regardless of their local tax base, a form of aid that provided considerable support for the expansion of suburban districts into formerly rural areas with small, one-room school districts.[86] Members of the Commission on School Districts also received support from university-based experts. Education scholar Hollis Allen, for example, lobbied Governor Warren, insisting that attempts to consolidate school districts in California had been harmed by the "tendency over the years, particularly evident now, to over subsidize *unnecessary* [emphasis in the original] small school districts."[87] If districts were helped to form a large enough tax base to pay for themselves, advocates for redistricting insisted, additional financial support from the state would be unnecessary.

With state aid framed as a last resort for helping districts cover what had been reimagined as local costs, dedicated sources of aid money and changes to the state's distribution formula were insufficient for addressing disparities. Moreover, these funds were primarily directed toward white suburbanites, reinforcing and extending the expansive network of governmental policies already underwriting white suburban affluence. Relative to the state's historical role in funding, for example, even aggregate increases in state funding during these years failed to keep up with growing costs or enrollments, and they never offset the shift toward local property taxes. Indeed, by 1949–50, the state was providing less than half the share of what it had provided in 1900.[88] If state lawmakers had simply maintained the same proportion of spending that they had provided in 1900, schools would have received an additional $44.2 million (about $550 million in 2022 dollars).[89]

Even the equalization program, created by the state in 1947, did more to expand the infrastructure on which postwar inequality was built than to soften even its most extreme impacts. Drawing on state revenues generated primarily from a sales tax, the equalization aid flowed disproportionately to suburban districts. While many Californians talked about the need to make school finance fairer, much of the rhetoric centered on the problems confronting expanding suburban districts, not impoverished rural or changing urban districts. The real trouble with finance, according to commentators, was unprecedented growth, not the way that the district property tax created inequalities. "Population shifts have caused unusual burdens," one group of educators lamented.[90] State aid followed this logic, defining need in terms of assessed valuation per student. With assessed valuations updated gradually but enrollment data updated annually, expanding suburban districts were getting credit in the state's aid formula for their growing student population but not the changes in overall taxable wealth accompanying suburbanization. With many of these districts created from rural districts that had been relatively small, suburban districts also benefited from the additional subsidies provided to districts for consolidating. The "net effect of the equalization program," historian John Philips explained in the years that followed, "was to divert a portion of state aid from the smallest rural districts and the largest urban districts . . . and to channel it into suburban districts."[91]

The way that state lawmakers equated school district financial need with growth in federally subsidized white suburbs was particularly obvious when they made San Lorenzo—a racially restricted white subdivision outside Oakland—the poster child of district need. Lawmakers graced the inside cover of the *Assembly Interim Committee on Public Education* report with an image of San Lorenzo. The caption of the image read, "This is a distressed school district. As more homes are built, the district will get more educationally impoverished." The report then repeatedly returned to San Lorenzo as an example of the challenges confronting similarly "distressed" districts.[92] Locally, San Lorenzo was understood as the exclusively white, flagship subdivision of the San Lorenzo Home Company, best known for the depth of their commitment to not only making places like San Lorenzo racially segregated, but trying to block the creation of racially integrated subdivisions nearby. For example, when the United Auto Workers introduced a plan to create Sunnyhills, a racially integrated suburb where Black union members could secure housing near the new Ford plant, the San Lorenzo Home Company tried to block the development and then offered to build a different subdivision restricted to Black residents in a different location. While these efforts by the San Lorenzo Home Company were unsuccessful, historian Robert Self has pointed out how they reflected the "deep investment of the real estate industry in segregation."[93]

Construction aid was another pillar of the reform program of the Warren administration, albeit secondary to district reorganization. Construction aid was deliberately guided toward suburban districts and away from rural and urban districts during the approval process. When the legislature drafted legislation for the aid, members of the State Commission on School Districts worked with members of the Schoolhouse Planning Commission to again prevent aid from flowing to districts that members of the reorganization commission deemed unworthy. Charles Bursch, the director of the Division of Schoolhouse Planning, met with members of the Commission on School Districts to encourage "cooperation" and prevent "one agency from retarding the efforts of another agency." The two bodies persuaded the legislature to allow the Commission on School Districts, in collaboration with the Division of Schoolhouse Planning, to prevent districts deemed inappropriately organized from receiving aid.

Rural districts were disfavored by the Commission on School Districts based on the claim that aid to those districts would discourage reorganization. Urban districts, meanwhile, were disfavored by the Division of Schoolhouse Planning because of how the division defined appropriate school locations.[94] Requirements like minimum lot sizes and a reliance on federal construction guidelines for school sites spread what historian Ansley Erickson has called a "prosuburban ideology," leading the Division of Schoolhouse Planning to reject smaller urban sites and approve large lots of the kind most readily available in new suburban tracts.[95] Here, the Division of Schoolhouse Planning also built on its own history of treating white communities as the best place for new school buildings. In its planning document outlining standards for public school sites in 1930, the Division of Schoolhouse Planning advised that "school sites should not be surrounded by high and overshadowing buildings," implicitly referring to urban school sites. "The most desirable environment for a city or village school site," the document continued, "is a good restricted residence area"—meaning one with racially restrictive covenants.[96]

Through the actual work of reorganizing the district boundaries—work that purportedly served as the rationale for limiting other reforms—policy makers further reinforced the idea that schools were local institutions while at the same time actively intervening in supposedly local decision making to ensure funding was unequal and conditioned on race. With guidance from the State Commission on School Districts, school district boundaries were redrawn again and again in California. The number of school districts in the state, as a consequence, was reduced by 57 percent between 1945 and 1972.[97] But the claim that district reorganization would "iron out" inequality seemed to go out the window. While the Commission on School Districts considered fiscal equalization, it made equalization secondary to maintaining homogeneous communities. Local tax bases were important, the commission insisted, but so were factors like "economic conditions, population changes, community structure, occupations, resources, and prospects for the future."[98] In the guidance provided to local survey committees, for example, the State Commission on School Districts included checklists with factors to contemplate when establishing new districts. The demographic composition of the families brought together in a new district and whether those families reflected "natural groupings" of people was one such factor. In a guide for local survey committees, officials explained that "a sense of community membership must be preserved in the larger area proposed."[99] The state commission instructed the local survey committees to be mindful of "natural barriers"—of a different sort from topography and geography—that could impact "community inclusiveness." Survey committees were also instructed to make sure new districts were composed of residents with "many common interests." New districts should never, the document advised, "include sharply contrasting centers of cultural, religious, or economic interests which would probably result in discrimination against some children."[100] The justification for ensuring discrimination in the reorganization process was the claim that discrimination would be ensured without it. One school official worried about how a proposed redistricting plan would "throw approximately 150 Anglo-Saxon children" into a school "entirely composed of children of Mexican extraction." Such a proposed redistricting plan, the official insisted, was liable to create "undesirable emotional problems on both sides" while creating a situation where the "safety and welfare of several hundred students would be jeopardized by a few prejudiced parents."[101]

In reports justifying various proposals for reorganization, local survey committees followed the state's guidance and devoted considerable space to how school district reorganization could support racial and economic segregation. Some proposals dedicated as much space to maintaining homogeneity in students as they did to tax bases. The San Mateo County Committee, for example, thought primarily about "population affinities" when considering where school district boundaries should be redrawn. "We found separation where union was needed and union of districts where separation was needed," the committee explained. In thinking about reorganization, they continued, "we divided the county into certain natural groupings of communities." These "natural groupings," unsurprisingly, fell along racial, ethnic, and economic lines. The Santa Clara County survey committee had similar concerns. It foregrounded its discussion of reorganization with a detailed account of how race and ethnicity would shape its efforts. The committee noted the "comparative freedom Santa Clara County enjoys from any racial problems" by detailing how there were only "730 Negros in the County in 1940," and those residents primarily lived in areas that could allow for the reorganization of districts without creating new districts educating Black and white students together.[102] The main concern facing the committee was the "rather large foreign-born population which has presented some difficult problems for certain schools in the past." The committee felt these "Portuguese, Mexican, Italian, Slavonian, or Japanese" children should not be placed in the same district, though they also expressed "reason to believe that the problem will soon cease to have any serious effect in the schools" because "the percentage of foreign born in the county . . . is declining with each decade."[103]

The areas where redistricting was most vehemently studied and discussed involved the handful of places where African Americans lived. The Contra Costa County survey committee treated the organization of boundaries in the city of Richmond as a "situation deserving special consideration."[104] The "situation," of course, was that Richmond's African American population had exploded between 1940 and 1945, from 270 to 14,000. At the same time, sections of the city were deliberately kept white. The solution was to organize attendance boundaries that could make the district writ large appear integrated while individual schools remained segregated by race. By the 1950s, Black students represented 22 percent of Richmond's elementary school population. The schools, however, were almost completely segregated. At six of the schools, over 95 percent of the students were African American.[105]

Even minor changes to district boundaries geared toward integration would have done much to alleviate racial apartheid. Dense suburban development meant that the rare communities where African American and Mexican American families were able to secure housing were almost always adjacent to exclusively white, affluent communities.[106] Simple changes to district boundaries would have easily integrated nearby schools, even if housing remained segregated. For instance, East Palo Alto shared a school district boundary with affluent Palo Alto. Reorienting the boundary from east to west, rather than north to south, would have created two integrated school districts.

Similarly, in 1954, through the influence of lawmakers from San José, the legislature passed a law overturning the requirement that newly incorporated cities and towns constitute new, independent school districts. The change could have aided district reorganization in support of integration, as the boundaries of new, segregated suburban communities could have been disconnected from the boundaries of school districts. Following the passage of the law, the connections were severed in many places; indeed, fewer than 10 percent of California's incorporated cities had school district and municipal boundaries with coterminous boundaries, according to one study of contemporary patterns.[107] Yet, in cities like San José, these changes helped to promote, rather than restrict, school segregation. Moreover, they promoted a form of segregation that was resistant to state intervention following *Mendez v. Westminster* (1947) and, later, federal intervention that localization had incentivized.

The tendency of education officials to "maintain separate schools by the simple device of adjusting boundary lines" was so widespread that in 1948, one observer used the manipulation of district boundaries as an example illustrating how Jim Crow could be found not just in the South but in California.[108] Similarly, a leader of the NAACP's West Coast branch noted the "gerrymandered" nature of school district boundaries in the state.[109] A few years later, the West Coast branch of the NAACP again explained that it was not simply housing patterns that had created racially segregated schools in the region, but "carefully drawn district boundary lines to enclose areas of Negro occupancy." These patterns, members of the NAACP insisted, represented their own "species of school segregation."[110]

Disparities Built to Last

Between the Great Depression and 1950, state lawmakers invested, legislatively, if not financially, in expanding the role of local financing in California's public education system. That investment was part and parcel of state investments in whiteness and suburbanization during these years.

As California entered the postwar period, there were many opportunities for challenging funding inequalities. State officials, however, pursued policies that entrenched and expanded disparities between school districts. A dense network of state, federal, and local policies had helped create segregated housing patterns across California. Efforts to maintain the school district system and reorganize district boundaries contributed to these baldly discriminatory patterns. The insistence of some state officials that district reorganization was more important than constructing new school buildings or equalization aid, and the ability of those officials to undermine policy proposals that did not direct aid to expanding suburbs, meant that educational policy in the state shaped patterns of unequal metropolitan development. Specifically, by accepting and expanding the logic of the district system, it was possible for Californians to translate housing inequalities into segregated schooling. That these reforms were pursued while supposedly addressing the inequalities of the district system only made funding inequality and segregation seem that much more natural and intractable.

The state of California refused to collect data on the demographic composition of its schools for much of the twentieth century. When the state finally gathered statistics on segregation in 1966, the effect of postwar policies was quite clear. In the largest school districts, 57 percent of Latino students were attending minority schools, 28 percent were attending "mixed" schools, and 15 percent were attending schools that were predominately white. For African Americans, segregation was much worse: 85 percent of African American students were attending minority schools, and 12 percent were attending "mixed" schools. Only 3 percent were attending predominately white schools.[111] Trends in school finance were just as bleak. This inequality in funding was challenged in California, and across the nation, throughout the late 1950s, 1960s, and 1970s. Yet the notion that the state had not been responsible for the creation of disparities between school districts—that they had emerged accidentally and organically—would allow courts to limit the scope of these challenges.

Epilogue
INEQUITY TRIUMPHANT

Between January and July 1851, members of a militia organized and funded by the newly formed California state government murdered approximately ninety-three Indigenous Californians while violently forcing bands of Miwok, Paiute, and Yokut people to cede their lands in the western Sierra Nevadas to the United States. The militia was composed of 518 recent migrants from elsewhere in the United States, all of them paid for their military service by the state of California. One of the men—a white lawyer from Boston who had arrived in California eleven months earlier—donated his military salary to help form California's school fund, the initial source of funding for American public education in the state. Notably, he was also the first superintendent of public instruction in the state, abandoning his post to help commit these atrocities.[1]

Racial Violence and Inequality from the Start

The precise mechanism through which the first dollars in California's school fund connected the financing of public schools with the invasion of Indigenous homelands by the United States was probably unique. It is doubtful any other state superintendent helped capitalize a state school fund in this way. The link these events forged between state-sponsored acts of racial violence, the seizure and sale of Indigenous land, and the institutional development of American public education is far from unique, however. It is, instead, where the story of funding for public education systems across much of the United States begins. The nearly 139 million acres of expropriated Indigenous lands used by federal and state governments to fund the US common school project, newly documented in this book, stand as testament to this larger truth.

This figure, representing about 7 percent of the landmass of the contiguous United States, remains an underestimate. There are several cases where Native American land was sold to finance what we consider early elementary and secondary education for which precise acreage figures do not exist. Furthermore, no number can capture what these links between Native American dispossession and common schooling meant for Indigenous people and white settlers alike. Quantification and its "lack of intimacy," Jill Lepore once observed, "represents not only a gain but also a loss of knowledge."[2]

Courts and Legislators

About a century later, Earl Warren, a California governor who had become chief justice of the United States Supreme Court, authored the court's unanimous decision on school segregation in 1954. In *Brown v. Board of Education of Topeka*, the Supreme Court declared education "a right which must be made available to all on equal terms," overturning the "separate but equal" doctrine established by *Plessy v. Ferguson* during the 1890s. Education was not provided on equal terms when students were segregated solely on the basis of race, the court declared. Even when the "physical facilities and other 'tangible' factors may be equal," racially segregated public schools were "inherently unequal" and unconstitutional.

Immediately following the *Brown v. Board of Education* decision, future Supreme Court justice Thurgood Marshall expressed optimism about desegregation. An attorney at the time who had helped secure the NAACP's victory in the case, Marshall predicted that school segregation would be eradicated in "up to five years."[3] Two decades later, Justice Marshall authored a dissent in both *San Antonio v. Rodriguez* and *Milliken v. Bradley*. As noted in the introduction, in *San Antonio v. Rodriguez*, the Supreme Court declared that a fundamental right to education does not exist under the United States Constitution. The following year the court also legalized racial segregation by school district boundary in *Milliken v. Bradley*, legitimizing the starkly unequal form of government-sponsored racial segregation common across the United States after World War II. Together, these decisions endorsed racial and economic apartheid via school district boundary. Physical facilities and other tangible factors for education—most notably per pupil expenditures and local tax rates for schooling—could be unequal yet not inherently unconstitutional.

While the US Supreme Court gave school funding disparities new legitimacy in *San Antonio v. Rodriquez*, civil rights groups across the country continued to pursue equalization through litigation on the state level. Drawing on the requirements to fund public school systems equitably and adequately contained in state constitutions, nearly every state has ruled on at least one legal challenge to how lawmakers have decided to fund schools inequitably. When successful, these challenges have provided much-needed aid to struggling school districts. They have also positively impacted the trajectories of students who would have been forced to attend underfunded schools in the absence of court intervention, with some studies finding that funding reforms increased intergenerational mobility and reduced the probability that children will experience poverty as adults.[4]

Yet courts have tended only to enforce rulings for short periods. Jurists have left the root sources of funding disparities untouched and given the same legislative bodies responsible for the initial constitutional violation wide latitude to re-create the same disparities down the road. A vicious cycle repeats itself. As legal scholar Laurie Reynolds points out, these rulings have created endless rounds of reform that do not alleviate inequities in the long run.[5] First, courts invalidate existing school finance systems for the disparities they create while leaving district taxation and spending intact. Next, state governments respond by providing assistance to districts with limited property wealth. Finally, over the next several years, changes in state budgets limit the scope of aid to impoverished districts, while wealthy districts continue to generate substantial amounts of new revenue until an "equilibrium" of inequality returns. Courts have attacked "the results of a school funding system while leaving untouched the source of the unconstitutionality," Reynolds concludes.[6]

In other cases, state high courts have upheld the idea that state governments can essentially condition the amount of funding they provide to school districts on the race and class of the students being educated. Courts are able to take this stance by glossing over or obfuscating the relationship between elected officials and the laws those officials pass and uphold. Laws exist regulating every aspect of local financing. In many states, those laws create material inequities in funding. They are re-created in each legislative session, over and over, budget after budget. In their outcomes, and in some cases their intent, they are racist and classist. Taking the position that passing and upholding those laws does not betray state constitutional obligations to create and maintain a public education *system* for all children requires imagining a world of laws without lawmakers, where budgets pass themselves and school funding formulas—weights, multipliers, indices—are spontaneous creations.

Who Constructs the Public?

Kelley Williams-Bolar, a Black woman and educator from Ohio, was arrested, fined, and sent to jail for ten days. The arrest was not in the 1840s or 1850s, a time when African American activists in Ohio challenged efforts to limit Black citizenship and access to an emerging common school system. Nor was she arrested during the civil rights era, a period when a large number of activists were arrested for acts of civil disobedience challenging the intersections of white supremacy and public education across the country. Williams-Bolar was arrested in 2011. She lived in a majority Black school district. She stole an education, according to state law, by sending her children to a predominately white public school in a more affluent suburban school district.[7]

When it comes to explaining why children of color and children from low-income families receive fewer educational resources than white children from affluent families in the United States, deeply rooted historical dynamics are critical. I have tried to concentrate on those historical dynamics and their relationship to education—white supremacy, wealth accumulation linked to predation, and the conversion of the state into an agent of private plunder—throughout this book. Following the foundational dispossession of Indigenous people that funded common school expansion, Progressive Era reforms articulated a narrow conception of the public, in which education could enrich one public at the expense of another. From the 1930s into the postwar era, local taxes helped create a sprawling and hidden welfare system for wealthy white suburbanites, corporations, and banks—all while shifting fiscal burdens onto low-income communities and communities of color.

As useful as these historical dynamics are for understanding where structural inequities in education come from, they cannot on their own explain why those inequities will continue into the future. We need to examine our collective role in upholding these dynamics or upending them. Both educational researchers and historians too often play the former role via inattention and silence.

False and misleading stories about the past abound in discussions of school finance in the popular media. *Education Week* and the *Atlantic* have trouble discussing school funding without referencing colonial Massachusetts and the supposedly eternal American tradition of funding schools through local taxes.[8] "Although the aims of public schooling have changed since the 17th century, the critical role of property taxation in funding education has endured," the authors of a recent article in the *Economist* similarly explain.[9]

If a broader notion of the public good is to be made possible, one in which vicious disparities along race and class lines may be interrupted, those of us in positions to create knowledge about educational systems must stop invisibilizing state actions that run counter to popular imagination. Policy makers re-create, tinker with, and rearrange school funding formulas each year. Budgets do not pass themselves. If the long history I have told of state actors dividing the public seems strange and foreign in its brazenness, perhaps it can also help us hear the echoes of history's brutality that reverberate in the choices Americans continue to make today.

Appendix

SCHOOL FINANCE DATA

Like all forms of quantitative school funding data, the values contained in the sources described in this appendix should be used with care because of inconsistencies in reporting across years. These data are imperfect. So, too, are contemporary funding data reported by the National Center of Education Statistics, though this point is missed by some researchers.

These data are useful for examining broad trends in how revenue for schools was generated. In this appendix, I briefly contextualize them and their imperfections. Scholars interested in conducting more extensive statistical analyses should not assume these data are measured with the level of precision requisite for techniques like hypothesis testing or a quasi-experiment. Further, I have not applied imputations in instances of missing data.

Estimated Acreage of Expropriated Native Land Used to Fund Early Public Schools

This estimate is based on federal and state expropriated land set aside for permanent state school funds, derived from several sources. I started by digitizing the acreage reported in Fletcher Swift, *A History of Public Permanent Common School Funds in the United States, 1795–1905* (New York: H. Holt, 1911), table 17, 100–106. I then included an additional 991,559 acres reported for New York State in the same volume, table 14, p. 85, but excluded from table 17. Note that the total figure reported includes acres of state lands in Texas that are not included in figure 1.1 because they were not technically used to capitalize a school fund.

Next, I estimated the acres of expropriated land that formed the federal budget surplus in the 1830s and which was then distributed to states and, in some states, then directed to permanent school funds. A federal budgetary surplus resulting in part from increased federal land sale revenues was passed on to states through the United States Surplus Revenue distributed in 1837, a portion of which some state legislatures then placed in their permanent school funds.

To estimate an acreage figure for those funds, I first estimate the increase in acres of expropriated land sold that accounted for the federal revenue surplus based on a slight modification of estimates from Paul Gates on the role of federal land sales in the surplus. Gates estimates that the increases in land sales in 1834, 1835, and 1836 (above and beyond previous years) were primarily responsible for the budget surplus.[1] At the same time, a gross budgetary surplus (including debt retirements) did not begin in 1834, and cash land sales (in acres) increased over cash land sales (in acres) the previous year each year leading up to the surplus revenue distribution act starting in 1833.[2]

Based on that pattern, I slightly modify Gates's estimate and calculate the total number of acres sold above and beyond 1832 levels in 1833, 1834, 1835, and 1836. This figure was approximately 31.5 million acres of additional land sold. Based on the assumption that 31.5 million acres of expropriated land were connected to the $28 million in surplus revenue distributed to states, I then determine the percentage of the $28 million that each state contributed to a permanent school fund and use that percentage with the ~31.5 million acre figure to produce an estimate for expropriated land. For example, if a state dedicated $2.8 million in surplus revenue to a permanent school fund, that would have represented 10 percent of the entire surplus distributed to all states. Based on the percentage, I would then estimate that this state was using ~3.15 million acres of expropriated land to finance education (10 percent of the 31.5 million acre estimate). While imperfect in relation to the federal budget, this estimate does capture the increased acres of expropriated land sold that would have contributed to the surplus revenue then used to finance schools.

Dataset 1: State-Level Expenditure and Revenue for the Entire United States, 1872–1920

Unless otherwise noted, data comparing individual states are from a dataset manually reconstructed by myself and research assistants from the reports of the US commissioner of education. These reports were issued as the *Annual Report of the Commissioner of Education* from 1870 to 1918. After 1917–18, they were released as the *Biennial Survey of Education in the United States* until 1957–58.

I expected inconsistencies to be more common in the earliest years of reporting. As a result, we digitized data from the 1870s and 1880s on a biennial basis for the school years ending in 1872, 1874, 1876, 1878, 1880, 1882, 1884, 1886, 1888, and 1890. After 1890, we digitized state-level data on a decennial basis until 1920.

The inconsistent treatment of certain revenue sources across years should be a concern for anyone using these data for purposes other than broad descriptions of the changing role state and local governments have played in funding over time. Revenue from state permanent school funds is reported in most years, and I treat it as a state revenue source in my analyses. Since revenue from the District of Columbia is sometimes considered "state" and sometimes considered "local," I excluded District of Columbia data from state comparisons.

We also collected and digitized decennial data from state annual reports for Arizona (as a territory and, after 1912, as a state), Minnesota, New Jersey, Ohio, Tennessee, and Utah (as a territory and, after 1896, as a state) for each decade between 1870 and 1920 to verify that county-level revenues were treated as local revenue in the Office/Bureau of Education reports. County revenue was reported as "local" in these reports, as are the current data released by the US Census Bureau and the National Center for Educational Statistics. As I point out in the text, scholars should consider the extent to which county taxes could facilitate a degree of redistribution between districts in large counties that might contradict the localism and local control they associate with a local tax.

Although the vast majority of states have data from the school year covered in each annual report, some states have data from the prior or following year. This is noted consistently in Office/Bureau of Education reports. While this is acceptable for a study of broad trends, scholars should consider the implications of this inconsistency if they wish to use data from these reports for analyses. I have tended to focus more on the proportional role of different revenue sources in education funding than per pupil or per capita figures, though at times I do reference such figures in the text and include details in the associated footnotes. Scholars intending to construct a reliable panel that uses a per pupil or per capita figure must decide whether to use school-age populations within a state or average daily attendance. School-age population is defined differently in different states. Per pupil figures are calculated in the California datasets using the census child as the pupil measure, a measure with a more consistent definition over time.

Dataset 2: National Percent Distribution of Public School Revenue by Source, 1872–1990

I aggregated "State-Level Expenditure, Revenue, and Teacher Salary Dataset for Entire United States, 1872–1920" at the national level to identify the proportion of public school revenue from state and local sources between 1872 and 1890. I combined these national totals with percentage distribution figures digitized from the National Center for Education Statistics (NCES) 1993 publication *120 Years of American Education: A Statistical Portrait* (Washington, DC: National Center for Educational Statistics). The NCES data cover the period between 1890 and 1990. Percentage distribution data are reported in "Table 21: Revenues for Public Elementary and Secondary Schools, by Source of Funds" on page 57.

Dataset 3: State of California Elementary School Funding Data Aggregated at County Level, 1870–1930

Data at the county level are reported in the biennial reports of the state superintendent of instruction for California. Although these data vary in what level of detail they provide, they consistently report revenue by source starting in the 1860s. These data report elementary and high school revenue sources, spending, and enrollment separately, allowing for comparisons that are not skewed by changes in high school enrollment and the costs associated with secondary education. With the help of research assistants, I digitized decennial data, starting in 1870, using the physical reports at Stanford University's Cubberley Library. Expenditure data exclude capital spending, as is the custom in school finance scholarship, because of the way onetime capital spending can skew data. Infrastructure spending is still considered in chapters 2, 4, and 6. In some years, the biennial reports of the superintendent of public instruction did not include revenue data broken down by source, and in those cases data from the most recent year with complete data were used. For example, the 1910 report did not separate data by source, and data from 1906 are used instead.

Dataset 4: District-Level Sample from California, 1870–1940

I digitized a sample of district-level elementary school funding data for the counties surrounding the San Francisco Bay from the county superintendent reports on file at the California State Archives in Sacramento. This included elementary school enrollment, elementary school revenue, elementary school expenditure, and school building valuation data for every school district in Alameda, Contra Costa, Marin, Napa, Solano, Sonoma, San Mateo, and Santa Clara Counties for the 1869–70, 1879–80, 1889–90, 1894–95, 1899–1900, 1904–5, 1909–10,

1914–15, 1919–20, 1929–30, and 1939–40 school years. Expenditure data again exclude capital spending.

Since I am concerned with how disparities in school funding evolved between communities, I selected these adjacent counties because of their diverse patterns of development throughout the period between 1870 and 1940. Throughout the nineteenth and twentieth centuries, virtually every kind of developed environment was contained in these counties. The region included every imaginable combination of urban, rural, suburban, and exurban communities.[3] Since these counties reflected patterns of development found across California and the nation during the nineteenth and twentieth centuries while located closely to one another, detailed district-level data from these counties provide a window into centralization, fragmentation, and disparities over time. In collecting revenue data, one of my main concerns was the use of the district property tax in the region. These data do not include San Francisco Public Schools as a result. San Francisco County contains only a single city and a single school district, making it impossible to disentangle district and county taxes. The sample includes, however, districts that were at various points urban like Antioch, Benicia, Oakland, San José, and Vallejo. The history of public finance in San Francisco has been considered in other histories readers may wish to consult.[4]

Each county superintendent report includes the amount each district received from district, county, and state taxes and the total number of pupils within each district. Assuming that county superintendents were consistent in their data collection, this dataset does not include money raised for capital projects funded through school bonds. In some cases, however, local districts may have needed to levy a local district tax to make interest payments on existing bond obligations.

Data points were missing or illegible in a handful of cases. At times this was because new districts had not yet received funds recorded by the county superintendent or because old districts, recently discontinued, were still listed as official districts in county reports. In other cases, data were simply missing or illegible. In both cases, the districts with missing data were dropped from the dataset. For 1890, missing or illegible data forced me to remove the Orinda district in Alameda County and the Laguna joint district in Marin County. After removing these districts, the dataset for 1890 had 480 school districts. For 1895, missing or illegible data forced me to remove the Pacheco district in Marin County, the Fairview, Sunnyside, and Pleasanton districts in Santa Clara County, and the Kidd Creek district in Sonoma County. After removing these districts, the dataset for 1895 had 547 school districts. For 1900, missing or illegible data forced me to remove the Knoxville and Lone Tree districts in Napa County, the Fairview district in San Mateo County, the Sunol, Purisima, and Agnew districts in Santa Clara County, and the Hot Springs and Joy School district in Sonoma County.

After removing these districts, the dataset for 1900 had 469 school districts. For 1905, missing or illegible data forced me to remove the Knoxville and Lone Tree districts from Napa County, the Fairview district in San Mateo County, the Comstock and Harve districts from Santa Clara County, the Blue Mountain and Olive school districts from Solano County, and the Crocker, Davis, Jenner, and Rodgers districts from Sonoma County. After removing these districts, the dataset for 1905 had 504 school districts. For 1910, missing or illegible data forced me to remove the Shafter district in Marin County, the Knoxville and Lone Tree districts in Napa County, the Pharis district in San Mateo County, the Blue Mountain district in Solano County, and the Tinite, Tan Bark, Litton, Guala, Frei, and Fort Ross districts in Sonoma County. After removing these districts, the dataset for 1910 had 508 school districts. For 1915, missing or illegible data forced me to remove the Vista district in Alameda County, the Fairview district in Santa Clara County, the Laguna and West Union districts in San Mateo County, the Morning Light district in Solano County, and the Creighton Ridge, Fort Ross, Ocean View, Plantation, Rose Hill, and Sacil districts in Sonoma County. After removing these districts, the dataset for 1915 had 511 school districts. For 1920, missing or illegible data forced me to remove the Alamo, Jersey, and Shelby districts in Contra Costa County, the Laguna district in San Mateo County, the Fairview and Las Mananitas districts in Santa Clara County, the American Canyon, King, Montgomery, and Mountain districts in Solano County, and the Fort Ross, Hot Springs, McMillen, and Mountain districts in Sonoma County. After removing these districts, the dataset for 1920 had 505 school districts. The final dataset for per pupil expenditures for all seven years had 3,524 total data points.

Measuring Disparities in Educational Resources

To assess disparities in educational resources between school districts, I often use the coefficient of variation (the ratio of the standard deviation to the mean). There are several reasons for my decision to use this metric. First, the coefficient of variation is resistant to inflation and thus provides a convenient way to compare per pupil expenditures over time. Second, Kaestle and Vinovskis (1986) use this metric in their study of nineteenth-century Massachusetts, one of the only detailed historical studies of variation in school spending between school districts. Finally, the coefficient of variation is an established metric used by contemporary scholars to assess equity in school finance.

Notes

INTRODUCTION

1. For example see Robert O. Self, *American Babylon: Race and the Struggle for Postwar Oakland* (Princeton, NJ: Princeton University Press, 2003); Becky Nicolaides, *My Blue Heaven: Life and Politics in the Working Class Suburbs of Los Angeles, 1920–1965* (Chicago: University of Chicago Press, 2002); Lisa McGirr, *Suburban Warriors: The Origins of the New American Right* (Princeton, NJ: Princeton University Press, 2001).

2. Serrano v. Priest, 5 Cal. 3d 584 (Cal. 1971). References to Beverly Hills and Baldwin Park at 594–95, 598, 611.

3. These figures were repeated in the national press and discussed directly in the California State Supreme Court opinion.

4. Serrano v. Priest, 5 Cal. 3d 584, 588 (Cal. 1971).

5. "School Funding: After Serrano What?," *Missoulian*, January 16, 1972, 26.

6. On *Serrano* and the wave of litigation during this period see Matthew Bosworth, *Courts as Catalysts: State Supreme Courts and Public School Finance Equity* (Albany: SUNY Press, 2001), 31; James Ryan, *Five Miles Away, a World Apart: One City, Two Schools, and the Story of Educational Opportunity in Modern America* (New York: Oxford University Press, 2010), 135–36; Paul A. Sracic, *San Antonio v. Rodriguez and the Pursuit of Equal Education* (Lawrence: University Press of Kansas, 2006), 43–47.

7. Matthew Bosworth, *Courts as Catalysts: State Supreme Courts and Public School Finance Equity* (Albany: SUNY Press, 2001), 31.

8. Anthony Harrigan, "Complete Federalization of Schools Possible," *Times and Democrat* (Orangeburg, SC), October 13, 1971, 4.

9. Harley Lutz, "Can the Property Tax Be Replaced?," *Wall Street Journal*, February 9, 1972, 14.

10. "Serrano Revisited," *Fremont (CA) Argus*, April 14, 1974, 4.

11. Lewis F. Powell Jr. to Mr. J. Harvie Wilkinson, August 30, 1972, San Antonio Independent School District v. Rodriguez, Supreme Court Case Files Collection, box 8, Powell Papers. Lewis F. Powell Jr. Archives, Washington & Lee University School of Law, Virginia.

12. San Antonio v. Rodriquez, 411 U.S. 1 (1973), 55.

13. San Antonio v. Rodriquez, 411 U.S. 1 (1973), 54, 8.

14. See, for example, Ryan, *Five Miles Away*, 124–25; Robert Berne and Leanna Stiefel, "Concepts of School Finance Equity: 1970 to the Present," in *Equity and Adequacy in Education Finance*, ed. Helen Ladd (Washington, DC: National Academy, 1999), 7–12; Sean Corcoran and William Evans, "Equity, Adequacy and the Evolving State Role in Education Finance," in *Handbook of Research in Education Finance and Policy*, ed. Helen Ladd and Edward Fiske (New York: Routledge, 2008), 332–33; "America's School Funding Is More Progressive Than Many Assume," *Economist*, December 23, 2017, https://www.economist.com/news/united-states/21732817-how-states-and-federal-government-offset-effects-local-inequality-americas.

15. For example, Thompson v. Engelking, 537 P. 2d 635—Idaho: Supreme Court 1975; Roosevelt Elementary School District No. 66 v Bishop, 877 P.2d 806, 813 (Ariz. 1994).

16. Richard Briffault, "The Role of Local Control in School Finance Reform," *Connecticut Law Review* 24 (1992): 783.

17. For example see reference to Cubberley in San Antonio v. Rodriquez, 411 U.S. 1 (1973), 8 n. 13. See also pages 48 and 49 in John Coons, William Clune, and Stephen Sugarman, *Private Wealth and Public Education* (Cambridge, MA: Harvard University Press) that Powell also cites in note 13. In *Private Wealth and Public Education*, five of the six notes on those pages are from various publications by Cubberley.

18. Lawrence Thomas Magee, "Historical Developments Affecting the Administration of the Los Angeles County Superintendent of Schools" (EdD diss., University of Southern California, 1955), 228.

19. For examples of the descriptions of the regulations discussed in this paragraph see the various legal provisions compiled in the school code across multiple years as they relate to school districting such as *Revised School Law, Approved March 24, 1866* (Sacramento: Department of Public Instruction, 1866), 10–12, 14, 16; *School Law of California: 1909* (Sacramento: Department of Public Instruction, 1909), 30–36, 60–72; *School Law of California: 1921* (Sacramento: Department of Public Instruction, 1921), 96–120; 217–81.

20. William Wesley Snider, "A Historical Study of School District Organization in Los Angeles County" (EdD diss., University of Southern California, 1959), 77.

21. "Baldwin Park Unified School District Asked," *Los Angeles Times*, September 25, 1958, pt. 3, p. 8.

22. Snider, "Organization in Los Angeles County," 154.

23. On the role of a dispute over the Canyon School in shaping incorporation see Nancie Clare, *The Battle for Beverly Hills: A City's Independence and the Birth of Celebrity Politics* (New York: St. Martin's, 2018), 37–38.

24. Snider, "Organization in Los Angeles County," 79–80, 151–52, 187.

25. For example see *School Law, Approved March 24, 1866*, 29–32; *School Law of California: 1909*, 30–36; *School Law of California: 1921*, 345–49.

26. Local taxation in western states often meant county-level taxation. In the statistics gathered by the US commissioner of education, no distinction is made in most years between these county taxes and a district or town-level tax farther east. However, this distinction is an important one for how much a community is imagining its funding, as for a local rather than geographically distant school. For example, there are twenty-three western counties that are each larger than the entire state of Massachusetts. The state of Connecticut is smaller than sixty-six counties in the West. If Delaware or Rhode Island were counties rather than states, neither would make the list of the one hundred largest counties in the nation. These figures are based on total state land area in square miles (table A-1) and total county land area in square miles (table B-1) ranked by size from data reported in US Census Bureau, *County and City Data Book: 2000*, 13th ed. (Washington, DC: US Department of Commerce, Bureau of the Census, 2001).

27. On racial covenants in Beverly Hills see Robert Fogelson, *Bourgeois Nightmares: Suburbia, 1870–1930* (New Haven, CT: Yale University Press, 2007), 76, 137.

28. See Area Description—Security Map of D16 (Los Angeles Area), dated 1939, in "Mapping Inequality: Redlining in New Deal America," Digital Scholarship Lab (University of Richmond), https://dsl.richmond.edu/panorama/redlining/#loc=10/34.003/-118.269&city=los-angeles-ca&area=D16&adview=full&adimage=4/16.847/-134.692.

29. For classic histories of postwar inequality that focused on segregation, racialization of poverty in the central cities of the Rust Belt, and the hand of the state see especially Arnold R. Hirsch, *Making the Second Ghetto: Race and Housing in Chicago, 1940–1960* (New York: Cambridge University Press, 1983), and Thomas J. Sugrue, *The Origins of the Urban Crisis: Race and Inequality in Postwar Detroit* (Princeton, NJ: Princeton University Press, 1996). For central accounts of suburban development and the hand of the state, especially the federal government, in underwriting postwar white affluence see especially

Kenneth T. Jackson, *Crabgrass Frontier: The Suburbanization of America* (New York: Oxford University Press, 1985); Self, *American Babylon*; Kevin Kruse, *White Flight: Atlanta and the Making of Modern Conservatism* (Princeton, NJ: Princeton University Press, 2005); David M. P. Freund, *Colored Property: State Policy and White Racial Politics in Suburban America* (Chicago: University of Chicago Press, 2007); Matthew Lassiter, *The Silent Majority: Suburban Politics in the Sunbelt South* (Princeton, NJ: Princeton University Press, 2007), and the essays in Kevin M. Kruse and Thomas J. Sugrue, eds., *The New Suburban History* (Chicago: University of Chicago Press, 2006). For a history that points out the still narrow map that defines the metropolis in these accounts and the importance of drawing an even wider map to include rural hinterlands see Andrew Needham, *Power Lines: Phoenix and the Making of the Modern Southwest* (Princeton, NJ: Princeton University Press, 2014).

30. In addition to the works cited above see also the role of the state through defense and research funding during World War II and the Cold War, especially Margaret Pugh O'Mara, *Cities of Knowledge: Cold War Science and the Search for the Next Silicon Valley* (Princeton, NJ: Princeton University Press, 2005).

31. On the falsity of the de facto and de jure distinction see especially Lassiter, *Silent Majority*, and as well as Ansley Erickson, *Making the Unequal Metropolis: School Desegregation and Its Limits* (Chicago: University of Chicago Press, 2016).

32. See especially Self, *American Babylon*, and Lassiter, *Silent Majority*, as well as work discussed below regarding California and the Sun Belt.

33. Mark Brilliant, *The Color of America Has Changed: How Racial Diversity Shaped Civil Rights Reform in California, 1941–1978* (New York: Oxford University Press, 2010); Shana Bernstein, *Bridges of Reform: Interracial Civil Rights Activism in Twentieth-Century Los Angeles* (New York: Oxford University Press, 2011), 11.

34. Brilliant, *Color of America*, 6, 14.

35. Robert Fogelson, *The Fragmented Metropolis: Los Angeles, 1850–1930* (Berkeley: University of California Press, 1967), 2.

36. For key examples of work on planning and land use see Greg Hise, *Magnetic Los Angeles: Planning the Twentieth-Century Metropolis* (Baltimore: Johns Hopkins University Press, 1997); Marc A. Weiss, *The Rise of the Community Builders: The American Real Estate Industry and Urban Land* (New York: Columbia University Press, 1987).

37. Robert Self, "City Lights: Urban History in the West," in *A Companion to the American West*, ed. William Deverell (Malden, MA: Blackwell, 2004), 37.

38. Kevin M. Kruse and Thomas J. Sugrue, introduction to *The New Suburban History*, ed. Kruse and Sugrue (Chicago: University of Chicago Press, 2006), 5.

39. Lisa McGirr, *Suburban Warriors: The Origins of the New American Right* (Princeton, NJ: Princeton University Press, 2001).

40. Nicolaides, *My Blue Heaven*.

41. Self, *American Babylon*.

42. Nicolaides, *My Blue Heaven*, 286.

43. For example see the following historiographic syntheses or essays: Nancy Beadie et al., "Gateways to the West, Part II: Education and the Making of Race, Place, and Culture in the West," *History of Education Quarterly* 57, no. 1 (February 2017): 94–126; Jack Dougherty, "Bridging the Gap between Urban, Suburban, and Educational History," in *Rethinking the History of American Education*, ed. William J. Reese and John L. Rury (New York: Palgrave Macmillan, 2008), 245–60.

44. Michael Bowman, "Learning Place: Education and Planning in Seattle and the Pacific Northwest, 1934–1955" (PhD diss., University of Washington, 2015); Karen Benjamin, "Suburbanizing Jim Crow: The Impact of School Policy on Residential Segregation in Raleigh," *Journal of Urban History* 38, no. 2 (2012): 225–46; Jack Dougherty, "Shopping for Schools: How Public Education and Private Housing Shaped Suburban Connecticut,"

Journal of Urban History 38, no. 2 (2012): 205–24; Ansley Erickson, "Building Inequality: The Spatial Organization of Schooling in Nashville, Tennessee, after *Brown*," *Journal of Urban History* 38, no. 2 (2012): 242–70; Walter Stern, *Race and Education in New Orleans: Creating the Segregated City* (Baton Rouge: LSU Press, 2018).

45. Emily E. Strauss, *Death of a Suburban Dream: Race and Schools in Compton, California* (Philadelphia: University of Pennsylvania Press, 2014), 4.

46. For an important exception that considers the mechanics of funding while examining the dynamics of postwar inequality see Tracy Steffes, "Assessment Matters: The Rise and Fall of the Illinois Resource Equalizer Formula," *History of Education Quarterly* 60, no. 1 (2020): 24–57. Destin Jenkins, too, notes debt financing for education in his history of racial capitalism and the bond market: Destin Jenkins, *The Bonds of Inequality: Debt and the Making of the American City* (Chicago: University of Chicago Press, 2021). Historians of education in the nineteenth and early twentieth centuries have also emphasized patterns in unequal funding in the late nineteenth and early twentieth centuries, at times attending more to the mechanics of taxation than historians have in accounts of inequality after World War II. See in particular Camille Walsh, *Racial Taxation: Schools, Segregation, and Taxpayer Citizenship, 1869–1973* (Chapel Hill: University of North Carolina Press, 2018), as well as work on "double taxation," in particular James Anderson, *Education of Blacks in the South, 1860–1935* (Chapel Hill: University of North Carolina Press, 1988), 156, 170, 179, 181, 183–85. On racial inequities in funding in the postbellum South see also Robert Margo, *Race and Schooling in the South, 1880–1895: An Economic History* (Chicago: University of Chicago Press, 1990). On the experience of African American communities determined to build excellent schools despite these oppressive public finance systems see Vanessa Siddle Walker, *Their Highest Potential: An African American School Community in the Segregated South* (Chapel Hill: University of North Carolina Press, 1996).

47. For an important recent exception focused on racial capitalism and the municipal bond market see Jenkins, *Bonds of Inequality*. For work rooted in the history of capitalism that also considers debt within the context of postwar suburban inequality and education see Michael Glass, "Schooling Suburbia: The Politics of School Finance in Postwar Long Island" (PhD diss., Princeton University, 2020); Esther Cyna, "Equalizing Resources vs. Retaining Black Political Power: Paradoxes of an Urban-Suburban School District Merger in Durham, North Carolina, 1958–1996," *History of Education Quarterly* 59, no. 1 (2019): 35–64.

48. In doing so I am indebted to work that does not consider the dynamics of school finance in detail but nonetheless illustrates how much can be learned from tracing the history of public finance, including Robin Einhorn, *Property Rules: Political Economy in Chicago, 1833–1872* (Chicago: University of Chicago Press, 1991), and *American Taxation, American Slavery* (Chicago: University of Chicago Press, 2006); Jenkins, *Bonds of Inequality*; Ajay K. Mehrotra, *Making the American Fiscal State: Law, Politics, and the Rise of Progressive Taxation, 1877–1929* (New York: Cambridge University Press, 2013); Isaac William Martin, Ajay K. Mehrotra, and Monica Prasad, eds., *The New Fiscal Sociology: Taxation in Comparative and Historical Perspective* (New York: Cambridge University Press, 2008); Julian Zelizer, *Taxing America: Wilbur D. Mills, Congress, and the State, 1945–1975* (New York: Cambridge University Press, 1998). Scholars have also considered the history of the general property tax in case studies of northeastern states and Kansas, though the connections between school finance and the fate of the general property tax are not part of this work. See Clifton K. Yearley, *The Money Machines: The Breakdown and Reform of Governmental and Party Finance in the North, 1860–1920* (Albany: SUNY Press, 1970), 27; Sumner Benson, "A History of the General Property Tax," in *The American Property Tax: Its History, Administration, and Economic Impact*, ed. George Benson et al. (Claremont, CA: Institute for Studies in Federalism, 1965), 37. See also Nicholas R. Parrillo, *Against the*

Profit Motive: The Salary Revolution in American Government, 1780–1940 (New Haven, CT: Yale University Press, 2013), 188.

49. For two examples that use the language of unintended consequence see Claudia Goldin and Lawrence F. Katz, *The Race between Education and Technology* (Cambridge, MA: Harvard University Press, 2008), 130–31; Sracic, *San Antonio v. Rodriguez*, 8.

50. See, to varying degrees, Carl Kaestle, *Pillars of the Republic: Common Schools and American Society* (New York: Hill & Wang, 1983), and David Tyack, "The Common School and American Society: A Reappraisal," *History of Education Quarterly* 26, no. 2 (1986): 301–6.

51. "School Department," *San José Municipal Record*, September 23, 1912, 8–9.

52. E. W. Davis to Board of Supervisors, May 19, 1895, box 69 (box without folders), row 10, bin 19, Sonoma County Board of Supervisors Records, Sonoma County Archives, Santa Rosa, CA.

53. This is true across a range of studies. See Kirabo Jackson and Claire Mackevicius, "The Distribution of School Spending Impacts," Working Paper 28517, National Bureau of Economic Research, Cambridge, MA, 2021, 50.

1. FUNDING FOR EDUCATION, SETTLER COLONIALISM, AND THE "CALIFORNIA EXPERIMENT" IN COMMON SCHOOL CENTRALIZATION, 1848–1865

1. The overused quote is from Horace Mann, *Twelfth Annual Report of the Secretary of the Massachusetts Board of Education* (Boston: Dutton and Wentworth, 1848), 59. This acreage estimate is based primarily on federal and state expropriated land set aside for permanent state school funds, summarized in Fletcher Swift, *A History of Public Permanent Common School Funds in the United States, 1795–1905* (New York: H. Holt, 1911), table 17, 100–106. It also includes 991,559 acres reported for New York State in Swift, *Common School Funds*, table 14, 85, but excluded from table 17. It also includes an estimate for the acres of expropriated land that formed the federal budget surplus in the 1830s and was then distributed to states and, by some states, to permanent school funds. The method for estimating that figure is described in greater detail in the appendix. Note that this figure also includes acres of state lands in Texas that are not included in figure 1.1 because they were not technically used to capitalize a school fund.

For a recent exploration of the connection between land-grant colleges and Native American dispossession see Margaret A. Nash, "Entangled Pasts: Land-Grant Colleges and American Indian Dispossession," *History of Education Quarterly* 59, no. 4 (November 2019): 437–67; Robert Lee and Tristan Ahtone, "Land-Grab Universities," *High Country News*, March 30, 2020, https://www.hcn.org/issues/52.4/indigenous-affairs-education-land-grab-universities.

2. For an important exception see Nancy Beadie, "Resource Extraction and Education Funding: Nature and Political Economies of State Formation in the United States," *Paedagogica Historica: International Journal of the History of Education* 56, no. 1–2 (2020): 150–70.

3. For a classic account on racial ideology and territorial expansion see Reginald Horsman, *Race and Manifest Destiny: The Origins of American Racial Anglo-Saxonism* (Cambridge, MA: Harvard University Press, 1981). For a more recent account of expansion and racial ideology in the US that brings the story of anti-Black racism into the narrative as well see Paul Frymer, *Building an American Empire: The Era of Territorial and Political Expansion* (Princeton, NJ: Princeton University Press, 2017).

4. John O'Sullivan, "Annexation," *United States Magazine and Democratic Review*, vol. 17 (New York, 1845), 5–6, 9–10.

5. For the historiographical critique of the myth of a "weak" American state see William J. Novak, "The Myth of the 'Weak' American State," *American Historical Review* 113, no. 3 (2008): 752–72. For other accounts of the period before the Civil War see William Novak, *The People's Welfare: Law and Regulation in Nineteenth-Century America* (Chapel Hill: University of North Carolina Press, 2000); Max M. Edling, *A Revolution in Favor of Government: Origins of the U.S. Constitution and the Making of the American State* (New York: Oxford University Press, 2003); Brian Balogh, *A Government Out of Sight: The Mystery of National Authority in Nineteenth-Century America* (Cambridge: Cambridge University Press, 2009); William H. Bergmann, *The American National State and the Early West* (New York: Cambridge University Press, 2012); Bethel Saler, *The Settlers' Empire: Colonialism and State Formation in America's Old Northwest* (Philadelphia: University of Pennsylvania Press, 2014).

6. On schools and American political development see Tracy Steffes, *School, Society, and State: A New Education to Govern Modern America* (Chicago: University of Chicago Press, 2012); Nancy Beadie, "War, Education, and State Formation: Problems of Territorial and Political Integration in the United States," *Paedagogica Historica: International Journal of the History of Education* 52 (2016): 58–75; Joan Malczewski, *Building a New Educational State: Foundations, Schools, and the American South* (Chicago: University of Chicago Press, 2016).

7. For examples of state and national funding that preceded the period typically associated with the rise of public education systems see Lawrence Cremin, *The American Common School: An Historic Conception* (New York: Teachers College Studies in Education, 1951), 93, 97; Carl Kaestle, *Pillars of the Republic: Common Schools and American Society* (New York: Hill & Wang, 1983), 10–12, 183–85; Nancy Beadie, *Education and the Creation of Capital in the Early American Republic* (New York: Cambridge University Press, 2010), 41–42; Johann Neem, *Democracy's Schools: The Rise of Public Education in America* (Baltimore: Johns Hopkins University Press, 2017), 70. See also the dates for the creation of permanent state school funds by state in Swift, *Common School Funds*, table 17, 100–106. For the creation of school districts by state legislatures and legislatures granting them power to raise local taxes see, for example, Cremin, *American Common School*, 91–93 on Massachusetts and 122–23 on Ohio. On courts granting school districts sufficient corporate powers to enter into contracts see an example from Massachusetts, in Inhabitants of Fourth School-District v. Wood, 13 Mass. 192, 12 Tyng 192 (1816).

8. On the small number of states that abolished rate bills by the end of the Civil War see Swift, *Common School Funds*, table 8. See also Kaestle, *Pillars of the Republic*, 149–51.

9. The practice was adopted in seven states. Swift reports requirements to raise a local tax as a condition for receiving a share of funding from permanent state school funds for Delaware, Massachusetts, New York, Rhode Island, Maine, Vermont, and Washington. See Swift, *Common School Funds*, 178.

10. On enrollments see, for example, Carl Kaestle and Maris Vinovskis, *Education and Social Change in Nineteenth-Century Massachusetts* (New York: Cambridge University Press, 1986); Albert Fishlow, "The American Common School Revival: Fact or Fancy?," in *Industrialization in Two Systems*, ed. H. Rosovsky (New York: Wiley, 1966). On the shift in compulsory school laws from symbolic to heavily enforced sites for the expansion of state power in the Progressive Era see Steffes, *School, Society, and State*, 119–53. On the lack of enforcement of early compulsory school laws and their symbolic nature see David Tyack, "Ways of Seeing: An Essay on the History of Compulsory Schooling," *Harvard Educational Review* 46, no. 3 (1976): 35–69.

11. See, for example, James Gordon Carter's comments on the history of Connecticut's state school fund in *Letters to the Hon. William Prescott, LL.D., on the Free Schools of*

New England, with Remarks upon the Principles of Instruction (Boston: Cummings, Hillard, 1824), 22, 54; "Report of the Trustees of the School Fund, Tuesday, November 5, 1839," in *Journal of the Proceedings of the Legislative Council of the State of New Jersey* (Somerville, NJ: S. L. B. Baldwin, 1840), 54; from Caleb Mills, "The First Address," quoted in Charles Moores, *Caleb Mills and the Indiana School System* (Indianapolis: Wood-Weaver printing, 1905), 405.

12. For example, note how the author generalizes about a pattern "throughout the United States" while discussing data from Massachusetts, in Maris Vinvoskis, *The Origins of Public High Schools: A Reexamination of the Beverly High School Controversy* (Madison: University of Wisconsin Press, 1985), 19.

13. For example see David Wallace Adams, *Education for Extinction: American Indians and the Boarding School Experience, 1875–1928* (Lawrence: University Press of Kansas, 1995); Brenda J. Child, *Boarding School Seasons: American Indian Families, 1900–1940* (Lincoln: University of Nebraska Press, 1998); Kim Cary Warren, *The Quest for Citizenship: African American and Native American Education in Kansas, 1880–1935* (Chapel Hill: University of North Carolina Press, 2010).

14. For a synthetic overview of the way ideas about the distinction between public and private have shifted over time see William Reese, "Changing Conceptions of 'Public' and 'Private' in American Educational History," in *History, Education, and the Schools* (New York: Palgrave Macmillan, 2007). On the unclear boundaries between public and private in the colonial era and early republic see Carl Kaestle, *The Evolution of an Urban System: New York City, 1750–1850* (Cambridge, MA: Harvard University Press, 1973). These boundaries were often the most unclear in relation to academies. See Mark Boonshoft, *Aristocratic Education and the Making of the American Republic* (Chapel Hill: University of North Carolina Press, 2020). On the early funding of academies see Beadie, *Education and the Creation of Capital*, and the chapters in Nancy Beadie and Kim Tolley, eds., *Chartered Schools: Two Hundred Years of Independent Academies in the United States, 1727–1925* (Routledge: New York, 2002). On the way distinctions between public and private became clearer in the years before the Civil War see Kaestle, *Pillars of the Republic*, 116–18, 166; Michael Katz, *Class, Bureaucracy, and Schools: The Illusion of Educational Change in America* (New York: Praeger, 1971), 23, 27–28. On the fuzzy distinction between public and private that persisted in relation to Catholic school systems see Robert Gross, *Public vs. Private: The Early History of School Choice in America* (New York: Oxford University Press, 2018). Similarly, Sherman Dorn points out how education for children with disabilities in the twentieth century can blur these boundaries as well. See Sherman Dorn, "Public-Private Symbiosis in Nashville Special Education," *History of Education Quarterly* 42, no. 3 (Autumn 2002): 368–94.

15. Kaestle frames his focus as "common-school systems" though also notes how his purpose is to retell the history of the "origins of public schooling"; see his *Pillars of the Republic*, ix. Katz at times discusses his focus as the origins of "public school systems" even as he makes clear his primary concern with the expansion of urban school bureaucracies. See, for example, his *Class, Bureaucracy, and Schools*, xix. Nancy Beadie's work on New York illustrates the state-level activity minimized by accounts that conceptualize the beginning of public schooling in this manner; see Beadie, "Education, Social Capital, and State Formation in Comparative Historical Perspective: Preliminary Investigations," *Paedagogica Historica: International Journal of the History of Education* 46 (April 2010): 19.

16. Katz, *Class, Bureaucracy, and Schools*, 23.

17. Kim Tolley, "Mapping the Landscape of Higher Schooling, 1727–1850," in Beadie and Tolley, *Chartered Schools*, 19–43.

18. On the blurred boundary between public and private and its connection to funding see Beadie, *Education and the Creation of Capital*, 107–22; Reese, *History, Education,*

and Schools, 95–112; Lawrence A. Cremin, *American Education: The National Experience, 1783–1876* (New York: Harper & Row, 1980), 164–71.

19. Reese, *History, Education, and Schools*, 97.
20. Kaestle and Vinovskis, *Education and Social Change*, 5, 208.
21. See Claudia Goldin and Lawrence F. Katz, *The Race between Education and Technology* (Cambridge, MA: Harvard University Press, 2008), 146.
22. Peter Lindert, *Growing Public: Social Spending and Economic Growth since the Eighteenth Century*, vol. 1 (New York: Cambridge University Press, 2004), 121.
23. Nancy Beadie, "Education, Social Capital," 19.
24. Beadie, 15.
25. Quoted in Kaestle, *Pillars of the Republic*, 52.
26. Boonshoft, *Aristocratic Education*, 132–33.
27. See the dates for when rate bills were outlawed in Swift, *Common School Funds*, table 8.
28. See, for example, the discussion of school districts in relation to *Rumford v. Wood* in Joan Williams, "The Invention of the Municipal Corporation: A Case Study in Legal Change," *American University Law Review* 34 (1985): 420–31.
29. Eric Hilt, "Early American Corporations and the State," in *The Corporation and American Democracy*, ed. Naomi Lamoreaux and William Novak (Cambridge, MA: Harvard University Press, 2017), 38.
30. For an overview see William Novak, "Public-Private Governance: A Historical Introduction," in *Government by Contract: Outsourcing and American Democracy*, ed. Jody Freeman and Martha Minow (Cambridge, MA: Harvard University Press, 2009), 23–40.
31. Henrik Hartog, *Public Property and Private Power: The Corporation of the City of New York in American Law* (Chapel Hill: University of North Carolina Press, 1983).
32. Novak, "Public-Private Governance," 30.
33. Hilt, "Early American Corporations," 58.
34. William G. Roy, *Socializing Capital: The Rise of the Large Industrial Corporation in America* (Princeton, NJ: Princeton University Press, 1999), 3.
35. See, for example, the quotes from Massachusetts in Henry Barnard, *Report of the Board of Education 1852–53* (Hartford, CT: State Printer, 1853), 157.
36. "Who Is My Neighbor?," *Common School Journal and Educational Reformer* 14, no. 21 (November 1852): 322–23.
37. Quoted in *Abstract of the Massachusetts School Returns for 1839–40* (Boston: Dutton and Wentworth, 1840), 323.
38. James Fraser, *Report to the . . . Commissioners Appointed by Her Majesty to Inquire into the Schools in Scotland, on the Common School System of the United States and of the Provinces of Upper and Lower Canada* (London: Her Majesty's Stationery Office, 1866), 50, 52.
39. George Boutwell, *Address by Hon. George S. Boutwell Delivered at the Dedication of Powers Institute* (Greenfield, MA: H. D. Mirick, 1858), 20.
40. *Report of the Iowa Secretary of the Board of Education* (Des Moines: State Printer, 1860), 18.
41. *Journal of the Assembly of Wisconsin Annual Session 1851* (Kenosha: State Printer, 1851), 833.
42. *Second Annual Report of the Superintendent of Public Instruction for the State of Indiana* (Indianapolis: State Printer, 1853), 5.
43. *Biennial Report of the Superintendent of Public Instruction of Illinois to the Seventeenth General Assembly* (Springfield: Lanphier & Walker, Printers, 1851), 67–68.
44. Christopher Morgan, *Annual Report of the Superintendent of Common Schools [Assembly, No. 21]* (Albany, NY: Charles Van Benthuysen, Printer to the Legislature, 1851), 4.

45. Quoted in Arthur Mead, *The Development of Free Schools in the United States as Illustrated by Connecticut and Michigan* (New York: Teachers College Press, 1918), 152.

46. On the square miles provided to each relevant state see Swift, *Common School Funds*, 57–58.

47. Carl Kaestle, "Public Education in the Old Northwest: 'Necessary to Good Government and the Happiness of Mankind,'" *Indiana Magazine of History*, March 1988, 60–74.

48. On Connecticut's school fund see Swift, *Common School Funds*, 228–37. On the dispossession of the Iroquois in New York after the Revolution see Laurence Hauptman, *Conspiracy of Interests: Iroquois Dispossession and the Rise of New York State* (Syracuse, NY: Syracuse University Press, 1999). On New York's fund see Beadie, *Creation of Capital*, 128.

49. Swift, *Common School Funds*, table 14.

50. *Annals of Congress*, 16 Cong., 2 sess., Jan. 30, 1821, p. 1771.

51. On 1820 proposal see John R. Van Atta, *Securing the West: Politics, Public Lands, and the Fate of the Old Republic, 1785–1850* (Baltimore: Johns Hopkins University Press), 99; Daniel Feller, *The Public Lands in Jacksonian Politics* (Madison: University of Wisconsin Press, 1984), 45. On the 1826 proposal see US Congress, House of Representatives, Committee on the Public Lands, School Fund for the Several States, 19 Cong., 1 sess., Feb. 24, 1826, Report No. 88, p. 2. On the 1827 and 1832 proposals see Magdalen Eichert, "Henry Clay's Policy of Distribution of the Proceeds from Public Land Sales," *Register of the Kentucky Historical Society* 52, no. 178 (January 1954): 25–32. On the 1833 proposal see "Education: The Reform Bill of the United States," *Vermont Chronicle*, November 1, 1833. On 1838 proposal see William Cost Johnson, *Speech of William Cost Johnson on Resolutions Which He Had Offered Proposing to Appropriate Public Land for Educational Purposes, Delivered in the House of Representatives February 1838* (Washington, DC: Gales and Seaton, 1838).

52. Michael Witgen, *Seeing Red: Indigenous Land, American Expansion, and the Political Economy of Plunder in North America* (Williamsburg, VA: Omohundro Institute for the Study of Early American History and Culture, 2022), 20.

53. Swift, *Common School Funds*, 74.

54. This figure includes some additional expropriated lands placed into state school funds after their initial capitalization in Texas. See the appendix for details on how I constructed this estimate. The percentage is based on an estimated total acreage for the 48 contiguous states of 1.9 billion acres.

55. Swift, *Common School Funds*.

56. *Proceedings of the California State Teachers' Institute and Educational Convention* (Sacramento: State Printer, 1861), 43.

57. Quoted in *Annual Report of the Superintendent of Public Instruction for the Year 1863* (Sacramento: State Printer, 1864), 168.

58. "Report of the County Superintendent of Public Schools," *Placer Herald*, November 20, 1858, 2.

59. See *Thirteenth Annual Report of the Superintendent of Public Instruction of the State of California for the Year 1863* (Sacramento: State Printer, 1863), 6.

60. Charles Loring Brace, *The New West: Or, California in 1867–1868* (New York: G. P. Putnam & Son, 1869), 79; "Education Matters in Other States," *Pennsylvania School Journal* 14, no. 12 (1866): 281.

61. "The California Experiment," *National Teacher: A Monthly Education Educational Journal* 3 (1873): 256; quoted in John Swett, *Public Education in California: Its Origin and Development, with Personal Reminiscences of Half a Century* (New York: American Book, 1911), 180.

62. Emerson White, "Addresses of Welcome," *Journal of the Proceedings and Addresses of the Thirty-Eighth Annual Meeting* (n.p.: National Education Association, 1899), 58–59.

63. For example, the US Commissioner of Education 1874 report records a territorial tax for Utah Territory, Idaho Territory, and Arizona Territory.

64. Richard White, *It's Your Misfortune and None of My Own: A New History of the American West* (Norman: University of Oklahoma Press, 1991), 192.

65. On connections between California's racial diversity and perceptions of the region as disorderly see Tomás Almaguer, *Racial Fault Lines: The Historical Origins of White Supremacy in California* (Berkeley: University of California Press, 1994), and Barbara Berglund, *Making San Francisco American: Cultural Frontiers in the Urban West, 1846–1906* (Lawrence: University Press of Kansas, 2007). On the fluidity of racial and gender hierarchies within the mines see Susan Lee Johnson, *Roaring Camp: The Social World of the California Gold Rush* (New York: W. W. Norton, 2000). On the importance of women in American settler colonialism see Laurel Clark Shire, *Threshold of Manifest Destiny: Gender and National Expansion in Florida* (Philadelphia: University of Pennsylvania Press, 2016). On gender and American empire building before the Civil War see Amy Greenberg, *Manifest Manhood and the Antebellum American Empire* (New York: Cambridge University Press, 2005).

66. Quoted in Berglund, *Making San Francisco American*, 4.

67. On the unique nature of race relations and the ambiguous status of Californios see Almaguer, *Racial Fault Lines*, and Michael Bottoms, *An Aristocracy of Color: Race and Reconstruction in California and the West, 1850–1890* (Norman: University of Oklahoma Press, 2013), 82.

68. Frymer, *Building an American Empire*, 172–219.

69. Quoted in Frymer, 195.

70. On "All Mexico" see Frymer, 172–219.

71. *Report of the Debates in the Convention of California on the Formation of the State Constitution, in September and October 1849* (Washington, DC: J. T. Towers, 1850), 353, 351, 347.

72. *Debates in the Convention of California*, 204–5.

73. "Address to the People of California," in John T. Frost, *History of the State of California from the Period of the Conquest by Spain to Her Occupation by the United States of America* (New York: Miller, Orton, 1857), 338.

74. *Debates in the Convention of California*, 348.

75. *Ninth Annual Report of the Superintendent of Public Instruction* (Sacramento: State Printer, 1860), 9.

76. *Ninth Annual Report*, 9.

77. *Fourth Annual Report of the Superintendent of Public Instruction of the State of California* (Sacramento: State Printer, 1855), 4.

78. *Fifth Annual Report of the Superintendent of Public Instruction of the State of California* (Sacramento: State Printer, 1856), 7.

79. Quoted in *Proceedings of the California State Teachers' Institute and Educational Convention*, 88.

80. "Education in California," *Marysville Daily Herald*, September 20, 1850, 3.

81. Quoted in Miriam Mead Hawley, "Schools for Social Order: Public Education as an Aspect of San Francisco's Urbanization and Industrialization Process" (MA thesis, San Francisco State College, June 1971), 4.

82. "Address of the Pacific Immigration Aid Association," *California Farmer and Journal of the Useful Sciences*, April 24, 1857.

83. Quoted in *Opinions of the Press of San Francisco and Sacramento on the Importance of Education* (n.p.: California Immigration Union, 1870).

84. C. T. Hopkins, *Common Sense Applied to the Immigration Question* (San Francisco: Turnbull & Smith, 1869), 22–23.

85. H. H. Haight, *First Biennial Message of H. H. Haight to the Legislature* (Sacramento: State Printer, 1869), 20.

86. Quoted in Lawrence Cremin, *The Genius of American Education* (New York: Vintage Books, 1965), 67.

87. Hilary Moss demonstrates a similar relationship between race and common school reform in antebellum Connecticut, Maryland, and Massachusetts: Moss, *Schooling Citizens: The Struggle for African American Education in Antebellum America* (Chicago: University of Chicago Press, 2009).

88. "The Public Schools and Colored Children," *San Francisco Bulletin*, February 24, 1858.

89. Berglund, *Making San Francisco American*, 8.

90. "Shall Negroes Go to School?," *Nevada City (CA) Journal*, April 6, 1855.

91. For Hubbs quotes see "Letter from the Superintendent of Public Instruction," *Sacramento Daily Union*, March 27, 1855.

92. "California Legislature," *Sacramento Daily Union*, March 12, 1855, 3.

93. "California Legislature," 3.

94. J. Holland Townsend, "American Caste, and Common Schools," *Anglo-African Magazine* 1 (March 1859), 81.

95. "Shall Negroes Go to School?," 2.

96. Townsend, "American Caste," 81.

97. On Peter Lester's activism, which included working to prevent Archy Lee from being enslaved and sent to Mississippi, see Quintard Taylor, *In Search of the Racial Frontier: African Americans in the American West 1528–1990* (New York: W. W. Norton, 1998), 78–79, 86–87, 91–92. For more on California's conventions see Bottoms, *Aristocracy of Color*, 30–31, and especially "Equality before the Law: California Black Convention Activism, 1855–65," https://coloredconventions.org/california-equality/.

98. "Negroes in the Public Schools," *San Francisco Globe*, February 10, 1858, 2.

99. "Colored Children in Public Schools," *Daily Alta California*, February 20, 1858, 1.

100. "The Public Schools and Colored Children," *San Francisco Bulletin*, February 24, 1858, 2.

101. Andrew Jackson Moulder, *Eighth Annual Report of the Superintendent of Public Instruction* (Sacramento: State Printer, 1859), 15.

102. "Diggers" was a slur used by Americans to describe California's Indigenous peoples. Moulder, 14.

103. Moulder, 14–15.

104. "Public Schools and Colored Children," 2.

105. Moulder, *Eighth Annual Report*, 14.

106. Nicolas Polos, "A Yankee Patriot: John Swett, the Horace Mann of the Pacific," *History of Education Quarterly* 4 (1964): 21.

107. "Statement of John Swett," *Sacramento Daily Union*, September 20, 1862, 3.

108. Quoted in "Education for People of Color in California," https://coloredconventions.org/california-equality/life-and-politics/education-for-people-of-color/.

109. On the 1866 law see Irving Hendrick, "Public Policy toward the Education of Non-white Minority Group Children in California, 1849–1970," unpublished report, National Institute of Education Project no. NE-G-003–0082, University of California Riverside, 1975, 36–39.

2. BUYING AND SELLING SCHOOLS AND RACIALIZING SPACE IN A WESTERN STATE

1. *Fourth Annual Report of the Superintendent of Public Instruction of the State of California* (Sacramento: State Printer, 1855), 6A.

2. "Minutes of Eden Vale School District No. 1," MS 637, California Historical Society, San Francisco.

3. Classified ad, *Daily Morning Chronicle* (San Francisco), June 6, 1869, 2.

4. This is the argument made in William Fischel, *Making the Grade: The Economic Evolution of American School Districts* (Chicago: University of Chicago Press, 2009).

5. The emphasis on efficiency is rooted in the Tiebout hypothesis. For the clearest historical accounts of funding that prioritize assumptions about efficiency over evidence of inequality see Fischel, *Making the Grade*. For an important recent account of the "economic style," its impact on policy making in recent years, and the kinds of evidence, questions, and outcomes it privileges see Elizabeth Popp Berman, *Thinking Like an Economist: How Efficiency Replaced Equality in U.S. Public Policy* (Princeton, NJ: Princeton University Press, 2022).

6. Quoted in Gunther Barth, *Instant Cities: Urbanization and the Rise of San Francisco and Denver* (Albuquerque: University of New Mexico Press, 1975), 134.

7. Hubert Howe Bancroft, *History of the Pacific States of North America: California Pastoral* (San Francisco: History Company, 1888), 732.

8. Roger Lotchin, *San Francisco, 1846–1848: From Hamlet to City* (New York: Oxford University Press, 1974), 242.

9. Quoted in *Fourteenth Biennial Report of the Superintendent of Public Instruction of the State of Illinois* (Springfield: State Printer and Binder, 1883), 139.

10. Quoted in George W. Knight, *History and Management of Land Grants for Education in the Northwest Territory* (New York: G. P. Putnam's Sons, 1884), 14.

11. "Deed for Benicia City," *Californian* (San Francisco), July 3, 1847, 3.

12. "Lots in Benicia City," *Californian*, June 19, 1847, 2.

13. *The Complete Tales of Henry James*, ed. Leon Edel, vol. 5, *1883–1884* (London: Rupert Hart-Davis, 1963), 32–33. "Robert Semple to Thomas Larkin, March 6, 1849," in *The Larkin Papers: Personal, Business, and Official Correspondence of Thomas Oliver Larkin*, ed. George Hammond, vol. 8 (Berkeley: University of California Press, 1962), 170.

14. "Multiple Real Estate Advertisements," *Alta California* (San Francisco), July 26, 1849.

15. Mel Scott, *The San Francisco Bay Area: A Metropolis in Perspective* (Berkeley: University of California Press, 1985), 33.

16. The schoolhouse was funded by Carpentier in what turned into a dubious deal for rights to the town's waterfront. See Edgar Hinkel and William McCann, *Oakland, 1852–1938: Some Phases of the Social, Political, and Economic History of Oakland, California* (Oakland: Works Progress Administration, 1939), 458.

17. Hinkel and McCann, 457.

18. Charles Falk, *The Development and Organization of Education in California* (New York: Harcourt, Brace & World, 1968), 127.

19. Falk, 127.

20. Falk, 127.

21. *History of Washington Township* (n.p.: Country Club, 1904).

22. "The Town of Searsville," *Journal of Local History* 1 (2009): 10; *History of Washington Township*, 61; "History: Pioneer School People," *Tri-City Voice* (Fremont, CA), September 18, 2007; Nicholas Perry and Kimberly Chan, *Mountain View* (Charleston, SC: Arcadia, 2012), 84; Thalia Lubin and Bob Dougherty, *Woodside* (Charleston, SC: Arcadia, 2012), 59; Claudine Chalmers, *Early Mill Valley* (Charleston, SC: Arcadia, 2005), 65; Philip Pezzaglia, *Rio Vista* (Charleston, SC: Arcadia, 2005), 69; Prudence Draper and Lloyd Draper, *Cotati* (Charleston, SC: Arcadia, 2004). Betty Gibson, "Alameda County's Educational Heritage," Alameda County Schools clipping file, Oakland History Room, Oakland Public Library; Philip Holmes and Jill Singleton, *Niles, Fremont* (Charleston, SC: Arcadia, 2004), 35; Marin History Museum, *Early San Rafael* (Charleston, SC: Arcadia, 2004), 32;

Contra Costa County Gazette, July 20, 1892, "Education Clippings," Contra Costa County Historical Society.
23. "Immigration," *Daily Evening Bulletin* (San Francisco), October 21, 1869.
24. Quoted in Richard Orsi, "Selling the Golden State" (PhD diss., University of Wisconsin, 1973), 387.
25. C. T. Hopkins, *Common Sense Applied to the Immigrant Question* (San Francisco: Turnbull & Smith, 1869), 58.
26. *Annual Report of the Board of Education to the Common Council of San Francisco* (San Francisco: Whitton, Towne, 1854), 14–15.
27. "Inaugural Address," *Stockton Independent*, May 11, 1869.
28. "School Trustees," *Weekly Colusa Sun*, June 26, 1869.
29. "Public Schools," *Los Angeles Daily News*, March 15, 1869, 2.
30. "Public Schools," 2.
31. "Encouragement of Immigration," *Daily Evening Bulletin*, November 12, 1870.
32. *San Francisco Chronicle*, June 23, 1869, 1.
33. "Santa Clara Valley," *San Jose Mercury-News*, November 30, 1869.
34. "Farm for Sale," *Contra Costa Gazette*, May 13, 1865.
35. "Miscellaneous: Julius Wetzlar," *Sacramento Bee*, July 18, 1870; "Farm for Sale," *Sacramento Bee*, September 9, 1861.
36. "Notes of Travel in California—No. 3," *Sacramento Daily Union*, July 9, 1860.
37. "Travel in Santa Clara, Santa Cruz and Monterey," *Daily Evening Bulletin*, January 19, 1860.
38. "Travel in Santa Clara, Santa Cruz and Monterey."
39. *Directory of the City of San Jose*, 1874, 16.
40. Classified ad, *Daily Morning Chronicle*, June 6, 1869, 2.
41. "Auction Sales," *Daily Alta California*, April 17, 1866, 3.
42. "Sebastopol Correspondence," *Russian River Flag*, July 29, 1869.
43. "Homes!," *Sacramento Daily Union*, July 31, 1869.
44. George Lipsitz, *How Racism Takes Place* (Philadelphia: Temple University Press, 2011), 15.
45. Quoted in Albert Shumate, *Rincon Hill and South Park: San Francisco's Early Fashionable Neighborhood* (Sausalito, CA: Windgate, 1988), 19.
46. Page & Turnbull Inc., *South of Market Area: Historic Context Statement* (report prepared for City and County of San Francisco Planning Department, 2009), 20.
47. John Whitmer, "Contesting the Golden Dream: The Shaping of San Francisco's Labor Landscape" (PhD diss., University of Idaho, 2002), 175.
48. William Warren Ferrier, *Ninety Years of Education in California, 1846–1936: A Presentation of Educational Movements and Their Outcome in Education Today* (Berkeley, CA: Sather Gate Book Shop, 1937), 43.
49. "City Intelligence," *Daily Alta California*, February 7, 1851, 2.
50. Quoted in Ferrier, *Ninety Years*, 44.
51. Happy Valley's reputation as a respectable neighborhood was short-lived, as manufacturing quickly developed in the area. Eventually the entire South of Market area was considered a slum. For a discussion of this transformation see Richard Rice et al., *Elusive Eden: A New History of California* (New York: McGraw Hill, 1996), 293.
52. Lotchin's analysis is based on land-use maps made by the Unites States Coast Survey in 1853, 1857, and 1869, a 10 percent sample of the 1857–58 San Francisco city directory compiled by Langley, and writing by San Franciscans discussing the spatial organization of the city at the time. Lotchin defines class as "a catalog of the groups which would have been considered in one group or another rather than a list of supposed characteristics

of a social stratum." Lotchin attempts to "let the contemporaries of the Gold Rush do their own defining" and considers artisans, laborers, sailors, and longshoremen working class. He considers merchants, clerks, and lawyers middle class. Lotchin, *San Francisco*, 22, 353nn28–30. Between Montgomery Street and Dupont Street the ratio of middle-class to working-class residents was roughly two to one. On Dupont Street the percentage of middle-class residents dropped to 60 percent, only to rise to 67 percent on Stockton Street and 75 percent on Powell Street. On Mason Street, 60 percent of the residents between Sutter Street and Greenwich Street were middle class. On Taylor Street 75 percent of the residents were middle class.

53. Lotchin, *San Francisco*, 22.

54. The elite residents of Rincon Hill would eventually flock to Russian and Nob Hills in the 1870s. For the history of Rincon Hill see Albert Shumate, *Rincon Hill and South Park: San Francisco's Early Fashionable Neighborhood* (Sausalito, CA: Windgate, 1988).

55. Gertrude H. Atherton, *Adventures of a Novelist* (New York: Liveright, 1931), 24–25.

56. Lotchin, *San Francisco*, 3–30.

57. For histories that frame the formation of urban school bureaucracies in these terms see Michael Katz, *The Irony of Early School Reform: Educational Innovation in Mid-nineteenth Century Massachusetts* (Cambridge, MA: Harvard University Press, 1968); Colin Greer, *The Great School Legend: A Revisionist Interpretation of American Public Education* (New York: Basic Books, 1972); Joel Spring, *Education and the Rise of the Corporate State* (Boston: Beacon, 1972); David Nasaw, *Schooled to Order: A Social History of Public Schooling in the United States* (New York: Oxford University Press, 1979). David Tyack, Ira Katznelson, and Margaret Weir all address the formation of San Francisco's school system in their histories, though they do not examine the spatial organization of the early schools. Tyack does, however, emphasize the formation of an "interlocking directorate" of reformers that, in some respects, are conceptually similar to the growth coalitions I describe.

58. *San Francisco City Directory . . . Compiled and Published by Harris, Bogardus, and Labatt* (San Francisco: Whitton, Towne, 1856), 135–36.

59. Lotchin, *San Francisco*, 25.

60. *Annual Report of the Board of Education* (1854), 4–5.

61. "Report of the Grand Jury," *Daily Evening Bulletin*, October 1, 1856.

62. North Beach would not remain a middle-class enclave for long, however, and the neighborhood would eventually become the center of San Francisco's Italian population. For a reference to North Beach as a middle-class community during the 1850s see Lotchin, *San Francisco*, 25.

63. Shumate, *Rincon Hill and South Park*.

64. "San Francisco Free Schools," *Daily Alta California*, March 22, 1852.

65. "Auction Sales," *Daily Alta California*, March 9, 1852.

66. James E. Vance, *Geography and Urban Evolution in the San Francisco Bay Area* (Berkeley, CA: Institute of Governmental Studies, 1964), 25.

67. Lotchin, *San Francisco*, 15.

68. "Airy Residences," *Daily Alta California*, September 9, 1951, 2.

69. *Annual Report of the Board of Education* (1854), 12.

70. Charles Dwight Willard, *The Herald's History of Los Angeles City* (Los Angeles: Kingsley-Barnes & Neuner, 1901), 279.

71. Quoted in Alexander Finkelstein, "Los Angeles's 1863–1876 Boom," *Southern California Quarterly* 99, no. 2 (Summer 2017): 148.

72. David Samuel Torres-Rouff, *Before L.A.: Race, Space, and Municipal Power in Los Angeles, 1781–1894* (New Haven, CT: Yale University Press, 2013), 139.
73. Torres-Rouff, 139.
74. William McClung, "Folio One: Southern California, 1900," in *Land of Sunshine: An Environmental History of Metropolitan Los Angeles*, ed. Greg Hise and William Deverell (Pittsburgh: University of Pittsburgh Press, 2005), 17.
75. Vierling Kersey, *Pioneer and Early Public Schools of California and of Los Angeles* (Los Angeles: Superintendent of Schools, 1948), 10.
76. Kersey, 10.
77. "Trees about the School House," *Los Angeles Star*, March 17, 1855.
78. "Brooklyn Heights," *Los Angeles Herald*, May 30, 1875.
79. "Brooklyn Heights."
80. *Annual Report of the Board of Education* (1854), 14–15.
81. "Public Schools," *Californian*, August 21, 1847, 3.
82. Robert Semple to Thomas Larkin, San Francisco, March 6, 1849, in *Thomas Larkin Papers*, ed. George P. Hammond, vol. 8, *1848–1851* (Berkeley: University of California Press, 1962), 170.
83. "Common Schools," *Sacramento Daily Union*, February 7, 1854, 2.
84. "Common Schools," 2.
85. George C. Mann and Ernest E. Oertel, *Study of Local School Units in California* (Sacramento: California State Department of Education, 1937), 7.
86. "Some Mistakes Corrected," *Oakland News*, October 14, 1872, 2.
87. "Board of Education," *Oakland Transcript*, May 8, 1872, 3.
88. *San Mateo County Gazette*, March 11, 1864, 2.
89. Lucille Lorge, Robert Phelps, and Devon Weston, *Images of America: Castro Valley* (San Francisco: Arcadia, 2005), 7.
90. "Our Public Schools," *Santa Cruz Weekly Sentinel*, January 21, 1865.
91. Byron C. Curry, "History of San Mateo County Public School Districts" (EdD diss., Stanford University, 1950), 95.
92. "Congressional Land Donations for Common Schools," *Sacramento Daily Union*, April 11, 1857.
93. "Speech of Hon. T. Laspeyre on the School Lands Question," *San Joaquin Republican*, March 29, 1860.
94. "Speech of Hon. T. Laspeyre."
95. "The Case Well Put," *Placer Herald* (Rocklin, CA), July 26, 1862.
96. Quoted in "A Few of the Counts," *Sacramento Bee*, June 18, 1861.
97. Quoted in "Few of the Counts," 4.
98. "California Legislature," *Sacramento Daily Union*, February 12, 1864, 1.
99. John Swett, *Public Education in California: Its Origins and Development, with Personal Reminiscences of Half a Century* (New York: American Book, 1911), 175.
100. "California Legislature," *Sacramento Daily Union*, March 3, 1864, 4; *Record of State Senators, 1849–2014* (Sacramento: California State Senate), http://secretary.senate.ca.gov/sites/secretary.senate.ca.gov/files/Senators%20and%20Officers%201849%E2%80%932014.pdf.
101. On the relationship between Bellows and Mann see F. Forrester Church, *God and Other Famous Liberals Reclaiming the Politics of America* (New York: Simon & Schuster, 1991), xv.
102. Henry Whitney Bellows, "Address of Rev. Dr. Bellows," *California Teacher* 2, no. 5 (November 1864): 113.
103. Bellows, 113.

3. FINANCE REFORM AND THE CONTESTED MEANING OF "PUBLIC" IN THE 1870S AND 1880S

1. *Hare's Guide to San Jose and Vicinity* (San José, CA: Geo. Hare, 1872), 17.

2. Quoted in Byron C. Curry, "History of San Mateo County Public School Districts" (EdD diss., Stanford University, 1950), 86.

3. Quoted in David Wallace Adams, *Education for Extinction: American Indians and the Boarding School Experience, 1875–1928* (Lawrence: University Press of Kansas, 1995), 52.

4. "School Law Amendments," *Contra Costa County Gazette*, February 28, 1874.

5. For further details on these figures see "National Data Aggregated at State Level" in the appendix.

6. See, for example, James Anderson, *Education of Blacks in the South, 1860–1935* (Chapel Hill: University of North Carolina Press, 1988); Robert Margo, *Race and Schooling in the South, 1880–1950* (Chicago: University of Chicago Press, 1990); Camille Walsh, *Racial Taxation: Schools, Segregation, and Taxpayer Citizenship, 1869–1973* (Chapel Hill: University of North Carolina Press, 2018).

7. See Kabria Baumgartner, *In Pursuit of Knowledge: Black Women and Educational Activism in Antebellum America* (New York: NYU Press, 2019), and Hilary Moss, *Schooling Citizens: The Struggle for African American Education in Antebellum America* (Chicago: University of Chicago Press, 2009).

8. Jarvis Givens, *Fugitive Pedagogy: Carter G. Woodson and the Art of Black Teaching* (Cambridge, MA: Harvard University Press, 2021), 13.

9. On that earlier tradition see, for example, Heather Andrew Williams, *Self-Taught: African American Education in Slavery and Freedom* (Chapel Hill: University of North Carolina Press, 2005). On reconstruction and Black education see Christopher Span, *From Cotton Field to Schoolhouse: African American Education in Mississippi* (Chapel Hill: University of North Carolina Press, 2009); Hilary Green, *Education Reconstruction: African American Schools in the Urban South, 1865–1890* (New York: Fordham University Press, 2016).

10. Anderson, *Education of Blacks in the South*, 19.

11. On Republican efforts to create a cabinet-level education position during the 1870s see Ward M. McAfee, *Religion, Race, and Reconstruction: The Public School in the Politics of the 1870s* (Albany: SUNY Press, 1998).

12. Quoted in McAfee, 20.

13. On origins of "Greater Reconstruction" see Elliott West, *The Last Indian War: The Nez Perce Story* (New York: Oxford University Press, 2009).

14. On the failure of these bills see Nancy Beadie, "The Federal Role in Education and the Rise of Social Science Research: Historical and Comparative Perspective," *Review of Research in Education* 44 (2016): 1–37; Nancy Beadie, "War, Education, and State Formation: Problems of Territorial and Political Integration in the United States," *Paedagogica Historica: International Journal of the History of Education* 52 (2016): 58–75.

15. For a broad overview, as well as how the practice was challenged in courts, see Camille Walsh, *Racial Taxation: Schools, Segregation, and Taxpayer Citizenship, 1869–1973* (Chapel Hill: University of North Carolina Press, 2018).

16. Ronald Butchart, *Northern Schools, Southern Blacks, and Reconstruction: Freedmen's Education, 1862–1875* (Westport, CT: Greenwood, 1980), 56, 60.

17. Michael Bottoms, *An Aristocracy of Color: Race and Reconstruction in California and the West, 1850–1890* (Norman: University of Oklahoma Press, 2013), 114–19.

18. Bottoms, 119.

19. Charles M. Wollenberg, *All Deliberate Speed: Segregation and Exclusion in California Schools, 1855–1975* (Berkeley: University of California Press, 1976), 19.

20. Bottoms, *Aristocracy of Color*, 124–25.
21. Wollenberg, *All Deliberate Speed*, 15–27.
22. Bottoms, *Aristocracy of Color*, 125–26.
23. Irving Hendrick, "Public Policy toward the Education of Non-white Minority Group Children in California, 1849–1970," unpublished report, National Institute of Education Project no. NE-G-003–0082, University of California Riverside, 1975, 71.
24. Bottoms, *Aristocracy of Color*, 132–34. The case was *Tape v. Hurley*. For a discussion of the Tape family that brought the case see Mae Ngai, *The Lucky Ones: One Family and the Extraordinary Invention of Chinese America* (Princeton, NJ: Princeton University Press, 2011). For a discussion of Chinese American educational activism in San Francisco see Victor Low, *The Unimpressible Race: A Century of Educational Struggle by the Chinese in San Francisco* (San Francisco: East/West, 1982).
25. For an overview see Richard White, *It's Your Misfortune and None of My Own: A New History of the American West* (Norman: University of Oklahoma Press, 1991).
26. See Fletcher Harper Swift, *A History of Public Permanent Common School Funds in the United States* (New York: H. Holt, 1911).
27. *Crofutt's Trans-continental Tourist* (New York: Geo. A. Croffut, 1874), 157.
28. Calculations based on public schools for western states and territories reported in 1870 and 1880 in Elliott West, *Growing Up with the Country: Childhood on the Far-Western Frontier* (Albuquerque: University of New Mexico Press, 2013), 190.
29. West, 190–91.
30. West, 189.
31. Quoted in William Deverell, *Railroad Crossing: Californians and the Railroad, 1850–1910* (Berkeley: University of California Press, 1994), 29.
32. Richard White, *The Republic for Which It Stands: The United States during Reconstruction and the Gilded Age, 1865–1896* (New York: Oxford University Press, 2017), 119.
33. See William C. Fankhauser, *A Financial History of California* (Berkeley: University of California Press, 1913), 207–11.
34. Deverell, *Railroad Crossing*, 29–32.
35. Tamara Venit Shelton, *A Squatter's Republic: Land and the Politics of Monopoly in California, 1850–1900* (Berkeley: University of California Press, 2013); David Igler, *Industrial Cowboys: Miller & Lux and the Transformation of the Far West, 1850–1920* (Berkeley: University of California Press, 2005).
36. Igler, *Industrial Cowboys*, 60–61.
37. Clifton K. Yearley, *The Money Machines: The Breakdown and Reform of Governmental and Party Finance in the North, 1860–1920* (Albany: SUNY Press, 1970), 27. In 1890 it accounted for 72 percent of state revenue and 92 percent of local revenue. Sumner Benson, "A History of the General Property Tax," in *The American Property Tax: Its History, Administration, and Economic Impact*, ed. George Benson et al. (Claremont, CA: Institute for Studies in Federalism, 1965), 37. See also Nicholas R. Parrillo, *Against the Profit Motive: The Salary Revolution in American Government, 1780–1940* (New Haven, CT: Yale University Press, 2013), 188.
38. Many states express tax rates on property in terms of a millage rate, the tax rate for each $1,000 of assessed property. The millage rate is the number of dollars of tax assessed for each $1,000 of property value. The term is derived from the Latin word for thousandth, *millēsimum*. Oxford English Dictionary, 3rd ed. (2002), s.v. "mill, n. 6."
39. Yearley, *Money Machines*, 16.
40. Parrillo, *Against the Profit Motive*, 190.
41. White, *Republic for Which It Stands*, 135; Leslie Decker, *Railroad Land Grants: The Taxation of the Railroad Land Grants, 1864–1897* (Providence, RI: Brown University Press, 1964).

42. Igler, *Industrial Cowboys*, 66.
43. People v. San Francisco & San Jose R. Co., 28 Cal. 254 (Cal. 1865).
44. Crosby v. Lyon, 37 Cal. 242 (Cal. 1869).
45. This eventually resulted in the decision to write a new constitution discussed later in this chapter. See Arthur Rolston, "Capital, Corporations, and Their Discontents in Making California's Constitutions, 1849–1911," *Pacific Historical Review* 80, no. 4 (November 2011): 521–56. See the following cases as well: Savings and Loan Society v. Austin (1873), 46 Cal. 473–74; Houghton v. Austin (1874), 47 Cal. 646; People v. Hibernia Sav. & Loan Soc., 51 Cal. 243 (1876).
46. Ezra S. Carr, *The Patrons of Husbandry on the Pacific Coast, Etc.* (San Francisco: A. L. Bancroft, 1875), 144.
47. Carr, 144.
48. Parrillo, *Against the Profit Motive*.
49. "The Support of Our Common Schools," *California Teacher* 11 (1873): 147.
50. Quoted in *Fourth Biennial Report of the Superintendent of Public Instruction* (Sacramento: State Printer, 1871), 145.
51. "Support of Common Schools," *California Teacher*, 153.
52. "Support of Common Schools," 141.
53. "Amending the School Law," *San Francisco Chronicle*, February 13, 1874, 2.
54. "Department of Public Instruction," *California Teacher* 11 (1874): 376.
55. "Support of Common Schools," 148.
56. "Tuttle's School Bill," *Sacramento Daily Union*, March 21, 1874, 2.
57. "Support of Common Schools," 153–54.
58. "School Law Amendments," *Contra Costa County Gazette*, February 28, 1874.
59. "Speech of Senator Tuttle on the School Bill," *Sonoma Democrat*, February 28, 1874, 1.
60. For background on the election see David Griffiths, "Anti-monopoly Movement in California, 1873–1898," *Southern California Quarterly* 52 (1970): 93–121.
61. "Speech of Senator Tuttle on the School Bill," 1.
62. See figures reported for both years in *Biennial Report of the Superintendent of Public Instruction of the State of California* (Sacramento: Department of Public Instruction, 1875), 19.
63. "Department of Public Instruction," *California Teacher* 11 (1874): 376.
64. Ellwood Cubberley, *School Funds and Their Apportionment: A Consideration of the Subject with Reference to a More General Equalization of Both the Burdens and the Advantages of Education* (New York: Teachers College Press, 1905), 174–98.
65. See, for example, the language in *Biennial Report of Hon. Cornelius Hedges, Superintendent of Public Instruction [Montana Territory] for the Years 1872–73* (Cincinnati: Robert Clarke, 1874), 9; *Annual Report of Territorial Superintendent of Public Instruction: Dakota Territory* (Yankton: Dakota Territory, 1882), 2; *Report of the Superintendent of Public Instruction of the Territory of Washington* (Olympia: C. B. Bagley, Public Printer, 1881), 9.
66. *First Biennial Report of the Superintendent of Public Instruction of the State of Colorado for the Two Years Ending August 31, 1878* (Denver: Daily Times Printing House and Book Manufactory, 1879), 127.
67. For further details on these figures see "State of California Elementary School Funding Data Aggregated at County Level, 1870–1930," in the appendix.
68. *First Biennial Report of the Superintendent of Public Instruction for the School Years 1869 and 1870* (n.p: n.p).
69. W. E. Metzger, "A History of State and Local Support of Nebraska Public Schools" (PhD diss., University of Nebraska, 1965).

70. Calculation based on *Report of the Superintendent of Public Instruction of the Territory of Washington* (1881), 9.

71. Some counties appear to have had districts with rate bills in 1877 because a tuition figure is reported, but the rate bills do not seem to correspond to having a special district tax or county tax. *Report of the Superintendent of Public Instruction [Montana Territory] for the Years 1877–78* (Helena: Independent Steam Power Print, 1879), 10–11.

72. *First Biennial Report of the Superintendent of Public Instruction* (Bismarck, ND: State Printers and Bonders, 1890).

73. *First Annual Report of the Superintendent of Public Instruction in the State of Montana for the Year Ending August 31, 1890* (Helena: Journal Publishing, 1891), 117.

74. *First Biennial Report of the Superintendent of Public Instruction of the State of Colorado for the Two Years Ending August 31, 1878* (1879), 127.

75. *Annual Report of Territorial Superintendent of Public Instruction: Dakota Territory* (1882), 2.

76. *Annual Report of Territorial Superintendent of Public Instruction: Dakota Territory* (1882), 2.

77. *Biennial Report of the [Utah] Territorial Superintendent of Common Schools for the Years 1874–5* (Salt Lake City: Desert New Steam Printing Establishment, 1876), 18.

78. *Biennial Report of the Superintendent of Public Instruction of the State of Nevada for the Years 1883 and 1884* (Carson City: State Printing Office, 1885).

79. See, for example, the summaries provided in the appeals made in *Sixteenth Report of the Vermont Board of Education* (Rutland: Tuttle, 1874), 439–48, and *Annual Report of the Superintendent of Public Instruction of the State of Wisconsin* (Madison: Atwood & Culver, 1874), lxxx–lxxxviii.

80. Elliott West, *Growing Up with the Country*, 195. West used census data. The patterns are consistent with US commissioner of education data used here.

81. For additional details on the underlying source data see "National Percent Distribution of Public-School Revenue by Source, 1872–1990," in the appendix.

82. In a curiously misleading account of early state aid programs, school finance scholar Paul Mort claims that compensatory state aid originated in Massachusetts in the 1870s: Mort, *State Support for Public Schools, School Administration Series* (New York: Teachers College, 1926), 32–33. Of course, as Fletcher Swift pointed out about Massachusetts in the 1920s, "No other state pursued so long and so completely the policy of placing almost the entire burden of school support upon the local communities": Swift, *Studies in Public School Finance: The East* (Minneapolis: University of Minnesota Press, 1922).

83. *Report of the [New Jersey] State Board of Education and the State Superintendent of Public Instruction for 1873* (Trenton: State Gazette, 1873), 11.

84. *San Francisco Chronicle*, February 20, 1874, 3.

85. "Tuttle's School Bill," *San Francisco Chronicle*, March 12, 1874, 2.

86. *San Francisco Chronicle*, March 18, 1874, 3.

87. Henry Bolander, *Fifth Biennial Report of the Superintendent of Public Instruction* (Sacramento: State Printer, 1873), 44.

88. For example see *Report of the Commission of Education for the Year 1879* (Washington, DC: Government Printing Office, 1889), 362; *First Biennial Report of the Superintendent of Public Instruction, State of Minnesota* (St. Peter, MN: J. K. Moore Printer, 1880), 214–15.

89. "School Lands," *Chicago Daily Tribune*, April 9, 1880, 3; "The State School Tax," *Chicago Daily Tribune*, February 15, 1875, 4; "The State School Tax," *Chicago Daily Tribune*, March 4, 1875, 4.

90. Ajay K. Mehrotra, *Making the Modern American Fiscal State: Law, Politics, and the Rise of Progressive Taxation, 1877–1929* (New York: Cambridge University Press, 2013).

91. *Annual Report of the Commissioner of Education for the Year 1889–1890, Volume 1* (Washington, DC: Government Printing Office), 24.

92. From *Report of the Connecticut State Board of Education for 1879* and reprinted in B. G. Northrop, *Schools and Communism, National Schools, and Other Papers* (New Haven, CT: Tuttle, Morehouse & Taylor Printers, 1879), 9.

93. On Wickersham's role in the NEA see *History of the National Education Association of the United States* (Washington, DC: National Education Association, 1892), 17.

94. J. P. Wickersham, "A Uniform State Tax," *Pennsylvania School Journal* 21 (1872): 400–401.

95. See the articles compiled in *A Bill to Promote Mendicancy: Facts and Figures That the South Does Not Need Federal Aid for Her Schools* (New York: Evening Post, 1886), and the analysis of editorials provided in Gordon Lee, *The Struggle for Federal Aid, First Phase: A History of the Attempts to Obtain Federal Aid for the Common Schools, 1870–1890* (New York: Teachers College, Columbia University, 1949). On broader significance of efforts see Beadie, "Federal Role in Education," and Beadie, "War, Education, and State Formation." On the idea of the pauper in the antebellum United States and the distinction between the deserving and undeserving poor see Michael B. Katz, *In the Shadow of the Poorhouse: A Social History of Welfare in America*, 10th anniversary ed. (New York: Basic Books, 1996).

96. "Connecticut's Warning against the Federal Education Scheme," *New York Evening Post*, February 6, 1886.

97. Quoted in Lee, *Struggle for Federal Aid*, 149; "The Blair Bill, Once More," *New York Evening Post*, December 31, 1887; "Connecticut's Warning against the Federal Education Scheme," *New York Evening Post*, February 6, 1886.

98. "Connecticut's Warning against the Federal Education Scheme."

99. E. W. Davis to Board of Supervisors, May 19, 1895, box 69 (box without folders), row 10, bin 19, Sonoma County Board of Supervisors Records, Sonoma County Archives, Santa Rosa, CA.

100. *Oakland News*, December 18, 1873, 3.

101. "San Jose Items," *Daily Alta California*, February 7, 1874, 2.

102. "Board of Supervisors," *Sacramento Daily Union*, August 9, 1872, 3.

103. Letter from E. Rousseau to Santa Clara County Board of Supervisors, April 28,1877, "DISTS School General Abandoned or Suspended, M–Z" folder, School District Records, Clerk of the Santa Clara County Board of Supervisors, San José, CA.

104. This is the argument made in William Fischel, *Making the Grade: The Economic Evolution of American School Districts* (Chicago: University of Chicago Press, 2009).

105. Claudia Goldin and Lawrence Katz, *The Race between Education and Technology* (Cambridge, MA: Harvard University Press, 2008), and Johann Neem, *Democracy's Schools: The Rise of Public Education in America* (Baltimore: Johns Hopkins University Press, 2017).

106. *Annual Report of the Commissioner of Education for the Year 1877* (Washington, DC: Government Printing Office, 1879), XXXIX.

107. *Sixteenth Annual Report of the Superintendent of Public Instruction of the State of New York* (Albany: Argus, 1870), 199.

108. *Report of the Board of Education of the State of Connecticut* (New Haven: Tuttle, Morehouse & Taylor, 1870), 162.

109. On the 1879 constitutional convention and higher education see John Douglass, "Creating a Fourth Branch of State Government: The University of California and the Constitutional Convention of 1879," *History of Education Quarterly* 32, no. 1 (Spring 1992): 31–72. For a historical account of constitutional conventions in the far West that includes both the 1850 and 1879 California constitutional conventions see David Johnson,

Founding the Far West: California, Oregon, and Nevada, 1840–1890 (Berkeley: University of California Press, 1992).

110. Kevin Starr, *Americans and the California Dream: 1850–1915* (New York: Oxford University Press, 1973), 132. For a discussion of the "Chinese question" that touches on the convention see Alexander Saxton, *The Indispensable Enemy: Labor and the Anti-Chinese Movement in California* (Berkeley: University of California Press, 1971), 127–32, and Andrew Gyory, *Race, Politics, and the Chinese Exclusion Act* (Chapel Hill: University of North Carolina Press, 1998), 169–171. On the dynamics of anti-Chinese violence and exclusion more broadly see Beth Lew-Williams, *The Chinese Must Go: Violence, Exclusion, and the Making of the Alien in America* (Cambridge, MA: Harvard University Press, 2018).

111. Rolston, "Capital, Corporations, and Their Discontents," 550.

112. Igler, *Industrial Cowboys*, 88.

113. William Reese, *The Origins of the American High School* (New Haven, CT: Yale University Press, 1995), 94.

114. *Eighth Annual Report of the Superintendent of Public Schools of the State of Missouri* (Jefferson City: State Printers, 1874), 65.

115. *Tenth Biennial Report of the Superintendent of Public Instruction of the State of Illinois, 1873–74* (n.p.: n.p., 1874), 75.

116. "No Room on Top," *Marin Journal* (San Rafael, CA), December 11, 1879, 2.

117. "High School," *Marysville Daily Appeal*, September 24, 1871, 2.

118. *Debates and Proceedings of the Constitutional Convention of the State of California* (Sacramento: State Printer, 1881), 1088.

119. *Constitutional Convention of the State of California*, 1095.

120. *Constitutional Convention of the State of California*, 1099.

121. *Constitutional Convention of the State of California*, 1098–99, 1104.

122. *Constitutional Convention of the State of California*, 1103.

123. "Mass Meeting of the San Francisco School Teachers in Opposition to the New Constitution," *Pacific School and Home Journal* 3 (May 1879): 175.

124. "Are Our People Attached to the Public School?," *Pacific School and Home Journal* 3 (May 1879): 172.

125. "The Truth of Our Position Demonstrated," *Pacific School and Home Journal* 3 (May 1879): 171.

126. "Truth of Our Position," 171.

127. John Napier, "Origin and Development of Public High School in California" (PhD diss., Stanford University, 1932), 322–41.

128. "Local Intelligence," *Marin Journal*, May 15, 1879, 3.

129. Ezra S. Carr, *Eighth Biennial Report of Superintendent of Public Instruction, 1877–1879* (Sacramento: State Printer, 1879), 25–27.

130. For a discussion of the impact of the new constitution on the University of California see John Douglass, "Creating a Fourth Branch of State Government: The University of California and the Constitutional Convention of 1879," *History of Education Quarterly* 32 (1992): 31–72, and John Douglass, *The California Idea and American Higher Education* (Stanford, CA: Stanford University Press, 2000).

131. Horace Davis, "The Relation of the University to the Public Schools," *Pacific Educational Journal* 5 (1889): 253.

132. Napier, "Public High School in California," 333.

133. R. Rudy Higgens-Evenson, *The Price of Progress: Public Services, Taxation, and the American Corporate State, 1872 to 1929* (Baltimore: Johns Hopkins University Press, 2003), 21.

134. Quoted in Higgens-Evenson, *Price of Progress*, 21.

135. Quoted in Higgens-Evenson, 21.

136. "The City Schools," *San Diego Union and Daily Bee*, March 28, 1884, 4.
137. "The Railroad Tax Question," *Placer Herald* (Rocklin, CA), March 25, 1882.
138. "Must Not Be Educated," *Daily Morning Times*, June 12, 1883.
139. For a classic view of the place of the case in the broader history of the Fourteenth Amendment's use for corporate personhood arguments by jurists see Morton Horwitz, *The Transformation of American Law, 1870–1960: The Crisis of Legal Orthodoxy* (New York: Oxford University Press, 1992), 67. More recently, historians have also emphasized limits to the protections corporations received under the Fourteenth Amendment until the second half of the twentieth century. See Ruth H. Bloch and Naomi R. Lamoreaux, "Corporations and the Fourteenth Amendment," in *Corporations and American Democracy*, ed. Naomi R. Lamoreaux and William J. Novak (Cambridge, MA: Harvard University Press, 2017), 286.

4. STATE-SPONSORED INEQUALITIES, BOOSTERISM, AND THE RACE FOR PROGRESSIVE ERA SCHOOL REFORM, 1890–1910

1. These statistics are from Jal Mehta, *The Allure of Order: High Hopes, Dashed Expectations, and the Troubled Quest to Remake American Schooling* (New York: Oxford University Press, 2013), 42.
2. The historiography of Progressive Era education reform is too extensive to list here. For useful historiographical essays that explore debates over the meaning and impact of "progressivism" in education see Ellen Condliffe Lagemann, "The Plural Worlds of Educational Research," *History of Education Quarterly* 29, no. 2 (Summer 1989): 185–214; William J Reese, "In Search of American Progressives and Teachers," *History of Education* 42, no. 3 (2013): 320–34; and the essays contained in William Reese, ed., "American Education in the Twentieth Century: Progressive Legacies," special issue, *Paedagogica Historica: International Journal of the History of Education* 39, no. 4 (August 2003): 415–97. For three canonical texts that each reflect the changing ways historians of education have thought about education reform in the Progressive Era see Lawrence A. Cremin, *The Transformation of the School: Progressivism in American Education, 1876–1957* (New York: Vintage Books, 1961); David B. Tyack, *The One Best System: A History of American Urban Education* (Cambridge, MA: Harvard University Press, 1974); William J Reese, *Power and the Promise of School Reform: Grassroots Movements during the Progressive Era* (New York: Teachers College Press, 2002). For excellent new accounts that have reframed education reform during the Progressive Era in new ways and shaped my own thinking see David Gamson, *The Importance of Being Urban: Designing the Progressive School District, 1890–1940* (Chicago: University of Chicago Press, 2019); Tracy Steffes, *School, Society, and State: A New Education to Govern Modern America* (Chicago: University of Chicago Press, 2012); Cristina Groeger, *The Education Trap: Schools and the Remaking of Inequality in Boston* (Cambridge, MA: Harvard University Press, 2021).
3. Campbell Gibson, "Population of the 100 Largest Cities and Other Urban Places in the United States: 1790 to 1990," Census Working Paper no. POP-WP027 (US Department of Commerce, Bureau of the Census, 1998).
4. Daniel T. Rodgers, *Atlantic Crossings: Social Politics in a Progressive Age* (Cambridge, MA: Harvard University Press, 1998), 113.
5. Ariane Liazos, *Reforming the City: The Contested Origins of Urban Government, 1890–1930* (New York: Columbia University Press, 2019), 3.
6. Richard Briffault, "Our Localism: Part I—The Structure of Local Government Law," *Columbia Law Review* 90, no. 1 (January 1990): 8.
7. Robert Wiebe, *The Search for Order, 1877–1920* (New York: Hill & Wang, 1967), 170.
8. Clifford Wheeler Patton, *The Battle for Municipal Reform: Mobilization and Attack, 1875–1900* (Washington, DC: American Council on Public Affairs, 1940), 71.

9. Liazos, *Reforming the City*, 3.
10. In re Lee Sing, 43 F. 359 (C.C.D. Cal. 1890).
11. For example, an ordinance from the early 1870s targeting Chinese San Franciscans, called the Cubic Air Ordinance, originated with an anti-Chinese organization. Eli Moore, Nicole Montojo, and Nicole Mauri, *Roots, Race, and Place: A History of Racially Exclusionary Housing in the San Francisco Bay Area* (Berkeley, CA: Haas Institute for a Fair and Inclusive Society, 2019), 30.
12. Yick Wo v. Hopkins, 118 US 356 (1886).
13. California Const. art. XI, § 11 (1879).
14. W. L. Pollard, "Outline of the Law of Zoning in the United States," *Annals of the American Academy of Political and Social Science* 155 (1931): 20.
15. Sonia Hirt, *Zoned in the USA: The Origins and Implications of American Land-Use Regulation* (Ithaca, NY: Cornell University Press, 2014), 130.
16. Kenneth Jackson, *Crabgrass Frontier: The Suburbanization of the United States* (New York: Oxford University Press, 1985), 141. For another classic account that discusses the growth of Progressive Era cities in relation to annexation and incorporation see Jon C. Teaford, *City and Suburb: The Political Fragmentation of Metropolitan America, 1850–1970* (Baltimore: Johns Hopkins University Press, 1979).
17. David Freund, *Colored Property: State Policy and White Racial Politics in Suburban America* (Chicago: University of Chicago Press, 2007), 46. See also Jackson, *Crabgrass Frontier*, 144–46.
18. For an older but still useful history of the growth of Los Angeles and the suburban fragmentation of the region see Robert Fogelson, *The Fragmented Metropolis: Los Angeles, 1850–1930* (Berkeley: University of California Press, 1993). See table 24, 226, for territorial expansion of the city.
19. Gamson, *Importance of Being Urban*, 72.
20. "Gardner Residents Gather at Meeting to Fix Definitely Boundaries of New Addition to City," *San Jose Evening News*, October 26, 1910, 1.
21. "City Official Paper," *San Leandro Reporter*, May 16, 1902, 2.
22. "Mackie Ousted by Chamber," *Alameda Daily Argus*, August 13, 1909, 1.
23. *Reasons for Consolidation* (Berkeley: Joint Committee on Consolidated City and County, 1910), 7. Pamphlet is in "Pamphlets and Clippings Related to Proposed Oakland/Berkeley Consolidation MSS 93/126c," Bancroft Library, University of California, Berkeley.
24. City and County Government Association, *Some of the Benefits That Would Accrue under a City and County Charter* (n.p., 1916).
25. "We Want Annexation as Slogan," *Alameda Daily Argus*, September 24, 1909, 1.
26. "Greater San Jose," *San Jose Evening News*, June 26, 1894, 2.
27. Paul Sandul, *California Dreaming: Boosterism, Memory, and Rural Suburbs in the Golden State* (Morgantown: West Virginia University Press, 2014), 2.
28. Teaford, *City and Suburb*, 9–10.
29. For example see Article 10 § 1662, in *School Law of California* (Sacramento: Department of Public Instruction, 1907), 47.
30. Charlotte Brooks, *Alien Neighbors, Foreign Friends: Asian Americans, Housing, and the Transformation of Urban California* (Chicago: University of Chicago Press, 2009), 26.
31. On integration in Los Angeles after 1880 see Judith Raftery, *Land of Fair Promise: Politics and Reform in Los Angeles Schools, 1885–1941* (Stanford, CA: Stanford University Press, 1992), 110. On Stockton and San José see Irving Hendrick, "Public Policy toward the Education of Non-white Minority Group Children in California, 1849–1970," unpublished report, National Institute of Education Project no. NE-G-003–0082, University of California Riverside, 1975, 74.

32. Brooks, *Alien Neighbors*, 27.

33. On Du Bois see Abigail Rosas, *South Central Is Home: Race and the Power of Community Investment in Los Angeles* (Stanford, CA: Stanford University Press, 2019), 26. See Josh Sides, *L.A. City Limits: African American Los Angeles from the Great Depression to the Present* (Berkeley: University of California Press, 2003), 11–35 on experience of Black residents in LA during the 1900s and early 1910s. On schools see especially *Los Angeles Times* quote on 17 and discussion of multiracial enrollment at schools like Jordan High, 18–21.

34. See Gene Slater, *Freedom to Discriminate: How Realtors Conspired to Segregate Housing and Divide America* (Berkeley, CA: Heyday Books, 2021), 56–66.

35. Slater, 64.

36. California courts outlawed racial covenants on property sales but upheld racially restrictive covenants on occupancy in Los Angeles Investment Co. v. Gary, 181 Cal. 680, 186 P. 596 (Cal. 1919), thus permitting people of color to purchase properties but allowing a prohibition on their residing in the properties they purchased when covered by a racial covenant, until *Shelley v. Kraemer*, 334 U.S. 1, 68 S. Ct. 836 (1948).

37. Quoted in Slater, *Freedom to Discriminate*, 63.

38. Slater, 64.

39. Marc A. Weiss, *The Rise of the Community Builders: The American Real Estate Industry and Urban Land* (New York: Columbia University Press, 1987), 82.

40. Moore, Montojo, and Mauri, *Roots, Race, and Place*, 31.

41. "Vote Monday for Extension," *San Mateo Leader*, June 9, 1909, 1; "Another Annexation Scheme Is Planned," *San Francisco Chronicle*, January 29, 1910, 4.

42. "Sunnyvale Tries to Annex Water Front," *San Francisco Call*, September 27, 1912, 2.

43. For references to Alameda's annexation plans see "Chamber of Commerce Favors Annexation," *San Francisco Call*, September 18, 1909, 12; "Oakland to Have First Chance to Annex Outside Territory," *Alameda Daily Argus*, September 28, 1909, 1. For San Leandro's plans see "For Greater San Leandro," *San Leandro Reporter*, March 14, 1908, 2; "Board of Trade to Change Name," *San Leandro Reporter*, March 14, 1908, 3; "Petition for Annexation Filed," *San Leandro Reporter*, April 25, 1908, 1.

44. "What Leading Businessmen Have to Say about Bond Issue," *Hayward Twice-a-Week Review*, September 4, 1911, 4.

45. Clipping in "Piedmont" clipping file, Oakland History Room, Oakland Public Library.

46. "Two Towns War over Annexation," *San Francisco Call*, October 4, 1912, 5.

47. "Chamber of Commerce Favors Annexation," *San Francisco Call*, September 18, 1909, 12.

48. "Not to Hold Election," *Alameda Daily Argus*, September 28, 1909, 4.

49. "We Want Annexation as Slogan," 1.

50. "The Argument for Greater San Jose as Presented by the Managing Board of the Chamber," *San Jose Mercury and Herald*, March 26, 1905, 21.

51. "City Official Paper," *San Leandro Reporter*, May 16, 1902, 2.

52. "City Official Paper," *San Leandro Reporter*, June 13, 1908, 2.

53. "Incorporation Committee Meets," *South San Francisco Enterprise*, January 19, 1907, 1.

54. "Annexation Is Again Discussed," *San Francisco Chronicle*, September 7, 1910, 9.

55. *Reasons for Consolidation* (Berkeley: Joint Committee on Consolidated City and County, 1910), 7, 9. Pamphlet is in "Pamphlets and Clippings Related to Proposed Oakland/Berkeley Consolidation MSS 93/126c," Bancroft Library, University of California, Berkeley.

56. "Greater Oakland Cry at Meeting," clipping in "Annexation" clipping file, Oakland History Room, Oakland Public Library.

57. *Reasons for Consolidation*, 9.

58. Quoted in *Shall Berkeley Annex Herself to Oakland: A Reply to the Arguments Presented by the "Committee of Two Hundred,"* unpaginated pamphlet in "Communication on Oakland Annexation or Consolidation," in "Pamphlets and Clippings Related to Proposed Oakland/Berkeley Consolidation MSS 93/126c," Bancroft Library, University of California, Berkeley.

59. "Problems Puzzle Hollywood City: School District Mix-Up Yet Unsolved," *Los Angeles Herald*, November 20, 1903, 11.

60. "School District Tangle Now Ended," *La Habra (CA) Star*, May 21, 1920, 1.

61. "Divide Town for Schools: Santa Monica Gets a Slice of Sawtelle," *Los Angeles Herald*, February 7, 1906, 8.

62. "Divide Town for Schools," 8.

63. See Slater, *Freedom to Discriminate*, 62–65.

64. "California Real Estate Association ____ Real Estate Board," responses for Redlands, Alhambra, and Montebello, c. 1927, in Survey of Race Relations, box 20, folder 16, Hoover Archives, Stanford University.

65. Aaron Cavin, "The Borders of Citizenship: The Politics of Race and Metropolitan Space in Silicon Valley" (PhD diss., University of Michigan, 2012), 23–24.

66. "Loses the School by Incorporating," *San Francisco Call*, September 27, 1900, 5.

67. On the idea of the "rural school problem" see Tracy Steffes, *School, Society, and State*, 47–82. On the continued existence of small, rural one-room schools beyond the Progressive Era and their subsequent transformation after World War II see Campbell Scribner, *The Fight for Local Control: Schools, Suburbs, and American Democracy* (Ithaca, NY: Cornell University Press, 2016). On their place in American myth see Jonathan Zimmerman, *Small Wonder: The Little Red Schoolhouse in History and Memory* (New Haven, CT: Yale University Press, 2009). On the history of rural schooling more broadly see Wayne E. Fuller, *The Old Country School: The Story of Rural Education in the Middle West* (Chicago: University of Chicago Press, 1982); William A. Link, *A Hard Country and a Lonely Place: Schooling, Society, and Reform in Rural Virginia, 1870–1920* (Chapel Hill: University of North Carolina Press, 1986); Paul Theobald, *Call School: Rural Education in the Midwest to 1918* (Carbondale: Southern Illinois University Press, 1995).

68. Author calculations from data described in "District-Level Sample from California, 1870–1940," in appendix.

69. For cities by initial incorporation dates see "California Cities by Incorporation Date," California Association of Local Agency Formation Commissions (CALAFCO), Incorporation Date, last accessed February 1, 2021, https://calafco.org/resources/incorporated-cities/california-cities-incorporation-date. For information on incorporation dates and subsequent annexations see Frank Jordan, *California Blue Book or State Roster 1913–1915* (Sacramento: State Printing Office, 1915). Information on Redwood City appears on 210.

70. Byron Curry, "History of San Mateo County Public School Districts" (EdD thesis, Stanford University, 1950), 170–71.

71. J. Harold Williams, *Reorganizing a County System of Rural Schools: Reports of a Study of the Schools of San Mateo County, California*, United States Bulletin of Education no. 16 (Washington, DC: Government Printing Office, 1916), 22.

72. Williams, 25, 26, 24.

73. "Census Marshals Find Boundaries Uncertain," *San Jose Mercury News*, May 15, 1908.

74. "Plea for Grant Schools Denied," *Sacramento Union*, February 11, 1911, 5.

75. "Census Reports Bone of Contention—Supervisors Refuse to Divide School Districts," *Red Bluff (CA) News*, January 12, 1906, 6.

76. William Reese, *America's Public Schools: From the Common School to "No Child Left Behind"* (Baltimore: Johns Hopkins University Press, 2005), 122.

77. Theodore MacDowell, *State versus Local Control of Elementary Education*, United States Bulletin of Education no. 22 (Washington, DC: Government Printing Office, 1915), 52.

78. Figures on school district debt aggregated to state levels for 1880 are derived from the data reported in *Report on Wealth, Debt, and Taxation at the Eleventh Census, 1890: Part I, Public Debt* (Washington, DC, Department of the Interior Census Office, 1892), 78. Figures for 1913 are derived from *Wealth, Debt, and Taxation 1913, Volume I Part II County and Municipal Indebtedness* (Washington, DC: Department of Commerce Bureau of the Census, 1915), table 1, 299. Author's calculations of national totals.

79. MacDowell, *State versus Local Control of Elementary Education*, 32–34.

80. Based on school debt figures described above and total state populations reported for 1880 in *Report on Wealth, Debt, and Taxation at the Eleventh Census, 1890*, 77. Figures for 1913 are derived from population total for states reported in *Wealth, Debt, and Taxation 1913, Volume I Part II County and Municipal Indebtedness* (Washington, DC: Department of Commerce Bureau of the Census, 1915), table 1, 299. Since the Bureau of Labor Statistics' Consumer Price Index begins in 1913, inflation adjustments are based on Robert Sahr's index starting in 1774. See Robert Sahr, "Inflation Conversion Factors for Years 1774 to Estimated 2028," https://liberalarts.oregonstate.edu/spp/polisci/research/inflation-conversion-factors-convert-dollars-1774-estimated-2024-dollars-recent-year.

81. Lawrence Chamberlain, *The Principles of Bond Investment*, 3rd ed. (New York: Henry Holt, 1913), 251.

82. For example see the information for school districts contained in John Moody, *Moody's Analyses of Investments, Part III Government and Municipal Securities* (New York: Moody's Investors Service, 1918).

83. MacDowell, *State versus Local Control of Elementary Education*, 33.

84. "The Board of Trade," *San Jose Evening News*, June 3, 1893, 3. For a reference to this trend in Berkeley see "Champion Cause of School Bonds," *San Francisco Chronicle*, July 29, 1906, 25. "A County Fair. The Board of Trade Will Take a Hand in It," *San Jose Evening News*, July 18, 1896, 4. For a discussion of the role boosters played in Hayward see "Chamber of Commerce Discusses High School," *Hayward Twice-a-Week Review*, September 4, 1911, 1; "High School Question Aired at Mass Meeting," *Hayward Twice-a-Week Review*, January 23, 1912, 1; "High School Bonds Carry with Twelve Acres," *Hayward Twice-a-Week Review*, April 2, 1912, 1.

85. "Many Matters Discussed at Chamber of Commerce: Urged Construction of New High School in San Jose," *San Jose Evening News*, May 1, 1912, 8.

86. "School Bonds Carry by Big Majority Here," *San Jose Evening News*, April 29, 1916, 5.

87. "Champion Cause of School Bonds," *San Francisco Chronicle*, July 29, 1906, 25; "A County Fair. The Board of Trade Will Take a Hand in It," *San Jose Evening News*, July 18, 1896, 4; "Chamber of Commerce Discusses High School," 1; "High School Question Aired at Mass Meeting," 1; "High School Bonds Carry with Twelve Acres," 1; "Board of Trade," *San Leandro Reporter*, February 1, 1908, 3; "News/Opinion," *Sunday Mercury and Herald*, September 12, 1909, 10; "Board of Trade Meets," *San Jose Mercury Herald*, February 27, 1916, 24.

88. "Progressive Merchants Endorse Bond and Annexation Elections," *Oakland Tribune*, November 14, 1906, 14.

89. "School Bond Election Fails to Carry in Burlingame," *San Mateo Times*, March 7, 1912, 5.

90. "High School Bonds Are Sure of Passage," *Hayward Twice-a-Week Review*, December 15, 1911, 1.
91. Untitled, *Marin Journal*, May 21, 1908, 2.
92. "What Leading Businessmen Have to Say about Bond Issue," 4.
93. Oakland Improvement League, *Vote for Progress: An Address to the Voters of Oakland* (Oakland, CA: n.p., 1892), 33.
94. "W. W. Garthwaite Says Vote for School Bonds," *Oakland Tribune*, April 21, 1904, 1.
95. "What Leading Businessmen Have to Say about Bond Issue," 4.
96. "What Leading Businessmen Have to Say about Bond Issue," 4.
97. "Woolsey Hotly Answers Stern," *Oakland Tribune*, June 14, 1914.
98. Oakland Improvement League, *Vote for Progress*, 2.
99. "Chamber of Commerce Discusses High School," 1.
100. Oakland Improvement League, *Vote for Progress*, 37.
101. "W. W. Garthwaite Says Vote for School Bonds," 1.
102. "Date of Bond Election Is May 15," *Gilroy Advocate*, April 8, 1911, 4.
103. Oakland Improvement League, *Vote for Progress*, 27.
104. Oakland Improvement League, 27–28.
105. Oakland Improvement League, 26.
106. "Non-resident Pupils in the High School a Source of Revenue," *San Jose Sunday Mercury and Herald*, March 19, 1911, 6.
107. Oakland Improvement League, *Vote for Progress*, 27.
108. Oakland Improvement League, 10.
109. "Boost for Bonds at Big Meeting," *Alameda Daily Argus*, January 31, 1910, 4.
110. "More School Money Needed," *San Jose Evening News*, November 15, 1919, 8.
111. Oakland Improvement League, *Vote for Progress*, 29.
112. "More School Money Needed," 8.
113. Oakland Improvement League, *Vote for Progress*, 40.
114. "Why You Should Vote for the School Bonds," *Gilroy Advocate*, May 20, 1911, 4.
115. "Chamber of Commerce Discusses High School," 1.
116. Oakland Improvement League, *Vote for Progress*, 24.
117. "Mayor Mott Defends Tax Levy as Necessary to Keep Oakland in the Front Rank of Cities," *Oakland Tribune*, September 19, 1911, 5.
118. "Why You Should Vote for the School Bonds," 4.
119. "Pertinent Facts on School Bond Issue," *Gilroy Advocate*, May 13, 1911, 4.
120. "Chamber of Commerce Discusses High School," 1.
121. "Chamber of Commerce Discusses High School," 1.
122. Oakland Improvement League, *Vote for Progress*, 33.
123. "Plenty of Basketball Thursday Evening," *Hayward-Twice-a-Week-Review*, February 13, 1912, 1.
124. "High School," *Marin Journal*, December 19, 1895, 3.
125. "School Board Makes Statement," *San Mateo Times*, November 12, 1910, 1.
126. "An Educational Necessity," *San Jose Evening News*, October 29, 1896, 2.
127. Oakland Improvement League, *Vote for Progress*, 25, 33.
128. "High School Question Aired at Mass Meeting," 1.
129. Oakland Improvement League, *Vote for Progress*, 26.
130. Fred Campbell, *Tenth Report of the Superintendent of Public Instruction* (Sacramento: State Printer, 1882), 31.
131. Campbell, 31.
132. Ira Hoitt, *Thirteenth Report of the Superintendent of Public Instruction* (Sacramento: State Printer, 1888), 27.

133. "Superintendents, Board of Education, and Trustees," *Pacific Educational Journal* 7, no. 8 (1891): 330.

134. John B. Clarke, "The New High Schools of California," *Pacific Educational Journal* 7, no. 9 (1891): 385.

135. "Union High Schools in Alameda County," *Pacific Educational Journal* 8, no. 8 (1892): 360.

136. John B. Clarke, "The New High Schools of California: Part III," *Pacific Educational Journal* 7, no. 9 (1891): 385.

137. Clarke, "New High Schools," 385.

138. Clarke, 390.

139. "The New High Schools of California," *Pacific Educational Journal* 7, no. 7 (1891): 270.

140. Campbell, *Tenth Report*, 32.

141. James Anderson, *Sixteenth Report of the Superintendent of Public Instruction* (Sacramento: State Printer, 1894), 22–48.

142. Clarke, "New High Schools," 389.

143. "Which Will Get It?," *Oakland Daily Tribune*, June 20, 1891, 5.

144. "Election Postponed," *Oakland Daily Tribune*, June 30, 1891, 6.

145. "The Union School," *Oakland Tribune*, 6.

146. "Union High School," *Marin Journal*, July 26, 1906, 1.

147. "Did Rivals Kill Antioch's High School?," *Contra Costa County Gazette*, July 20, 1895, education clippings, Contra Costa County Historical Society, Martinez, CA.

148. "Not by Foul Means," *Contra Costa County Gazette*, August 17, 1895, education clippings, Contra Costa County Historical Society.

149. "The High School Not a Political Issue," *Contra Costa County Gazette*, October 31, 1894, education clippings, Contra Costa County Historical Society.

150. "Alameda County," *San Francisco Call*, September 3, 1891, 3.

151. "Brief Local Notes," *Marin Journal*, March 13, 1902, 5.

152. "Rejoicing at Esparto," *Woodland Daily Democrat*, August 17, 1898, 5.

153. "Joint High School for Southern Towns," *Marin Journal*, July 27, 1905, 3.

154. "Sonoma County," *San Francisco Call*, June 30, 1891, 2.

155. "That High School," *Ukiah (CA) Republican Press*, July 10, 1891, 2.

156. "The Proposed Union High School," *Sausalito News*, July 29, 1905, 2.

157. "As Others See Us," *Oakland Tribune*, June 18, 1895, 8.

158. "Rejoicing at Esparto," 5.

159. "That High School," 2.

160. Anderson, *Sixteenth Report of the Superintendent of Public Instruction* (1894), 19–63.

161. Hubert Staffelbach, "Cultural Influences Affecting the Development of High Schools in California" (PhD diss., Stanford University, 1950), 28.

162. *Annual Report of the Public Schools of the City of Oakland for the Year Ending June 20, 1893* (Oakland, CA: Jordan Printing, 1893, 38–39.

163. *Annual Report of the Public Schools of the City of Oakland for the Year Ending June 20, 1893*, 38–39.

5. THE RISE OF THE DISTRICT PROPERTY TAX, EDUCATIONAL EXPERTISE, AND RATIONALIZED INEQUALITY, 1910–1928

1. C. L. Phelps, "Points on School Taxation and Control," *Sierra Educational News* 14 (May 1918): 260.

2. Unless otherwise noted, the finance data discussed in this chapter was obtained from data at the California State Archives in Sacramento. For a description of the

district-level data see "District-Level Sample from California, 1870–1940" in the appendix. For a description of patterns across the state see "State of California Elementary School Funding Data Aggregated at County Level, 1870–1930" in the appendix.

3. Ajay K. Mehrotra, *Making the Modern American Fiscal State: Law, Politics, and the Rise of Progressive Taxation* (Cambridge: Cambridge University Press, 2013), 186.

4. For a discussion of the early failure of state income taxes and the writing of tax experts on its fundamental flaws see Jon C. Teaford, *The Rise of the States: Evolution of American State Government* (Baltimore: Johns Hopkins University Press, 2002), 55–56.

5. Quoted in Mehrotra, *Modern American Fiscal State*, 41.

6. Most notably in 1903 and 1909. See William C. Fankhauser, *A Financial History of California* (Berkeley: University of California Press, 1913), 331.

7. Fankhauser, 335.

8. See Roger Lister, *Bank Behavior, Regulation, and Economic Development: California, 1866–1910* (New York: Routledge, 1993), table 2-2.

9. Quoted in "No Tax on Land for State Purposes," *San Francisco Chronicle*, February 17, 1899.

10. Edward Gallagher, "Nonsense and the Junior College: Early California Development," Hoover Institute Working Papers in Education, March 1994, 5–8.

11. *Journal of California State Senate* (Sacramento: State Printer, 1901), 261.

12. Quoted in Mansel Blackford, *The Politics of Business in California* (Columbus: Ohio State University Press, 1976), 148.

13. Mehrotra, *Modern American Fiscal State*, 215n73.

14. *Inaugural Address of Governor George C. Pardee* (Sacramento: State Printer, 1903), 19.

15. *Inaugural Address of Governor George C. Pardee*, 10.

16. Carl Plehn, *The Plan for Tax Reform in California: A Paper Presented at the Annual Convention of the Bankers Association of California* (San Francisco: Press of W. N. Brunt Co., 1905), 10.

17. Blackford, *Politics of Business in California*, 150–54.

18. Carl Plehn to R. M. Welch (secretary of the California Bankers Association), February 14, 1906, box 59, folder 2, George Pardee Papers, Bancroft Library, University of California at Berkeley.

19. Carl Plehn to George Pardee, July 17, 1906, box 59, folder 2, George Pardee Papers, Bancroft Library, University of California at Berkeley.

20. Blackford, *Politics of Business in California*, 151.

21. Carl Plehn to L. E. McPherson, December 15, 1905, box 59, folder 2, George Pardee Papers, Bancroft Library, University of California at Berkeley.

22. Quoted in Marvel M. Stockwell, *Studies in California Taxation 1910–1935* (Berkeley: University of California Press, 1939), 17.

23. "Corporations Rap Tax Amendment," *San Francisco Call*, February 7, 1907, 3.

24. *Preliminary Report of the Commission on Revenue and Taxation of the State of California* (Sacramento: State Printer, 1906), 27.

25. *Preliminary Report of the Commission on Revenue and Taxation*, 42.

26. *Preliminary Report of the Commission on Revenue and Taxation*, 17–18.

27. Mehrotra, *Modern American Fiscal State*, 215.

28. Henry Carter Adams, *Science of Finance: An Investigation of Public Expenditure and Public Revenues* (New York: Holt, 1899), 70.

29. Adams, 327.

30. "Proposed Taxation Amendments," *Transactions of the Commonwealth Club of California* 3, no. 4 (May 1908): 118.

31. Franklin Hichborn, *Story of the Session of the California Legislature of 1921* (San Francisco: Press of the James H. Barry Co., 1922), 26.

32. Quoted in Hichborn, 27.
33. Quoted in Hichborn, 27.
34. "The Constitutional Amendments and Bond Propositions," *Los Angeles Herald*, November 6, 1910, 6.
35. "Amendment No. 1 Is Assailed by Boynton," *San Francisco Call*, October 28, 1910, 4.
36. Carl Plehn to George Pardee, January 4, 1906, box 59, folder 2, George Pardee Papers, Bancroft Library, University of California at Berkeley.
37. Hichborn, *California Legislature of 1921*, 36
38. R. Rudy Higgens-Evenson, *The Price of Progress: Public Services, Taxation, and the American Corporate State, 1872 to 1929* (Baltimore: Johns Hopkins University Press, 2003), 99–100.
39. George Mowry, *The California Progressives* (Berkeley: University of California Press, 1951), 289.
40. Hichborn, *California Legislature of 1921*, 29.
41. "S.F. Schools Face $104,000 Deficit," *Los Angeles Herald*, January 5, 1915, 1.
42. "New Bill Increases Public School Funds," *Mariposa Gazette*, June 12, 1915, 1.
43. "Teachers Must Wait for Part of Salary till July," *Sacramento Union*, April 17, 1915, 9.
44. "Fall River Mills Schools to Close," *Sacramento Union*, March 8, 1915, 5.
45. "State Plus Local School Support," *Sierra Educational News* 15 (March 1919): 121.
46. "Teachers and Poll Tax," *Red Bluff (CA) Daily News*, April 23, 1915, 2.
47. Mark Keppel, "Adequate Support for Elementary Schools," *Sierra Educational News* 14 (December 1918): 587.
48. For early accounts suggesting that many western states went through a deliberate process of shifting school funding sources from the state level to local districts see Fletcher Harper Swift, *A History of Public Permanent Common School Funds in the United States* (New York: H. Holt, 1911), 11.
49. Hichborn, *California Legislature of 1921*, 36, 33, 39.
50. "School Department," *San Jose Municipal Record*, September 23, 1912, 8–9.
51. "Coyote School District," "Franklin School District," "DIST Meridian," "Jefferson Union: Boundary Changes: Midway Annexation," School District Records, Santa Clara County Clerk's Office, San José, CA.
52. "Los Gatos," "Meridian," "Mayfield," School District Records, Santa Clara County Clerk's Office, San José, CA.
53. "State Plus Local School Support," *Sierra Educational News* 15 (March 1919): 121.
54. "Increasing School Funds," *Sierra Educational News* 14 (January 1918): 25.
55. C. L. Phelps, "Points on School Taxation and Control," *Sierra Educational News* 14 (May 1918): 260.
56. "Coghlan Defeats Benedict Measure," *San Francisco Call*, March 10, 1911, 5.
57. "South Is Beaten in School Fight," *Los Angeles Herald*, March 10, 1911, 6.
58. "Bay City Protest Will Be Unheeded," *Sacramento Union*, February 26, 1911, 12.
59. "Amend School Bill for Cities," *Sacramento Union*, March 10, 1911, 2.
60. Hichborn, *California Legislature of 1921*, 36.
61. "Case of 17 Million Children," *Ladies' Home Journal*, August 1912, 3.
62. Robert Craford, "Local Taxation a National Problem: Are Our Cities and Rural Districts Spending Too Fast?," *Barron's*, July 12, 1926, 3.
63. Tracy Steffes, *School, Society, and State: A New Education to Govern Modern America* (Chicago: University of Chicago Press, 2012), 95.
64. Quoted in S. Alexander Rippa, "The Business Community and the Public Schools on the Eve of the Great Depression," *History of Education Quarterly* 4, no. 1 (March 1964): 37.
65. Quoted in Rippa, 37.

66. Henry Pritchett, "The Rising Cost of Education," *American Law School Review* 5, no. 3 (May 1923): 171–90.

67. "Cost of Education," *Washington Post*, May 1, 1927, SM3.

68. For a classic account of how a concern for business concepts of efficiency influenced education reform during the Progressive Era see Raymond E. Callahan, *Education and the Cult of Efficiency: A Study of the Social Forces That Have Shaped the Administration of the Public Schools* (Chicago: University of Chicago Press, 1962).

69. Carl C. Plehn, "Expenditures for Schools," *Proceedings of the Annual Conference on Taxation under the Auspices of the National Tax Association* 17 (September 1924): 98.

70. See, for example, James F. Walsh, "Public Education: Its Quality and Its Costs," *Bulletin of the National Tax Association* 13, no. 4 (January 1928): 113–16; H. J. Harman, "Controlling Expenditures in New Mexico," *Bulletin of the National Tax Association* 9, no. 5 (February 1924): 133–35; L. M. Livengood, "Why It Costs That Much," *Bulletin of the National Tax Association* 9, no. 7 (April 1924): 208–14.

71. Quoted in Callahan, *Education and the Cult of Efficiency*, 116. The Taxpayers Association of California was founded in 1916 by representatives from corporations and banks in the state. It was not the same organization as the California Taxpayers Association that operates today. In the 1930s, the journalist Franklin Hichborn emphasized the continuities in the financing and support of the original Taxpayers Association of California, a successor group called the Tax Investigation and Economy League, and the California Taxpayers Association that was founded in 1926 and exists today. On the origins of the organization that was founded in 1916 see Hichborn, *California Legislature of 1921*, 41–42, n. 22. On the continuities between the Taxpayers Association of California, the Tax Investigation and Economy League, and the California Taxpayers Association see "Tax Conference Is Accused of Ignoring Issues," *Sacramento Bee*, February 8, 1936, 6.

72. Wilford Talbert, "Are We Spending Too Much Money on Our Schools?," *California Taxpayers' Journal* 1, no. 4 (1918): 22.

73. Ellwood Cubberley, *School Funds and Their Apportionment: A Consideration of the Subject with Reference to a More General Equalization of Both the Burdens and the Advantages of Education* (New York: Teachers College Press, 1905), 4. For overview of Cubberley's role in education as an academic discipline see Ellen Condliffe Lagemann, *An Elusive Science: The Troubling History of Education Research* (Chicago: University of Chicago Press, 2000), 76–80. For an uncritical biographical account see Jesse B. Sears, *Cubberley of Stanford and His Contribution to American Education* (Stanford, CA: Stanford University Press, 1957). For an overview of the history of school finance as an area of formalized study see R. L. Johns, "State Financing of Elementary and State Secondary Education," in *Education in the States: Nationwide Development since 1900*, ed. Edgar Fuller and Jim B. Pearson (Washington, DC: National Education Association of the United States, 1969).

74. Johns, "State Financing of Elementary and State Secondary Education," 183.

75. Cubberley, *School Funds and Their Apportionment*, 73.

76. Cubberley, 82, 123.

77. Jesse B. Sears and Ellwood P. Cubberley, *The Cost of Education in California: A Report Reviewed and Presented by the Educational Finance Inquiry Commission* (New York: Macmillan, 1924), 265.

78. Ellwood Cubberley, *Public Education in the United States* (Boston: Houghton Mifflin, 1919), viii.

79. Cubberley, *Public Education*, 168, 169.

80. Cubberley, *Public Education*, 546.

81. Fletcher Harper Swift, "The Declining Importance of State Funds in Public-School Finance," *School Review* 29, no. 7 (September 1921): 541.

82. For report and quotation see Sears and Cubberley, *Cost of Education*, 347. The report was the seventh volume in a series produced by the American Council of Education's Educational Finance Inquiry Commission. For an account of the committee's work and its connection to a broader national movement to increase state and federal contributions to education see Steffes, *Schools, Society, and State*, 99–106.

83. Sears and Cubberley, *Cost of Education*, 347.

84. California Department of Public Education, *Financing Education in California* (Sacramento: Department of Public Education, 1926), 719.

85. Sears and Cubberley, *Cost of Education*, 348.

86. *Report of the Special Legislative Committee on Education* (Sacramento: State Printer, 1920), 10.

87. Hichborn, *California Legislature of 1921*, 41.

88. "School System to Be Analyzed," *Sacramento Union*, June 21, 1919, 9.

89. "Relative to the Appointment of a Legislative Committee to Examine and Report upon a Committee of Education in This State," box 19, folder 169, Herbert C. Jones Papers, Special Collections, Stanford University.

90. "School System to Be Analyzed," 9.

91. Mark Keppel, "Adequate Support for Elementary Schools," *Sierra Educational News* 15, no. 1 (January 1919): 47, 25–26.

92. UC Regional Cultural History Project, *Herbert G. Jones on California Government and Public Issues* (Berkeley: University of California, 1958), 98.

93. Letter, Ellwood Cubberley to Herbert C. Jones, October 13, 1920, Herbert Jones Papers, Special Collections, Stanford University.

94. Quoted in Sears, *Cubberley of Stanford*, 182.

95. *Report of the Special Legislative Committee on Education* (1920), 36.

96. *Report of the Special Legislative Committee*, 36.

97. *Report of the Special Legislative Committee*, 95.

98. Letter, Marshall Mott to Herbert C. Jones, April 15, 1920, box 21, folder 185, Herbert Jones Papers, Special Collections, Stanford University.

99. "To Give Schools Much Attention," *Madera (CA) Tribune*, January 10, 1921, 4.

100. Letter, Guy V. Shoup to Herbert Jones, March 31, 1921, Herbert Jones Papers, Special Collections, Stanford University.

101. *Report of the Special Legislative Committee*, 44.

102. John David Philips, "The Politics of State School Support: California as a Case Study, 1919–1960" (PhD diss., Stanford University, 1965), 74–164.

103. *Journal of California State Senate* (Sacramento: State Printers, 1919), 1563.

104. For quotation see "Statement Issued on Amendment 16," *Marin Journal*, October 29, 1920, 8. For other editorials supporting the amendment see "Many Support Amendment 16," *Madera Tribune*, October 15, 1920, 1; "Vote Yes on Amendment 16," *Sausalito News*, October 20, 1920, 4.

105. Quoted in Higgens-Evenson, *Price of Progress*, 100.

106. On Plehn's work as a lobbyist against increased corporation taxation see Higgens-Evenson, *Price of Progress*, 100, 46–49; Hichborn, *California Legislature of 1921*, 45–49.

107. For a description of Cubberley as a delegate see "Minutes of San Rafael Conference," *California Taxpayers' Journal* 4 no. 1 (January 1920): 8. For references to rural school inefficiencies drawing on Cubberley and explicitly framed in opposition to the initiative campaign for increased school funding see "Making the Rural School Efficient," *California Taxpayers' Journal* 4, no. 6 (September 1920): 3.

108. Helen Halter, "The Educational Programs of Selected Taxpayers Associations and Their Influence on Public Education" (PhD diss., New York University, 1937), 130.

109. California Department of Public Education, *Financing Education in California* (Sacramento: Department of Public Education, 1926), 719.

110. See, for example, Mehrotra, *Modern American Fiscal State*, 217, and Teaford, *Rise of the States*, 52–54.

111. See, for example, *Report of the Proceedings of the Bar Association of Arkansas* (Bar Association of Arkansas, 1916), 114; *State of Nebraska Report of the Special Commission on Revenue and Taxation* (Lincoln: Woodruff), 134.

112. Sears and Cubberley, *Cost of Education*, 348. For a discussion of the broader finance inquiry commission nationally see Steffes, *Schools, Society, and State*, 98, 240n38.

6. THE ART OF ADDRESSING INEQUALITY WHILE EXPANDING IT, 1928–1950

1. For example, Jack Dougherty, "Shopping for Schools: How Public Education and Private Housing Shaped Suburban Connecticut," *Journal of Urban History* 38, no. 2 (2012): 205–24; Ansley Erickson, *Making the Unequal Metropolis: School Desegregation and Its Limits* (Chicago: University of Chicago Press, 2016).

2. For a classic account of urban education in the years after World War II, attending to funding disparities, see Jeffrey Mirel, *The Rise and Fall of an Urban School System: Detroit, 1907–91* (Ann Arbor: University of Michigan Press, 1993). For more recent work examining the role of schooling in shaping the stratification of communities after World War II see Erickson, *Making the Unequal Metropolis*; David García, *Strategies of Segregation: Race, Residence, and the Struggle for Educational Equality* (Oakland: University of California Press, 2018); Andrew Highsmith, *Demolition Means Progress: Flint, Michigan, and the Fate of the American Metropolis* (Chicago: University of Chicago Press, 2015); John Rury, *Creating the Suburban School Advantage: Race, Localism, and Inequality in an American Metropolis* (Ithaca, NY: Cornell University Press, 2020); Emily Straus, *The Death of the Suburban Dream: Race and Schools in Compton, California* (Chicago: University of Chicago Press, 2014).

3. See, for example, Margaret Pugh O'Mara, *Cities of Knowledge: Cold War Science and the Search for the Next Silicon Valley* (Princeton, NJ: Princeton University Press, 2005).

4. David Freund, "Marketing the Free Market: State Intervention and the Politics of Prosperity in Metropolitan America," in *The New Suburban History*, ed. Kevin Kruse and Thomas Sugrue (Chicago: University of Chicago Press, 2006), 22.

5. Dick Netzer, *Impact of the Property Tax: Its Economic Implications for Urban Problems; Supplied by the National Commission on Urban Problems to Joint Economic Committee, Congress of the United States* (Washington, DC: Government Printing Office, 1968), 24. This was true of every California city included in the study with the exception of San Francisco, which was unique in the relative diversity and poverty of the cities around it at the time.

6. "Pupil Costs below State Average in Contra Costa," *Oakland Tribune*, December 5, 1954.

7. Assessed valuations and tax rates are from "Pupil Costs below State Average in Contra Costa." Spending differences are from state funding data for 1948 described in appendix.

8. Dougherty, "Shopping for Schools."

9. Robert O. Self, *American Babylon: Race and the Struggle for Postwar Oakland* (Princeton, NJ: Princeton University Press, 2003).

10. See, for example, the advertisements for the subdivision "Plantation Acres" featured in the *Press Democrat* (Santa Rosa, CA), November 2, 1945, 15. The advertisement for Vista de Vallejo is from 1932 and reprinted in Brendan Riley, "Racial Redefining in Vallejo,"

Vallejo Times-Herald, March 25, 2022, https://www.timesheraldonline.com/2022/03/25/brendan-rileys-solano-chronicles-racial-redefining-in-vallejo/.

11. For an overview across communities and time periods of school segregation and resistance to it in California see Charles Wollenberg, *All Deliberate Speed: Segregation and Exclusion in California Schools, 1855–1975* (Berkeley: University of California Press, 1978).

12. See, for example, the origins of a separate school in Santa Ana in Gilbert Gonzalez, *Chicano Education in the Era of Segregation*, 2nd ed. (Denton: University of North Texas Press, 1990), 177; in Santa Paula in Martha Menchaca, *The Mexican Outsiders: A Community History of Marginalization and Discrimination in California* (Austin: University of Texas Press, 1995), 67; and in Oxnard in García, *Strategies of Segregation*, 12–37.

13. Irving Hendrick, "Public Policy toward the Education of Non-white Minority Group Children in California, 1849–1970," unpublished report, National Institute of Education Project no. NE-G-003–0082, University of California Riverside, 1975, 207–8.

14. Richard Valencia, *Chicano Students and the Courts: The Mexican American Legal Struggle for Educational Equality* (New York: NYU Press, 2008), 11.

15. On the complaint see Menchaca, *Mexican Outsiders*, 66.

16. "Wood Denies Charge Made by Mexicans," *San Francisco Examiner*, June 28, 1919, 3. For more on the charge and the role of the Mexican consulate in Mexican American civil rights challenges see Francisco Balderrama, *In Defense of La Raza: The Los Angeles Mexican Consulate and the Mexican Community* (Tucson: University of Arizona Press, 1982), 56–57.

17. Gonzalez, *Chicano Education*, 15.

18. See, for example, Carlos Kevin Blanton, "From Intellectual to Cultural Deficiency: Mexican Americans, Testing, and Public School Policy in the American Southwest, 1920–1940," *Pacific Historical Review* 72, no. 1 (2003): 39–62.

19. On education structuring pathways into work in the 1930s and 1940s see Cristina Groeger, *The Education Trap: Schools and the Remaking of Inequality in Boston* (Cambridge, MA: Harvard University Press, 2021).

20. García, *Strategies of Segregation*, 2.

21. In some accounts, including a newspaper account at the time, Montoya's first name is recorded as Frank, but his daughter has clarified his name was Fred. See David G. García and Tara J. Yosso, "'Strictly in the Capacity of the Servant': The Interconnection between Residential and School Segregation in Oxnard, California, 1934–1954," *History of Education Quarterly* 53 (2013): 84n95.

22. "Schools for Mexicans Only Held Illegal," *Fresno Morning Republican*, October 1, 1929, 13.

23. Quoted in "Segregation of Mexican Pupils Thought Lawful," *Gridley (CA) Herald*, February 7, 1930.

24. Quoted in Menchaca, *Mexican Outsiders*, 75.

25. On *Alvarez v. Lemon Grove* see Richard Valencia, *Chicano Students and the Courts: The Mexican American Legal Struggle for Educational Equality* (New York: NYU Press, 2008), 19–21; Victoria-María MacDonald, ed., *Latino Education in the U.S.: A Narrated History, 1513–2000* (New York: Palgrave Macmillan, 2004), 117–82.

26. For example see Gonzalez, *Chicano Education*, 17, 38.

27. Section 8004, California Education Code. On the repeal see Mark Brilliant, *The Color of America Has Changed: How Racial Diversity Shaped Civil Rights Reform in California, 1941–1978* (New York: Oxford University Press, 2010), 82–84.

28. Hendrick, "Education of Non-white Minority Group Children," 213.

29. John Sides, *LA City Limits: African American Los Angeles from the Great Depression to the Present* (Berkeley: University of California Press, 2004), 161–62.

30. For Santa Paula see Menchaca, *Mexican Outsiders*, 65–74; for Oxnard see García, *Strategies of Segregation*; for Santa Ana, Lisbeth Haas, *Conquests and Historical Identities in California* (Berkeley: University of California Press, 1995), 184–96.

31. Sides, *LA City Limits*, 30; "NAACP Fights Injustices in Monrovia, Cal.," *California Eagle*, October 26, 1934, 3; "Decision of Monrovia Court Reversed thru N.A.A.C.P. Attorney," *California Eagle* (Los Angeles), March 1, 1935, 1.

32. Jackson v. Pasadena City School Dist., 59 Cal.2d 876 (1963).

33. Aaron Cavin, "The Borders of Citizenship: The Politics of Race and Metropolitan Space in Silicon Valley" (PhD diss., University of Michigan, 2012), 85–86.

34. "Districting of Schools Is Announced for Coming Year," *San Bernardino Sun*, September 5, 1920, 10.

35. Quoted in Gene Slater, *Freedom to Discriminate: How Realtors Conspired to Segregate Housing and Divide America* (Berkeley, CA: Heyday Books, 2021), 228–29.

36. Netzer, *Impact of the Property Tax*, 17–18.

37. Quoted in Richard Slitor, *The Federal Income Tax in Relation to Housing* (Washington, DC: National Commission on Urban Problems, 1968), 6.

38. Quoted in Slitor, 6.

39. For example, Susanna Loeb and Miguel Socias, "Federal Contributions to High-Income School Districts: The Use of Tax Deductions for Funding K–12 Education," *Economics of Education Review* 21, no. 1 (February 2004): 85–94.

40. David Freund, *Colored Property: State Policy and White Racial Politics in Suburban America* (Chicago: University of Chicago Press, 2010), 181.

41. Slater, *Freedom to Discriminate*, 105.

42. See table 6, p. 30, and table 9, p. 32, in *Summary Report of the California Tax Research Bureau* (Sacramento: State Board of Equalization, 1932). The counties were Alameda, Butte, Glenn, Imperial, Inyo, Lake, Nevada, Sacramento, San Diego, San Joaquin, Siskiyou, Sonoma, Sutter, Tulare.

43. "Legislative Expert Attacks Proposed Income Tax Repeal," *Sacramento Bee*, October 24, 1942, 17.

44. For rates see *Franchise Tax Board Annual Report for 1950* (Sacramento: Franchise Tax Board, 1951), 10. For examples of deductibility see *Regulations Relating to the Personal Income Tax Act of 1935 as Amended in 1937* (Sacramento: Charles McColgan, Franchise Tax Commissioner, 1938), 90, and *Regulations Relating to California Personal Income Tax Law as Amended 1941* (Sacramento: Charles McColgan, Franchise Tax Commissioner, 1942), 82.

45. "State Taxes," *Bakersfield Californian*, April 21, 1943, 16.

46. On the history of teacher union efforts to increase education funding and conflicts with conservative taxpayer groups in the later part of the twentieth century see Kelly Goodman, "Tax the Rich: Teachers' Long Campaign to Fund Public Schools" (PhD diss., Yale University, 2021).

47. Bradford Trenham, "School Reorganization: Local Taxpayers Should Solve Local Problems," *California Tax Digest*, April 1935, 123.

48. "Distribution of Funds Inequitable," *Reedley (CA) Exponent*, August 29, 1930, 4.

49. "County School Merger Sought," *Los Angeles Times*, April 21, 1928, pt. 2, p. 3.

50. Trenham, "School Reorganization," 123.

51. "State Appropriates School Funds," *Anaheim Gazette*, August 28, 1930, 5.

52. Walter F. Dexter, "Streamlining the Public Schools," address delivered at the Twelfth Annual Meeting of the California Taxpayers Association, *California Tax Digest*, April 1938, 118.

53. *Petaluma (CA) Argus-Courier*, December 10, 1932.

54. "State Chamber Announces Program to Facilitate a Reduction [in] State Expenses," *Visalia (CA) Times-Delta*, December 13, 1932, 2.

55. "California Tax Body Assailed," *San Francisco Examiner*, March 22, 1932; "Coast Committee of Welfare Work Will Make Study," *Peninsula Times Tribune* (Palo Alto), May 22, 1931, 9.

56. "Discusses Economics of Public Education," *Peninsula Times Tribune*, February 27, 1933, 4.

57. Quoted in "Tax Conference Is Accused of Ignoring Issues," *Sacramento Bee*, February 8, 1936, 6.

58. "Tax Conference Leaves Questions Unanswered," *Sacramento Bee*, February 11, 1936, 20.

59. Dennis W. Johnson, *Democracy for Hire: A History of American Political Consulting* (New York: Oxford University Press, 2016), 24.

60. Quoted in Johnson, 25.

61. "A Mean Man with Your Money," *Fortnight: The Newsmagazine of California*, March 4, 1949, 9.

62. See, for example, the cartoons and data visualization in "Education for a Changing World," *Tax Digest*, April 1937, 116–17.

63. "Facts about Taxpayers' Association Told by Franklin Hichborn," *Modesto (CA) News-Herald*, April 14, 1928, 1, 9.

64. "A Mean Man with Your Money," 8–9.

65. For example see "Vandegrift Opposes Sales and Income Tax for School Fund," *Press Democrat*, April 16, 1932, 1.

66. See, for example, "Seventeen Named to Chart Course of School Finance Study," *School Life*, September 1931, 113.

67. For example, A. G. Grade and G. A. Moe, *State Aid and School Costs: Report of the Regents Inquiry* (New York: McGraw Hill, 1938), viii.

68. For an overview see John Philips, "The Politics of State School Support: California as a Case Study" (PhD diss., Stanford University, 1965), 297–334. For the text of the proposition and final vote count see *Statement of Vote at General Election Held on November 8, 1932 in the State of California* (Sacramento: Secretary of State, 1932), 43. See Proposition 9, "School Funds. Income Sales Tax."

69. For example see "How to Vote on Proposition No. 9," *Burbank (CA) Daily Review*, 2.

70. Philips, "Politics of State School Support," 302–3.

71. See *Biennial Report of the California State Department of Education 1936* (Sacramento: California State Department of Education, 1937), 33, table 11. Percentages reported for all districts. For just elementary schools the pattern is the same.

72. Based on table no. 3a, Consolidated Revenue Statement, All Government Cost Funds (Net Revenues after Elimination of Inter-fund Transfers), in *Biennial Report of the State Controller for Fiscal Years Ending June 1937 and 1938* (Sacramento: State Printer, 1938). Expressed as percentage using total reported under "Grand Total Revenue." Bank and corporation tax reported as "Bank and Corporation Franchise Tax," income tax reported under "Personal Income Tax," and sales tax is sum of consumption taxes reported under "Gasoline Tax" and "Retail Sales and Use Taxes."

73. Quoted in Philips, "Politics of State School Support," 347.

74. "Plan Is Offered to Lift Small Taxpayer's Burden," *Modesto Bee*, February 5, 1940.

75. See, for example, the sources cited in Philips, "Politics of State School Support," 330n54.

76. See Irving Hendrick, "'The Impact of the Great Depression on Public School Support in California," *Southern California Quarterly* 54 (1972): 190.

77. Quoted in Richard B. Harvey, "Governor Earl Warren of California: A Study in 'Non-partisan' Republican Politics," *California Historical Society Quarterly* 46, no. 1 (March 1967): 45. On Warren and education see John Aubrey Douglass, "Earl Warren's 'New Deal': Economic Transition, Postwar Planning, and Higher Education in California," *Journal of Policy History* 12, no. 4: 473–512.

78. State Reconstruction and Reemployment Commission (SRRC), *The Administration, Organization, and Financial Support of the Public School System, State of California* (Sacramento, 1945), 2.

79. SRRC, 54.

80. SRRC, 32.

81. George H. Geyer, "Review of Activities and Progress of Local Survey Committee in the Calendar Year 1947," 1948 meeting minutes, Commission on School District Files, California State Archives, Sacramento.

82. "Legal and Financial Problems Affecting District Reorganization," September 27, 1948, 1948 meeting minutes, Commission on School District Files, California State Archives, Sacramento.

83. *A Report on School District Reorganization in California, 1946–1948* (Sacramento: State Commission on School Districts, 1949), 90.

84. Letter from George Geyer, December 5, 1946, to "Members of Statewide Committee on Apportionment," appendix in "Minutes of the Meetings of State Commission on School Districts, December 14, 1946," contained in bound "Minutes of the Meetings of the State Commission on School Districts January 1946 to December 1947," box 2, Documents of the Commission on School Districts, State of California, 1945–1949, Stanford University Library.

85. "Commission on School Districts Minutes of the Meeting December 3 and 4, 1948," contained in bound "Minutes of the Meetings of the State Commission on School Districts from February 1948 to December 1948," box 2, Documents of the Commission on School Districts, State of California, 1945–1949, Stanford University Library.

86. "Commission on School Districts Minutes of the Meeting December 3 and 4, 1948."

87. Quoted in *Report of the Cooperative Committee on School Finance* (Sacramento: California State Department of Education, 1949), RSD-1.

88. See, for example, *Biennial Survey of Education in the United States, 1948–50: Statistics of State School Systems* (Washington, DC: US Department of Health, Education, and Welfare, 1954), table 25, p. 76.

89. Estimated based on difference between state revenue total from Revenue Biennial Survey of Education in the United States, 1948–50, and percentage of total revenue that would have hypothetically come from the state using percentage derived from Report of the Commissioner of Education, table 12, 75, state tax revenue (column 3) and income from state permanent school fund (column 2) as percentage of total revenue (column 7).

90. "Financing Public Education," *Sierra Educational News* 39 (January 1943): 9.

91. Philips, "Politics of State School Support," 400.

92. For example, *Second Report of the Assembly Interim Committee on Public Education* (Sacramento: Assembly of the State of California, 1949), inside cover, 46–52.

93. Self, *American Babylon*, 114.

94. Patricia Hill, *Check List for a Healthful and Safe School Environment* (Sacramento: California State Department of Education, 1957).

95. Charles Bursch, *Forty Years of Schoolhouse Planning* (Sacramento: State Department of Education, 1969), 33.

96. Division of Schoolhouse Planning Bulletin, *Standards for Public School Sites* (Sacramento: State Printing Office, 1930), 15.

97. Charles Benjamin, "School District Reorganization in California: A Study of State Politics of Education" (PhD diss., Stanford University, 1980), 367.
98. "Commission on School Districts Minutes, February 5, 1948," 1948 meeting minutes, Commission on School District Files, California State Archives, Sacramento.
99. *Program for Optional Reorganization of School Districts, Bulletin Number 1* (Sacramento: State Commission on School Districts, 1946), 8.
100. "Some Guides, with Comments and Questions, for an Evaluation of the Proposed Unified School District and Considerations in Marking the Accompanying Check Sheet," box 6, part 1, Documents of the Commission on School Districts, State of California, 1945–1949, Stanford University Library.
101. "School Redistricting Proposal Develops Segregation Problem," *San Bernardino Sun*, December 7, 1946, 7.
102. "Report of Santa Clara County Local Survey Committee regarding the Organization of the East Side Union High School District," box 5, part 2, Documents of the Commission on School Districts, State of California, 1945–49, Stanford University Library.
103. "Report of Santa Clara County Local Survey Committee regarding the Organization of the East Side Union High School District."
104. "Progress Report of Local Survey Committee, Alameda County," box 5, part 2, Documents of the Commission on School Districts, State of California, 1945–49, Stanford University Library.
105. Richard Rothstein, *The Color of Law: A Forgotten History of How Our Government Segregated America* (New York: Liveright, 2017), 211.
106. Examples of places where African Americans could secure housing include Richmond, Oakland, Russel City, and eventually East Palo Alto. There were also a handful of Mexican American *colonias* in Decoto, Niles, Washington, and Gardner.
107. William Fischel, *Making the Grade: The Economic Evolution of American School Districts* (Chicago: University of Chicago Press, 2009), 203.
108. "Jim Crow Is Dying," *Los Angeles Sentinel*, October 7, 1948, 25.
109. Quoted in Brilliant, *Color of America*, 234.
110. Quoted in Brilliant, 234.
111. Gary Orfield and Jongyeon Ee, *Segregating California's Future: Inequality and Its Alternative 60 Years after* Brown v. Board of Education (Los Angeles: UCLA Civil Rights Project, 1994), 14–15.

EPILOGUE

1. On the militia and its atrocities see Benjamin Madley, *An American Genocide: The United States and the California Indian Catastrophe* (New Haven, CT: Yale University Press, 2016), 530. On the donation to help form the school fund see David Ferris, *Judge Marvin and the Founding of the California Public School System* (Berkeley: University of California Press, 1962), 53.
2. Jill Lepore, "Richer and Poorer," *New Yorker*, March 9, 20015, https://www.newyorker.com/magazine/2015/03/16/richer-and-poorer.
3. Quoted in James T. Patterson, *Brown v. Board of Education: A Civil Rights Milestone and Its Troubled Legacy* (New York: Oxford University Press, 2002), 71.
4. On income mobility see Barbara Biasi, "School Finance Equalization Increases Intergenerational Mobility: Evidence from a Simulated Instruments Approach," *Journal of Labor Economics* 41 (forthcoming). On wages and poverty see C. Kirabo Jackson, Rucker C. Johnson, and Claudia Persico, "The Effects of School Spending on Educational and Economic Outcomes: Evidence from School Finance Reforms," *Quarterly Journal of Economics* 131 (February 2016): 157–218.

5. Laurie Reynolds, "Full State Funding of Education as a State Constitutional Imperative," *Hastings Law Journal* 60 (2008): 751–52; Bradley W. Joondeph, "The Good, the Bad, and the Ugly: An Empirical Analysis of Litigation-Prompted School Finance Reform," *Santa Clara Law Review* 35 (1995): 763, 814.

6. Laurie Reynolds, "Uniformity of Taxation and the Preservation of Local Control in School Finance Reform," *University of California–Davis Law Review* 40 (2007): 1857.

7. Annie Lowrey, "Her Only Crime Was Helping Her Kids," *Atlantic*, September 13, 2019, https://www.theatlantic.com/ideas/archive/2019/09/her-only-crime-was-helping-her-kid/597979/.

8. Alana Semuels, "Good School, Rich School; Bad School, Poor School," *Atlantic*, August 25, 2016, https://www.theatlantic.com/business/archive/2016/08/property-taxes-and-unequal-schools/497333/; Debra Viadero, "School Finance: Slowly, the Burden Shifts to the States," *Education Week*, November 17, 1999, https://www.edweek.org/ew/articles/1999/11/17/12finance.h19.html.

9. "America's School Funding Is More Progressive Than Many Assume," *Economist*, December 23, 2017, https://www.economist.com/news/united-states/21732817-how-states-and-federal-government-offset-effects-local-inequality-americas.

APPENDIX

1. Paul Wallace Gates, *History of Public Land Law Development* (Washington, DC: United States Public Land Law Review Commission, 1968), 13–15.

2. On the budget surplus/deficit by year see *Historical Statistics of the United States, Colonial Times to 1970*, pt. 2 (Washington, DC: Bureau of the Census, 1975), 1104 (Series Y 335–38). On land sales see also 76 Cong. Rec. H10453 (1940) (Year and Cash Sales Table).

3. For an overview of these development patterns see Mel Scott, *The San Francisco Bay Area: A Metropolis in Perspective* (Berkeley: University of California Press, 1985).

4. In particular see Terrence McDonald, *The Parameters of Urban Fiscal Policy: Socioeconomic Change and Political Culture in San Francisco* (Berkeley: University of California Press, 1986); Destin Jenkins, *The Bonds of Inequality: Debt and the Making of the American City* (Chicago: University of Chicago Press, 2021).

Index

Abrahamson, Hugo, 125
academies, 27
access (to education), 20. *See also* civil rights activism; geography; race; school districts; segregation (racial); white supremacy
Adams, Edson, 54, 145
Adams, Henry Carter, 142
Alabama, 122
Alameda County, 11, 48–50, 69, 113, 115, 118, 133, 150, 172, 181
Alameda Daily Argus, 125
Alcatraz Island, 52
Alder Glen, 150
Allen, Hollis, 190
Alpine School, 74–76
Alviso District, 153
American Journal of Education, 36
American political development (APD), 22–25
"American Progress" (Gast), 80
Anderson, James, 78, 132
Andrus, Washburn, 125
annexation (of neighboring municipalities), 107–21, 177. *See also* incorporation (of surrounding land); local taxes; real estate
Antioch College, 72
Antioch Ledger, 134
Apache, 80
Arapahos, 80
Arizona, 2, 90
Arkansas, 167
Assembly Interim Committee on Public Education report, 191
assimilation, 24–25
Atherton, Faxon, 49
Atherton, Gertrude, 62
Atlantic, 200
attendance zones, 176–77
Augus, William, 123–24

Baldwin Park, 1–2, 5–6, 9–10
Bancroft, Hubert Howe, 51
banks, 17, 84–87, 98, 140–43, 151, 155, 170–71, 181–87, 200, 239n71
Bannock people, 80
Barnard, Henry, 36, 160

Beadie, Nancy, 27, 78, 215n16
Beadle, W. H. H., 89
Bedford Inquirer, 95
Bellows, Henry Whitney, 72
Belshaw, C. M., 134
Benicia, 51–56, 68
Berkeley, 110, 113, 115–16, 123–24, 128
Bernstein, Shana, 11
Beverly Hills, 1–2, 5–6, 117
Beverly Hills Unified School District, 6
Bingham Ordinance, 109
Black Americans: citizenship status of, 42–44, 46–47, 77–81, 173; educational claims of, 45–47, 112, 173–74, 176–77, 194; free schools and, 75–76, 78–81
Blackmer, Eli, 101–2
Black nationalism, 11–12
Board of Equalization, 98, 140, 146
Boas, Franz, 136
Bolander, Henry, 93
bonds, 30, 107, 121–28, 139
boosterism, 53–59, 67–73, 80–81, 100–101, 107, 113–15, 122–37, 143–44
Booth, Newton, 75, 79, 83
boundaries (district): exclusion and, 48–50, 69–73, 95–97, 102–5, 107–21, 128–31, 135–40, 153–65, 169–77; modification of, 5–6, 14–17, 48–50, 69–73, 94–97, 102–5, 151–54, 163–70, 177, 188–95. *See also* geography; school districts
Boutwell, George, 29
Boynton, A. E., 146
Brace, Charles Loring, 36
Brannan, Sam, 60
Briffault, Richard, 4, 108
Brillian, Mark, 11
Briones Valley, 172
Brooklyn Land and Building Company, 66–67
Brown, Joseph, 42
Brown v. Board of Education, 176, 198–99
Bryant, Edwin, 60
Bureau of Educational Investigation, 157
Burlingame, 113, 119
Butler, John, 156
Butte County, 86

249

INDEX

Calaveras County, 35
Calhoun, John, 38
California: as archetypal postwar state, 10–11, 36; corporate policies and, 82–88; county taxation policies and, 54–55; as funding model for eastern states, 7; higher education system of, 103–5; Indigenous expropriation and, 34–35, 50–52, 197–98; as national governance model, 36, 89–90, 158–62, 167; need-adjusted school funding in, 18, 188–95; new state constitution of, 18, 97–105, 108–9, 111, 226n45; original state constitution of, 35, 38; racialized belonging in, 1–4, 11, 17, 41–46, 78–79, 112–13, 173–78, 199–200; school funding policies in, 1–4, 9–10, 34–35, 39–47, 76–77, 102–5, 122–28, 140–54, 162–67, 192–95; settler colonialism and, 15–17, 22–25, 36–41; State Archives of, 20; state income tax and, 179–81; state-sponsored regional competition and, 113–37; statewide property tax and, 6–7, 14, 18–21, 25–31, 70–73, 81–88, 97, 138–47, 225n38
California Bankers' Association, 143
California Black Convention, 46
California Chamber of Commerce, 185
California Immigration Union, 41
The California Progressives (Mowry), 147
California State Board of Agriculture, 83
California State Board of Equalization, 84
California Taxpayers Association (CTA), 184–88, 239n71. *See also* Taxpayers Association of California
California Tax Research Bureau, 181
California Teacher, 85–86, 133
California Teachers Association, 154, 163, 166
Calkins, Thomas, 124
Cambrian, 55
Caminetti, Anthony, 141
Campbell, Frederick, 129–30, 132
Carlisle Indian Industrial School, 75
Carpentier, Horace W., 54
Carpinteria Union School District, 175
Carr, Ezra, 85
Carter, Alexander, 186
Casey, Lewis, 55
Centerville, 133
Central Pacific Railroad, 82–84
Chamberlain, Lawrence, 122
Cheyenne, 80
Chicago Daily Tribune, 94
Chilean migrants, 38
Chinese migrants, 38, 41, 44, 63, 79, 98, 108–9, 111–13, 231n11

Church, Edward, 63
citizenship, 41–42, 67–68, 75–88
civilization discourses, 16–17, 22–25, 32–34, 36–41. *See also* education (public); Indigenous land (expropriation of); settler colonialism; white supremacy
civil rights activism, 1–4, 11, 17, 44–46, 78–79, 112, 173–78, 198–200
Civil War, 45, 73, 75
Clark, J. G., 55
Clarke, John, 130–31
class: race and, 13–14, 59–67, 177–83; spatial inequalities and, 13–21, 60–67, 85–95, 102, 107–21, 181–83
Coates, Frank, 135
colonialism, 15–17
colonias, 117
Colorado, 88–89
colorblindness, 15
Comanches, 80
Commission on Revenue and Taxation, 144–48
Commission on School Districts, 190
commodification (of education), 50–59, 93–105, 123–35, 143–48, 154–57, 167–83, 191
Common School Journal, 29
Commonwealth Club of California, 145–46
Compton school district, 13
Connecticut, 28–32, 94–95, 97, 160, 210n26
Conness, John, 71
consolidation (of rural districts), 118–21, 129–31, 164–65, 188–92
Constitution (US), 1–3, 5, 75, 79, 104–5, 109
Contra Costa County, 118, 134, 194
Contra Costa County Gazette, 134
Cook County (IL), 94
Corporation of the City of New York, 28
corporations, 17, 27–30, 84–87, 98, 140–43, 151, 155, 170–71, 181–87, 200, 239n71. *See also* banks; intangible forms of wealth; lobbying (corporate); public service corporations; railroad corporations; taxation
Corte Madera, 134
counties (as administrative unit), 6–7, 13–14, 35, 54–55, 150–54, 210n26. *See also* school districts; *specific California counties*
County High School Act, 129–32
County of San Mateo v. Southern Pacific Railroad Company, 105
County of Santa Clara v. Southern Pacific Railway Company, 105
covenants (real estate), 9–10, 112–13, 117, 172–73, 232n36

Covina Union High School District, 6
Cowdery, J. F., 79
Coyote School District, 153
Crawford, Robert, 155
Cremin, Lawrence, 160
Crocker, Charles, 125
Cubberly, Ellwood: expertise of, 5, 18, 158–62, 166–68, 184; local control rhetoric and, 139–40, 160–62; Special Legislative Committee on Education and, 163–65; teacher unit and, 87–88
Cubic Air Ordinance, 231n11
Culver City, 117

Daily Alta Californian, 40, 44, 53, 60, 64, 68
Daily Morning Times, 105
Dakota Territory, 89
Dartmouth College v. Woodward, 28
Davis, E. W., 95–96
debt financing. *See* bonds
Delaware, 210n26
Del Norte County, 132
Denman Grammar School, 72–73
desegregation, 12, 169–70, 177, 198–99. *See also* civil rights activism; Fourteenth Amendment; race; school districts
development. *See* boosterism; commodification (of education); local taxes; real estate
Dexter, Walter, 185
"Dillon's Rule," 108
Division of Schoolhouse Planning, 192
domestic science, 106–7
Du Bois, W. E. B., 112
Dwight, Theodore, 27

Eastland School District, 118
Eaton, John, 97
Economist, 200
Eden Vale, 48–50, 68, 150
education (public): assimilation and, 24–25; civilizing mission of, 15–17, 22–25, 32–34, 36–41, 48–50, 54–55, 72, 80–81; county taxes and, 6–7, 187; desegregation efforts and, 11–12, 169–70, 177, 198–99; expertise and, 5, 18, 140–47, 155–64, 184–89; historiography and, 10–17, 25–27, 212n46; ideational struggles over the meaning of, 13–17, 34–36, 41–47, 68–77, 81–88, 95–96, 98–99, 102, 122–23, 145–49, 158–60, 167–68, 183–95, 199–201; Indigenous expropriation as foundational fund for, 15–17, 22–25, 29, 31–36, 46–52, 70, 197–98, 200–201; labor market outcomes and, 174–75; local control ideologies and, 2–4, 67–73, 92–95; need-adjusted funding and, 18, 188–95, 199, 227n82; racial inequalities and, 1–4, 11, 17–18, 44–47, 59–67, 77–81, 108–10, 112, 170–71, 173–78, 199–200; real estate's connection to, 15–19, 21, 48–50, 52–59, 67–73, 93–95, 100, 103–5, 116–17, 121–28, 130–31, 134–35, 143–44, 147–57, 162–68, 171–88, 191; as semipublic good, 13–14, 17–18, 35–36, 41–47, 50–52, 56–59, 67–73, 81–88, 92–95, 105, 121–28, 139–47, 158–60, 162–70, 184; spatial segregation and, 1, 4, 11–12, 36–41, 44–47, 49–50, 56, 59–73, 77–81, 93–97, 103–5, 110–21, 131–37, 169–96; state-building capacity of, 106–7; statewide property tax support for, 6–7, 14, 18–21, 25–31, 70–73, 81–88, 97, 104, 138–57; tuition charges and, 14, 26; whether funding matters for student outcomes and, 20–21
Educational Finance Inquiry Commission, 167
educational opportunity (definition), 20
Education Week, 200
Elk Grove School District, 96
Elmhurst, 113
Ely, Richard T., 141, 145
Erickson, Ansley, 192
European migrants, 38
expertise, 18–19, 140–47, 155–64, 184–86, 188–89

Federal Housing Authority, 171, 181
Fifteenth Amendment, 75, 79
Filipino Americans, 175
Fisher, Maturin, 30
Fogelson, Robert, 11
Folsom, Joseph L., 60
Fort Point, 52
Fourteenth Amendment, 2, 75, 79, 104–5, 109
Franklin School District, 153–54
Fraser, James, 29
free-market mythologies, 1–4, 10–17, 23–35, 46–47, 122–23, 183–88, 200–201
Frémont, John C., 60
Freund, David, 109, 171, 180
Fruitvale, 113
fugitivity, 77–78
Fullerton, 116
funding disparities (definition), 20

Gaddis, Henry, 35
Gage, Henry, 141
Galt School District, 120
Gardner District, 153

Garthwaite, W. W., 124
Gast, John, 80
Gentlemen's Agreement of 1907, 112
geography: class inequalities and, 20, 60–67, 85–95, 102, 107–21, 181–83, 198–99; district-level taxation's effect on, 7–8; private property regimes and, 15–16; public goods and, 14–15, 121–123, 128–37, 139–49; racial inequalities and, 1, 10–12, 15, 41–47, 49–50, 52–53, 59–67, 109–10, 129–31, 183–95; state action's division of, 10, 13–14, 53–56, 102–5, 131–37, 147–57, 164–66, 170–95. *See also* commodification (of education); local taxes; school districts
Georgia, 32, 42
Gerlough, L. S., 185
Geyer, George, 190
GI Bill, 180
Gilroy, 58, 124, 126–27
Gilroy Advocate, 126
Givens, Jarvis, 77–78
Glascock, John, 128
Glendale, 117
gold rush, 37–39, 53, 60
Gonzalez, Gilbert, 174
Grace, A. G., 186
Graham, A. L., 123
Grass Valley, 43–44

Hager, John, 102
Haight, Henry, 41, 82–83
Halleck, Henry, 63
Happy Valley Public School, 60, 62, 221n51
Harrigan, Anthony, 2
Harris, William T., 94
Hawthorne, 117
Hayward, 48–50, 58, 68, 113–14, 123, 126–27, 135
Hayward Review, 123–24
Hichborn, Franklin, 147, 151, 154, 162, 181, 185, 188, 239n71
Hickman, L. M., 56
Higgens-Evenson, R. Rudy, 147
high schools, 97–105, 123, 128–37
Hihn, F. A., 59
Hillsborough, 113, 119
Hilt, Eric, 28
historiography, 10–17, 25–27, 212n46
Hoitt, Ira, 129–30
Hollywood City, 116
homeownership: district boundaries and, 16; public education as capitalized with, 15, 17–19, 21; racialized policies encouraging, 9–10, 171–73, 180–81, 191–92; renters and, 177–83; schooling's connection to, 11–12, 18–19. *See also* commodification (of education); geography; race; real estate; renters
home rule, 108–9. *See also* local taxes; school districts; statewide property taxation
homestead associations, 58–59
Hopkins, C. T., 41
Hoppe, Jacob David, 38
Howard, W. D. M., 60
Hubbs, Paul, 39–40, 43

Idaho, 90
Igler, David, 98–99
Illinois, 30, 52, 100
incorporation (of surrounding land), 27–30, 37, 75–76, 111, 113–14
Indiana State Teachers Association, 99
Indigenous land (expropriation of), 15–17, 22–36, 46–52, 70, 80–81, 197–201
Indigenous people (as students), 44, 111, 175–76
intangible forms of wealth, 83–88, 98–99, 104, 139, 157, 162–67. *See also* corporations; statewide property taxation

Jackson, Kenneth, 109
Japanese migrants, 112–13, 174, 177
Jertberg, Gilbert, 190
Jim Crow laws, 195
Johnson, Hiram, 148, 162
Jones, Herbert C., 162–63, 165
Jones, Wilson W., 43
Joyce, Peter, 102

Kaestle, Carl, 32, 215n16
Kansas, 2
Kansas City, Missouri, 112
Kartznelson, Ira, 222n57
Katz, Michael, 25–26, 215n16
Keller, M. J., 126
Keppel, Mark, 161, 163
Kern County, 132
Kirkland, D. W., 124
Kruse, Kevin, 11

Ladies' Home Journal, 155
La Habra Star, 116
Laine, Thomas, 101–2
Lakota, 80
land grants, 16–17, 31–34, 54, 83
Larkin, Thomas, 53, 60, 68
Laspeyre, Thomas, 71
Lebron, Harvey, 185

INDEX

Lemon Grove School District, 175–76
Lepore, Jill, 198
Lester, Peter, 44
Lester, Sarah, 44–45
Lick, James, 60
Lippitt, Francis, 39
Lipsitz, George, 60
lobbying (corporate), 147–54, 162–67, 181, 184–87. *See also* taxation
local control rhetoric, 15, 65–73, 92–97, 121–28, 139–40. *See also* annexation (of neighboring municipalities); boosterism; free-market mythologies; incorporation (of surrounding land); race; real estate; school districts; white supremacy
local taxes: annexation efforts and, 107–21, 177; antiredistributive quality of, 6–7, 18, 138–40, 144–45, 149, 162–67, 169–70, 188–95; California's new constitution and, 18, 138–40; corporate tax avoidance and, 147–54, 162–67, 181–82, 184, 187; county funding and, 6–7, 210n26; exclusion and, 48–50, 69–73, 95–97, 102–5, 107–21, 128–31, 135–37, 139–40, 153–54, 158–65, 169–77; expertise and, 5, 18–19, 155–64, 184–89; high school and, 99–100, 102–5, 123, 125, 131–37; mythology of, 1–4, 10, 13–14, 17, 23–31, 34–35, 46–47, 122–23, 183–88, 200–201; opposition to, 29, 34–35, 70–73, 88–92; origins of, 6; policy debates over the levying of, 5–6, 88–92, 140–47; as private funding, 35–36, 71–73, 85–86, 92–95; renters and, 177–81; rural schools and, 85–86, 118–21, 162–64, 192; school construction and, 96–102, 123–24; as special tax, 14, 30, 76–77, 88–92, 104; state policies creating, 20–21, 24–31, 160–67, 170–95; statewide tax contributions and, 6–7, 14, 18–21, 25–31, 70–73, 81–88, 97, 104, 138–57; subsidization of affluent districts and, 13–14, 18–19, 170–73, 177–81, 183–96; as unattractive to white settlers, 36–47. *See also* boosterism; geography; municipal services; public goods; race; school districts; taxation
London Times, 104
Los Angeles, 64–67, 112–13
Los Angeles City School District, 6, 12
Los Angeles County, 6–8, 116, 153–54
Los Angeles Daily News, 56
Los Angeles Herald, 116, 146
Los Angeles Star, 65
Los Angeles Times, 154
Los Angeles Unified School District, 176

Lotchin, Roger, 52, 61, 64, 221n52
Lutz, Harley, 3

MacDowell, Theodore, 121–22
Maine, 32
manifest destiny, 22–24
Mann, Horace, 72
Marin County, 103, 118, 133, 150
Marin Journal, 103, 123–24, 127, 133, 166
market forces rationale, 14–15, 18–19. *See also* commodification (of education); free-market mythologies; race; real estate
Marshall, Thurgood, 198
Maryland, 33, 122
Marysville, 100
Marysville Herald, 40
Massachusetts, 7, 24, 26–29, 32, 34–35, 90–91, 94, 200, 227n82
Maxcy, Virgil, 33
Mayfield, 123, 150
McCarver, M. M., 39
McClymonds, John, 136–37
McDougal, John, 38
McDuffie, Duncan, 112
McGirr, Lisa, 11
McWilliams, Carey, 186
Mehrotra, Ajay, 140, 167
Mellus, Henry, 60
Melrose, 113
Mendez v. Westminster, 176, 195
Mendocino County, 132
Merced County, 84
Meridian School District, 153
Mexican Americans, 1–2, 37, 41, 112, 117, 174–76, 193
Mexican-American War, 37–38, 42–43, 51–53
Mexican migrants, 38
Midway District, 153
Miles, H. E., 156
Millbrae School District, 119, 120
Miller & Lux, 83–84
Millette, Percival, 35
Milliken v. Bradley, 198
Mill Valley, 118, 123, 133–35
Minnesota, 2, 108
Missouri, 99, 108
Modoc, 80
Monrovia School District, 176–77
Montana (state), 90
Montana Territory, 88
Montbello, 117
Montoya, Fred, 175
Moody's, 122
Moon, Alexander, 54

254 INDEX

Moon District, 121
More, G. A., 186
Morrill Land-Grant Acts, 31
Mort, Paul, 227n82
mortgage markets, 9–10, 171–73, 180–81, 191–92
Moss, Hilary, 219n88
Mott, Frank, 126
Moulder, Andrew Jackson, 39, 44–45
Mount Dell, 96
Mowry, George, 147
municipal services, 109–11, 113–15, 117–21. *See also* boosterism; local taxes
Muwekma Ohlone, 48, 51

NAACP (National Association for the Advancement of Colored People), 176–77, 195
Napa County, 150
National Association of Manufacturers, 156
National Education Association, 94–95
National Grange of the Order of Patrons of Husbandry, 85
National Municipal League, 108
National Survey of School Finance, 186
National Tax Association, 157
Nebraska, 88, 167
Nevada, 88–90
Nevins, Thomas, 56, 68
New Deal, 169, 183, 186, 188
New Hampshire, 32–34, 122
New Jersey, 2, 32, 91–92
New Right, 11
New York (state), 30, 32, 36
New York Times, 64–65
Nez Perce, 80
Nicolaides, Becky, 11–12
Nilson, J. P., 153
nonresident pupil, 96–97. *See also* boundaries (district)
Norris, Frank, 82
North Carolina, 32
North Dakota, 88
Northrop, Birdsey, 94
Northwest Ordinance, 31–32
Novak, William, 23, 28

Oak Grove District, 153–54
Oakland, 11–12, 54, 69, 79, 96, 100, 110, 114, 115–16, 123–28, 136–37, 191
Oakland Bank of Savings, 124
Oakland Daily Tribune, 133, 135
Oakland News, 69
O'Grady, William, 62–64

Ohio Company of Associates, 32
Ohlone people, 48, 51
Ontario School District, 177
Orange County, 116, 176
O'Sullivan, John, 22–24

Pacific Coast Conference on Public and Private Responsibility in Welfare Work, 185
Pacific Education Journal, 130
Pacific Grove, 123
Pacific Immigrant Aid Association of California, 40–41
Pacific Mail Steamship Company, 52
Pacific School and Home Journal, 102
Palo Alto, 120, 194
Pardee, George C., 142–43
Park Homestead Union, 58
Parrillo, Nicholas, 85
Parsons, J. B., 127
Pasadena School District, 176
Patton, Clifford, 108
Pennsylvania, 32, 94–95
Pennsylvania School Journal, 36
People's Independent Party, 98
Peralta, Vicente, 54
Pershing Square, 65
Phelps, C. L., 139–40
Phelps, Timothy Guy, 43
Piedmont, 114
Pierce, Franklin, 53
Placer County, 35, 84, 104
Placer Herald, 71
Plantation Acres subdivision, 173
Pleasant Grove School District, 96, 143
Plehn, Carl, 18, 142–45, 147–48, 150–51, 154–58, 160, 162, 167
Plessy v. Ferguson, 75, 198–99
Poett, J. H., 60
policing, 117
Powell, Lewis, 3–5
Price, Rodman, 60
private property regimes, 31–36, 40–41, 46–50, 67–73, 81–88, 100, 147–54. *See also* boundaries (district); Indigenous land (expropriation of); public goods; real estate
privatization: business corporations and, 27–30, 37, 75–76, 81–88, 113–31; local taxes and, 2–6, 20–31, 35–36, 71–73, 85–86, 92–95; school district boundary-making and, 96–97, 171–83. *See also* intangible forms of wealth; local taxes; race; school districts; statewide property taxation
Progressive Era: educational inefficiency discourses and, 139–40, 154–57, 162–67,

184–85, 190–91; public finance's birth in, 140–47; rural school districts and, 118–21, 163–64; schoolings' expansion during, 106–7, 121–28, 136–37; school reform funding in, 18, 106–7, 121–28; status hierarchies' entrenchment during, 10, 12–13, 18, 164, 169–70; tax policy rhetoric and, 76–77, 97, 115, 140–57

Public Education in the United States (Cubberly), 160

public finance (discipline), 18, 140–47, 155–62, 184–86, 188–89

public goods: common school movement and, 25–31; corporations and, 17, 27–28, 30, 75–76, 81–88, 98, 104–5, 140–43, 151, 155, 170–71, 181–87, 200, 239n71; finance reform and, 74–77, 81–88, 95–96, 127–28; Indigenous land theft as creating, 15–17, 22–25, 29–36, 46–52, 70, 197–98, 200–201; localization politics and, 65–73, 107, 158–60, 188–95; privatization and, 81–88, 92–95, 98–99, 113–28, 130–31; racial monopolization of, 11–12, 41–47, 82–88, 92–95; spatialization of, 14–17, 51–53, 67–73, 93–97, 102, 121–37, 139–49, 158–59, 162–68, 188–95, 199–201. *See also* boundaries (district); education (public); geography; race

public service corporations, 6–7. *See also* corporations; public goods

Pullman Company, 143

race: California's multiracial status and, 10–11, 25, 37–42, 75–79, 173; citizenship and, 41–42, 75–81; civilization discourses and, 16–17, 22–25, 32–34, 36–41; class and, 13–14, 59–67; education funding disparities and, 13–21, 169–78; homeownership benefits and, 9–10, 16–17, 171–73, 177–81, 191–92; immigration narratives and, 55–56, 98; Indigenous expropriation and, 15–17, 22–25, 29–36, 46–52, 70, 75, 197–98; private property regimes and, 16–17, 32–35, 82–88; Reconstruction Amendment challenges and, 75–76, 79–81; renter status and, 177–83, 195–96; residential segregation and, 9–10, 14–17, 112–13, 169–70, 172–73, 182–83, 232n36; school integration and, 79–81, 194–95; settler colonial logics and, 24–25, 36–41, 52–64, 68–73, 80–81; spatial inequalities and, 1, 4, 15–17, 20, 36–50, 52–53, 56–73, 77–81, 93–97, 103–5, 107–21, 131–37, 169–96, 198–201; state policies' consciousness of, 45–50, 108–9; tax-base segregation and, 8–10, 39–40, 78–81, 113–21, 172–77, 183–95. *See also* civil rights activism; desegregation; geography; school districts; segregation (racial); settler colonialism; white supremacy

railroad corporations, 81–83, 104–5, 185. *See also* corporations

rate bills, 26, 30, 35–36

real estate: district property taxes and, 147–54, 171–73; home rule provisions' effects on, 108–21; land monopolism and, 83–88; racial integration efforts and, 191–92; renter exploitation and, 177–83; restrictive covenants and, 112–13, 117, 232n36; schools as commodities and, 50–59, 67–73, 80, 93–95, 100, 103–5, 116–17, 121–28, 130–31, 143–44, 147–57, 167–68, 171–88, 191; spatial inequalities and, 1, 15–17, 20, 41–53, 58–67, 70, 107–10, 116–21, 135–37, 176–77, 181–83; state and federal policies regarding, 9–10, 18–19, 49–50, 52–53, 100–101; as taxable wealth, 113–21, 139–54, 162–68. *See also* boosterism; commodification (of education); school districts

Reconstruction, 18, 73, 75
Redlands, 117
redlining, 9
Redwood City, 110
Reese, William, 99, 121
renters, 177–83
repopulation (racial), 36–41
residency requirements, 16, 176, 200. *See also* boundaries (district); local taxes; school districts
Reynolds, Laurie, 199
Rhode Island, 90, 210n26
Riley-Stewart Amendment, 187–88
Rincon Point Grammar School, 63
Rincon School, 45
Rodeo Land and Water Company, 6
Rolph, James, 186–87
Rolston, Arthur, 98–99
Roy, William, 28
rural districts, 85–86, 118–22, 132, 150, 163–64, 192

Sacramento, 68
Sacramento Bee, 71
Sacramento County, 120
Sacramento Daily Union, 70–71
San Antonio v. Rodriguez, 3–5, 198–99
San Benito, 132

San Bernadino County, 7, 117
San Bruno, 119
San Diego, 104
San Diego Union and Daily Bee, 104
San Dimas School District, 174
Sandul, Paul, 111
San Francisco, 44, 51–56, 60–73, 79, 93–95, 98, 109, 111–12, 148, 174, 187, 222n57
San Francisco and San José Railroad, 84
San Francisco Bulletin, 44, 56
San Francisco Call, 41, 135, 154
San Francisco Chronicle, 86
San Francisco Herald, 44
San Joaquin Republican, 71
San Joaquin School District, 96
San José, 58, 68, 74–75, 96–98, 110–15, 123, 125, 127–28, 150, 153, 177, 194–95
San Jose Tribune, 71
San Leandro, 113, 115, 123, 127
San Leandro Reporter, 115
San Lorenzo Creek, 48–50, 57–58, 69
San Lorenzo Home Company, 191–92
San Luis Obispo County, 132
San Mateo, 119, 127
San Mateo County, 69, 84, 97, 113, 118, 151–52, 193
San Pablo Elementary School District, 172
San Rafael, 100, 103, 127
Santa Barbara County, 175
Santa Clara, 58, 113
Santa Clara County, 96, 118, 151–52, 193–94
Santa Clara Street School, 74–76
Santa Cruz, 59
Santa Cruz Weekly Sentinel, 69
Santa Monica, 117
Santa Paula Chronicle, 175
Santa Paula School District, 174
Santa Rosa, 103, 150
Sather, Peder, 63
Saturday Evening Post, 95
Sausalito, 133–35
Sausalito News, 135
Sawtelle, 117
school administration (discipline), 158–62, 164–65, 184–86, 188–89
school districts: annexation efforts and, 107–21, 177; bond sales and, 121–28, 139; boundary modifications and, 5–6, 14, 16–17, 48–50, 69–73, 94–97, 102–5, 107–21, 128–31, 151–54, 163–65, 169–70, 177, 188–95; county policies and borders and, 6–7; funding disparities between, 4, 7–8, 74–77, 85–87, 102–5, 116–17, 131–37, 139–40, 143–68, 170–88, 190–96, 198–99;

high school buildings and, 97–105, 129–31, 192; public good notions and, 14–15, 121–28, 140–47; racialization and, 8–9, 113–21, 129–31, 135–37, 171–77, 183–96, 198–99; rural districts as disfavored versions of, 118–22, 132, 150, 163–64, 192; state policies' creation of, 5–6, 65–73, 95–97, 107, 109–10, 117–21, 170–71; as tax boundaries, 6–8, 10, 12–13, 18–19, 75–77, 84, 92–95, 97–102, 147–54, 162–68, 184–95, 198–99. *See also* geography; local taxes; race; real estate; *specific districts*
school finance: bonds and, 30, 107, 121–28; data appendix on, 203–8; district unification and, 129–31, 164–65, 188–92; Indigenous expropriation and, 15–17, 22–25, 29–36, 46–52, 70, 197–98; inefficiency discourses and, 154–57, 161–67, 184–85, 190–91; the meaning of "public" and, 74–77; need-adjusted funding and, 18, 188–95, 199, 227n82; permanent state school funds and, 28–41, 53, 70–71, 84–89, 93–95, 146–48, 160, 197–201; per-pupil funding mechanisms and, 113–21, 191; Progressive Era boosterism and, 121–28; racial exclusion and, 36–47, 121–28, 169–70, 188–96; sales taxes and, 190–91; statewide property taxes and, 6–7, 14, 18–21, 25–31, 70–73, 81–92, 97, 104, 138–57; teacher units and, 87–88. *See also* bonds; consolidation (of rural districts); public goods; real estate; school districts; taxation
School Funds and Their Apportionment (Cubberly), 158
Science of Finance (Plehn), 145
Seal Beach, 117
Sears, Jesse, 160–61, 168
Sebastopol, 59, 135
segregation (racial), 110, 174, 190–95, 198–99
Selby, Thomas, 63
Self, Robert, 11–12, 172–73, 192
Seligman, Joseph, 141, 145
semipublic good (education as), 13–14, 18–19
Semple, Robert, 39, 53, 68
Serrano v. Priest, 1–3
settler colonialism, 22–25, 31–34, 36–64, 68–73, 80–81
Shattuck, F. K., 123
Sherman, William Tecumseh, 51
Shumate, Albert, 63
Sierra Educational News, 140, 148
Siskiyou County, 132
siting (of schools), 59–67
Smith, G. E., 59

INDEX 257

Smith, George A., 153
Solano County, 150
Sonoma County, 16, 95–96, 150
Soquel, 59
Southern Pacific Railroad, 82, 84, 104, 125, 135, 141, 185
South San Francisco, 119
space. *See* geography
Special Legislative Committee on Education, 162–63
"special taxes," 14
Starr, Kevin, 98
State Commission on School Districts, 193–94
State Reconstruction and Reemployment Commission (SRRC), 188–90
state school funds, 28–41, 53, 70–71, 84–89, 93–95, 146–48, 160, 197–201
statewide property taxation, 1, 4, 36–50, 56–81, 93–97, 103–5, 110–21, 131–37, 169–96
Stephens, William, 162–63
Stockton, 54, 56, 112
Story, Joseph, 28
Strauss, Emily, 12–13
Strayer, George, 188–90
Strobridge, Edward, 128
Sugrue, Thomas, 11
Sullivan, Matt, 146
Sullivan, Raymond, 2
Sunnyhills, 191
Sunnyvale, 114
Surplus Revenue Act, 33
Swett, John, 40, 45, 90
Swift, Fletcher Harper, 160, 214n10

Talbert, Wilford, 157
Tape family, 75–76, 79–81
taxation: annexation and incorporation and, 107–21, 177; California's constitutional convention and, 98–102; California state income tax and, 179–82; corporate avoidance of, 104–5, 139–40, 145–54, 162–67, 181–82, 184, 187; county-level taxes and, 150, 210n26; general property taxes and, 83–92; historiography and, 10–17, 25–27, 212n46; intangible forms of wealth and, 98–99, 104, 113–15, 139–47, 157; Progressive Era reform efforts and, 140–47, 154–57; racial disparities and, 78–81, 171–73; regressive character of property taxes and, 177–83; sales taxes and, 190–91; school funding disparities and, 1–7, 25–31, 75–77, 88–92, 98–102, 107–21, 129–31, 140–62, 170–83, 188–95; state policies and, 4–7, 23–24, 35, 39–40, 76–77, 88–92, 94–95, 104, 107, 129–31, 140–54, 158–67, 170–95; subsidies and, 84–88, 177–81. *See also* boosterism; corporations; local taxes; public goods; real estate; school districts; state school funds
Tax Investigation and Economy League, 239n71
Taxpayers Association of California, 139, 157, 162, 166, 239n71. *See also* California Taxpayers Association (CTA)
Taylor, Bayard, 38
teacher training, 28–29
Teaford, Jon, 167
Tehama County, 120
Temple, Jonathan, 65
Tennessee, 33–34
territories, 37
Texas, 2
Thirteenth Amendment, 75
Thompson, Robert, 35
Tompkins, Edward, 82
Treaty of Guadalupe Hidalgo, 38, 43
Trenham, Bradford, 184, 186
tuition charges, 14, 26, 30, 35–36, 96–97
Tuttle, B. F., 76, 87–93, 98, 102, 105
Tyack, David, 222n57

Ukiah Press Record, 135
unified school districts (definition), 6
Union Fusion Party, 45
Union High School Act, 129–30, 132, 134
Union School District, 96
United Auto Workers, 191
urbanization, 107–21
US Supreme Court. *See specific cases*
Ute people, 80

Vallejo, Mariano, 53
Vance, James, 64
Vandegrift, Rolland, 186–87
Ventura, 110
Ventura County, 174
Veterans Administration, 171, 180
vocational education, 106–7

Wall Street Journal, 3
Warren, Earl, 169–70, 182, 190, 192, 198–99
Washington State, 108
Washington Territory, 88
Washington Township, 133
wealth. *See* intangible forms of wealth; statewide property taxation; taxation

Weber, Charles, 54
Weekly Colusa Sun, 56
Weir, Margaret, 222n57
Westgate, 117
Wetzlar, Julius, 57
White, Emerson, 36
White, William P., 156
white supremacy, 25–34, 36–64, 68–73, 112–13, 176, 200–201
Wickersham, James P., 78, 94–95
Wiebe, Robert, 108
Williams, J. Harold, 119
Williams-Bolar, Kelley, 200
Wilson, Henry, 78
Wilson, John, 63
Wisconsin, 30
Witgen, Michael, 33
Wonds, Fred, 124
Wood, William, 174
Woodhams, Maurice, 97
Workingmen's Party of California, 98, 104

Yearley, Clifton K., 140
Yerba Buena, 51–52, 60
Yolo County, 35

zoning practices, 9, 16, 109, 113, 117, 176. *See also* geography

Milton Keynes UK
Ingram Content Group UK Ltd.
UKHW012051201223
434735UK00006B/437